# Emotions in History

*General Editors*
UTE FREVERT    THOMAS DIXON

# Emotional Arenas

*Life, Love, and Death in 1870s Italy*

MARK SEYMOUR

UNIVERSITY PRESS

Great Clarendon Street, Oxford, OX2 6DP,
United Kingdom

Oxford University Press is a department of the University of Oxford.
It furthers the University's objective of excellence in research, scholarship,
and education by publishing worldwide. Oxford is a registered trade mark of
Oxford University Press in the UK and in certain other countries

© Mark Seymour 2020

The moral rights of the author have been asserted

First Edition published in 2020

Impression: 1

All rights reserved. No part of this publication may be reproduced, stored in
a retrieval system, or transmitted, in any form or by any means, without the
prior permission in writing of Oxford University Press, or as expressly permitted
by law, by licence or under terms agreed with the appropriate reprographics
rights organization. Enquiries concerning reproduction outside the scope of the
above should be sent to the Rights Department, Oxford University Press, at the
address above

You must not circulate this work in any other form
and you must impose this same condition on any acquirer

Published in the United States of America by Oxford University Press
198 Madison Avenue, New York, NY 10016, United States of America

British Library Cataloguing in Publication Data

Data available

Library of Congress Control Number: 2019955135

ISBN 978–0–19–874359–0

Printed and bound by
CPI Group (UK) Ltd, Croydon, CR0 4YY

Links to third party websites are provided by Oxford in good faith and
for information only. Oxford disclaims any responsibility for the materials
contained in any third party website referenced in this work.

*For Grant, Matthew, Justine, Ella, and Phillipa,
with love.*

# Acknowledgements

Emotionally speaking, both pride and a tinge of shame make themselves felt at the point in this book project when the author can formally acknowledge those who helped along the way. The shame relates to the sheer duration of the process, which now means that practically everyone who knows me has wondered when (and even if) this book would see the light of day. Its genesis goes back to the late 1990s, when I was in Rome researching debates over divorce from 1860 to 1900 for a PhD thesis. My advisor, John A. Davis, wisely suggested that I look through newspapers for examples of what a seriously unhappy couple might do about a bad marriage prior to the advent of a divorce law in Italy. The 1878 murder of a decorated Risorgimento soldier by his wife's lover stood out as a variation on the theme of 'divorce, Italian-style', and the incident became an example in my thesis and first book.

The story continued to intrigue me, but the possibility of writing a monograph about it was only able to emerge during my first period of research leave from the University of Otago in 2007, when I worked on the records of the murder trial at the Archivio di Stato di Roma for the first time. Countless visits later, I remain grateful to the dedicated staff at the archive's annex off the Via Tiburtina for their help and advice. Particular thanks go to Luca Saletti, Maddalena Mele, and director Maria Temide Bergamaschi. More recently, at the ASR's headquarters, Ida Manola Venzo assisted with images from the file and facilitated contact with Rita Venanzi, who efficiently helped me obtain permission to reproduce them. I also very gratefully acknowledge the permission of Allan Ceen, of the fascinating Studium Urbis, for permission to reproduce a section of one of his marvellous maps of Rome.

The challenges of Rome's libraries, laden with treasure but not easy to negotiate, can only be met with help from their staff. At the Biblioteca Storica dell'Amministrazione Penitenziaria, I was ably assisted by Luca Morgante, and at the Biblioteca Centrale Giuridica, Cristina Ivaldi went well beyond the call of duty. Staff at the Biblioteca di Storia Moderna e Contemporanea were unfailingly helpful, particularly Rosanna De Longis. I spent most time at the library of the Archivio Capitolino, where director Vincenzo Frustaci placed me into the care of the ever-resourceful Loredana Magnanti. The fact that the library's building had housed Rome's Court of Assizes at the time of the trial I was researching made working there an uncanny experience. I am very grateful for two visits to the main hall of Borromini's oratory (abandoned but still magnificent), which allowed me to inhabit the trial's historic space and helped me to think about the event's emotional dynamics.

Seeking to understand the broader context of the story behind the trial, I received extraordinary hospitality and assistance in Calabria. My hosts in Corigliano Calabro, Luigi and Barbara Pisani, arranged for me to meet the Mayor of Cassano allo Ionio, Gianluca Gallo, who entrusted me to the former librarian of the Biblioteca Diocesana, Enrico Cirianni. His tour of the town, including the probable abodes of key figures in the story, was unforgettable—as was the lunch provided at short notice almost magically by his wife Rosaria Cirianni.

Weaving the varied spaces of this narrative into a story centred around 'emotional arenas' would probably never have happened but for Benno Gammerl's 2010 workshop on 'Emotional Styles—Communities and Spaces', hosted by the Center for the History of Emotions at Berlin's Max Planck Institute for Human Development. I shall always be grateful to Benno for organizing that event, as well as to the Center's director, Ute Frevert, and staff, especially Karola Rockmann, for hospitality and organization. Thanks to Professor Frevert's further generosity, I enjoyed a fellowship at the Center in 2011, benefiting enormously from exchanges with its researchers, particularly Gian Marco Vidor. During that stay, 2010's workshop paper became an article titled 'Emotional Arenas'. Barbara Rosenwein's warm response to its publication, sent spontaneously by e-mail, made all the difference after the physical and emotional upheaval of the Christchurch earthquakes.

Thomas Dixon catalysed the transformation of 'Emotional Arenas' into a book, and he has been a wonderful mentor and supporter throughout the process. From his suggestion that I submit a proposal to OUP's History of Emotions series, to his eagle-eyed yet kid-gloved commentary on each chapter, it has been an extraordinary privilege to work with him. Robert Faber, senior history editor at OUP during the early stages, was also kindly encouraging. Since his departure, Cathryn Steele has been a patient, warm, and helpful editor. The three anonymous referees who read the original proposal were trenchant in their critiques, and the book has been shaped by their comments. David Laven also read the entire manuscript, and I am grateful for his very attentive reading. He helped tighten my prose and saved me from many errors. I take full responsibility for remaining flaws and weaknesses, but any strengths owe much to the input of all the readers who looked at some, most, or all of my manuscript before the final submission.

I am deeply grateful to Robert Aldrich, who introduced me to history when I was an undergraduate, and has been a mentor and friend ever since. He believed in this book well before it began to be written, and in 2015 devised a memorable 'boot camp' to help me launch the writing. He has read and commented on almost all of the manuscript with characteristic acumen. A different form of collegial friendship came from Barbara Rosenwein. Since her first generous message of 2012, she has periodically reminded me that she awaited the book version. Once it was finally completed she made comments on the entire manuscript, with a unique combination of warmth and rigour. I have yet to meet Barbara in person, which makes me feel all the more privileged by the way she has shared her insights.

Fellow members of the 'Rome Writing Club 2015', Giacomo Lichtner, Sally Hill, and David Capie, formed when we were all on research leave, helped keep the spirit of Robert Aldrich's boot camp alive despite Rome's distractions. Giacomo and Sally are my key Italianist mates in New Zealand, and collaborating with them is always a pleasure. Giacomo made incisive comments on the book's introduction, which benefited greatly from his sensitive reading.

The University of Otago has been generous in its support of my work. This book could not have been written without regular research leave, and I was also assisted by University of Otago research grants, including a Prestigious Writing Grant, which gave me a semester free of teaching in 2016. Three superb heads of department, Barbara Brookes, Tony Ballantyne, and Takashi Shogimen, have helped guide my work on this project, and I am deeply grateful for their very engaged support. The same goes for colleagues in and outside my department, particularly Annabel Cooper (who helped greatly at the proposal stage), Brian Moloughney, John Stenhouse, Jon Hall, and Catherine Fowler. Special appreciation goes to Paola Voci, who provided rays of Italian sunshine by way of sustenance, friendship, and intellectual acuity. I gratefully acknowledge all the cheerful help provided by administrators Sue Lang, and more recently, Sandra Burgess. Otago's librarians have efficiently made sure that distance proved no obstacle when it came to interlibrary loans, and thanks to Donald Kerr for helping me purchase a rare 1879 book on the trial.

Some of the work was carried out during visiting fellowships at other institutions. In 2013 I was a guest at the University of Cagliari, and I thank Cecilia Dau Novelli for inviting me to apply and hosting my stay, as well as Alessandro Pes and Valeria Deplano and their colleagues, who made it a very congenial visit. In 2016 I received an Australian Research Council International Visitorship, divided between the Melbourne and Adelaide nodes of the ARC's Centre of Excellence for the History of Emotions. Both visits were enormously constructive and I thank the Centre's academic and administrative staff, above all Lisa Beaven for suggesting I apply and being my main host, and Grace Moore and Katie Barclay for looking after me so well.

In Italy over the years I have benefited from the nurturing warmth and support of friends in and outside academia. In Sardinia, the family Virdis-Sechi, particularly Silvia, Ester, Anna, and Gavino, have been welcoming me for nearly thirty-five years. Colleagues and friends from Trinity College's Rome Campus helped me establish myself as a scholar. Thanks to Livio and Wendy Pestilli, Ivana Rinaldi, and Francesco Lombardi, for making Rome feel like home since 1997. If ever Rome got dull, Gabriella Rienzo always welcomed me in Naples, and continues to do so. A special mention goes to Virginia Jewiss, not just for a long friendship, translation advice, and much encouragement on this book, but for entrusting her

Rome apartment to me on many occasions. And in Milan, Angelo Ascari and Juri Franchi showed that northern hospitality can be as warm as southern.

One of the pleasures of academic life is the way it integrates sociability and professional life such that the boundaries are sometimes undetectable. I value John and Elaine Davis's ongoing friendship and interest, expressed over regular and generous dinners, usually in Rome. Marjan Schwegman and Jaap Talsmar have been wonderful friends as well as wise sounding boards for this project. Seen less often, but much valued for their ideas and the moral support generated by their interest are Valeria Babini, Chiara Beccalossi, Cristina Bon, Sean Brady, Paolo Colombo, Peter Cryle, Roy Domenico, Paul Garfinkel, Mary Gibson, Alessandra Gissi, Domenico Rizzo, Arianna Arisi Rota, Milena Sabato, and Joseph Viscomi.

The UK's Association for the Study of Modern Italy (ASMI) has been like a family to me since the early days, and I particularly thank Philip Cooke, John Foot, Stephen Gundle, Lucy Riall, and Perry Willson for making me feel welcome at my first ASMI conference in 2002, and ever since. Penelope Morris (co-editor of ASMI's journal *Modern Italy* with me since 2015) and I have shared the ups and downs of professional and personal life over the period of our co-editorship and this book's writing in a uniquely intense way.

I owe most though, to the friends and family who constitute my thinly spread but most personally felt emotional constellation. Peter Briggs, Sue Burton, Imelda Craglietto, and Thomas Mayer, have always been there for me, even as things Italian drew me away from them. My eldest niece, Marlene Melchior, has shared in this project since it began, always with a wisdom beyond her years. My father John and second mother Sylvia, have always lovingly welcomed me on my way into and out of Europe, and they stand close behind this work—as does the memory of my mother Antonia. My siblings, Matthew, Justine, Ella, and Phillipa, scattered as they are across the continents, are a fundamental and adored presence. And my partner Grant Midgley, who has lived with this book since it was just a set of characters in a story, has long meant 'home' for me, wherever we are in the world.

# Contents

*List of Illustrations*   xiii

   Introduction   1

1. Intimate Arenas: A New Couple for a New Kingdom   20
2. Arena of Desire: The Circus   50
3. Virtual Arenas: Illicit Love by Letter   78
4. Arenas of Mortality: From Eros to Thanatos   113
5. Arena or Temple? The Trial in Rome's Court of Assizes   150
   Conclusion   204

*Bibliography*   213
*Index*   223

# List of Illustrations

| | | |
|---|---|---|
| 0.1 | Map of the murder locality, indicating the assassin's escape direction (arrow), and the most likely route by which the victim was carried from the Via dei Carbonari to the Ospedale della Consolazione, over the ancient Forum | xiv |
| 0.2 | Giovanni Fadda pointing to his attacker | 2 |
| 1.1 | Raffaella Saraceni | 21 |
| 1.2 | Giovanni Fadda | 22 |
| 1.3 | Fadda reprimanding his wife for addressing a letter to 'Caro Edoardo', a man he did not know | 40 |
| 2.1 | Pietro Cardinali | 57 |
| 2.2 | Antonietta Carrozza | 58 |
| 3.1 | Photograph of Giovanni Fadda discovered in Pietro Cardinali's trunk | 85 |
| 3.2 | The sacred heart near the signature on the letter of 22 March 1866 | 89 |
| 3.3 | The front page of M. N. +'s first letter to Cardinali | 99 |
| 4.1 | The letter found on Fadda's floor after the murder, and the official envelope in which it was stored | 129 |
| 4.2 | Pietro Cardinali having lunch with old friends in Bari, on his way to Rome | 130 |
| 5.1 | The crowd seeking entry to the Court of Assizes on the first day of the Fadda murder trial, Rome, 30 September 1879 | 170 |
| 5.2 | The Court of Assizes of Rome during the Fadda trial | 177 |
| 5.3 | An advocate addresses the rapt audience during the Fadda murder trial | 196 |
| 5.4 | Raffaella faints during the reading out of the verdicts | 200 |
| 6.1 | Antonietta Carrozza performing in the circus at Rome's Politeama, days after her release from the court | 210 |
| 6.2 | Raffaella bids farewell to her mother as her prison sentence begins | 211 |

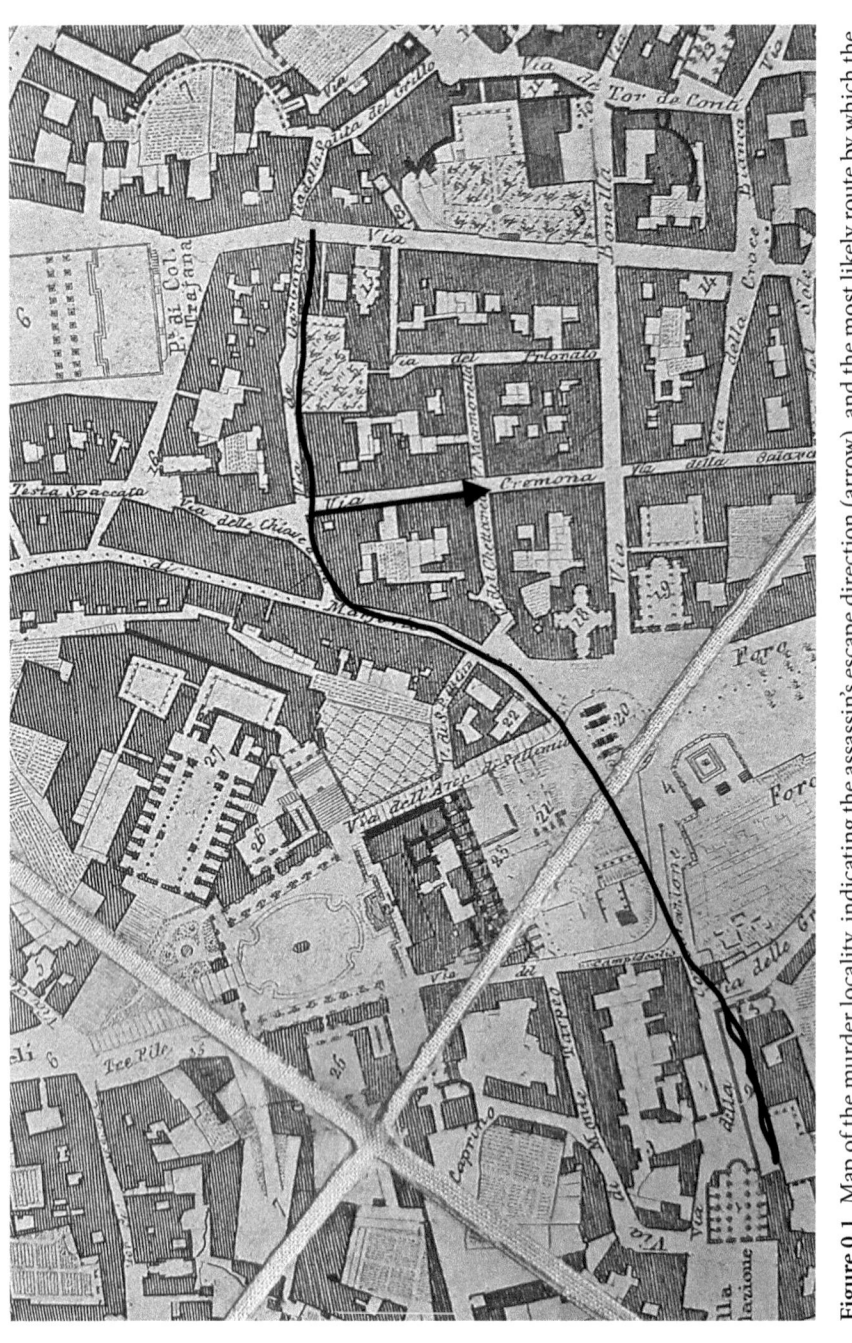

**Figure 0.1** Map of the murder locality, indicating the assassin's escape direction (arrow), and the most likely route by which the victim was carried from the Via dei Carbonari to the Ospedale della Consolazione, over the ancient Forum

*Source:* Pianta Topografica di Roma, Direzione Generale del Censo, 1866, reproduced with the kind permission of Allan Ceen, Studium Urbis, Rome.

# Introduction

## Prologue

Early on a Sunday morning in October 1878, the densely populated area on the urban side of Rome's ancient Forum was coming to life for a day of worship and rest. To the southeast, the Colosseum loomed over the cityscape, as it had for the last eighteen centuries. Just after 7 a.m., a 'sinister looking' individual in knee-high boots emerged surreptitiously from a doorway in the Via dei Carbonari. After looking up and down the street, he stalked off towards the Piazza delle Chiavi d'Oro. Moments later, a second figure, dressed in long white underwear splotched with what looked like blood, staggered out from the same doorway. He called for help and tried to pursue the first figure, who, sensing himself followed, took flight down the Via Cremona. The wounded man lurched to the street corner, where, with a supreme final effort, he pointed, with both finger and gaze, to his aggressor. His last force spent, he then collapsed onto the local baker's doorstep.[1]

The man's pained calls had been heard. Some residents got to their windows in time to see the bloody figure point to the fugitive. At a barbershop on the Via Cremona, two off-duty civic guards were waiting for their Sunday shave. Hearing a commotion, they dutifully sprang into the street, where they instinctively waylaid the man in boots as he sped towards them. Assorted citizens rushed up from behind shouting 'Assassin, assassin!' The captive struggled to escape the officials' grasp, but they managed to handcuff him, alarmed to see smears of fresh blood on his hands as they did so. Following their glances downwards, the captive saw the blood too. Quickly he sought to wipe his chained hands, jabbering that he had simply been passing by, that the bloody man had leapt upon him, that he was innocent.[2] The guards gripped him tighter, already suspecting that they held the perpetrator of a violent crime.

---

[1] Archivio di Stato di Roma, Tribunale Civile e Penale di Roma (henceforth ASR,TCPR), 1879, busta 3659. This 'busta' (literally an envelope, but in this case an archival unit consisting of four volumes, each containing several hundred folios) records the investigative work on the crime carried out by public prosecutors Michele Finizia and Flaminio Felici. The volumes are numbered IA, IB, II, and (due to an archival quirk), IV. Within each, nearly all individual folios are numbered. My account of the crime scene is based on the first document in Volume IA, Finizia's 'Compendium', a synthesis of witness statements and summary of the case amounting to some thirty unnumbered pages; and a second 'compendium', written by Felici, in Volume II, ff. 360–72. All translations are my own unless otherwise indicated.

[2] ASR, TCPR, 1879, b. 3659, vol. II, ff. 16–17, statement by Giuseppe Ozzella (civic guard), 10 October 1878; and ff. 18–19, statement by Angelo De Marco (civic guard), 10 October 1878.

*Emotional Arenas: Life, Love, and Death in 1870s Italy.* Mark Seymour, Oxford University Press (2020). © Mark Seymour.
DOI: 10.1093/oso/9780198743590.001.0001

**Figure 0.2** Giovanni Fadda pointing to his attacker
Source: *Processo Fadda illustrato. Dibattimento alla Corte d'Assise di Roma* (Rome: Giovanni Bracco Editore, 1879), pp. 116–17.

On the baker's doorstep, members of the public gathered around the unconscious victim. A stretcher was found and locals carried him to the Ospedale della Consolazione, on the other side of the Forum. Nothing could be done to save him, and he died a short time later, due to blood loss from multiple stab wounds.[3] The guards delivered the presumed attacker to the police station, where he was locked in a cell, 'trembling with nerves'.[4] As the visceral responses to this ghastly scenario began to settle, the more dispassionate rhythms of official procedure took over, establishing a sense of order and control. First and foremost, it was essential to identify those involved, as an initial step towards establishing a narrative that would lead to the law courts, and, hopefully, justice.

The stabbed man was Giovanni Fadda, aged thirty-five, originally from Cagliari, Sardinia, and a captain of the 32nd Infantry Regiment of the Italian army. He had married one Raffaella Saraceni, of Cassano allo Ionio, Calabria, in Naples in 1871, but the couple had been estranged for some time. These details were confirmed by various witnesses over subsequent days, but it is likely that the chief prosecutor, Michele Finizia, was able to piece together key outlines of the

---

[3] ASR, TCPR, 1879, b. 3659, vol. II, ff. 360–72, Felici's compendium.
[4] ASR, TCPR, 1879, b. 3659, vol. II, ff. 78–81, statement by Gaetano Rossi, Cardinali's cell mate, 20 October 1878.

victim's life on the basis of reports received by midday that Sunday. At 11 a.m., Finizia visited Fadda's modest apartment, where he met the victim's servant and landlady. The prosecutor noted the disarray of furniture and blood stains everywhere. He sifted through the dead man's belongings, and took various documents away. These included letters, photographs, and a medical certificate. The latter related to wounds sustained by the captain at Solferino in 1859, site of a major battle in the Risorgimento, Italy's struggle for independence and national unity.[5]

Police interrogated the man who had attacked Fadda soon after he was delivered into their custody. His name was Pietro Cardinali, and he reported his profession as 'equestrian artist'. Until recently he had been the leading performer in a circus with his two brothers, touring the southern half of Italy. Cardinali had come to Rome, he claimed, in search of a new job. He attempted to explain his dealings with Fadda by telling a garbled story about having met a man in the town of Chieti who asked him to deliver a parcel to the captain. Cardinali signed a statement to this effect with an unsteady hand.[6] The story did not add up, and to the cell mate who had noted his jittery nerves, Cardinali gave a rather different account, about being in love with Fadda's independently wealthy wife.[7] Meanwhile, police followed another lead.

Residents near Fadda's apartment reported that they had seen the sinister stranger in riding boots lurking around their streets for some days before the attack. He had been in the company of another man whose main distinguishing features were an outfit of black corduroy and a soft black hat. This description was sufficient to lead to the arrest of the second man soon after the attack.[8] He was found by police at Rome's main railway station, seeking to escape the city on the next train south. Terrified, he identified himself as Giuseppe De Luca, stablehand in the Cardinali circus. Under questioning, De Luca did not try to dissimulate, unlike his boss. He told the police that he had accompanied Cardinali to Naples, ostensibly to buy horses, but instead they pressed on to Rome. Only then had Cardinali revealed that the real purpose of the journey was to commit a 'great act of vendetta' against Captain Fadda on behalf of his wife.[9]

De Luca obligingly elaborated that Fadda and Raffaella had lived apart for quite some time, he in Rome, she with her mother and stepfather in Cassano. Raffaella and her brother came from a prominent and well-to-do family, and it

---

[5] ASR, TCPR, 1879, b. 3659, vol. IA, ff. 3–4, Inspection report of Fadda's apartment by Finizia, 11 a.m., 6 October 1878: ff. 5–13 list all documents taken, f. 14, medical certificate, and ff. 15–44, letters, photographs, and other documents.
[6] ASR, TCPR, 1879, b. 3659, vol. IA, ff. 78–83, first statement by Pietro Cardinali, 6 October 1878.
[7] ASR, TCPR, 1879, b. 3659, vol. II, ff. 78–81, statement by Gaetano Rossi, Cardinali's cell mate, 20 October 1878.
[8] ASR, TCPR, 1879, b. 3659, vol. IA, f. 75, account of the arrest of Giuseppe di De Luca, stablehand, 10.15 a.m., 6 October 1878.
[9] ASR, TCPR, 1879, b. 3659, vol. IA, ff. 84–7, statement by De Luca, 6 October 1878.

was thought that they had inherited a large amount of money from their father, who had died some time ago. The circus had spent a month in Cassano the previous summer, and Raffaella attended all their performances assiduously. De Luca claimed that she and Cardinali were involved in an illicit affair. The murder, he said rather chillingly, could have been predicted some time ago: Raffaella had let it be known that she found her husband 'tiresome', and no one would be surprised to hear that she and Cardinali were conspiring to have Fadda 'done away with'.[10]

This rather operatic story had yet to be corroborated, but it meant that within hours of the murder, the public prosecutor possessed the outlines of a compelling narrative. At its centre lay the unsatisfactory marriage of a wealthy young woman to a battle-scarred veteran of Italian unification. Unusually for the time, the couple had separated. Even more unusually, the young wife had allegedly taken up with an equestrian circus artist. The illicit couple, to be rid of an irksome husband and perhaps make way for their own marriage, had conspired to end Fadda's life. Lines that linked remote parts of southern Italy, Sardinia, Naples, and Rome, through a headstrong woman, an honourable soldier, and a knavish circus acrobat, had emerged. The story was to change little as a result of deeper investigation over the coming months. It was destined to make a profound impression on all of Italy when it finally reached a courtroom, one year after that murderous morning in October 1878.

## An Emotional Microhistory

There were many murders in 1870s Rome, but for various reasons the killing of Captain Fadda stood out.[11] The trial, held in October 1879, was the most sensational witnessed in the city since courts were opened to the public in 1871, shortly after Rome became the capital of Italy.[12] The case was followed assiduously by the local public, and, through newspapers, by the rest of Italy and even beyond. As a public event, the trial provided contemporaries with an opportunity to witness the lives, loves, and deaths of a range of relatively ordinary, even representative figures, who happened to have come together in an intensely emotional constellation.

---

[10] ASR, TCPR, 1879, b. 3659, vol. IA, ff. 84–7, statement by De Luca, 6 October 1878, here f. 87. De Luca said Raffaella was 'anojata' with her husband, which can mean both bored, and irritated.

[11] For example, an in-house archival index at the ASR, titled Corte di Assise di Roma, Elenco alfabetico degli imputati, Fascicoli processuali, 1871–1898, 325 bis I, indicates that Rome's Court of Assizes heard 102 murder trials in 1879. Daniele Boschi claims that Rome's murder rate between 1872 and 1879 was 12.3 per 100,000 population (compared with London's 0.5 per 100,000), 'Homicide and Knife-Fighting in Rome, 1845–1914', in *Men and Violence: Gender, Honor and Rituals in Modern Europe and America*, edited by Pieter Spierenburg (Columbus: Ohio State University Press, 1998), pp. 128-58, here p. 133.

[12] After Italian unification in 1861, Turin was capital of the new kingdom until 1865, then Florence until late 1870. It was only once Rome was taken from the pope by the Italian state (in September 1870), that the city became its capital.

To posterity, the trial exemplifies the sort of case that from the 1970s Italian microhistorians dubbed 'exceptional-normal', where a body of evidence from an unusual event provides a keyhole through which historians are able to examine aspects of 'normal', everyday life.[13]

The trial's setting was an Italy still very much in the process of being 'made' after its formal political unification of 1861. Preparation by prosecutors was impressive, generating an archive of over two thousand folios of great complexity and richness. The itinerant professions of the accused and the victim meant that witnesses were called from a wide range of occupations and locations. As well as numerous interviews with over one hundred ordinary men and women, police seized a variety of rather personal documents. The most striking of these are dozens of letters that bring to life a range of everyday social relationships, and some that were more unusual. Fadda's job as an army quartermaster had resulted in postings to diverse parts of the new nation, including Sicily, Calabria, Abruzzo, and Rome. Raffaella seldom accompanied him, and during periods of separation, the couple exchanged letters. Their early correspondence was tender and dutiful, and the letters give a sense of what it was like, at the time of Italy's nation-building, for a couple to build married life and kinship networks through written words.

These letters were of as much interest to the public of the 1870s as they are to a social historian in the present. Prior to and during the trial, some of the Faddas' correspondence was published in newspapers, particularly later letters that testified to increasing marital tensions. Just like a subsequent historian, contemporary officials and the public were eager to sound the emotional depths of the Fadda–Saraceni marriage to know what had gone wrong. Nor were these dutiful letters the only ones unearthed by the police. From Cardinali's travelling trunk, investigators seized a cache of missives written by secret admirers, and perhaps even lovers, sent over the course of his circus career. Collectively, these letters express torrents of love and desire, and sometimes jealousy, anger, and disappointment. They still seem saturated with the feelings of their anonymous authors, despite having been sewn tightly into their archival resting place for nearly one and a half centuries.

In terms of emotional expression, the love letters sent to Cardinali were very different from those exchanged by Fadda and Raffaella. These contrasting sets of correspondence provided the first impetus towards my interpretation of the Fadda case as a contribution to the history of emotions. To an innocent in the archive, the letters, particularly the illicit ones, had apparently done the work of amber, preserving emotions of the past in a way that made them seem alive

---

[13] Edoardo Grendi, 'Micro-analisi e storia sociale', *Quaderni storici*, vol. 12, no. 35(2) (1977): 506–20; Carlo Ginzburg, 'Microhistory: Two or Three Things that I Know about it', trans. John and Anne C. Tedeschi, *Critical Inquiry*, 20 (Autumn 1993): 10–35.

decades after their authors had died. Did my response amount to the sort of 'sensual archive experience', as Emily Robinson has put it, that overshadows doubt, misleadingly elevating a set of documents to the status of proof of the existence of those emotions?[14] Or, were these letters the sort of raw material that might genuinely enable me to take a small step towards meeting Lucien Febvre's 1941 challenge to the discipline to 'reconstitute the emotional life of the past'?[15]

Febvre's essay, written during the depths of World War Two, was itself reconstituted in the early twenty-first century due to new interest in the history of emotions. It is sometimes regarded as a founding document for the field, even if its central proposal may represent an impossible task.[16] *Annaliste* history of *mentalités* and a first wave of Anglophone social and cultural historians in the 1960s and 1970s did pay close attention to collective feelings rather promisingly.[17] But individual emotions remained difficult terrain for historians—a zone of methodological discomfort somewhere between mentalities and biology. The cultural turn of the later twentieth century further deepened humanities scholars' wariness of anything that might smack of biological 'essentialism', and their analytical emphases shifted further away from the subject, towards the ways emotions were represented, particularly through language and texts.[18]

This tendency put something of an embargo on ambitions to try to bring emotions as they were experienced by living subjects in the past back to life. Serious collective efforts to meet the general challenge of historicizing emotions did not begin to register as mainstream historiography until about sixty years after Febvre's essay was first published. Then, over the first two decades of the twenty-first century, pioneering research opened new historiographical receptiveness to the possibility that aspects of past emotional experience might at least be partially reconstituted. That new intellectual environment encouraged my research on episodes of life, love, and death in 1870s Italy to move in this direction.

---

[14] Emily Robinson, 'Touching the Void: Affective History and the Impossible', *Rethinking History*, vol. 14, no. 4 (2010): 503–20, here 507.

[15] Lucien Febvre, 'Sensibility and History: How to Reconstitute the Emotional Life of the Past', in *A New Kind of History: From the Writings of Lucien Febvre*, edited by Peter Burke, trans. K. Folca (London: Routledge and Kegan Paul, 1973 [orig. Annales ESC, vol. 3, 1941]), pp. 12–26.

[16] Jan Plamper, *The History of Emotions: An Introduction* (Oxford: Oxford University Press, 2015 [in German, 2012]), pp. 40–3; Joanna Bourke, 'Fear and Anxiety: Writing about Emotion in Modern History', *History Workshop Journal*, vol. 55, no. 1 (2003): 111–33, esp. pp. 113–14. For a critique of Febvre's status, see Barbara H. Rosenwein, 'Worrying about Emotions in History', *American Historical Review*, vol. 103, no. 3 (June 2002): 821–45, here, pp. 821–3.

[17] Representative are E. P. Thompson's *The Making of the English Working Class* (London: Victor Gollancz, 1963), and, in a similar vein, Douglas Hay, 'Property, Authority and the Criminal Law', in *Albion's Fatal Tree: Crime and Society in Eighteenth-Century England*, edited by Douglas Hay, Peter Linebaugh, John G. Rule, E. P. Thompson, and Cal Winslow (London: Allen Lane, 1975), pp. 17–63. Both are notable for the close attention they pay to the emotional experience of their subjects.

[18] Ruth Leys, 'The Turn to Affect: A Critique', *Critical Enquiry*, vol. 37, no. 3 (2011): 434–72, here p. 440.

The specific case study is made possible by the felicitous archival lode generated as a result of Giovanni Fadda's misfortune. Had it not been for his murder, all those letters would probably have been lost to history. The thoughts, observations, and feelings expressed in the extensive investigative interviews would have gone unrecorded. But because of Fadda's death, letters were preserved, and records were created. This work uses the resulting repository, as well as extensive journalistic commentary, to explore the emotional lives of a small cast of characters with microhistorical intensity. But it also tells a larger story about Italy early in the nation's history. The scope of the book echoes the way Tommaso Astarita, in *Village Justice* (1998), wrote both a microhistory of a crime and a broader history of early modern Calabrian life.[19] There is still much to be learned about Italy's social history in the early decades after unification, particularly in relation to patterns of interaction, geographical mobility, feelings, and sexual relationships.[20] One of this book's two main aims is to contribute to our understanding of Italian life in the 1870s.

The second main aim is to extend ways of visualizing and thinking about historical change in emotional cultures. If two sets of personal letters prompted an emotions-history interpretation of Fadda's world, the judicial court that staged the trial for his murder suggested the paradigm at the heart of the book: 'emotional arenas'. At the time of the hearing, criminal proceedings open to the public were still a novelty in Rome, dating back only to 1871. The trial, which ran for the entire month of October 1879, seized the imaginations of the city and much of Italy, arguably at an unprecedented level. It stimulated collective engagement in a way that reminded many observers of ancient Rome's lengthy public festivals, generating great emotional intensity at peak moments.

It was through looking at the trial for Giovanni Fadda's murder as a form of spectacle, as a 'stage' where emotions were generated, performed, expressed, and explored—in ways distinctive to that particular social space—that the 'emotional arena' concept began to take shape in my mind.[21] Its development was driven by the need for an emotions-history paradigm that had an inherent sense of physical boundaries, and, equally importantly, an intrinsic sense of human scale. Moreover, as explained later in the Introduction, it became clear that viewing not just the court but a range of other social spaces as distinctive 'emotional arenas' might well contribute to the way we discern emotional dynamics in a given culture. As a

---

[19] Tommaso Astarita, *Village Justice: Community, Family and Popular Culture in Early Modern Italy* (Baltimore and London: The Johns Hopkins University Press, 1999).

[20] A notable step was Valeria P. Babini, Chiara Beccalossi, and Lucy Riall (eds), *Italian Sexualities Uncovered, 1789–1914* (Basingstoke: Palgrave Macmillan, 2015).

[21] As discussed in chapter 5, the notion of courts as theatres goes back to ancient Greece and Rome, but the first scholarly work I came across that drew on the idea in the context of modern Italy was Angela Groppi, 'Il teatro della giustizia. Donne colpevoli e opinione pubblica nell'Italia liberale', *Quaderni storici* 111 (2002): 649–79. My 2012 article, 'Emotional Arenas', represents an early attempt to map out the paradigm that this book develops.

result, the 'emotional arena' became an organizing principle of the book, with each chapter treating distinct spaces from the lived experience of 1870s Italy.

Post-unification Italy, still in the throes of transition from one historical phase to the next, provides a promising context for enquiries into the history of both social life and the emotions. The new nation-state had largely been put together in the late 1850s through a combination of shrewd diplomacy, fortunate battles led by Giuseppe Garibaldi and King Victor Emmanuel II of Piedmont, and wider geopolitical shifts that aided the cause of Italian unification. Because the diverse inhabitants of the peninsula had only recently come together as a national community, cultural norms, including those relating to the expression and experience of emotion, were notably varied and fluid. This meant that competition for hegemony over such norms between the new polity and older patterns and power structures—from folkloric ways to old-regime hierarchies to Catholic orthodoxies—was particularly marked. For these reasons and because of the nature of Fadda's story, the trial brought forth debate about the role of emotions in both private and public arenas in a way that was unusually historically legible.

## Emotions and Historians

Scholarly understanding of the emotions can be plotted along a spectrum at one end of which human feelings are universal and timeless, and at the other, they are socially constructed and culturally contingent. Few if any humanities scholars would place themselves at the 'universal' end, but much of the historical debate about emotions has been over where on the spectrum they sit, and what can be said about emotions when those whose experience they were part of are long dead. As indicated earlier, it is a debate that historians came to only quite recently. In seeking to historicize emotions, scholars of the past have moved into terrain traditionally occupied by their colleagues in literature, art, philosophy, anthropology, and sociology on the one hand, and by tendentially more present-focused biological, psychological, and neuroscientific disciplines on the other.

While scholars of literature and art possess enviably rich sources of various types, social scientists have their own range of promising possibilities, and psychologists and neuroscientists can avail themselves of experiments and data from living subjects, for historians, emotions have posed particular methodological challenges. The first obviously concerns sources. Despite recognition from at least Febvre's time that emotions profoundly shape history, their importance in the past has not always been recognized, and there has been no guarantee of emotions' abundant preservation in the archives. Archivists and historians, as Barbara Rosenwein has observed, long had a preference for 'hard rational things'. As a result, emotional material has not often been a prominent feature of archival repositories.²² Even if some rich lode is struck, interpretive challenges can make it as difficult for a historian to reconstitute emotions, as it would be for an entomologist to bring an insect preserved in amber back to life.

If it is unlikely that we will ever truly reconstitute, on a broad scale, the emotional experience of the past, or chart concisely how those experiences changed over time, what historians have done very fruitfully is explore change in emotional language, expression, 'style', and norms.²³ Rosenwein's *Emotional Communities in the Early Middle Ages* (2006) was particularly felicitous for the way it helped historians of all periods visualize how emotional norms might be formed and contained within particular social groups. The corollary was that if the community changed, or merged with another, emotional ways would do so too.²⁴ Despite the highly specialized research behind Rosenwein's 'emotional communities' idea, its elegance and transferability help to explain why the book influences scholars working far beyond the chronological and geographical boundaries of her specific subject.

Less elegant, less cohesive, but ultimately perhaps the most influential monograph in the history of emotions so far is William Reddy's magisterial *The Navigation of Feeling* (2001).²⁵ Several of the tools it laid out for 'navigating' emotions in the past have, like 'emotional communities', become entrenched in the scholarly lexicon. Among Reddy's key terms were 'emotional regime' (meaning a set of broad norms about emotions, connected to the regime in power), and 'emotional refuge' (a 'relationship, ritual or organization' where such norms were evaded and new ones elaborated). These terms, as well as others, have been welcomed and used by historians, who were more than familiar with regimes and refuges in other contexts.²⁶

The more abstract but ultimately most powerful of Reddy's ideas is summed up in his term 'emotive', coined with the aim of reconciling (or at least reducing the gap between) the universal biological concept of emotions and the idea that they are exclusively socially constructed.²⁷ The term does so by drawing attention to the 'performative', reifying aspects of what people say about their emotions, as

---

²² Rosenwein, 'Worrying about Emotions', p. 821.
²³ On language, Thomas Dixon, *From Passions to Emotions: The Creation of a Secular Psychological Category* (Cambridge: Cambridge University Press, 2003); and Ute Frevert et al., *Emotional Lexicons: Continuity and Change in the Vocabulary of Feeling 1700–2000* (Oxford: Oxford University Press, 2014). On emotional style, among many, see particularly Peter N. Stearns, *American Cool: Constructing a Twentieth-Century Emotional Style* (New York: New York University Press, 1994); and Benno Gammerl, 'Emotional Styles—Concepts and Challenges', *Rethinking History*, vol. 16, no. 2 (2012): 161–75 (and the ensuing articles in that special issue of *Rethinking History*).
²⁴ Barbara H. Rosenwein, *Emotional Communities in the Early Middle Ages* (Ithaca, NY: Cornell University Press, 2006).
²⁵ William M. Reddy, *The Navigation of Feeling: A Framework for the History of Emotions* (Cambridge: Cambridge University Press, 2001).
²⁶ Reddy, *The Navigation of Feeling*, p. 129.   ²⁷ Plamper, *The History of Emotions*, p. 252.

well as the descriptive elements of such statements. An example is the declaration 'I love you'. Such a statement, probably coming to the surface out of a range of contradictory feelings, itself represents a dynamic attempt to arrive at the essence of what the speaker feels.[28] Jan Plamper's helpful gloss on such processes is to suggest that choosing one's emotion verb has the effect of 'overwriting' or diminishing the others.[29] In this way, as Reddy puts it, 'emotives do things to the world'. They are 'instruments for directly changing, building, hiding, intensifying emotions'—in both the subject and others.[30] Only the subject knows exactly how an emotion, or set of emotions, feels, but as a term, 'emotive' draws attention to the nexus between the inner feeling, and the speaker's (or writer's) efforts to manage or shape its outward manifestations. These efforts will inevitably also be shaped by cultural and social expectations.

Reddy's work persuaded many historians that, instead of seeking to sift reconstitutable emotions from the records of past lives, the most productive site for working on the history of emotions would be the interface between individual emotional experience and the physical, social, and cultural worlds. It was not, of course, that historians had never thought of this; more that Reddy's work provided a confidence that came from possessing a well-calibrated set of navigational instruments that were informed by the work of disciplines that had been exploring emotions for longer than historians—principally anthropology. In the wake of *The Navigation of Feeling*, there has been a notable increase in historical exploration of the social meanings of emotions, investigating the ways they have been expressed, enacted, 'performed', and received, in the past.

One of the most persuasive theoretical developments along the lines suggested by Reddy's work was a much-cited 2012 article by Monique Scheer, which additionally harnessed some of Pierre Bourdieu's theories for the benefit of emotions historians. Scheer invited scholars to see emotions as 'a kind of practice'. This requires acknowledgement that 'pure' physical human bodies are always 'infused' with social and cultural elements, and thus by history itself.[31] Accordingly, those bodies' emotional responses must also be infused with social structure and history. More specifically, drawing on Bourdieu's notion of habitus (which might be crudely summarized as the active presence of the past in current culture), Scheer argued that the human body's 'automatic, spontaneous' responses, among which emotions must figure, are habits that emerge 'where bodily capacities and cultural requirements meet'.[32] Regarding emotions as 'a kind of practice' takes a further

---

[28] Reddy, *The Navigation of Feeling*, p. 102.   [29] Plamper, *The History of Emotions*, p. 252.
[30] Reddy, *The Navigation of Feeling*, p. 105.
[31] Monique Scheer, 'Are Emotions and Kind of Practice (and is That What Gives Them a History)? A Bourdieuian Approach to Understanding Emotion', *History and Theory*, 51 (May 2012): 193–220, here p. 199.
[32] Scheer, 'Are Emotions and Kind of Practice', p. 202.

step towards reconciling the idea of emotions as universally visceral on the one hand, and socially constructed on the other.

Scheer's argument also outlines ways in which emotions might have histories, and reinforces the idea that the most promising place to look for those histories is at the interfaces between emotional experience and cultural, social, and political developments. *Emotional Arenas* seeks to build upon the work of Reddy, Rosenwein, Scheer, and many others who have stressed the dynamic relationship between human emotions and more tangible elements of the past. That body of scholarly work has provided a rich set of concepts and a vocabulary, among which emotives, emotional regimes, refuges, communities, and emotions-as-practice are now indispensable. What *Emotional Arenas* seeks to add, in a nutshell, is more flesh and blood, with a clearer sense of boundedness and human scale, in the context of lived experience in particular social spaces. Although there is a growing body of more empirically focused work, there is still room for research anchored in the specific social spaces where 'bodily capacities and cultural requirements' might regularly meet—places where once living bodies were 'infused' in a context of historical change.

Linking distinctive social spaces, a key feature of western societies since the mid-nineteenth century has been their mobility. More than in previous centuries, people began to move from one social setting to another, one community to another, one town to another, one country to another, one continent to another. In such a context, emotional regimes, refuges, communities, and practices can be difficult to pin down or even discern. According to some of the most persuasive arguments about emotions, they are linked to various distinctive social settings—from communities to particular spaces. They depend on those spaces for their body-infusing cues. Most people who have been to school, a church, a museum, a graveyard, or a war memorial, for example, will have some sense of how spaces can 'infuse' emotions. Indeed, in modern societies, distinct social spaces may be the key *loci* in which cultural standards and requirements about emotions are learned.[33] Yet, while the analytical category of space is beginning to establish itself among historians of the emotions, work which examines concrete instances remains relatively scarce.[34]

So far, one of the strongest contenders for systematic consideration as an emotional space has been the court of law.[35] There are some straightforward reasons for this, one being that legal processes tend to generate rich, reliably archived

---

[33] Also drawing on the notion of emotions as practice, Andreas Reckwitz makes a persuasive theoretical argument about the relationship between emotions and space in 'Affective Spaces: a Praxeological Outlook', *Rethinking History*, vol. 16, no. 2 (2012): 241–58.

[34] A nice exception is Margrit Pernau's examination of Delhi, 'Space and Emotion: Building to Feel', *History Compass*, vol. 12, no. 7 (2014): 541–9.

[35] Laura Kounine, 'Emotions, Mind, and Body on Trial: A Cross-Cultural Perspective', *Journal of Social History*, vol. 51 no. 2 (2017): 219–30, here 219–20.

sources about people's lives. Another is that, particularly in criminal and family court cases, the emotional stakes for those involved are often very high. Moreover, courts themselves are likely to have similar atmospheres across a range of cultures. Indeed it may be that the western legal world's historical tendency to cultivate an image that draws a stark line between the emotional and the cognitive, resulting in the ideal of courts as arenas with a singularly sober 'emotional style', has itself made the exploration of the emotional side of 'the law' irresistible to historians.[36] In any case, in recent years law courts, as a key institution of western societies, are one of the few genres of space *as spaces* that have received focused attention from historians interested in the emotions.[37]

## Emotional Arenas

The term 'arena' may work particularly well for a courtroom, but this book seeks to extend the concept beyond those confines, using a variety of scenarios from everyday life in 1870s Italy to build its case. The argument it develops is that the evolving social spaces of a young nation—and by extension of western life more generally—function as a range of 'emotional arenas', where interplays between subjective feelings and the external world are continuously shaped and staged. In the broadest sense the term 'emotional arenas' denotes contemporaneously existing but defined social spaces, where the experience and expression of emotions, and their staging and shaping, are likely to follow patterns distinctive to that space. Together, the book's examples point to how we might see particular social spaces as 'infusing' distinctive emotional tenors, and thus shaping historical emotional change.

Even well prior to the emergence of a specific historiographical focus on emotion, historians laid the groundwork for the notion of associating particular spaces with distinctive feelings and modes of expression. The best example is perhaps the large body of research on the family home, often driven by the twin

---

[36] A seminal early collection which deconstructs the myth of the alienation of emotions from the law is Susan A. Bandes (ed.), *The Passions of Law* (New York: New York University Press, 1999). Thomas Dixon, 'The Tears of Mr Justice Willes', *Journal of Victorian Culture*, vol. 17, no. 1 (2012): 1–23, represents a rich concrete example. On law and emotion more generally, see Terry A. Maroney, 'A Field Evolves: Introduction to the Special Section on Law and Emotion', *Emotion Review*, vol. 8, no. 1 (2015): 3–7.

[37] See, for example, David Lemmings (ed.), *Crime, Courtrooms and the Public Sphere in Britain, 1700–1850* (Farnham: Ashgate, 2012); Mark Seymour, 'Emotional Arenas: From Provincial Circus to National Courtroom in Late Nineteenth-Century Italy', *Rethinking History*, vol. 16, no. 2 (2012): 177–97; Marianna Muravyeva, 'Emotional Environments and Legal Spaces in Early Modern Russia', *Journal of Social History*, vol. 51, no. 2 (2017): 255–71; Gian Marco Vidor, 'Rhetorical Engineering of Emotions in the Courtroom: the Case of Lawyers in Modern France', *Rechtsgeschichte—Legal History* 25 (2017): 286–95; Katie Barclay, *Men in Court: Performing Emotions, Embodiment, and Identity in Ireland, 1800–1845* (Manchester: Manchester University Press, 2019).

imperatives of social history and gender history.[38] Early findings were often structured around a private-sphere/public-sphere dichotomy, which argued that as economies industrialized and work was separated from the domestic sphere, the home became a female-gendered, emotionally intimate retreat from an increasingly competitive commercial world.[39] The home is one of the emotional arenas to be examined in this book.

At first glance, one of Reddy's terms, the emotional 'refuge', might seem to fit the emerging modern home well. It was constituted by a set of relationships among which the stringent emotional norms of the working world were relaxed. On the other hand, the 'refuge' idea, while certainly not describing a still life, may be insufficiently dynamic to describe the emotional life of domestic space. Research has shown that the home itself was a place of emotional negotiation, of adjusting to and working out emotional patterns and practices. There, for men as well as women, family relationships continued to become a more intense locus for the experience and expression of emotions, particularly love.[40] Perceiving the home as an 'emotional arena', even if it was also a refuge, places analytical emphasis on the dynamic processes whereby the home both staged and shaped a range of sentiments in ways that were increasingly distinct from other social spaces. Such processes have continued to change over time.

Of course, private life was by no means the exclusive arena in which historical actors experienced emotions and learned about cultural requirements. A sense of how 'emotional arenas' might be applied more broadly is illustrated by an imaginary tour through more public examples, selected from this book's historical setting. The most important non-religious cultural space in nineteenth-century Italy was the opera theatre, and it had a profound role in 'the emotional education of Italians'.[41] Popular not just with elites, the theatre was a place where emotions were literally staged, and which the audience attended in the hope of having their heartstrings gratifyingly pulled. Emotions might sometimes burst forth from the audience, expressed in tears, shouts, or even more tangibly, as eggs or tomatoes launched as signs of anger or disappointment.[42] The culture of this arena as a whole both staged and shaped the expression of emotions. In turn, the space represented a theatrical culture that was shaped—by librettists, composers, singers,

---

[38] See, for example, Barbara Brookes (ed.), *At Home in New Zealand: History, Houses, People* (Wellington, NZ: Bridget Williams Books, 2000).
[39] The seminal work is Leonore Davidoff and Catherine Hall's *Family Fortunes: Men and Women of the English Middle Class, 1780–1850* (London: Routledge, 2002 [1987]).
[40] John Tosh, *A Man's Place: Masculinity and the Middle-Class Home in Victorian England* (New Haven: Yale University Press, 2007 [1999]).
[41] Carlotta Sorba, *Teatri. L'Italia del melodramma nell'età del Risorgimento* (Bologna: Il Mulino, 2001), pp. 13–14.
[42] See David Gentilcore, *Pomodoro! A History of the Tomato in Italy* (New York: Columbia University Press, 2010), p. 64, which explains that Italians even had a word for a pelting with tomatoes as an expression of disappointment: *pomodorata*.

and the audience itself—around the experience of emotions.[43] Members of the public grasped that the opera was a distinctive emotional arena. Within it, they behaved, and probably experienced their feelings, in distinctive ways.

By contrast, the morning after a night at the opera, many members of the audience may well have gone to Mass. Churches are also spaces of emotion, and while that potentially rich subject awaits more specific historical analysis, we can safely assume that the feelings parishioners experienced in religious 'arenas' were likely to have been of a different ilk from those of the opera theatre.[44] The ways they expressed those emotions, or kept them within, almost certainly differed from the ways of the theatre, with an emphasis on inward spiritual reflection, and clerical officiations addressed to the congregation in a much more direct way. This simple duo of the church and the theatre, with time at home probably fitting between the two, illustrates how historical actors might move through several different emotional arenas over a very short time. In each, they would have felt and behaved in ways that were distinctively staged, and at least to some extent shaped, by the boundaries of the arenas themselves.

In this context, the importance of boundaries inherent in 'emotional arenas' can be brought into sharper focus by thinking about a particular facility offered in Catholic churches: the confessional box.[45] A small bounded space, publicly visible yet confidential, its purpose is to stage, shape, and ultimately dissolve, specific emotions, particularly guilt,[46] and more particularly still, guilt over sexual matters.[47] Michel Foucault argued that the ritual of confession and the confessional box created guilt too, by constructing discourses about sin.[48] Even for those who do not kneel at the confessional, its obtrusion into the space of the church reminds parishioners of their sins and their duty to confess. Within Italian and Catholic culture, the confessional box can be seen as a microcosmic emotional arena, a tiny space that nevertheless exerted a powerful influence over the interplay

---

[43] Susan Rutherford, *Verdi, Opera, Women* (Cambridge: Cambridge University Press, 2013), pp. 11–13.

[44] Works such as Dixon's *From Passions to Emotions*, and Susan C. Karant-Nunn's *The Reformation of Feeling: Shaping the Religious Emotions of Early-Modern Germany* (Oxford: Oxford University Press, 2012), have of course placed religion at the centre of the cultural shaping of emotions, but the role of religious space in this process has yet to receive concentrated analysis. John Kieschnick presents brief but stimulating ideas in 'Material Culture', in *The Oxford Handbook of Religion and Emotion*, edited by John Corrigan (Oxford: Oxford University Press, 2007), pp. 223–38, here pp. 228–9; see also Caitlin Cihak Finlayson, 'Spaces of Faith: Incorporating Emotion and Spirituality in Geographic Studies', *Environment and Planning A*, vol. 44 (2012): 1763–1778.

[45] John Cornwell, *The Dark Box: A Secret History of Confession* (London: Profile Books, 2014).

[46] John Bossy, 'The Social history of Confession in the Age of the Reformation', *Transactions of the Royal Historical Society*, vol. 25 (1975): 21–38, here p. 30.

[47] Fernanda Alfieri, *Nella camera degli sposi. Tomás Sánchez, il matrimonio, sessualità (secoli XVI-XVII)* (Bologna: Il Mulino, 2010).

[48] Michel Foucault, *The History of Sexuality Volume I: An Introduction*, trans. Robert Hurley (New York: Vintage Books, 1990 [1978], p. 19.

between subjective feelings and the external world.⁴⁹ The substance of exchanges within the confessional are hidden from history, but merely considering the box as an emotional arena lets us visualize how defined social spaces might shape interplays between feelings and experience.

In nineteenth-century Italy, theatres and churches were long-standing institutions and familiar landmarks, and, the emotional styles associated with particular aesthetic epochs certainly changed over time. As examples for my argument, their main purpose here is to illustrate how the idea of viewing social spaces as 'emotional arenas' helps us to conceptualize the contours and boundaries of a particular society's emotionally variegated culture at a given moment. By looking at several emotionally distinctive arenas—whether a box at the opera or a confessional box in a church—we grasp what it might mean for historical actors to 'navigate' their feelings, as William Reddy would put it, between emotionally discrete arenas, within a given culture and historical epoch.

If the emotional arena idea helps us understand the complex emotional requirements of a particular moment, it also provides a focus for the analysis of shifting emotional patterns and cultures across time. For example, among the legacies of both the Reformation and Counter-Reformation are church buildings the emotional styles of which diverged distinctly over ensuing centuries, the emergence of the Baroque style being a familiar example. Similarly, the political revolutions and national unifications of later centuries witnessed new emotional arenas, such as parliaments, gaining hegemony over older ones, such as royal courts. Historians have already conducted convincing explorations of the relationship between political, cultural, and emotional change.⁵⁰ This book's focus on a narrow chronological window reflects my own particular interest in the intersections of social history, lived experience, broader political and institutional shifts, and the way these influenced emotions.

In the context of recently unified Italy, viewing the courts of law through an 'emotional arenas' lens focuses the general argument. From the 1860s, in line with the new state's liberal ideology, the Italian legal system instigated more systematic public participation in the proceedings in courts of law, partly to underscore its own legitimacy. Criminal trials were notably one of the few processes of the new state in which women could participate, though only as members of the audience. For major criminal cases, juries, consisting of men, became the norm, as did an eager public audience.⁵¹ In Rome from the early 1870s, after

---

⁴⁹ Pino Lucà Trombetta, in *La confessione della lussuria. Definizione e controllo del piacere nel Cattolicesimo* (Genoa: Costa & Nolan, 1991), notes the distinctive 'habitus' of the confessional space, p. 7.

⁵⁰ As well as the second half of Reddy's *The Navigation of Feeling*, on eighteenth-century France, see also Daniel Wickberg, 'What is the History of Sensibilities? On Cultural History, Old and New', *American Historical Review*, vol. 112, no. 3 (2007): 661–84.

⁵¹ Floriana Colao, Luigi Lacchè, and Claudia Storti, 'Premessa', in Colao, Lacchè, and Storti (eds), *Processo penale e opinione pubblica in Italia tra Otto e Novecento* (Bologna: Il Mulino, 2008), p. 8.

a Saturday evening at the opera and a Sunday morning in church, on Monday, some members of the same public might have participated in a trial. They may have been members of a jury, plaintiffs, or defendants, or more likely, simply interested members of the public. In court, Italian men and women would have encountered a new type of 'emotional arena' that had the potential to stage and shape their emotions in new ways.

Courts of law were neither opera theatres nor churches, but in many ways they could be reminiscent of both, a blend of the histrionic and the sacred.[52] What would a public that was unfamiliar with courts make of the cultural requirements, behavioural and emotional, of this new arena? To complicate matters, in some cases, such as the one this book treats, the intimate emotional arenas of one married couple, involving their homes, lives, loves, and families, were laid out in court so that they became a form of spectacle that was as emotionally intense as an opera. Perhaps even more so, given that real lives were at stake. Yet the atmosphere was supposed to be as serious as a church or even a confessional box. There could be no tomatoes in court. Not even any applause. The appropriate emotional timbre for the new space had to be established by the state, and grasped by the public. In short, the court of law emerged, relatively quickly in the Italian case, as a new and complex emotional arena, governed by a distinctive set of liturgies and rituals.

## Arenas Real and Virtual

Although buildings and tangible spaces are clear examples through which today's reading public might grasp the idea of the 'emotional arena', this book also deploys the idea in a metaphorical, virtual way. In an age of social media, suggesting that emotions can be generated, experienced, and expressed in distinctive ways in virtual 'spaces' is uncontroversial. But it is not anachronistic to perceive similar phenomena in a past that well predates the internet. Since Benedict Anderson's *Imagined Communities* of 1983, scholars have accepted that the 'profound emotional legitimacy' of an idea (such as nationalism) can be established via the collective imagination—that is, by virtual means.[53] And the idea can be taken further back than Anderson's focus on the nineteenth century. For example, Rosenwein has suggested that in early modern Europe, emotions values were

---

[52] Scholarly literature on this topic for Italy seems to be limited to critiques of 'excessive theatricality' in courts (e.g. see Colao, et al., n. 48, p. 9), but conceptual and technical overlap between theatres and courts has certainly been examined in other contexts. See, for example, Simon Devereaux, 'Arts of Public Performance: Barristers and Actors in Georgian England', in *Crime, Courtrooms and the Public Sphere in Britain, 1700–1850*, edited by David Lemmings (Farnham: Ashgate, 2012), pp. 93–117.

[53] Benedict Anderson, *Imagined Communities: Reflections on the Origin and Spread of Nationalism* (London: Verso, 1991).

shared via 'textual' as well as real communities.⁵⁴ This book is structured around five examples of types of emotional arena, some concrete, and some more metaphorical or imagined, across five chapters. All could potentially have been experienced by ordinary Italians of the 1870s.

Chapter 1 is an exploration of marriage as the key emotional arena experienced by Giovanni Fadda and Raffaella Saraceni after their wedding. Cohabiting only for short periods, they spent most of their married life apart. Their marital arena may have consisted of four walls on occasion, but it was much more often textual, based on letters. In the early stages, this seems to have been a harmonious arrangement, and the correspondence was a proxy for togetherness. It displays tenderness, affection, and a sense of commitment, revealing much about the construction of emotional ties between kin in 1870s Italy. The pair represent the new Italy's virtuous 'modern couple', working to banish the nation's lingering indolence and other vices.⁵⁵ But as Raffaella persistently refused to settle into the homes that Fadda established for her, their correspondence expresses increasing amounts of anger, frustration, and jealousy. Ultimately, their marital arena came apart in a rather bitter separation that caused Giovanni great anxiety.

Raffaella's alleged affair with Pietro Cardinali opens a peephole onto an emotional arena very different from her marriage: that of an itinerant circus. This troupe's performances and lives form the basis of chapter 2. There are two main aspects to the circus as an emotional arena. First, as a spectacle, or 'spettacolo', it brought emotional excitement to the audience, evoking joy, admiration, anxiety, and desire. Moreover, the circus artists lived and socialized, apparently promiscuously, among the people of the towns they visited. This raises questions about where one style of emotional arena ended and others began. Secondly, the official investigation brought to light some of the intimate dynamics of the families that made up the circus. The picaresque group was marked by passions less bridled than those between Giovanni and Raffaella. Because of the exceptional circumstance of the criminal investigation, some of these were brought into the light of day. In a more general sense, the circus's sojourn in Cassano allo Ionio reveals much about regional social and community life in the small towns of 1870s southern Italy.

For various reasons, sexual desire in those small towns, especially among women, might be the most difficult emotion to 'reconstitute' historically. But we know that the circus evoked desire because several women fell in love with Pietro Cardinali during his performances at the circus. After the troupe had departed, some of these women wrote passionate letters to him, sometimes for periods

---

⁵⁴ Barbara H. Rosenwein, 'Problems and Methods in the History of Emotions', *Passions in Context: International Journal for the History and Theory of Emotions* [online journal], 1 (2010). http://www.passionsincontext.de (accessed 27 April 2019); see also Plamper, *The History of Emotions*, p. 69.

⁵⁵ Silvana Patriarca, *Italian Vices: Nation and Character from the Risorgimento to the Republic* (Cambridge: Cambridge University Press, 2010), p. 78.

lasting months. These women created, unbeknownst to each other, virtual emotional arenas of illicit amorous correspondence. Their letters, written in utmost secrecy, and mailed anonymously through third parties, provide historical access to a rarely visible emotional world. This is the subject of chapter 3. Even though each author was her own person, what is striking is that the emotional tenor of their letters is similar enough to be able to view the genre of the illicit love letter as belonging to a distinct emotional arena. Moreover, although never sexually explicit, the intensity of the letters invites revision of what we currently know of women's inner lives in nineteenth-century Italy.

Chapter 4 moves from Eros to Thanatos. Grief over death is the emotional corollary of love, and several instances of death punctuate the story of Fadda's marriage. The chapter explores physical and cultural responses to death using the idea of 'arenas' to focus on cultural changes in this intense area of emotional life. This is particularly relevant at a time when the Italian state sought to govern areas of experience that had previously been the preserve of the Catholic Church. While Fadda was alive he had to contend with the death of his own mother. Though her death generated scant written evidence, it is enough to reveal Fadda's performance of self-control and forbearance. On a completely different scale, in January 1878, Italy's first king died. The nation's first state funeral has been extensively analysed by historians as an official exercise in fostering public emotional engagement, a step towards 'making Italians'. The chapter, as well as arguing that Rome, and even all of Italy, became a momentary emotional arena during the funeral, also analyses the way the king's death inflected the lives of ordinary living subjects: Fadda, Raffaella, and some of their relatives. An emotional lockdown was imposed on their lives, such that grieving for the king took precedence over all other matters.

Then there was the death of Giovanni Fadda. His murder, planned with an almost inscrutable blend of insouciance and cold blood, raises questions about what his life meant to those who contrived his demise. The crime tested the new state's investigative and forensic arenas over a very wide area of national territory. In marked contrast to the 1710–11 trial for murder in Astarita's *Village Justice*, whose distinctive point is that it was held in a feudal court, the Fadda murder was dealt with by a new, centralized, national administrative apparatus.[56] Official mechanisms were nevertheless swift and competent, with an emphasis on secular and scientific values. For example, the morgue where an autopsy on Fadda's body was carried out was an arena for the performance of an altogether dispassionate emotional style that portends the prestige of scientists and other professionals, in no small part because of their capacity for emotional self-control.

---

[56] Astarita, *Village Justice*, p. xv.

Once the prosecution's preparations were complete, the narrative that explained Fadda's murder, barely different from the one established by Michele Finizia on the day of the crime, arrived at the Court of Assizes one year later. This extraordinary event is the subject of chapter 5. In the context of an Italian state that faced significant challenges in engaging the commitment of its citizens, events such as the Fadda trial presented opportunities for the public to derive emotional gratification from official processes. For the duration of the trial, the courtroom, filled to bursting point with people, excited yet restrained, was a definitive emotional arena for modern Italy, almost a state theatre for the values of liberalism.

Commentary on the trial, and Italian criminal trials in general, has often either implied or expressed criticism of 'excessive' degrees of theatricality.[57] This chapter, although it eagerly portrays the court as a highly emotional arena, develops an alternative interpretation. Drawing from broader scholarship on courtrooms and trials across Europe over a broad time span, it argues that legal spaces are necessarily arenas of intense but distinctly managed emotions. Italy, in opening its courts to the public, re-joined a long tradition of courts as a form of theatre that was well established elsewhere in Europe by the 1870s, and was an important aspect of the relationship between state and citizen.

Ultimately, by examining some of the evolving institutions, cultures, and social spaces of 1870s Italy as emotional arenas—from marriage to circuses to secret loves and grief-laden deaths—in which we can see the staging and shaping of interplays between subjective feelings and the external world, it is my hope that we will develop a clearer sense of some of the dynamics that give emotions a history.

---

[57] See, for example, Thomas Simpson, *The Fadda Affair: Murder and Media in the New Rome* (New York: Palgrave Macmillan, 2010); but also Groppi (n. 38) and Colao et al. (n. 51 and n. 52).

# 1
# Intimate Arenas
## A New Couple for a New Kingdom

### A Spring Wedding

Naples in the 1870s, as today, was a place of enthralling beauty, particularly when viewed from the escarpment high above the old city. Looking out across the famous bay, the cityscape is dominated by Mount Vesuvius, an active volcano at once magnanimous in its climatic influence and ominous with violent potential. In this quintessential southern Italian setting, it is easy to visualize a picture-book late-spring wedding in May 1871, uniting Lieutenant Giovanni Fadda with one Signorina Raffaella Saraceni. The bride was a nubile eighteen years of age, and her groom, smart and bemedalled in a soldier's uniform, was in the prime of life in his late twenties. The happy occasion, attended by family and friends, including several of the groom's fellow officers, merged two sets of kin, making the couple into a new familial cell.[1] The pair embodied the aspirations of an emergent bourgeois class that, via the unification of Italy, had become key protagonists in one of Europe's newest nations. Raffaella and Giovanni, married under the new civil code of 1866, represented many new couples who found themselves at the vanguard of Italy's national springtime.

Raffaella came from the rugged southern region of Calabria. Her mother's family had property and her stepfather was a director of the area's nascent railway system. Their home town, Cassano allo Ionio, located on the instep of Italy's boot-shaped peninsula, perches on a hilltop looking south over the Ionian Sea. Naples was an arduous 250 kilometre journey to the northwest by horse-drawn coach, or even further on the new railway, via the less mountainous region of Puglia. Despite the distance, Raffaella's family had close ties to the southern metropolis, passing frequent sojourns there. They kept an apartment in the densely populated Spagnoli district,[2] and the tailor used by Raffaella and her mother, Federico

---

[1] *Processo Fadda Illustrato. Dibattimento alla Corte d'Assise di Roma dal 30 settembre al 31 ottobre 1879* (Rome: Giovanni Bracco Editore, 1879), p. 139. The witness was a young lawyer and friend of the couple, Pietro Rosano, who, in 1879, recalled attending the wedding.

[2] Probably located at Vico Tre Re a Toledo, Naples, from the address on a postcard from Giovanni Fadda to Carolina Nola, dated Chieti, 9 August 1877, held in the Archivio di Stato di Roma, Tribunale Civile e Penale di Roma (henceforth ASR, TCPR), 1879, busta 3659, vol. IV, f. 172. In line with Italian custom, Raffaella's mother Carolina was generally referred to by her original surname, Nola, not her

**Figure 1.1** Raffaella Saraceni (ASR, TCPR, 1879, b. 3659). Reproduced with permission from the Ministero dei Beni e Attività Culturali e del Turismo, ASRM 56/2015. Further reproduction prohibited.

Schiavone, had an atelier in nearby Via Roma.[3] It was during a stay in Naples that Raffaella met her future husband. As she recalled their courtship, Giovanni Fadda was 'presented at home, we mutually liked each other', he then requested her hand, and they were married.[4]

Fadda was originally from Cagliari, capital of the island of Sardinia. His father was a notary, but the family was not especially distinguished or well-to-do. Before

---

married surname, Saraceni. Though there are some exceptions, I have chosen to use Nola throughout to avoid confusion.

[3] ASR, TCPR, 1879, b. 3659, vol. IV, ff. 205–7, report by Naples prosecutor of visit to Schiavone's atelier, 13 October 1879. Numerous letters from Raffaella Saraceni and Carolina Nola to their tailor (ASR, TCPR, 1879, b. 3659, vol. IV, ff. 208–21) not only reveal great concern about sartorial matters but indicate that the tailor was the women's confidante. Naples' Via Roma was renamed Via Toledo in the 1980s, and remains one of the city's most important commercial streets.

[4] ASR, TCPR, 1879, b. 3659, vol. IA, ff. 120–6, interrogation of Saraceni by prosecutor Michele Finizia, Rome, 10 October 1878. One of Fadda's friends, a captain in the same regiment who probably attended the wedding, recalled the engagement in a very similar way—ASR, TCPR, 1879, b. 3659, vol. II, ff. 11–12, witness statement by Alberto Pontiroli Gobbi, 43, of Modena, 9 October 1878.

**Figure 1.2** Giovanni Fadda (ASR, TCPR, 1879, b. 3659). Reproduced with permission from the Ministero dei Beni e Attività Culturali e del Turismo, ASRM 56/2015. Further reproduction prohibited.

the unification of Italy, Sardinia had been part of Victor Emmanuel II's Kingdom of Piedmont-Sardinia, centered in Turin, northern Italy. In 1859, Giovanni Fadda, at only sixteen years of age, had volunteered to serve his king in the wars against Austria that paved the way for Italian unity. Wounded in the celebrated battle of San Martino and later decorated, Giovanni carried about him the air of a man who had earned his stake in the nation. In Raffaella's family's estimation, this military valour, augmented by a secure position as an army quartermaster in the new state, may have made up for the Sardinian soldier's somewhat humbler family stock. On paper at least, Giovanni and Raffaella looked like a promising match.

To sensitive observers, conscious of allegory and symbolism, the marriage must have been more than just a happy private alliance. Raffaella and Giovanni each came from areas of the Italian peninsula that, until recently, had been entirely unrelated polities. The decade prior to the couple's wedding had seen all that change rapidly. Victor Emmanuel II of Piedmont's wars against Austria, seeking to consolidate a northern Italian state, unexpectedly catalysed Giuseppe Garibaldi's almost miraculous conquest of the southern half of the peninsula in the name of Italy in late 1860. That famous expedition was followed by the foundation of the Kingdom of Italy in March 1861, the acquisition of the Veneto from Austria in 1866, and ultimately the conquest of Rome as a fitting capital for the nation in the autumn of 1870. The new couple's lives, as witnesses of and participants in this process for more than a decade, were profoundly entwined with the Italian Risorgimento. Their marriage could well have been seen by contemporaries as both a product and an intimate symbol of Italy's unification.

For historians too, the Fadda marriage might epitomize the intertwining of kinship and nationhood that was so persuasively analysed in the Italian context by cultural historian Alberto Mario Banti.[5] The symbolic links between marriage and the nation have been explored in other western contexts in a similarly convincing way. Nancy Cott has observed that the public quality of marriage means that as an institution, it 'participates in the public order', shaping community life and facilitating 'the government's grasp on the populace'. Yet Cott also proposed, with a striking simile, that marriage was 'like the Sphinx': a conspicuous public monument, but also inscrutably private and often 'full of secrets'.[6] In the preparatory phase of Italy's Risorgimento, kinship, as Banti argued, became an instrumental metaphor of future national unity, precisely because of its powerful emotional resonance.[7] And as Cott's insights suggest, particularly in a new nation such as Italy, couples like the Faddas continued that symbolic national labour in their everyday lives.

But the work of a married couple was not only symbolic. Beyond official blessings for their union to contribute offspring to the newly constituted body politic, Giovanni was a nation-builder in another way. As a state functionary, he was deeply involved in the development of Italy's infrastructure, and Raffaella was expected to support him in the task. Although no longer in combat, Giovanni remained a soldier attached to his regiment, a fact that was clearly central to his identity. The marriage was to bear some of the burdens of an essential incompatibility, as Myna Trustram has put it, between soldierly life and the domestic arena.[8] For Raffaella, expected to accompany Fadda from one posting to the next, the marriage meant exchanging the secure realm of her extended family for the loneliness of a soldier's wife in the nation's outposts. Married 'coupledom',

---

[5] Alberto Mario Banti, *La nazione del Risorgimento. Parentela, santità e onore alle origini dell'Italia unita* (Turin: Einaudi, 2000).

[6] Nancy Cott, *Public Vows: A History of Marriage and the Nation* (Cambridge, MA: Harvard University Press, 2000), p. 1. On the 'eager desire for domesticity and nationality to cleave together' in Britain, see Karen Chase and Michael Levenson, *The Spectacle of Intimacy: A Public Life for the Victorian Family* (Princeton: Princeton University Press, 2000), p. 3. And on the power of secrets in marriage and family life, see Deborah Cohen, *Family Secrets: Living with Shame from the Victorians to the Present day* (London: Viking Books, 2013).

[7] Banti, *La nazione del Risorgimento*, p. 110.

[8] Myna Trustram, *Women of the Regiment: Marriage and the Victorian Army* (Cambridge: Cambridge University Press, 1984), p. 1.

ideally a unique emotional arena whose intimate joys were enough to make it a sentimentally self-sufficient unit, was the pair's new life. But it was not to be easy for either spouse.

Hindsight reveals that, like the beautiful city in which the marriage had been solemnized, the relationship was shadowed by ominous and destructive tensions from a relatively early stage. For Raffaella, marriage was to be a painfully constrained state whose potential intimate pleasures did not make up for the loss of the world constituted by her parents, brother, servants, and the vibrant social life of their family home. She found married life limited and lonely. The transition was arguably less of an emotional shift for Fadda, since armies and regiments themselves had a universal tradition of constituting family-like arenas of attachment and security.[9] As the bread-winning male who moved with his comrades, Fadda's life changed less than Raffaella's, and he had more to fall back on, emotionally speaking. Nevertheless, in the long run, the strain of juggling allegiances between diverse and perhaps incompatible emotional arenas told on Fadda just as it did on Raffaella.

Over a period of seven years, inner tensions gradually transformed the marriage from a promising symbol of national unity into a prison. The union was ultimately put asunder through Giovanni's murder. Its private domains were explored by officials and their findings became part of the public record. The violent death that parted the couple forced the sphinx to reveal some of the usually inscrutable emotional textures, contours, and experience of their marriage. In this sense, the preservation of correspondence and other types of personal testimony made the relationship into a classic example of the terrain that is so rich with microhistorical possibilities: the violent conclusion of an apparently normal relationship resulted in the exposure of its exceptionalism. Those revelations allow the exploration of feelings that are likely to have been experienced at least to some degree by most 'normal' couples of the time and place.[10]

Based on the records of that judicial investigation, this chapter explores marriage as an 'emotional arena' in 1870s Italy. The qualities of this arena had a great deal to do with the ideology of marriage at the time. In many types of western discourse, the couple in late nineteenth-century bourgeois society increasingly took on the character of an emotionally self-contained unit.[11] This was reflected

---

[9] Trustram, *Women of the Regiment*, for example pp. 10 and 22–3.

[10] Edoardo Grendi, 'Micro-analisi e storia sociale', *Quaderni storici*, vol. 12, no. 35(2): 506–20 (here p. 512). In this essay Grendi was referring to 'exceptional-normal' documents, but the term soon came to be applied to 'exceptional-normal' events: see Carlo Ginzburg, 'Microhistory: Two or Three Things that I Know about it', trans. John and Anne C. Tedeschi, *Critical Inquiry*, 20 (Autumn 1993): 10–35 (here p. 33).

[11] Like many historians, my interest in the politics of marriage and family was given great impetus by Leonore Davidoff and Catherine Hall's *Family Fortunes: Men and Women of the English Middle Class, 1780-1850* (London: Routledge, 2002 [1987], esp. ch. 7, '"Our family is a little world": family structure and relationships'. An early essay on the politics of intimacy that had much to say about

in concrete spatial terms as the marital home developed culturally into a private and distinctive emotional arena. For too long viewed simplistically as a 'female' and therefore emotional space, John Tosh's work brought to light masculine investment in the emotional arena of the marital home.[12] As we will see, Fadda's concern with providing a suitable nest for Raffaella suggests that the phenomenon Tosh describes in Victorian England had its counterpart in Italy. What is also clear though, is that Fadda was largely frustrated in his attempts to make his marriage into a self-contained unit based on hearth and home. Because of this, the physical spaces of the Fadda's marriage play a relatively minor role in this analysis.

Instead, because Fadda and Raffaella spent so much time apart, it is largely as a metaphorical emotional arena that their marriage presents itself. As a result of their separations, the couple lived their marriage largely through letters. The emotional features of a marital relationship come across in a correspondence that largely took the place of cohabitation. In this written record many of the emotions that might be expressed in a marital home are visible: affection, love, desire, pride, fear, anger, and even jealousy. The Fadda's marriage relationship represents an emotional arena despite the fact that often, and unusually, it was not contained within four walls. Indeed it is because it did not do so that so much more than usual of the thoughts and feelings involved were preserved in writing for posterity.

Alas, the correspondence does not yield all the marriage's secrets. For all the historical and official sifting of Raffaella and Giovanni's relationship, parts of it remained sphinx-like, particularly in relation to their sexual experience.[13] We will never know the exact nature of their most intimate secrets. What became clear from the judicial process is that for Raffaella and Giovanni, their union was dominated not by gratification, but by emotional suffering. For some time, they sought to manage this, but ultimately they failed. The marriage, which had emerged hand-in-hand with the Italian Risorgimento as a promising emotional arena for shaping and staging the couple's sweetest joys, concluded with Fadda's death. It

---

'the couple' was a cultural history of 'drives and emotions' ahead of its time: Peter Gay's *The Bourgeois Experience. From Victoria to Freud: Vol. I, The Education of the Senses* (Oxford: Oxford University Press, 1984), esp. 'Sweet Bourgeois Communions', pp. 109–68.

[12] John Tosh, *A Man's Place: Masculinity and the Middle-Class Home in Victorian England* (New haven: Yale University Press, 2007 [1999]).

[13] Historiographical explorations of this topic have been limited by scant source materials and perhaps institutional impediments. Notable exceptions are Bruno Wanrooij's pioneering *Storia del pudore. La questione sessuale in Italia, 1860–1940* (Venice: Marsilio editori, 1990); and Antonia Pasi and Paolo Sorcinelli's edited volume, *Amori e trasgressioni. Rapporti di coppia tra '800 e '900* (Bari: Edizioni Dedalo, 1995). The introduction stresses the difficulties of exploring this historical terrain, precisely because of the intimate, private nature of the subject for most couples (pp. 5–6). More recently, *Italian Sexualities Uncovered, 1789–1914*, edited by Valeria P. Babini, Chiara Beccalossi, and Lucy Riall (Basingstoke: Palgrave Macmillan, 2015), marks an important step forward.

## The New Civil Law and a Mobile Couple

After Italy's unification in 1861, the new government's eagerness to wrest jurisdiction over the institution of marriage from the Catholic Church was demonstrated by the relatively hasty introduction of a unified civil code for the new nation, effective from 1 January 1866. This replaced the disparate laws and customs of the numerous polities that had been brought together to form the new kingdom. The process exemplified Cott's notion of marriage law as a tool for 'sculpting' the body politic.[15] Italy's new code, though, did not represent a radical alteration to the concept of marriage, since it essentially recast from a secular mould the ecclesiastically based laws it replaced. Although the code stipulated that a marriage was only valid if conducted by an official of the state, rather than the church, it replicated the Christian principles of marriage by reinforcing its indissolubility and casting the bride as subject to the groom's authority.[16] It was this law that regulated Saraceni's marriage to Fadda.

If marriage law was principally concerned with property and propriety, folklore still saw matrimony as a passport to the gratifying duties of conjugal intimacy. It is of course difficult to explore that aspect of the historical experience of matrimony because of the scarcity of direct personal accounts. Typically, contemporary documentation of Raffaella's and Giovanni's marriage arrangements leaves no trace of the personal feelings that may well have been uppermost in the minds of the betrothed. Rather, the records suggest that this conjunction of middle-class Italian families was typical of established historiographical understandings of the phenomenon. These views were, until recently at least, shaped by the nature of traditional historical records of marriage and personal life, in which subjective matters such as sentiment and sexuality can only be discerned, if at all, between the lines.

In Raffaella and Giovanni's case, as was customary, financial and material concerns dominate the union's written arrangements. These are exemplified by the marriage agreement's details of Raffaella's dowry, from the handsome sum of

---

[14] Liberal Italy's collective anxiety about a national lack of 'mettle' has long been a theme in the historiography. See Silvana Patriarca, *Italian Vices: Nation and Character from the Risorgimento to the Republic* (Cambridge: Cambridge University Press, 2013).
[15] Cott, *Public Vows*, p. 5.
[16] Michela De Giorgio and Christiane Klapisch-Zuber (eds), *Storia del matrimonio* (Rome-Bari: Laterza, 1996); Mark Seymour, *Debating Divorce in Italy: Marriage and the Making of Modern Italians, 1860–1974* (New York: Palgrave Macmillan, 2006), pp. 11–17.

19,500 lire, down to the sheets and blankets provided for the marriage bed.[17] There is little to be gleaned anywhere about the future partners' emotions, hopes, and desires, just as there is no direct evidence about how things felt for the couple in a key emotional locus of marriage: between those carefully inventoried sheets. However, in their case, even early historical traces suggest that the union's ominous shadows originated from that marriage bed. Fadda's professional colleagues knew that the wounds he had received on the battlefield of San Martino had been in the genital region, and had resulted in a 'certain physical imperfection'.[18] One colleague even claimed that before assenting to the marriage, Raffaella's parents had required Fadda's 'viripotenza' to be medically investigated.[19]

That claim reflected the previous Catholic legal regime's preoccupation not only with a woman's virginity, but with the successful consummation of marriage. According to the Catholic principles that informed marriage law in most Italian states before 1866, perpetual impotence existing prior to a marriage was one of the few grounds on which an annulment could be granted. The provision remained unchanged under Italy's new civil code. Obviously, sexual capacity remained of vital importance personally and socially, and Angus McLaren's skilful cultural history of impotence leaves no doubt that centuries of religious law and folk wisdom shaped indelible popular notions on the subject across the western world.[20] This was certainly the case in Italy as much as anywhere, as popular interpretations of the Fadda marriage were to reveal.

It turns out that there was an element of truth to the rumour of the medical investigation of the soldier's virility, but the check probably took place several months after the May 1871 wedding, not prior. In October 1871, Fadda requested a medical certificate from the army, which outlined that during 1859's battle of San Martino, he had been wounded by a bullet that seriously damaged his left testicle.[21] The certificate did not touch on the question of his virility, but the date of the certificate is interesting, almost as if Fadda felt the need for an official explanation for what may have been an intimate shortcoming. Furthermore, Raffaella's parents may have had nothing to do with the check-up, since another friend recalled meeting the bride's mother, Carolina Nola, in Naples a year after the wedding. Noting that Raffaella had yet to become pregnant, he hinted at the

---

[17] ASR, TCPR, 1879, b. 3659, vol. IB, ff. 98–101, marriage agreement between Raffaella Saraceni and Giovanni Fadda, dated 2 May 1871.
[18] ASR, TCPR, 1879, b. 3659, vol. IV, f. 317, testimony of Mariano Labriola, in court, 10 October 1879.
[19] ASR, TCPR, 1879, b. 3659, vol. II, ff. 11–12, witness statement by Alberto Pontiroli Gobbi, 43, of Modena, also a captain of the 32nd Fanteria, 9 October 1878.
[20] Angus McLaren, *Impotence: A Cultural History* (Chicago: University of Chicago Press, 2007), pp. 31–5.
[21] ASR, TCPR, 1879, b. 3659, vol. IA, f. 14, certificate attesting to Fadda's war injuries (inflicted on 24 June 1859), dated Cagliari, 2 October 1871.

alleged premarital check-up of Fadda's 'capacity'. It appeared to the friend that this was the first Signora Nola had heard of the problem.[22]

In any case it was not really until after the marriage had started to appear problematic that the story of Fadda's war wound, and speculation about its effects on the sexual aspects of the marriage, could take on a causal role in any explanatory narrative. All we can be certain about is that the couple's relationship somehow limped along rather than flourished. The pair do not seem, in retrospect, to have become an emotionally self-sufficient unit. The difficulty probably did have a sexual aspect from the outset, but it was not something the couple ever mentioned directly in writing. What observers noticed is that for young newlyweds, Fadda and Saraceni spent surprising amounts of time apart. Documentary evidence that accrued after the marriage, in the form of letters exchanged between the couple during their many periods of separation, provides a way of observing how they sought to construct their relationship during these separations, and of gauging its emotional climate and style, particularly for the second half of the marriage's seven-year duration.

Technically the civil code obliged a woman to live with her husband wherever he chose to establish their marital home, and much has been made of the subaltern position in which this and other aspects of the code placed an Italian married woman.[23] At the time of his marriage Giovanni was an official of a newly established state whose central government faced the enormous task of bringing its far-flung provinces under the control of unified administration. Just as Giovanni had played a part in unifying the nation through war, he continued to have a role in the consolidation of the state once it was made, and it was a role he took very seriously. In his position as army quartermaster, he was required to take postings around the southern areas of the Italian peninsula, relocating periodically for much of his married life.

Given marriage law, custom, and the symbolic potential of the couple itself, we might expect to witness the pair travelling around the distant reaches of the new body politic like a diplomatic couple. Instead, after about fifteen months together spent in Naples, Giovanni was sent to Caltanissetta, in the heart of Sicily. He spent a year there, but Raffaella only joined him for the final month of his posting. Prior to that she stayed with her parents in Calabria. After Sicily, Giovanni's next long-term station was the town of Chieti, in the Abruzzi region, on the Adriatic coast due east of Rome. He was based there for about three years, during which Raffaella only lived with him for limited periods. Looking back on her marriage, Raffaella admitted that she spent a lot of time with her parents in Calabria, and

---

[22] ASR, TCPR, 1879, b. 3659, vol. IV, f. 317, Mariano Labriola's statement in court, 11 October, 1879.
[23] For example, Anna Maria Isastia, 'La questione femminile nelle discussioni parlamentari postunitarie: il Codice Civile del 1865', *Dimensioni e problemi della ricerca storica*, no. 2 (1991): 167–84.

made short-term attempts to live with Giovanni only occasionally during the seven years of their union.[24] The couple never created an emotional arena in the form of a marital home.

Raffaella's recollections of her married life are vague about her reluctance to cohabit with her husband. Between the lines, the main explanatory possibilities are the unsuitability of Giovanni's busy peripatetic lifestyle, and, on the other hand, Raffaella's intense attachment to the emotionally gratifying arena represented by her lively, sociable, parental home. As some of Giovanni's letters confirm, the hinterland towns of 1870s southern Italy offered few facilities for short-term sojourners, and there would have been little to amuse or comfort the young wife of a busy officer. As will also become obvious, Raffaella remained particularly attached to her mother, and was deeply embedded within the life of her extended family at home in Cassano. There is also the strong possibility of sexual difficulties with her husband. Any and all of these factors might explain Raffaella's reluctance to live with him. Equally, her reluctance to join him may have exacerbated the difficulties, particularly from Giovanni's point of view.

Either way, the troubled emotional dynamics of Giovanni's and Raffaella's marriage are of interest. Historians of Italy and other places of emigration are familiar with the challenges created for couples, and women in particular, by long-distance relationships resulting from men taking employment opportunities abroad.[25] Yet, despite the sociologically familiar phenomenon of internal migration in Italy itself (particularly in the 1950s and 1960s), little is known about the nature of such distanced relationships in the previous century, even for the mobile social class to which Raffaella and Giovanni belonged. During that period of earnest nation-building, with the deployment of civil and military personnel to recently incorporated outposts, there must have been many couples in similar situations. Nevertheless, Saraceni spent so little time with her husband that it 'excited the marvel' of the townsfolk of Cassano allo Ionio, and was also noted by observers in the towns where Giovanni was stationed.[26]

## Couples and Kin by Correspondence

In the absence of cohabitation, letters became an important element of Giovanni and Raffaella's family life, and in writing them the couple played their part in a

---

[24] ASR, TCPR, 1879, b. 3659, vol. IA, ff. 120–6, interrogation of Raffaella Saraceni by prosecutor Michele Finizia, Rome, 10 October 1878. Raffaella claimed the couple spent eighteen months together in Naples, but Giovanni began to send letters from Sicily in early August, 1872, approximately fourteen or fifteen months after the wedding.
[25] Donna R. Gabaccia and Loretta Baldassar, *Intimacy and Italian Migration: Gender and Domestic Lives in a Mobile World* (New York: Fordham University Press, 2010).
[26] ASR, TCPR, 1879, b. 3659, vol. II, f. 210, witness statement by Raffaele De Vincentis, 52, doctor and mayor of Cassano, 21 November 1878. See also the testimony of observers in Chieti, below.

broad trend in unified Italy. As Gabriella Romani has shown, the 1861 unification marked a turning point in the growth of Italian 'postal culture'. The nationalization of Italy's mail service gave rise to a marked increase in epistolary traffic across the peninsula, from 71 million letters in 1863, to 156 million twenty years later.[27] Romani suggests that as more Italians participated in epistolary exchanges, their 'perceptions of space and notions of personal as well as collective boundaries' were transformed.[28] Raffaella and Giovanni's marriage correspondence exemplifies such transformations.

In essence, correspondence was to provide an intimate, crucial part of the couple's 'togetherness': given the time they spent apart, rather than their shared domestic space, letters became a foundation of the emotional arena represented by their marriage. Through the letters, the couple created an imagined space in which to share exchanges of sentiment. The couple's personal letters were augmented, particularly in the early days, by those exchanged between Giovanni and Raffaella's mother, Carolina Nola. Carolina played a significant role in fostering the marriage long after the wedding had taken place. Indeed, she tended the relationship as if it were an ailing houseplant, meaning that even in their correspondence the married couple were not an emotionally self-sufficient unit.

Collectively the trio's letters attest to broader dynamics in the shaping and arrangement of family life. They document arrivals and departures, health and illness, general affection, and sometimes, emotionally charged events such as engagements, weddings, illness, and death. Many of these family letters were ferreted out by the authorities during the criminal investigation into Giovanni's murder. The epistles are neither numerous nor celebrated, unlike some famous correspondence.[29] But they are sufficient to provide an unusual glimpse into one couple's careful epistolary 'performance' of familial emotions, centered around their own marriage, then extending to members of both families, across many leagues of land and sea.

In early August 1872, Giovanni was posted to Caltanissetta, central Sicily. Rather than accompany him, Raffaella returned to her parental home in Calabria. One of the earliest of Giovanni's Sicilian letters to survive was sent to his mother-in-law, Carolina. He addressed her intimately as 'Cara Madre' (Dear Mother), but used the formal third-person-singular verb form, a normal sign of intergenerational respect. Writing into existence a familial network across wide swathes of national territory, Giovanni recounted to Carolina that a letter had arrived from

---

[27] Gabriella Romani, *Postal Culture: Writing and Reading Letters in Post-Unification Italy* (Toronto: University of Toronto Press, 2013), p. 23.
[28] Romani, *Postal Culture*, p. 14.
[29] For example, see Susan K. Foley and Charles Sowerwine, *A Political Romance: Léon Gambetta, Léonie Léon, and the Making of the French Republic, 1872–1882* (Basingstoke: Palgrave Macmillan, 2012); and Paola Carlucci, 'Il filo interrotto della vita: Sidney Sonnino e Natalia Morozzo della Rocca', in *Scrivere d'amore. Lettere di uomini e donne tra Cinque e Novecento*, edited by Manola Ida Venzo (Rome: Viella, 2015), pp. 233–70.

Cagliari from his uncle, as well as a telegram. Some sort of setback, the nature of which is unclear, had foiled efforts on his part that he had been convinced 'would be good for the family'. Later letters confirm this early hint that Giovanni was always conscious of trying to do what he thought was right, according to a strenuous personal sense of obligation. The letter concludes by sending greetings to 'la Nonna' (the Grandma) and the whole family, and he signs off 'Your very affectionate Giovanni'.[30]

How much feeling lay behind the affection Giovanni expressed for his mother-in-law? The formulaic nature of his closing and indeed the correspondence as a whole raises an immediate question about how much emotion can be read into these letters. In the 1990s, a group of cultural historians set an influential theoretical bar on the extraction of authors' 'inner feelings' from personal letters. Informed by post-structuralist concerns about documents as texts, they warned that letters revealed more about the social customs of the day than they did of their writers' true sentiments.[31] In the wake of such insights and the linguistic turn more generally, scholars wary of 'essentialism' learned to be sceptical of the idea that personal writing might offer direct insights into an author's emotions.[32] Historians felt they could analyse the emotional shells they found—the social structures—but not the sentient mollusc within.

From early in the twenty-first century, ideas about the relationship between language and emotions, pioneered by William Reddy's concept of the 'emotive', have tended to dissolve this impasse. Reddy argued persuasively that emotional utterances may record inner feeling because they were in fact constitutive of them.[33] Monique Scheer's argument that emotions are 'a kind of practice', that is, not just something people experience in consciousness but 'something they do', moves even further towards fusing the binary notion of bodily experience of emotions on the one hand, and social structures on the other.[34] Cumulatively, theoretical work in this vein has given historians greater confidence to write about the personal emotions they discern in the nets they cast over private correspondence or personal utterances—even if they remain highly attuned to the influence of cultural forms.[35]

---

[30] ASR, TCPR, 1879, b. 3659, vol. IV, f. 157, letter from Giovanni Fadda to Carolina Nola, dated Caltanissetta, 3 August 1872.
[31] Exemplary of the approach is Roger Chartier, Alain Boureau and Cécile Dauphin, *Correspondence: Models of Letter-Writing from the Middle Ages to the Nineteenth Century* (Cambridge: Polity Press, 1997 [1991]).
[32] Ruth Leys, 'The Turn to Affect: A Critique', *Critical Enquiry* 37 (Spring 2011): 434–72, here p. 440.
[33] William M. Reddy, *The Navigation of Feeling: A Framework for the History of Emotions* (Cambridge: Cambridge University Press, 2000), pp. 104–11.
[34] Monique Scheer, 'Are Emotions a Kind of Practice (and is that what Makes them have a History)? A Bourdieuian Approach to Understanding Emotions', *History and Theory*, 51 (May 2012): 193–220, here p. 195.
[35] See, for example, Manola Ida Venzo, 'Documenti del sé: usi e abusi', and Roberto Bizzocchi, 'Decodificare le emozioni', both in Manola Ida Venzo (ed.) *Scrivere d'amore*, pp. 11–18 and 19–24

Such questions will appear again in chapter four, which explores an altogether more passionate genre of correspondence, but the argument here about Fadda's writing is that it engages rituals that underlined his sense of the importance of affective family ties in nineteenth-century Italy.[36] He engaged emotionally according to the standards of the emotional arena of the extended family, which he also helped to construct and maintain. The fact that Carolina in Calabria was informed by her son-in-law stationed in Sicily of the doings of an uncle in Sardinia also bears witness to an emerging national consciousness that was partly ushered into being by familial correspondence. Giovanni contributed to both projects at every possibility, with meticulously conscientious attention to the extended family into which he had married. He never failed to send greetings, solicitations, and gallant gestures—such as kisses upon the hand—to a wide range of Raffaella's relatives.

In a more detailed letter, also addressed to his mother-in-law, Giovanni describes the challenges and discomfort of life in Caltanissetta and his hope that he would not have to stay in the district. He reported that the administration was in disarray and the accounts were behind. Though unremarkable observations, in the light of a developing sense of Giovanni's character, these words give an early indication of a certain fastidiousness. Giovanni described the town as 'horrendous' and, providing an indication of the difficulties of daily life in the Sicilian heartland, laments that even water cost a fortune. Rents, if a place could be found at all, were even worse. One colleague had just taken an unfurnished house for the exorbitant sum of 900 francs a year. Giovanni himself had searched for an apartment, without luck, and was lodging in a hotel paying one franc per day.[37] Although the varied units of currency thwart attempts to compare, it was clearly cheaper to stay in a hotel than to rent an apartment.

It may not have been Giovanni's intention, but his descriptions make it clear that Raffaella had good reason not to join her husband in those early days at least. Only at the end of the letter, though, did Giovanni mention Raffaella by name. He assured Carolina that he had received his wife's letter and would now write to her, as well as 'la nonna' and 'Peppino'. The latter was a typically affectionate family diminutive for Raffaella's older brother, Giuseppe. An even more extensive salutation concluding this letter bade Carolina to greet the uncle and aunts and kiss

---

respectively; Martin Lyons, '"Questo cor che tuo si rese": the Private and the Public in Italian Women's Love letters in the Long Nineteenth Century', *Modern Italy*, vol. 19, no. 4 (2014): 355–68; Roberto Bizzocchi, *A Lady's Man: The Cicisbei, Private Morals and National Identity in Italy* (Basingstoke: Palgrave Macmillan, 2014), e.g. pp. 89–114.

[36] My understanding of letter-writing in Italy owes much to the literature that has built up from the early 2000s, particularly Maria Luisa Betri and Daniela Maldini Chiarito(eds), «*Dolce donor graditissimo*». *La lettera privata dal Settecento al Novecento* (Milan: Franco Angeli, 2000); Angela Russo, «*Nel desiderio delle tue care nuove*». *Scritture private e relazioni di genere nell'Ottocento risorgimentale* (Milan: Franco Angeli, 2006); and other works cited in this chapter.

[37] ASR, TCPR, 1879, b. 3659, vol. IV, ff. 158–9, letter from Giovanni Fadda to Carolina Nola, dated Caltanissetta, 26 August 1872.

grandma's hand, then finally declared its writer her 'very affectionate son, Giovanni'.[38] It is clear, at the very least, that such affections were held in high regard by the families of the time, and they were enacted repeatedly.

In the context of 1870s Italy, marriage, though constituting the couple as the fundamental cell of society, was also a link in the chain of extended family ties. This couple was the object of particular concern for a worried mother, although we only glean this through Giovanni's conscientious responses. A shorter letter from Fadda in Caltanissetta, dated 17 September 1872, addressed again to 'Cara Madre', acknowledges hers of 13 September and seeks to put to rest her evident concern about his lack of correspondence with Raffaella. Giovanni assures Carolina that he writes to his wife every two days to let her know 'about his state of health'. He goes on to mention an impending ministerial decision, perhaps about an imminent change of work location, and signs off with an embrace only to her and Peppino, with no mention of the extended family on this occasion.[39]

Nearly all of these letters survive in the archive without their original envelopes, so it is not possible to know to which addresses they were sent. In this case though, two things point to the fact that the letter was addressed to Carolina at a place other than her main residence in Cassano. If she had been at home, there would have been no need for Giovanni to reassure her that he wrote to Raffaella every second day, since the women lived in the same house. Furthermore, knowing that Carolina was away obviated the need for Giovanni to send his habitual conscientious salutations to the extended family. Judging by the greetings, Giovanni knew that Carolina was only in the company of her son, and the most likely possibility is that the pair were sojourning in Naples.

The key points confirmed by the letter though, are that Giovanni had an independent relationship with his mother-in-law, and that, for her part, she nurtured and tended her daughter's marriage even from a distance of hundreds of kilometres. Giovanni's next letter removes any doubt that Carolina was away from home. Brief, it was written by Giovanni from Cassano, where he was paying a surprise visit. Confirming the importance of Carolina's coordinating presence at the centre of the extended family, the letter's opening lines referred to Giovanni's telegram telling her of his arrival and saying he had found the whole family in good health. The letter recounted that this had given him great pleasure, and he added that he too was in good health, despite the lack of a cloak during his journey, which had made it a chilly one.[40]

---

[38] ASR, TCPR, 1879, b. 3659, vol. IV, ff. 158–9, letter from Giovanni Fadda to Carolina Nola, dated Caltanissetta, 26 August 1872.
[39] ASR, TCPR, 1879, b. 3659, vol. IV, ff. 160–1, letter from Giovanni Fadda to Carolina Nola, dated Caltanissetta, 17 September 1872.
[40] ASR, TCPR, 1879, b. 3659, vol. IV, ff. 162–3, letter to Carolina Nola, undated but sent from Cassano.

The constant references to health in this family correspondence make the news repetitive, but they are a reminder that the precariousness of good health made it a ubiquitous concern at a time when even minor illnesses could become life-threatening. For this reason, individual emotional well-being, in the form of the absence of fear, was closely tied to the health of family members. Additionally, Giovanni seems rather pleased that he managed to keep the visit to Cassano a surprise for all, and particularly mentions that Raffaella was amazed by the way he had managed to pull the whole thing off. Giovanni often seems a rather staid character, but the value he places on surprise in this case suggests that he also had a lighter side. His signature refers to the uncles, aunt Isabella, and even a female servant. He signs off by sending his mother-in-law and brother-in-law, Peppino, the usual embraces.[41]

The surprise visit brought the spouses together again, perhaps only for a few days. The couple also recorded this momentary togetherness on paper, since Raffaella added a message to her mother beneath Giovanni's words. This would have saved paper and postage, but it may also have been reassuring to the worried mother to see her daughter and son-in-law united on paper. Compared with Fadda's rather formal and reserved tone, there is a vivid warmth to Raffaella's expression. She addresses her mother as 'Carissima mamma mia' (dearest mother of mine), and launches straight into an account of the great pleasure she felt upon seeing 'her Giovannino', whom she 'truly had a need to see'. But Raffaella clearly felt an equal if not greater emotional need to see her mother. If she came home too, wrote Raffaella in the second line of the letter, she would be even happier. She expressed the hope that this would happen soon, and reinforced the message by asking her mother to return home. The kiss on her own mother's hand underlines that Giovanni's identical earlier gesture to his grandmother-in-law was not a prim affectation but a customary way of honouring women held in high esteem.[42]

Raffaella's words convey the impression of a filial relationship that is at once emotionally deep, yet formal and hierarchically structured. This family, and very probably many others at the time, was like a living tapestry: their affective bonds were constantly woven and re-woven through the exchange of gestures and written words, and the young couple was very much enmeshed within a living emotional fabric. No doubt in daily life these connections were woven afresh with quotidian speech and interaction, but of course evidence of those transactions is much less likely to be preserved for historical analysis. For now, making allowance for the formulaic qualities of epistolary style, it is clear that the Fadda couple's ties were the product of consistent labour, a constant shuttling back and forth between the warp and woof of family feelings.

---

[41] ASR, TCPR, 1879, b. 3659, vol. IV, ff. 162–3, letter to Carolina Nola, undated but sent from Cassano.

[42] ASR, TCPR, 1879, b. 3659, vol. IV, ff. 162–3, letter to Carolina Nola, undated but sent from Cassano, Raffaella's addition to Giovanni's main letter.

After his brief visit to Cassano, Giovanni returned to Sicily to resume the duties of his post in Caltanissetta. The earliest surviving letter he wrote directly to Raffaella came from Caltanissetta in late April 1873, almost two years after the wedding. Giovanni addresses his wife as 'Raffaelluccia', using a similar affectionate diminutive to the one he used earlier for her brother, 'Peppino'. The first line assures her that his health is good, that he eats and drinks 'like a Turk', and sleeps as much as his duties allow. Giving a glimpse of the professional life of a military employee, he says he will soon travel to the northern city of Parma for a period of two months, to learn about a new type of rifle, after which he would return to train officers how to use it.[43]

The letter is rather brief and businesslike. There are no metaphysical disquisitions about love or romance, though it ends somewhat tenderly: on his way to Parma he would be able to make a stop in Cassano, 'for just enough time to embrace you', and he signs off 'I draw you tightly to my heart, your very affectionate husband, Giovanni.' Acting as a brusque conclusion to this modest scene of written intimacy, Giovanni continues immediately beneath his words to Raffaella with a note addressed to his mother-in-law. Delighted to gather that she had a good Easter, Giovanni reports in turn that for him the festivity had passed pleasantly enough in the company of a colonel and other officers, though he regretted not having been able to share the occasion with his 'dear half'. Confirming that he had no particular expectations of privacy in the matrimonial correspondence above, he mentions, 'As you will have gathered from what I wrote to Raffaella, I will be coming to Cassano soon.'[44] There was no impermeable membrane separating the couple from the family fabric.

The passing visit to Cassano came and went without a written trace. When Giovanni next wrote to his wife, it was from Parma, in June 1873. Addressing the letter 'Beloved Raffaelluccia', its opening lines assured her that he was putting into practice her advice, 'impelled by the affection you hold for me', not to tear himself apart with overwork. He took her counsel 'as seriously as if it had come from an angel', and mentioned that he was in a perfect state of health. Referring to a question she had evidently put to him about the city, which until recently had been part of a foreign and distant polity from both their points of view, Giovanni explained that his duties limited the scope for exploration. He complained about the number of generals lurking about in civilian clothes checking to see if soldiers had their gloves on (it would have been hot in June), foreshadowing twentieth-century clichés about Italian military priorities.

---

[43] ASR, TCPR, 1879, b. 3659, vol. IV, ff. 164–5, letter from Giovanni Fadda to Raffaella, and Carolina Nola, dated Caltanisetta, 26 April 1873.
[44] ASR, TCPR, 1879, b. 3659, vol. IV, ff. 164–5, letter from Giovanni Fadda to Raffaella, and Carolina Nola, dated Caltanisetta, 26 April 1873.

During his time off, Giovanni chose to go for walks outside the city. Implying a stark contrast with the landscape of much of southern Italy, he describes the paths he takes as 'delicious, very clean, and shaded by extremely tall trees'. With a touch of smugness, he opines that such walks were a better use of time than stretching out in cafes, as his fellow officers did, giving superiors the impression that they loved to laze about doing very little. It also suggests that Giovanni felt himself somewhat removed from the ranks of his colleagues, and was possibly something of a loner. Concluding the letter with a greeting to 'Mother, Father, Peppino, grandma, uncles, and aunt Isabella', he bade Raffaella goodbye with 'A very affectionate embrace from he who loves you so much, Your Husband, Giovanni.'[45] The letter from Parma, written after just over two years of marriage, bears witness to Raffaella's solicitations over her husband's health, as it does to his affection for her. Even if the expressions that convey this affection were partly the product of ritualized habit, the genuine qualities of the emotional bonds expressed in the letters—respectful rather than passionate—are confirmed retrospectively by the difficulties that were to come.

## Early Marital Tribulations

Over succeeding years the correspondence began to be marked by declining affections and increasing tension. By May 1874, Giovanni was stationed in Cosenza, one of the principal cities of Calabria. About 90 kilometres from Cassano, it was relatively close to Raffaella's home, albeit separated by some very rugged territory. It was from here that Giovanni wrote the first letter to his mother-in-law in which there are hints that his marriage to Raffaella was fraught with unexpressed difficulties and even emotional turmoil. The letter's tone is distinctly different from previous examples, beginning with the salutation, 'Cara Suocera' (dear mother-in-law), an altogether cooler and more distant term than the earlier 'Cara Madre'.[46] The issue was Raffaella, who had moved to Cosenza to join him. Giovanni is 'content that she has come', and reminds Carolina of what he had declared three years ago (presumably at the time of the wedding). Alas what he said back then is not repeated, but it must have been something about his commitment to Raffaella. In the meantime 'if there have been a few moments of misunderstanding, that has not detracted in the least' from what Giovanni felt for her. He asks Carolina never to believe what she might hear, suggesting that gossip-mongers were spreading rumours.[47]

---

[45] ASR, TCPR, 1879, b. 3659, vol. IV, ff. 166–7, letter from Giovanni Fadda to Raffaella Saraceni, dated Parma, 15 June 1873.
[46] ASR, TCPR, 1879, b. 3659, vol. IV, ff. 168–9, letter from Giovanni Fadda to Carolina Nola, dated Cosenza, 10 May 1874.
[47] ASR, TCPR, 1879, b. 3659, vol. IV, ff. 168–9, letter from Giovanni Fadda to Carolina Nola, dated Cosenza, 10 May 1874.

In particular, Giovanni warns that those who wish harm will avail themselves of all possible means, and, not having been able to accuse him of anything concrete, they have insinuated to Raffaella that he went 'to the hotel' even when the couple were together—as if frequenting a hotel were in some way a betrayal of their marriage. It would be easy to jump to the conclusion that the 'hotel' stood for a brothel, but this seems an unlikely meaning, as Giovanni hastens to explain to Carolina that while Raffaella was not in residence with him, he would go to the hotel to eat, or have coffee, but then he 'assiduously' made sure he left the premises in the company of 'serious people of higher rank', so that if anyone wanted to gossip about his habits, he would have excellent alibis. In truth, he says, he would far prefer to have taken food home to eat, but feared that if he altered his habits, it could provoke 'calumny'.[48]

Here is a man who seems to live in fear about what others might think or say, and who dreaded any form of shame. Either he did not want to be seen living a dissolute life, or, more likely, he was burdened with horror about the idea that anyone might speak ill of his marriage, thus casting aspersions on his own masculine honour. Giovanni's fear of shame dictated much of his daily behaviour. This interpretation is reinforced by the final section of the letter, in which he wrote about the way he had kept the apartment 'hermetically sealed' since the day Raffaella departed, convinced that this would be the best way to express 'a deference' to his wife. As if to confirm the fearsome alacrity of the rumour mill, he mentioned that the day before Raffaella arrived, he had opened the place up, and immediately 'throughout the entire building word spread of her imminent arrival.'[49]

It is difficult to know whether all marriage relationships in southern Italy were the subject of such intense public scrutiny and discussion, but it seems that there was something unusual about Giovanni and Raffaella's relationship that attracted particular attention. Alternatively, Giovanni might have been hypersensitive about his reputation, possibly for reasons of self-doubt. Either way, the idea of public scrutiny obviously weighed heavily on Giovanni, who has revealed himself to be attentive and even fastidious about his image. The letter to Carolina suggests that the relationship was revealing signs of strain and awkwardness, but Giovanni was the more intent on keeping its inner workings hermetically sealed from the public eye, at the same time wishing to assure his mother-in-law that his own attitude and comportment, despite rumours, were beyond reproach.

The cooling of the language of emotional connection between Giovanni and his in-laws, adumbrated in the opening salutation, 'Dear mother-in-law', is

---

[48] ASR, TCPR, 1879, b. 3659, vol. IV, ff. 168–9, letter from Giovanni Fadda to Carolina Nola, dated Cosenza, 10 May 1874.
[49] ASR, TCPR, 1879, b. 3659, vol. IV, ff. 168–9, letter from Giovanni Fadda to Carolina Nola, dated Cosenza, 10 May 1874.

echoed in its conclusion: 'Accept an embrace extendable to all the relatives, your very affectionate, Giovanni.' A small shift perhaps, but this is notably different from Giovanni's affectionate salutations to scrupulously listed uncles, aunts, grandma, and brother-in-law, in earlier letters. This missive, with its pained discussion of relationship difficulties and the public image that might surround them, stands out from the previous correspondence, which was virtually unmarked by chinks in the armour of an apparently successful marriage carefully managed by husband, wife, and mother-in-law.

As well as a shift in emotional tone, the letter of May 1874 marks the beginning of a hiatus in the correspondence, at least in the judicial file's collection. The silence could simply be a sign that the couple were cohabiting again. Yet Giovanni's anxious tone and desire to defend his marriage against rumour-mongers portended the tribulations that were to be more clearly visible in later years of the couple's marriage. At some stage, perhaps later in 1874, Fadda was posted to Chieti, in the far-off Abruzzo region of central Italy. Raffaella claimed that she had followed him on this posting and lived with him for three years, although she admitted she had often returned to Calabria, sometimes for 'several months'.[50] Fadda's posting in Chieti spanned some notable family events, including his brother-in-law's engagement to be married, and the death of his mother in Sardinia. Although there is minimal correspondence about the period, this is made up for by the fact that later, local witnesses provided fairly consistent recollections of Fadda's and Raffaella's married life together.

## Marriage Observed in a Regional Town

In late August 1876 Giovanni wrote to Raffaella explaining how to get the most advantageous tariff to transport large amounts of luggage from Calabria to Chieti, suggesting that she had still not fully committed to the move.[51] Fadda's landlord in Chieti, one Luigi Majo, recalled that Raffaella arrived some months after her husband, in the company of her mother. Majo paid the family a courtesy visit and remembered Raffaella's mother telling him that her daughter suffered from nervous headaches.[52] Whether the couple's cohabitation in Chieti was long-term or not, local testimony such as that from their landlord suggests that the pair were perceived as a normally married couple. Nevertheless, it was during the couple's sojourn in Chieti that the authorities retrospectively spied cracks in the marriage

---

[50] ASR, TCPR, 1879, b. 3659, vol. IA, ff. 120–6, interrogation of Raffaella Saraceni by prosecutor Michele Finizia, Rome, 10 October 1878.

[51] ASR, TCPR, 1879, b. 3659, vol. IV, f. 170, letter from Giovanni Fadda to Raffaella Saraceni, dated Chieti, 28 August 1876.

[52] ASR, TCPR, 1879, b. 3659, vol. II, f. 94, witness statement by Luigi Majo, 54, Chieti, 19 October 1878.

vessel, and some flickers of information about the couple's sex life also started to take on a certain consistency from the Chieti period.

Doubts about the solidity of the marriage were raised in the official mind by several witnesses shortly after the murder had taken place. Influential testimony was provided by Giovanni's brother Cesare Fadda, who was an inspector of public lands. Cesare recounted that at first he thought that with marriage to Raffaella, his brother 'had found his happiness', and he even requested an employment transfer to Calabria in order to be close to his brother's family of marriage. Eventually, Cesare received a transfer to Castrovillari, an administrative centre in Calabria just 16 kilometres from Cassano allo Ionio. Although by the time he moved there his brother had been transferred to Chieti, Cesare was nevertheless drawn into Raffaella's family's orbit. Within a couple of years, perhaps around 1876, Cesare realized that his brother's marriage was troubled, and his overall impression was that Raffaella was very reluctant to depart from her parental home to go and live with her husband.[53]

Giovanni Fadda did not confide in his brother about his marriage until a late stage, when it had begun to break down, from about the end of 1877. A detail Cesare particularly recalled was that during the couple's cohabitation in Chieti, Giovanni had once found an unfinished letter written by Raffaella addressed to one 'Caro Edoardo'. Immediately suspicious of his wife writing to a man whose name he did not recognize, he had tried to read the letter, but Raffaella had 'jumped on him like a tiger', and destroyed it before he could grasp the contents.

According to Cesare, the incident had raised suspicions about her 'conduct'. Furthermore, Cesare claimed that Raffaella had circulated rumours around both Chieti and Cassano to the effect that the groin injury received during 'a battle in 1859' had left her husband impotent. Giovanni feared that she was using this story as an excuse for 'immodest liaisons', and he clearly feared the damage to his honour. Cesare alleged that in Chieti, in addition to a liaison with the said Edoardo, Raffaella had also been close to a hairdresser by the name of Di Sciullo. He indicated to authorities that the local pharmacist, Raffaele Aloè, could confirm all this.[54]

Cesare Fadda's claims prompted further investigation into perceptions of the Fadda–Saraceni marriage among Chieti's residents. What emerges is an impression of local observation of others by the townsfolk that hovers somewhere between the sort of community scrutiny to be expected in a small town, and a Foucauldian panopticon that made the most intimate details public knowledge— just the sort of intense observation that Fadda himself seemed to fear. Either way,

---

[53] ASR, TCPR, 1879, b. 3659, vol. IA, ff. 136–42, statement by Cesare Fadda to Michele Finizia, Rome, 11 October 1878.
[54] ASR, TCPR, 1879, b. 3659, vol. IA, ff. 136–42, statement by Cesare Fadda to Michele Finizia, Rome, 11 October 1878.

**Figure 1.3** Fadda reprimanding his wife for addressing a letter to 'Caro Edoardo', a man he did not know

*Source: L'Epoca* (Genoa), 5–6 October 1879, p. 1, reproduced with permission from the Biblioteca di Storia Moderna e Contemporanea, Rome.

while tending to confirm some of the peculiarities of the Fadda marriage, nothing emerged from the locals in direct support of Cesare Fadda's allegations. For example, Raffaele Aloè, the pharmacist that Cesare indicated would be able to confirm Raffaella's 'immodest liaisons', did rather the opposite. His shop was close to Fadda's home, and he got to know the man quite well, as Fadda would drop in for a chat on the way home.[55]

The pharmacist's impression was that during her sojourns in Chieti, Raffaella rarely went out, and she struck him as an 'honest woman'. He was aware that Fadda was pained by Raffaella's reluctance to depart from Calabria, always finding an excuse to stay longer, but there is no sense of her ever having cast aspersions on her husband's sexual vigour. On the contrary, Aloè said that in fact he had learned of Fadda's groin injury from the soldier himself. The fact that Aloè learned of this very personal information from Fadda, rather than via rumours started by Raffaella, gives a very different impression from Cesare's claim. In any case, the pharmacist was uncertain about 'whether this prevented Fadda from performing his marital duties'. Such testimony precisely captures Nancy Cott's idea that marriage was a conspicuous institution inviting public scrutiny, while always preserving at least some sphinx-like secrets.

Yet, Aloè was certain about other things that were not much less intimate. He testified that 'even during his wife's long absences', Fadda never visited a 'casa di piacere', a house of pleasure. In fact, he said, whenever the younger men hatched a plot to go out to find a 'pretty girl', Fadda would 'change the subject and try to detach himself'. All told, Aloè's testimony tended towards a picture of an outwardly regular marriage with some internal tribulations, though he muddied the waters, perhaps unintentionally, with a comment that further fuelled the authorities' suspicion: he said that after the news of Fadda's murder had reached Chieti, a young man had mentioned to him that Raffaella Saraceni often used to gaze out of her window towards the office of the Bank of Naples, 'perhaps trying to catch a glimpse of Signor Lombardi', a member of the bank's staff.[56]

Another witness interviewed in the search for marital secrets was the pharmacist's brother, a lawyer by the name of Giuseppe Aloè. The lawyer affirmed that he had met Fadda in his brother's shop and liked him so much that they developed a friendship. He reported that when Raffaella was in Chieti, the two couples would exchange visits. Giuseppe Aloè said he never had any reason to suspect Raffaella, and in public streets and at the theatre her behaviour was always 'honest and dignified'. Clearly reflecting a question inspired by his pharmacist brother's closing observations, he said he had never seen Raffaella on her balcony or looking out of

---

[55] ASR, TCPR, 1879, b. 3659, vol. II, ff. 85–7, statement by pharmacist Raffaele Aloè, Chieti, 17 October 1878.
[56] ASR, TCPR, 1879, b. 3659, vol. II, ff. 85–7, statement by pharmacist Raffaele Aloè, Chieti, 17 October 1878.

windows. The one thing he affirmed is something we know already: it was true that Raffaella only came to Chieti with reluctance. The most intimate detail that Fadda had confided in him, more than once, was that this had to do with her 'great love for her mother'.[57]

Further witnesses embellished this picture of regional town life but did not alter the impression that Raffaella's wifely conduct was beyond reproach. A weaver named Rosa Panella lived in the Faddas' building, and it turned out that it was her son who had claimed that he frequently saw Raffaella looking towards the Bank of Naples. The idea that merely looking out of a window could have constituted an act of impropriety for a married woman is confirmed by the fact that the authorities sought further information about the alleged gazing. Rosa Panella explained it away by saying that Raffaella was probably looking out for an acquaintance, and she never had any reason to suspect Raffaella of any sort of marital irregularity.[58] Still, the bank manager himself was duly interviewed. His name was Edoardo Donzelli, and it would turn out that Fadda himself was intensely jealous of the possibility that Raffaella might have been attracted to him. He probably suspected that the 'Caro Edoardo' of Raffaella's mysterious letter was the selfsame bank manager.

Donzelli affirmed that it would have been impossible for Raffaella to gaze at any of his staff because the bank's windows faced a different direction. He admitted that his own apartment, in the same building as the bank, faced the Faddas' residence. His impression of Raffaella, made during 'the short time she lived here', was that she tended to be withdrawn. He had gathered, during one or two conversations with her, 'justified by the friendship I had with her husband', that she was bored in Chieti and wanted return to Cassano and 'the affection of her relatives'.[59] All of this tends to confirm that for whatever reason, Raffaella was not gratified by the limited emotional arena of her married life, and yearned for her mother and her extended family. In this she was probably little different from many a soldier's wife, obliged to live in an unfamiliar town in an unfamiliar part of the country, far away from the people with whom she felt most at home. In short, she was unwilling to accept the more modern emotional arena of the mobile couple in exchange for her extended family.

Adding different perspectives to the views of Fadda's professional peers, two servants were called upon to give evidence about the couple's period in Chieti. One, Teresina Pacchini, was in service to Carolina Labriola, wife of a local judge. Teresina explained that since the judge was an old friend of the Saraceni family,

---

[57] ASR, TCPR, 1879, b. 3659, vol. II, ff. 88–9, statement by Giuseppe Aloè, lawyer, Chieti, 17 October 1878.
[58] ASR, TCPR, 1879, b. 3659, vol. II, f. 90, statement by Rosa Panella, weaver, 58, Chieti, 17 October 1878.
[59] ASR, TCPR, 1879, b. 3659, vol. II, f. 92, statement by Edoardo Donzelli, director of the Bank of Naples, Chieti, 18 October 1878.

she had been sent to keep Raffaella company and help her with some domestic work. In Teresina's view, Raffaella was a good wife, and she had seen her and Giovanni 'joking together lovingly'. Raffaella never had visitors and knew few people, though she did see the wives of people 'such as the director of the Bank of Naples'. Teresina said that Raffaella had once mentioned that her husband had been injured in the groin during a battle, and as a result 'only occasionally fulfilled his conjugal duties'. She added that Raffaella never showed any signs of displeasure over this, and nor could she ever imagine her 'betraying the conjugal bed'.[60] The judge himself seconded everything said by his maid. He too had heard about Fadda's injury, but 'did not know whether this had rendered him less apt to the duties of marriage'.[61]

These views confirm that to observers—even quite intimate confidantes such as the maid—Giovanni and Raffaella's marriage was one that may have had more than the usual share of emotionally challenging problems at its heart. On the other hand, the impression is that these troubles were successfully contained and managed within the marriage. To those who observed the couple, there was no great sense of marital storminess, and Raffaella was not perceived as wayward or inclined to 'immodest liaisons'. Rather, any reluctance she had to spend time with Fadda was more likely attributed to her attachment to her family of origin, particularly her mother. Privileged with hindsight, historian-observers would sympathize with the loneliness of a married woman in a deeply unfamiliar town, made claustrophobic by the fact that even gazing out of the windows had the potential to be seen as an act of impropriety.

Despite the outward calm, Fadda himself was almost certainly plagued by angst and jealousy, suspicious that Raffaella indulged in flirtatious associations with other men while he was away from home. Several sources bear witness to Fadda's emotions about his wife, an early example being testimony from his own domestic attendant during the couple's sojourn in Chieti. Giovanni Bellino-Rocci recalled that after returning home from a period away, Fadda had specifically asked him if he had been aware of Raffaella engaging in anything resembling an amorous liaison. Bellino-Rocci claimed that Raffaella had used various excuses to encourage him to leave the house. He also told Fadda that Raffaella and her maid seemed always to be at the window, chatting with an employee of the Bank of Naples. Fadda, possibly thinking of 'Caro Edoardo', asked his attendant if he had ever seen this person in their building's stairwell, but the answer was no.[62] This did not reassure Fadda, who continued to be haunted by the fear of his wife's

---

[60] ASR, TCPR, 1879, b. 3659, vol. II, f. 97, statement by Teresina Pacchini, 26, maid to Carolina Labriola, Chieti, 22 October 1878.
[61] ASR, TCPR, 1879, b. 3659, vol. II, f. 99, statement by Mariano Labriola, Judge of the Court of Chieti, 22 October 1878.
[62] ASR, TCPR, 1879, b. 3659, vol. II, ff. 124–5, statement by Giovanni Bellino-Rocci, former attendant to Captain Fadda, Turin, 3 November 1878.

attraction to 'Edoardo' for a long time after he discovered her writing to a man of that name.

The period at Chieti was punctuated by more public matters of family emotion, particularly the arrangements for the wedding of Raffaella's brother, Giuseppe. Peppino was engaged to be married to a local Calabrian woman, Teresina Lamengo, in the summer of 1877. The news occasioned a rare letter from Fadda to his father-in-law, Raffaella's stepfather. Addressed to 'Caro suocero' (dear father-in-law), the letter announces politely that the news of the imminent wedding gave him and Raffaella great pleasure. As for their presence at the wedding, they would do their utmost to be there. Indeed, Fadda could assure him that Raffaella would attend, but his own desire to do so would have to be 'subordinated to the timing of the event and whether it was possible to be absent from the regiment'.[63] Both the tone and the facts typified Fadda's self-control and sense of duty to work coming before all else.

After Giovanni had signed off, Raffaella wrote on the same sheet to her 'Carissimo Papà mio', immediately mentioning that the previous day they had received her mother's letter letting them know she had returned safely and in good health (very probably from a visit to Chieti). Raffaella then asked her father to tell Peppino that she would 'not write to him now', saving her letter for the moment when she could write to the couple-to-be together. It may be that the etiquette of the day required a formal engagement announcement before a letter could legitimately be addressed to a new couple. In any case it is clear that Raffaella attached symbolic importance to writing to the pair collectively, lending support to the interpretation that when she and Giovanni wrote a letter together, there was more to it than saving paper and postage.

The joint letter-writing was thus part of the daily weaving of a married couple into the broader affective ties of an extended family. In that sense, this letter embodied more than the usual number of layers of togetherness. Under Raffaella's message to her father, Giovanni, unlike Raffaella, did take the opportunity to write to Giuseppe immediately. He used the reverse side of the letter addressed to Raffaella's stepfather. In typically stiff language Fadda formally congratulated Giuseppe on his decision to marry a 'woman whose rare virtues make her worthy of the choice'. He signed off 'Accept an embrace from your affectionate brother-in-law, Giovanni.'[64] Hindsight tinges the letter with irony, for it was to be over continual delays to the wedding, and Raffaella's determination to stay in Calabria until the event, that the incipient tensions within Giovanni's and Raffaella's relationship finally came to a head.

---

[63] ASR, TCPR, 1879, b. 3659, vol. IV, f. 171, letter from Giovanni Fadda and Raffaella Saraceni to Raffaella's father and brother, dated Chieti, 14 July 1877.
[64] ASR, TCPR, 1879, b. 3659, vol. IV, f. 171, letter from Giovanni Fadda and Raffaella Saraceni to Raffaella's father and brother, dated Chieti, 14 July 1877.

## Rome, or Death!

During the autumn of 1877, the emotional tensions brewing over Raffaella's brother's wedding were exacerbated by major changes in Giovanni's life. His mother had died in August, and there are indications that this was emotionally disturbing, but it is difficult to grasp to what extent that was so, because the event was soon eclipsed by preparations for Giovanni's transfer to a new position in Rome. After years of difficult postings in regional towns, a position in Rome must have promised as much to Giovanni as had the dream of wresting Rome from the pope—expressed in the slogan 'Roma, o morte!' at the time of Garibaldi's ill-fated 1862 expedition to try and take the city for Italy.[65] With Rome established as the new national capital after September 1870, Giovanni's aspirations in relation to the city were more personal than political. Not only did a post in Rome signify that the arduous phase of Giovanni's career was behind him, but the amenities of the city and the stability of his position there allowed him to dream of finally establishing a more stable life with Raffaella.

Prior to the couple's move to Rome from Chieti, Raffaella had gone to stay with her mother, who was visiting Naples for the purpose of ordering bridal clothes for the coming wedding.[66] Giovanni, as well as doing his best to console his father for the loss of his wife in long letters, earnestly busied himself with preparations for the move to Rome. On 4 September 1877 he wrote to Raffaella from Chieti, telling her and her mother that his departure was imminent. He expressed his hope that Raffaella would join him there soon afterwards. Meanwhile, he said he would find and establish their home-to-be, and prepare it for her arrival. On the adjoining page he wrote a separate note to Raffaella's mother, apologizing for the lack of letters and saying how busy he was getting ready to move.[67]

A week later, the momentous transfer had been made, and Fadda wrote to Raffaella from Rome on 10 September, expressing a degree of anxiety, not having heard from her. He said he had sent a telegram to Cassano the previous day, impatient to know whether she had returned there from Naples. He then described the difficulties and expense of finding a suitable apartment in Rome for the pair of them. Some landlords had had the temerity to ask 200 lire quarterly for a four-room apartment. Giovanni thought if he had to pay that much—more than his salary—he may as well resign.[68] Portending both the real-estate bonanza that Rome

---

[65] Christopher Duggan, *The Force of Destiny: A History of Italy since 1796* (London: Allen Lane, 2007), p. 245. On Garibaldi's dreams for Rome, see Daniel Pick, *Rome or Death: The Obsessions of General Garibaldi* (London: Jonathan Cape, 2005).
[66] Corroborated by Cesare Fadda, ASR, TCPR, 1879, b. 3659, vol. IA, f. 136, statement to Michele Finizia, Rome, 11 October 1878.
[67] ASR, TCPR, 1879, b. 3659, vol. IV, ff. 175–6, letter from Giovanni Fadda to Raffaella Saraceni, dated Rome, 4 September 1877.
[68] ASR, TCPR, 1879, b. 3659, vol. IV, ff. 177–8, letter from Giovanni Fadda to Raffaella Saraceni, dated Rome, 10 September 1877.

underwent as a result of becoming Italy's capital, as well as the aura of privilege that settled over Italy's governing classes, Fadda was told simply that that was what parliamentary deputies were willing to pay. Ultimately, he contented himself with an apartment that cost 90 lire per quarter. Fadda may have counted himself fortunate in having found an affordable place to live, but the final line of the letter was plaintive: 'Dear Raffaella, I beg you write to me often or else you will make me feel ill.'[69]

With the opening and closing lines of that first letter from Rome, Giovanni gave brief vent to the anxieties that Cesare Fadda had claimed were constant features of his brother's emotional inner life. Giovanni was still concerned about the possibility of Raffaella's lingering in Naples, and the lack of letters from her aggravated his angst. His worry about Naples may have been that there, Raffaella had more opportunity to participate in social and festive occasions, perhaps increasing her chances of meeting others like 'Edoardo'. Just over a month later, in mid-October, Fadda had finally received a letter from Raffaella, which made him feel a little more optimistic about the next phase of their future together. Rather stiffly though, he wrote 'My dear Raffaelluccia, I have received your letter and am content to hear the good news about your health; I too am well.' He then described the apartment he had found and prepared for her arrival, hoping that she would like it. It was somewhat cramped, he admitted, but emphasized again that paying '200–300 lire a quarter is nothing, so I feel lucky spending 90.'[70]

Giovanni mentioned rather proudly that the apartment was on one of the principal streets, the stairway was 'all lit with gas, and the other residents in the building all civil'. After signing the letter with a particular intense expression of affection, 'Addio dear Raffaelluccia embracing you strongly to my heart', he added an uncharacteristic postscript explaining what exactly he meant by 'somewhat cramped': three rooms, two of which were quite respectable, with carpet, and a third for 'any use, for meals and so on'. On the adjoining page he addressed seven lines to his mother-in-law, mentioning his own and his brother Cesare's states of health.[71]

Fadda had found a small Roman nest for Raffaella, but over the autumn and into the winter of 1877, it sheltered only one occupant. The outlook for the pair's domestic harmony deteriorated as Raffaella resisted Giovanni's pleas to join him in Rome. The main obstacle was the continued postponement of her brother's wedding. According to Cesare Fadda, speaking to the public prosecutor, his brother made repeated requests to the Saraceni family that they bring his wife to Rome, but the reply was always that she would wait until after the wedding.[72]

---

[69] ASR, TCPR, 1879, b. 3659, vol. IV, ff. 177–8, letter from Giovanni Fadda to Raffaella Saraceni, dated Rome, 10 September 1877.
[70] ASR, TCPR, 1879, b. 3659, vol. IV, ff. 179–80, letter from Giovanni Fadda to Raffaella Saraceni and her mother, dated Rome, 17 October 1877.
[71] ASR, TCPR, 1879, b. 3659, vol. IV, ff. 179–80, letter from Giovanni Fadda to Raffaella Saraceni and her mother, dated Rome, 17 October 1877.
[72] ASR, TCPR, 1879, b. 3659, vol. IA, ff. 136–42, statement by Cesare Fadda to Michele Finizia, Rome, 11 October 1878.

Raffaella's own story was similar, with the explanatory emphasis on 'all her relatives' wanting her to stay in Cassano until after the wedding. She claimed that in her letters to Fadda she had begged that he should come and join them in the festivities.[73] One of the letters from this tense period was written to Giovanni by the intending groom, Raffaella's brother Giuseppe. It corroborates both Raffaella's and Cesare's accounts of the marital tension, and reveals much about the dynamics within the Saraceni family.

Dated 25 November 1877, the letter says

Dearest Giovanni,

you'll take me for importunate, impertinent, and anything else; but I too turn to you to implore you to permit Raffaella to stay until after my wedding, which I swear will take place in December. You know how punctilious my mother is, and how my father lets her lead him by the nose [...]. And you know what an influence on both of them your wife is, so I am sure that in her presence everything will go well. So if you care about my peace and my tranquility, don't deny me the only thing I ask of you, and which I hope for from you as a special grace.

We are talking about a delay of a fortnight or so. Please do me this favour and I shall be eternally grateful.

I will see this as new proof of the affection you have for all of us, and me especially. Please don't mention this to Raffaella [...].

I embrace you awaiting a favourable response and am always

Your affectionate

G Saraceni.[74]

Giuseppe's letter confirms impressions suggested by other correspondence about the dynamics within Raffaella's family, particularly that Carolina was a matriarch whose will (at least in relation to family matters) prevailed over that of her husband. This may have been a cultural norm for the time, place, and class of the Saraceni family, but it seems that even for a contemporary historical subject within the family milieu, such as Giuseppe, Carolina Nola exercised unusual influence. Equally though, Giuseppe's letter suggests that Raffaella herself was influential over both parents.

We do not know if Fadda replied to Giuseppe, but he did write to Raffaella about the problem of the wedding, just two days after his brother-in-law's letter, in all likelihood before receiving that one. Giovanni expressed his frustration, not so much over Raffaella's failure to come to Rome, but the constant prevarication

---

[73] ASR, TCPR, 1879, b. 3659, vol. IA, ff. 120–6, Interrogation of Raffaella Saraceni by Michele Finizia, Rome, 10 October 1878.
[74] ASR, TCPR, 1879, b. 3659, vol. IA, f. 42, letter from Giuseppe Saraceni to Giovanni Fadda dated [Cassano] 25 November 1877.

over the wedding. He had delayed his departure for Cassano to attend the wedding until 4 or 5 December, but at that point would only have fifteen days of leave, so hoped the ceremony would actually take place since he would not be able to stay any longer. He said his colonel asked him each day when he planned to depart. The uncertainty was embarrassing to Fadda, who told Raffaella that his superior was not trying to make life difficult, but rather, 'we who are lightweight in asking for leave and then delaying it'.[75] Fadda once again revealed himself to be acutely conscious about his public image, fearing personal shame if it were in any way compromised.

Fadda evidently made the planned December visit to Cassano, but the wedding did not take place while he was there. According to Raffaella, her husband came to Cassano and ordered her 'to follow him to Rome within 15 days'. Discussions involving all the family members led to an agreement that Raffaella would stay until after the wedding, sealed with a formal promise from her father that he would accompany her to Rome personally.[76] Cesare Fadda's account of the same event provided more insight into his brother's pain over this occasion. On the way back to Rome after visiting Cassano, Giovanni stayed with his brother in the nearby town of Castrovillari. In conversation with Cesare, Giovanni revealed for the first time the full measure of his emotional pain over Raffaella. Giovanni was convinced his wife did not love him, saying that she had given him a cold reception in Cassano, and had insisted that she would not go to Rome until after the wedding. It was on this visit, too, that Giovanni first confessed to Cesare that he had doubts about Raffaella's 'conduct', mentioning his discovery, some months earlier in Chieti, of her half-written letter to the mysterious 'Edoardo'.[77] Fadda's visit to Cassano in early December 1877 was to be the last time her ever saw Raffaella.

## Conclusion

After Giovanni Fadda's murder ten months later, questions about the emotional qualities of his marriage to Raffaella were given high priority in the judicial investigation. In particular the authorities wondered whether Raffaella had a motive to release herself from the marriage by instigating an assassination. From an early stage, the prosecutor took a keen interest in the emotional reasons for Raffaella's apparent reluctance to separate herself from her family of origin and go forth with Fadda to build a new and independent family centred around their marriage.

---

[75] ASR, TCPR, 1879, b. 3659, vol. IV, f. 181, letter from Giovanni Fadda to Raffaella Saraceni, dated Rome, 29 November 1877.

[76] ASR, TCPR, 1879, b. 3659, vol. IA, ff. 120–6, interrogation of Raffaella Saraceni by Michele Finizia, Rome, 10 October 1878.

[77] ASR, TCPR, 1879, b. 3659, vol. IA, ff. 136–42, statement by Cesare Fadda to Michele Finizia, Rome, 11 October 1878.

Ultimately, these questions came to preoccupy the Italian public more generally, as the inner workings of the relationship were revealed in tantalizing snippets by newspaper reportage. The prospect of a marital sphinx being forced to reveal at least some of its secrets encouraged the public to follow the case with zeal. The couple's entwined emotional and sexual woes became a hinge on which the case seemed to hang in the court of popular opinion, as well as the Court of Assizes.

The epistolary evidence and personal impressions which formed the basis of the judicial enquiry—and this chapter—suggest a marriage that to both social peers and from the more intimate perspective of a servant or confidante, did not give obvious signs of emotional discomfort or imminent upheaval. An answer to the question mark over the couple's sexual bond, or lack of it, was never clearly established. But the possibility of an insuperable physical problem at the heart of the marriage was mentioned so many times that it could not be dismissed as hearsay or misguided folk wisdom left over from more superstitious times. That the problem may have been a direct result of a young volunteer soldier's self-sacrifice for the national cause only made the matter more poignant and tragic.

Whether there was a physiological obstacle to a successful and enduring marriage between Giovanni Fadda and Raffaella Saraceni, their letters, and impressions from observers, bear witness to earnest and enduring efforts to conjure, shape, and stage sentiments appropriate to the emotional arena of a new couple in a new nation. Just as the couple represented the unification of diverse elements of the Italian peninsula, so too did each member seem to represent different ideals about what constituted an ideal family. Giovanni epitomized the nation's bourgeois avant-garde, a nation-builder who aspired to professional success and independent intimacy for his marriage. He dutifully performed the rituals of affection amongst his own and Raffaella's family, but being alone with his wife was his heart's principal desire. Yet the bride he chose was a woman who clung to the warmer, broader arena represented by her family of origin, with its strong intergenerational and social bonds. Ultimately, for whatever reason, she could never fully exchange that for the independent ways of Liberal Italy's ideal modern couple.

Thus by Christmas 1877, after seven years of fitful married life, Giovanni settled unhappily into a half-empty apartment in Rome, having dreamt of creating a space within four walls that represented his ideal emotional arena, while Raffaella remained in hers, with her extended family, ostensibly waiting for her brother to wed. Unable to resolve their marital differences legally, in early 1878, the couple accepted that their relationship could not go on. They gave up all pretence of building the arena of marriage together, and entered into a relatively unusual state in nineteenth-century Italy: the awkward limbo of a married couple living separate lives.[78]

---

[78] On personal separations in Italy, see Mark Seymour, *Debating Divorce in Italy*, pp. 62–4.

# 2
# Arena of Desire
## The Circus

### A Circus Comes to Town

While Giovanni Fadda sought to come to terms with living alone in Rome, Raffaella seemed to be fully absorbed back into her beloved family and the community of Cassano allo Ionio. Cassano was one of the many hilltop towns that mark Calabria's forbidding landscape. In the 1870s, these ancient settlements had outwardly changed little as a result of the region's incorporation into the new Italian nation over a decade earlier. But in the new Italy, as elsewhere in much of the late nineteenth century, the development of railways was beginning to alter the relationship between local settlements and the outside world.[1] Not long after unification, the iron horse began to reach even the peninsula's most distant regions, connecting them to a slowly emerging national geography and culture.[2] By the late 1870s, travellers and the ideas and news they carried were able to come and go in the remoter parts of Italy more easily than ever before.[3] Centuries of relative isolation began to be overcome, and, as we shall see, even such things as the arrival of a small circus, facilitated by the railway, had the potential to draw distant citizens into a nascent national community.

In June 1878, a train brought the members of a small itinerant circus to the station at Sibari, on the coastal plains some 14 kilometres from Cassano allo Ionio. Viewed from Sibari, Cassano was a typical 'streak of white at the summit of a bare hill', as Carlo Levi was to describe such settlements some sixty years later.[4] The journey had begun at the circus's last port of call, the city of Taranto, in Puglia, the region that forms the heel of Italy's boot. The train had followed the

---

[1] Christopher Duggan, *The Force of Destiny: A History of Italy since 1796* (London: Allen Lane, 2007), p. 271.

[2] Stefano Maggi, 'I treni e l'unificazione d'Italia: l'epoca delle costruzioni ferroviarie', *TeMA. Trimestrale del Laboratorio Territorio Mobilità e Ambiente*, vol. 4, no. 1 (March 2011): 7–14, here p. 8.

[3] Albert Schram, in *Railways and the Formation of the Italian State in the Nineteenth Century* (Cambridge: Cambridge University Press, 1997), emphasizes the slower development of railways in the south (pp. 87–8), though the main southern trunk lines were laid in the 1870s and by the mid-1880s the south had over 4000 km of railways, not far behind the north's 5000 km (p. 76).

[4] Carlo Levi, *Christ Stopped at Eboli*, trans. Frances Frenaye (London: Cassell, 1948), p. 2. Levi's portrait of the landscape and culture of the Basilicata region (where he was exiled by the fascist government), just to the north of Calabria, remains perhaps the most influential literary work in shaping modern perceptions of the Italian south.

*Emotional Arenas: Life, Love, and Death in 1870s Italy*. Mark Seymour, Oxford University Press (2020). © Mark Seymour.
DOI: 10.1093/oso/9780198743590.001.0001

arch of the boot along the coast of the Ionian Sea, Sibari being about halfway towards the peninsula's toe.[5] The circus artistes were already much missed by some of their keener fans in towns where they had performed, but they would quickly gain new ones in Cassano.

After arriving at the station, the twenty-five souls who constituted this intriguing troupe made their arduous way up the hillside to Cassano by horse and cart, weighed down by the extensive equipment of their craft. They also had several horses of their own, which may have served as packhorses for the last leg of the day's travel. Despite the advent of railways, the circus's journeys from town to town in the southern half of the Italian peninsula remained slow and difficult, and this helps explain why the company would take up residence for several weeks at a time even in small towns like Cassano. Over this period, their 'spettacolo' would bring pleasure and excitement to the townsfolk on an almost daily basis, and the circus visit would intensify the rhythms of local social life.

The arrival of a circus company was indeed a promising event for the inhabitants of isolated towns in regional Italy of the nineteenth century. Larger and more cosmopolitan centres had theatres that staged operatic and theatrical performances, as well as circuses. Small towns, particularly in the South, had to do more to invent their own entertainment, as visiting performers came less frequently.[6] Though settlements like Cassano had rich and ancient cultural and folk traditions, acts such as the circus might be the only amusement from the outside world that many members of the population ever saw. When such a show did arrive, the circus had broad appeal that brought the town together, to be collectively thrilled by daredevil equestrian acrobatics, the circus's principal speciality.[7] On this visit, the circus arena was to become the epicentre of a particularly intense web of emotional stimulation.

The circus that arrived in the summer of 1878, known as the Cardinali Brothers' Equestrian Company, had previously visited Cassano, more than a decade earlier, probably in 1865 or 1866.[8] Suggesting the relative rarity of circus visits to such towns, some of Cassano's families still remembered that earlier visit by the Cardinali Brothers, and they welcomed their return with special warmth. Those

---

[5] The circus's itinerary is reconstructed from accounts provided by its members, who were questioned by officials: Archivio di Stato di Roma, Tribunale Civile e Penale di Roma (henceforth ASR, TCPR), 1879, busta 3659, vol. IV, folio 223, statement by Carlo Bartone (a circus clown), 21 October 1879. See also ASR, TCPR, 1879, b. 3659, vol. IA, ff. 94–100, statement by Giuseppe De Luca (circus stablehand), 8 October 1878.

[6] Carlotta Sorba, *Teatri. L'Italia del melodramma nell'età del Risorgimento* (Bologna: Il Mulino, 2001), pp. 23–32.

[7] Alessandro Cervellati, *Questa sera grande spettacolo. Storia del circo italiano.* (Milan: Edizioni Avanti! Collezione 'Mondo Popolare', 1961), p. 28.

[8] ASR, TCPR, 1879, b. 3659, vol. IA, ff. 120–6, interrogation of Raffaella Saraceni. She thought the circus had last come to Cassano 'about 14 years ago'. Other anecdotal evidence suggests the circus probably toured this area in the summer or autumn of 1865, which would have made it thirteen years earlier. See ASR, TCPR, b. 3659, vol. 1A, f. 270, letter to 'Girolamo', dated Catanzaro, 22 March 1866.

who had witnessed the circus in the 1860s as children, Raffaella Saraceni and her brother Giuseppe among them, were now young adults. They felt particular joy upon the Cardinalis' return, anticipating the revival of intense childhood memories. Later on, it was to become clear that certain members of this circus had a particular knack for establishing relationships with members of the local community that would grow into lasting emotional bonds.[9] Less certain is whether this was a special feature of the Cardinali circus, or quite normal in an epoch before the advent of more impersonal forms of entertainment.

Circuses such as the Cardinali Brothers' represented a long tradition of travelling entertainment in Europe and North America that had its heyday in the second half of the nineteenth century.[10] In Italy, circuses like this normally stayed for a few weeks, and then moved to the next town, usually leaving no trace other than happy memories of excitement and entertainment. This early summer visit to Cassano was to be different, because the types of emotions that were normally circumscribed within the arena pounded by galloping horses were destined to spill over the symbolic boundary of the circus ring. This overflow took the shape of a love affair that triggered a set of events whose emotional magnitude far exceeded a thrilling equestrian display, or even the most melodramatic of contemporary operas.

The events precipitated by the Cardinali Brothers' 1878 visit to Cassano were ultimately also to expose, for a national and even an international audience, the barren hinterlands of Giovanni Fadda and Raffaella Saraceni's marriage. They also revealed a set of emotional regimes peculiar to the nomadic troupe itself, more sinister and less disciplined than those displayed within the circus's public arena. The aftermath of the circus's visit even brought to light an obscure virtual arena of 'emotional refuges'—William Reddy's term for spaces where strongly felt private emotions could take shelter or even hide from the exigencies of established emotional regimes.[11] But that virtual arena is the subject of the next chapter.

This one charts the landscape—historical, emotional, and geographical—surrounding the Cardinali Bros Circus' fateful visit to Cassano allo Ionio in the summer of 1878. Ultimately, it presents the circus as a familial emotional arena that contrasted starkly with the ideal of the couple represented by Giovanni and Raffaella. It begins with an exploration of the way circuses exemplify the idea of a particular social space representing a distinctive emotional matrix.

---

[9] The trial archive contains many references to close friendships between members of the circus and the public, from children to adults. Raffaella Saraceni mentioned it in her first interrogation by the prosecutor: ASR, TCPR, 1879, b. 3659, vol. IA, ff. 120–6, Rome, 10 October 1878.

[10] Helen Stoddart, *Rings of Desire: Circus History and Representation* (Manchester: Manchester University Press, 2000), p. 16; Yoram S. Carmeli, 'The Invention of Circus and Bourgeois Hegemony: A Glance at British Circus Books', *Journal of Popular Culture*, vol. 29, no. 1 (1995): 213–21.

[11] William Reddy, *The Navigation of Feeling: A Framework for the History of Emotions* (Cambridge: Cambridge University Press, 2001), p. 128.

## An Ancient 'Emotional Arena'

As Marian Murray wrote in a pioneering work on the circus first published in 1956, 'Not so long ago, innumerably small or isolated communities saw almost no entertainment except that provided by the periodic visits of the circus.'[12] Although Murray's context was the nineteenth-century United States, the notion is just as apt for the same era in southern Italy. Grand antecedents of the humble circus that entertained Cassano allo Ionio in 1878 are to be found in the famous amphitheatres of the Roman empire. The Romans were the first to construct distinctive circular or oval spaces for chariot races and other forms of public entertainment. They also gave those spaces the name 'arena', from the Latin for sand, the ideal surface to cushion the hooves of galloping horses.[13] Although the arena's association with sand has disappeared from the English use of the word, the notion of an arena as a particular space, defined by material textures and boundaries and dedicated to public spectacle, remains. Connotations of competition and collective emotional arousal are still very much associated with the word in its present usage.

Competition and emotional arousal of various kinds were fundamental elements in the Roman arenas, forming an integral part of their social purpose in both the Republican and Imperial eras. Dangerous races involving horses hitched to chariots provided the classic form of public entertainment in ancient Rome. Such competitions were usually held during the final days of the city's frequent and lengthy public festivals. They were intended to bring public excitement and jubilation to a climax during the festivities' closing moments. The extreme levels of audience engagement and excitement generated by such races—of public, shared emotion—are known to have verged on the fanatical.[14] As Rupert Croft-Cooke and Peter Cotes put it in a classic work on the circus, after the first chariot race, the air was thick with 'danger, confusion and excitement. The crowds grew ecstatic in their shouts of encouragement' and were 'hysterical in their jubilation when a favourite won.'[15]

Chariot races were extremely dangerous, and the emotions they generated had a great deal to do with fear. Injury and death regularly befell participants: contemporary mosaics of accidents suggest a public fascination with risk and violence.[16] The spectacle of danger stimulated a range of responses such as anxiety, relief, and

---

[12] Marian Murray, *Circus! From Rome to Ringling* (Westport, CT: Greenwood Press, 1973 [1956]), p. 25.
[13] Murray, *Circus!*, p. 41.
[14] Kathleen Coleman, 'Entertaining Rome', in *Ancient Rome: The Archeology of the Ancient City*, edited by Jon Coulston and Hazel Dodge (Oxford: Oxford University School of Archeology, 2000), p. 215.
[15] Rupert Croft-Cooke and Peter Cotes, *Circus: A World History* (London: Elek, 1976), p. 23.
[16] Coleman, 'Entertaining Rome', p. 216.

joy in the audience—but also horror and grief. Seen in this way, it is easy to understand why the Roman masses developed an insatiable love for the culture of the circus. It was an arena of gratifying emotional engagement, the intensity of which was clearly magnified as it was shared among thousands of citizens at the same moments. Regular and extravagant offerings of 'bread and circuses' came to be intrinsically associated with both Republican and Imperial Rome because Roman magistrates and emperors found that guaranteed sustenance and emotional gratification were the two most powerful instruments of political pacification and legitimization.[17]

More than a millennium after the fall of Roman civilization, the story that began with the arrival of a small circus in Cassano was to have a brutal climax within a few hundred metres of Rome's Colosseum. Nevertheless, the historical line connecting the Cardinali Brothers' Equestrian Circus with the traditions of ancient Roman amphitheatres was a relatively indirect one. After the fall of Rome in the fifth century, its extravagant circuses disappeared too, and it was not until the eighteenth century that recognizably similar forms of entertainment came into fashion again. They did so first in England in the 1760s, when 'trick-riders' began to stage public spectacles whose central attraction was the performance of daring equestrian feats. Philip Astley, a brilliant horse rider who had fought in the Seven Years War and reached the rank of sergeant major in King George II's army, is credited with having established the type of performance space that would soon become known once again as the circus.[18] Echoing Roman traditions, Astley called the arena he established in Lambeth, London, 'Astley's Amphitheatre'.[19]

The same genre of collective emotional gratification that had mesmerized the ancient Romans quickly appealed to the English public too, and the principal features of the modern circus were laid down within a few years of Astley's early experiments. In 1772, Astley's former employee, Charles Hughes, established 'The Royal Circus and Equestrian Philharmonic Academy'. This was the first modern use of the term 'circus', and Hughes also established the circus's standard performance space, consisting of a circular ring with a diameter of 13 metres, or 42 feet, with the audience around it. This diameter was found to generate the ideal degree of centrifugal force to aid the riders' balance.[20] Despite being temporarily upstaged by Hughes, Astley's entrepreneurial skills soon returned him to the

---

[17] Paul Veyne, *Bread and Circuses: Historical Sociology and Political Pluralism*, ed. Oswyn Murray, trans. Brian Pearce (London: Allen Lane, 1990 [1976]), esp. pp. 208–9 (Republican Rome), and 398–401 (Imperial Rome).

[18] Marius Kwint, 'The Legitimization of the Circus in Late Georgian England', *Past and Present* 174 (2002), pp. 72–115, here p. 76.

[19] Brenda Assael, *The Circus and Victorian Society* (Charlottesville: University of Virginia Press, 2005), p. 3.

[20] Helen Stoddart, *Rings of Desire: Circus History and Representation* (Manchester: Manchester University Press, 2000), p. 14.

forefront of developments in the circus as a form of entertainment, not just in Britain but also in Continental Europe.

In 1783 Astley established the 'Amphithéâtre Astley' in Paris, and in 1787, he was granted the right to build the 'Cirque du Palais Royale' at Versailles.[21] Astley's Continental career was soon thwarted by the French Revolution, during which he retreated back to England. But the circus as a form of entertainment remained popular, and Astley's Paris buildings were taken over by an Italian-born impresario, Antonio Franconi. Franconi established a monopoly over circus entertainment in Paris during the decade following the Revolution. Illustrations from the early nineteenth century indicate that Franconi's 'Cirque Olympique' was lavishly decorated, and attracted aristocratic patrons.[22] During this period, Franconi and his two sons also exported the recently established circus format to much of the rest of Continental Europe, their routes assisted by Napoleon's conquests.[23] In this way, the ancient Roman traditions of the circus returned to Italy via territories once conquered by the Roman empire: Britain and France.

In Italy, the entertainment traditions of Roman amphitheatres had developed during the medieval period under names such as *saltimbanchi* (acrobats), and during the Renaissance, as the *commedia dell'arte*, using mime in masks. Both were variations on centuries-old traditions.[24] But it was via France that the modern circus came to Italy in the nineteenth century. While Franconi and his sons were important in northern Italy, in more southern parts, the French Guillaume family was the most prominent circus dynasty. Their company was a favourite of Joachim Murat while he was King of Naples between 1808 and 1815, and the Guillaumes continued to entertain Italians for nearly ninety years. From the 1860s the key figure was Emilio Guillaume, probably born in Italy. His company was based in Rome and he became friendly with the first king of united Italy, Victor Emmanuel II. After unification in 1860 there was a proliferation of small, family-based circuses over the peninsula.[25] In its humble way, the Cardinali circus was a descendant of millennial traditions, and a typical example of Italy's provincial circuses after unification.

## Family, Sex, and Money in the Provinces

The circus that arrived in Cassano allo Ionio in June 1878, like other small family-based troupes, was a diminutive relative of the great companies that regularly toured Europe's large cities. Its make-up was typical of the self-contained, family-based

---

[21] Stoddart, *Rings of Desire*, p. 15.
[22] Pascal Jacob, *The Circus: A Visual History* (London: Bloomsbury Visual Arts, 2018), pp. 58–66.
[23] Stoddart, *Rings of Desire*, p. 15.
[24] Giorgio Torselli, *Il Circo* (Rome: Fratelli Palombi Editore, 1970), p. 12.
[25] Cervellati, *Questa sera grande spettacolo*, p. 58.

groups of the period that plied their entertainments in the smaller regional towns of Italy. Its core members were the three Cardinali brothers, Lorenzo, Luigi, and Pietro, and their sister Antonietta. The circus entourage included the brothers' wives, a total of fourteen children, and four other members: two clowns, and two men to look after the horses.[26] In all, the circus gave livelihoods to twenty-five people. Collectively, they constituted, depending on the observer's point of view, either a reasonably regular extended family, or a picaresque nomadic tribe. Perhaps part of the group's mystique was that it could have been either.

For its members, the circus was a way of life as well as a way of earning a living. The standard mode of business was for the company to sign a contract with a local theatrical promoter in each town they visited. The promoter paid the circus a fixed fee, in return for assuming the risk of a loss, but just as likely making a profit. One impresario reported that he paid the Cardinali company 60 lire per day.[27] Considering that average earnings for a labourer in larger northern cities at the time were about 2 lire per day, this gave the circus a respectable income.[28] There are no details about how the money was divided among the performers, but there was almost certainly a hierarchy. Emilio Guillaume himself estimated the equestrian performer Pietro Cardinali's income potential in a major city circus at about 400 lire per month—several times as much as a labourer.[29] He would certainly have earned less than this in the humble towns visited by his family, and no doubt the circus also faced considerable expenses. Probably aware that the work would get harder as he aged, circus members like Pietro always kept an eye out for other income opportunities.

Pietro, the youngest of the Cardinali brothers, was the circus's star performer.[30] As might be expected from a successful showman from such a milieu, there was something of the cocky rogue about him. A contemporary photograph (figure 2.1) which he signed and gave to a friend as a memento shows him posing confidently in a skin-tight outfit that outlines athletic proportions. His arms are raised above his head, rather dramatically holding a whip or sword that is curved with tension as a result of the pressure exerted at each end by his hands. The overall impression is the sort of athletic virility and bravura to be expected of an accomplished equestrian artist. Cardinali was clearly a man who made a living out of being looked at, and a good part of his work was to provoke intense feelings among

---

[26] ASR, TCPR, 1879, b. 3659, vol. IA, f. 247, interview with Antonietta Carozza, Rome, 19 October 1878.

[27] *Processo Fadda illustrato. Dibattimento alla Corte d'Assise di Roma dal 30 settembre al 31 ottobre 1879* (Rome: Giovanni Bracco Editore, 1879), p. 39.

[28] Paolo Murialdi, *Storia del giornalismo italiano* (Bologna: Il Mulino, 1996), provides earnings figures in relation to the cost of newspapers, p. 65.

[29] ASR, TCPR, 1879, b. 3659, vol II, ff. 42–3, witness statement by Emilio Guillaume, 11 October 1878.

[30] ASR, TCPR, 1879, b. 3659, vol. IA, 'Compendio', 6 February 1879.

**Figure 2.1** Pietro Cardinali (ASR, TCPR, b. 3659, 1879). Reproduced with permission from the Ministero dei Beni e Attività Culturali e del Turismo, ASRM 56/2015. Further reproduction prohibited.

those who paid to watch him: tingling fear as he faced the dangers of the ring, then admiration, and in some cases perhaps, even desire.

Professionally, this handsome horseman performed in partnership with the young female rider, Antonietta Cardinali. Presented as the Cardinali brothers' young sister, she, like the brothers, had learned the circus arts from a very young age. When the group arrived to entertain Cassano in 1878, she was in her early twenties, and the acts she performed with Pietro received top billing among the Cardinali company's repertoire. We have no photographs of Antonietta, only artists' impressions and eye-witness accounts. Unsurprisingly, these affirm that she too had an athletic physical appearance, and that, like Pietro's, her performance costumes were designed to reveal much more of her physique than the standard feminine fashions of the day normally allowed (see figure 2.2).

This was a period, for example, when women, if they bathed at beaches in public, wore voluminous costumes that thwarted any attempt to discern bodily contours. By contrast, a contemporary sketch of Antonietta shows her in a brief tutu, her legs clad in tights, and a close-fitting bodice narrowing her waist and

**Figure 2.2** Antonietta Carrozza. Source: *Processo Fadda illustrato* (Rome: Giovanni Bracco Editore, 1879), p. 33.

emphasizing her bust. One of her legs is raised high as she steps on to the back of a clown who crouches on his hands and knees. The look on the clown's face is somewhere between impish and forbearing. Antonietta is about to use the clown's back as a step from which to mount her steed, but not far beneath the surface of the image lie possibilities of an erotic nature.

Together, images of Pietro and Antonietta, outlining their shapely bodies and foreshadowing performances of great physicality, suggest that their double act undeniably contrived to project an erotic dimension. Somewhere on the palette of the audience's emotional engagement with the equestrian performers' art— mounting excitement, pangs and gasps of fear when risks were taken, then relief and joy when they were overcome—there are likely to have been elements of desire and even outright lust. Looking back from a present that is saturated with images that strive to elicit such emotions, there is reason to be cautious about too easily discerning the same elements in nineteenth-century precursors of modern western culture. But even though the commodification of sexual desire had yet to become commonplace in 1878, especially in a remote Calabrian town, later events affirm that arousing sexual desire was indeed a key aspect of Pietro and Antonietta's craft.

These artists were anything but unique in this way, as becomes obvious if Pietro and Antonietta's performances are viewed in a larger context. We may know little of the erotic currents of nineteenth-century life in small Italian settlements, but understandings derived from research on social and entertainment patterns of larger population centres, both in Italy and elsewhere, can be plausibly mapped onto even the remotest southern town. For example, in terms of sexual allure, Antonietta was the provincial, low-culture version of the types of diva figures who had established a leading role in Italian theatrical and operatic culture from early in the nineteenth century.[31] Such figures were not just sexualized objects for consumption by the 'male gaze', but, as Katharine Mitchell has argued, were sexually desiring subjects in their own right.[32]

Antonietta could also be seen in more popular culture as akin to the famous Adah Isaacs Menken. Menken thrilled audiences in the early 1860s, first in New York, and later all over England, as the eponymous heroine in Byron's play *Mazeppa*. In the climactic scene, she was strapped to a horse, clad only in scanty 'fleshings' that contrived to make her appear naked, as the horse careered off. This exciting finale, together with Menken's reputation as a 'dangerous woman' in her private life, earned her a huge following.[33] Apart from her physical beauty, Menken was also admired for playing the equestrian scene herself, rather than being substituted by a stuntwoman. Antonietta combined sexual allure with physical bravura in a similar, though less notorious way. Looking beyond Antonietta's heyday towards the later nineteenth century, she might prefigure the showgirls who would make Paris's Moulin Rouge theatre famous.

Such female performers would have been a rare spectacle indeed in Cassano, and this made the physicality of the circus performance, inflected as it was with an erotic charge, all the more exciting. No doubt a good portion of the townsfolk would have been transfixed as Antonietta mounted her steed and performed acrobatics. Whether or not there was the occasional flash of underclothing as she cartwheeled across the back of a horse, or leapt from one horse to another, guided by Pietro's strong arms, at least some of the audience are likely to have experienced *frissons* made the more piquant for their erotic elements. The phenomenon would have been a rudimentary relative of the more rarefied performances of the

---

[31] See Susan Rutherford, *The Prima Donna and Opera, 1815–1930* (Cambridge: Cambridge University Press, 2006), who writes that by the 1840s, the operatic prima donna in Italy was regarded as a combination of '*demi-mondaine*, professional artist and exalted diva' (p. 31).

[32] Katharine Mitchell, 'Literary and Epistolary Figurations of Female Desire in Early Post-Unification Italy, 1861–1914', in *Italian Sexualities Uncovered, 1789–1914*, edited by Valeria P. Babini, Chiara Beccalossi, and Lucy Riall (Basingstoke: Palgrave Macmillan, 2015), pp. 125–42 (here p. 126).

[33] Michael Diamond, *Victorian Sensation, Or, the Spectacular, the Shocking, and the Scandalous in Nineteenth-Century Britain* (London: Anthem Press, 2003), pp. 268–9.

operatic stage, and not too far off those that were becoming available as a form of popular entertainment in more worldly cities on a regular basis.

## The Female Gaze

Historians, particularly those working on periods before the twentieth century, are probably more familiar with the idea of males 'gazing' at female sexuality in performance and entertainment than they are with the notion of women gazing at masculine sex appeal.[34] But the work of cultural studies scholars, particular on cinema, suggests that it would be a mistake to overlook the fact that Pietro Cardinali clearly had just as powerful an erotic effect on his provincial audiences as did Antonietta. A range of evidence makes it plain that Cardinali provoked high levels of admiration and even desire in many of the women who watched him, in a way that prefigures the masculine allure of cinema figures such as Rudolph Valentino.[35] Indeed, circus performers like Cardinali may have been the precursors of modern male film stars. Though notable strides in the exploration of sexual dynamics in nineteenth-century Italy have recently been made,[36] the continuing relative historical unfamiliarity of the phenomenon of Italian women's desire, not to mention the ramifications of Pietro's allure, make further analysis of his appeal indispensable.

As with the question of Antonietta's attractiveness, it is worth placing Cardinali's magnetic effect within a broader context of sexually appealing men in the nineteenth century, both in Italy and elsewhere. It may seem inappropriate to compare a knave like Cardinali to a hero like Giuseppe Garibaldi, but as Lucy Riall's pioneering biography demonstrated unarguably, the Italian Risorgimento's most charismatic figure self-consciously cultivated much of his personal appeal, including at the sexual level. Riall showed how this self-fashioning helped to forge an emotional bond between Garibaldi and his followers, particularly among women but not solely, that could be parlayed into political support.[37] In a similar

---

[34] The seminal article on the female body as an object of the 'male gaze' is Laura Mulvey, 'Visual Pleasure and Narrative Cinema', *Screen*, vol. 16, no. 2 (1975): 6–18; for a counterpoint on the male as the gaze's object, see Steve Neale, 'Masculinity as Spectacle: Reflections on Men in Mainstream Cinema', *Screen*, vol. 24, no. 6 (1983): 2–16.

[35] Miriam Hansen, in 'Pleasure, Ambivalence, Identification: Valentino and Female Spectatorship', *Cinema Journal*, vol. 25, no. 4 (1986): 6–32, credited Valentino with making women into 'a socially and economically significant group' for the first time in film history (p. 6). The example of Jules Léotard, discussed below, suggests that awareness of the value of the 'female gaze' may well pre-date the advent of cinema. I thank Catherine Fowler for help with the material in this and the previous note.

[36] Valeria P. Babini, Chiara Beccalossi, and Lucy Riall (eds), *Italian Sexualities Uncovered, 1789-1914* (Basingstoke: Palgrave Macmillan, 2015) is the best recent example, but see also Perry Willson (ed.), *Gender, Family and Sexuality: The Private Sphere in Italy, 1860-1945* (Basingstoke: Palgrave Macmillan, 2004), and Bruno P. F. Wanrooij, *Storia del pudore. La questione sessuale in Italia, 1860-1940* (Venice: Marsilio Editori, 1990).

[37] Lucy Riall, *Garibaldi: Invention of a Hero* (New Haven: Yale University Press, 2007), pp. 185–8 and pp. 342–4.

and even more obviously staged way, though on a smaller scale, Cardinali flaunted his physical attractiveness and cultivated the emotions it provoked. This was part of what gave his performances particular intensity.

Though there has been little historical investigation of the erotic aura of the circus, particularly in relation to its male performers, Cardinali's appeal does have more famous precedents. The best example is provided by Jules Léotard, the French acrobat who invented the skin-tight, flexible costume that has borne his name ever since, and a version of which Cardinali himself wore. In the mid-1850s, Léotard pioneered an extraordinary flying act using three trapezes. He took the act to Paris in 1859 and became an overnight sensation, subsequently touring other major European cities. Contemporaries particularly noted Léotard's effect upon women. In Paris, they reportedly crammed the passageways to the arena in the hope of touching their idol, prefiguring the sort of fandom that was in store for the twentieth-century kings of popular music from Elvis Presley onwards. After Léotard's performances, Parisiennes showered him with 'enflamed letters', expressing their desire to know him.[38]

Nor was it only Latin women who were susceptible to Léotard's physical appeal and athletic skill. In May 1861 he appeared in London, garnering similar acclaim, and again causing a sensation among the city's women.[39] Léotard's sexual magnetism was so pronounced that it inspired one of the most popular British music hall songs of the 1860s, 'That daring young man on the flying trapeze':

> He smiled from the bar on the people below
> And one night he smiled on my love.
> She winked back at him and she shouted 'Bravo!'
> As he hung by his nose up above!
> He'd fly through the air with the greatest of ease,
> A daring young man on the flying trapeze,
> His movements were graceful; all girls he could please;
> And my love he purloined away.[40]

No one knows how many London women Léotard might have purloined away, but the music hall song immortalized the sexual allure of the male circus acrobat. It told of Léotard's emotional hold on members of the female public in a way that uncannily foreshadowed events in Cassano in 1878—for, by all accounts, Pietro Cardinali purloined away the loves of many a man.

---

[38] Dominique Jando, *Histoire mondiale du cirque* (Paris: Jean-Pierre Delarge, 1977), pp. 35–6.
[39] Diamond, *Victorian Sensation*, p. 263.
[40] 'The Man on the Flying Trapeze', by George Leybourne and Alfred Lee. Quoted in Diamond, p. 263.

Moving from historical precedents to a more specific focus on the desire elicited by the Cardinali circus in Cassano takes us into less certain historical territory for many reasons. For all their intensity, fleeting *frissons* of desire were not the type of emotion that was conscientiously expressed, shared, or recorded for posterity by those who experienced them. Such fundamental and widely if not universally felt emotions have generally been challenging for historians to discern in the places and cultures of the past, except through works of culture such as art, opera, theatre, and fiction.[41] Yet, in the wake of the Cardinali Circus' visit to Cassano in 1878, information that came to light after the circus's departure confirmed in a vivid and unusual way what images of Pietro and Antonietta have already suggested: excitement related to desire was a fundamental aspect of the circus's emotional arena.

Several women left traces of the emotions generated as a result of watching Pietro Cardinali perform. The only one whose real name we know was Raffaella Saraceni, disconsolate wife of Giovanni Fadda. Aged only twenty-three, but estranged from her husband, by June 1878, Raffaella had effectively settled back in Cassano to live with her parents. 'Neither a wife nor a spinster', as her mother put it pithily, Raffaella may have been particularly susceptible to the sexual energy offered by the Cardinali circus.[42] During its sojourn the circus put on frequent shows, probably on several occasions each week, and it was common for people to frequent the arena night after night. Witnesses claimed that in June 1878, one of the most assiduous audience members was Raffaella. Not only was she said to have attended performances very regularly, but she always had a front row seat. When the question of her zeal for the circus came up for scrutiny by state officials, she claimed that it did not distinguish her in any way from her fellow citizens, who all went equally regularly.[43]

Conversely, some of these fellow citizens insisted that there was something distinctive about Raffaella's eager attendance, one aspect of which was that she notably 'overdid' her *toilette* on those occasions.[44] Differences of opinion about the appropriateness of Raffaella's assiduous attendance or overdone *toilette* probably reflect a degree of social rivalry between women, as they argued over the boundaries of propriety in public arenas. Raffaella may have been the victim of resentment by those who wanted to keep her in her place as a married woman, despite the unhappiness of her union. Tensions of this type are familiar in communities even today, but the more unusual and interesting observations expressed by

---

[41] See, for example, Alberto Mario Banti, *Eros e virtù. Aristocratiche e borghesi da Watteau a Manet* (Rome-Bari: Laterza, 2016).

[42] ASR, TCPR, 1879, b. 3659, vol. IA, ff. 37–9, letter from Carolina Nola to Giovanni Fadda, dated 30 March 1878.

[43] ASR, TCPR, 1879, b. 3659, vol. IA, ff. 120–6, interrogation of Raffaella Saraceni by public prosecutor Michele Finizia, 10 October 1878.

[44] ASR, TCPR, 1879, b. 3659, vol. IA, 'Compendio', 6 February 1879.

members of the public in Cassano concern the alleged emergence of an illicit bond between Raffaella as a member of the audience, and Pietro as a performer. Fellow members of the audience claimed to have been alerted to this through observing intense levels of eye contact between Raffaella and Pietro during the performance.[45]

It is worth keeping in mind the comparative intimacy of the circus ring, whose diameter was only 13 metres, or 42 feet. The fact that the audience encircled the performers meant that its members, as well as watching the artists, could also observe each other directly—much more so than in the boxes of theatres, for example. No lorgnettes were needed in the best seats of the circus. Observers claimed that during performances, Pietro and Raffaella exchanged frequent 'segni d'intelligenza'—signs of intelligence, or, more simply, knowing looks.[46] Fellow citizens observed Raffaella's and Pietro's apparent desire to 'know' each other. What they might mutually have known is not difficult to guess: put politely, the pair were suspected of having wanting to 'know' each other in the biblical sense. Whether that was the case or not, the public observed the generation of sexual electricity. It was also discovered that, while Raffaella was ultimately singled out, she was not the only member of the audience who experienced these feelings.

## Arenas Licit and Illicit

The sexual electricity apparently generated by the eye contact between Raffaella Saraceni and Pietro Cardinali and the knowledge that she was not the only one to experience it raises questions about what channels of release such emotions may have found at the end of the evening among those—both male and female—who experienced kindred feelings. To what extent did the circus arena, whose boundary was little more than notional, effectively circumscribe the audience's feelings of arousal, desire, or even lust, within the space enclosed by the big top? Were these emotions simply left behind to cool and dissipate at the end of the performance? Or did they provoke thoughts and impressions that could be memorized, secreted away, and taken home, to be revisited, reimagined, and perhaps even shared, in more private settings?

In turn, did the townsfolk, whose sense of morality was at least to some extent determined by the teachings of the Catholic religion, wonder about the sexual dynamics between those alluring members of the nomadic tribe itself, once they finished their show and moved beyond the spatial and temporal arenas that

---

[45] ASR, TCPR, 1879, b. 3659, vol. IA, ff. 120–6, interrogation of Raffaella Saraceni by public prosecutor Michele Finizia, 10 October 1878.
[46] Reflected in questions put to Raffaella Saraceni by public prosecutor Michele Finizia, ASR, TCPR, b. 3659, ff. 120–6, 10 October 1878, and Finizia's 'Compendio' of 6 February 1879.

framed their nightly performances for the public? And to what extent might the members of the nomadic tribe who constituted the circus have mingled socially with the townsfolk beyond the bounds of the ring? Could Pietro and Raffaella have come to know each other in a different context? Could that sexual electricity have been conducted to a more private and even intimate emotional arena?

Not all these questions can be answered, but some can, and the answers are surprising. The situations were more layered than they appeared. Superficially at least, the connections of kinship between the main members of the circus—with three brothers, their wives, and fourteen children—resembled those of an extended family. The circus members' self-presentation as three married couples with children reinforced that interpretation. But beneath the surface were legacies of emotional and sexual complexities that would have given pause to any Catholic priest who heard them whispered during confession.[47] It is improbable that within the micro-arena of the 'dark box' any such confessions were made by members of the Cardinali clan, and even if they had been, they would not be accessible to posterity.[48] But in due course, at least some of these complexities were to be confessed in a more secular arena: to an investigating magistrate of the Italian government.

What these confessions revealed was that the relationship between Pietro and Antonietta had several quite contradictory guises. To their circus audience they were the glamorous and beautiful brother and sister. Their stage act stressed their physical attunement and played on the sexual tensions that took on a life of their own during the intense corporeal interactions of this lithe pairing of man and woman. In this guise, perhaps the supposed fraternal relationship in fact helped to defuse, rather than augment, the sexuality of their performance, and thus steered it away from anything approaching scandal or immorality. However, kept hidden from the public was the fact that the pair were not true siblings. Even better hidden was the fact that in the past, Pietro and Antonietta had been drawn into a sexual relationship of their own.

Antonietta was adopted at an early age by the Cardinali brothers' parents as a foundling, when the circus had once passed through Messina, Sicily. Although raised as a family member, Antonietta was not a blood relative. Furthermore, the sexual energy that was part of the pair's appeal during their circus performances was not purely conjured up for the benefit of the audience. The couple had had an

---

[47] As well as the canonical statement by Michel Foucault in *The History of Sexuality Vol. I: An Introduction*, trans. Robert Hurley (New York: Vintage Books, 1978 [1990]), pp. 59–67, several more recent studies have examined confession as an instrument of the control of marriage and sexuality. See for example Daniela Lombardi, *Storia del matrimonio. Dal Medioevo a oggi* (Bologna: Il Mulino, 2008), p. 120, and Fernanda Alfieri, *Nella camera degli sposi. Tomás Sánchez, il matrimonio la sessualità (secoli XVI-XVII)*, (Bologna: Il Mulino, 2010), pp. 48–70.

[48] John Cornwell, in *The Dark Box: A Secret History of Confession* (London: Profile Books, 2015), pp. 46–7, provides a glimpse of the confessional box as an intimate space potentially charged with eroticism.

intense sexual relationship, beginning in the late 1860s, when Antonietta was sixteen years old. The sexual contact may only have been occasional, but the relationship had gone on for at least a year, and probably much longer. Antonietta initially believed Pietro loved her, and she claimed that early on she had had confidence that her adoptive mother and the Cardinali brothers would oblige Pietro to marry her.[49]

Unsurprisingly, and with the knowledge of the circus members, Antonietta had fallen pregnant twice as a result of the relationship with Pietro, once in 1870, and again in 1871. She had given birth to both infants, but, as was so common at the time, they were subsequently given up, just like Antonietta herself had been, to be adopted out as foundlings.[50] So, behind the scenes of the circus arena, Pietro and Antonietta's relationship was not only fraternal, but they were rather a pair of sometime lovers. Their circus act flirted, consciously or unconsciously, with this taboo reality, and may have given their performances an element of occult emotional energy. Like a Catholic priest, and perhaps reflecting confessional culture, in due course the Italian government magistrate was drawn to explore the hidden contours of this taboo relationship. Unlike a Catholic priest, he left a written record of what he uncovered.

When placed under the cool spotlight of legal interrogation almost a decade after the sexual encounters, the erstwhile lovers' personal accounts of their emotional experience were notably divided along gender lines. Above all the differences throw into relief the contrasting implications of sexual relationships for males and females before the advent of reliable birth control. For Pietro the relationship offered access to sexual enjoyment, albeit tinged, but perhaps also intensified, by the guilt associated with breaking the incest taboo implied by the adoptive relationship. In the context of the extended family, the risks to family honour through Antonietta falling pregnant were cushioned by the nature of the circus group. As a nomadic tribe, their morality was not subject to the usual standards of sexual honour, and Antonietta seemed to feel little shame about the illegitimate births.[51] Pietro, for his part, flatly denied both the conception and the birth of the two children, dismissing the claims as 'absolutely false'. His decisiveness suggested emotional distance from the entire matter, whether the lovemaking or the birth of his children.[52]

How much Pietro's detachment represented his inner feelings is unclear, but in all likelihood he carried few emotional scars as a result of giving up his offspring.

---

[49] ASR, TCPR, 1879, b. 3659, vol. IB, ff. 131–2, interrogation of Antonietta, 12 November 1878.

[50] David I. Kertzer, *Sacrificed for Honor: Italian Infant Abandonment and the Politics of Reproductive Control* (Boston: Beacon Press, 1993). Sicily and Calabria had the highest ratios of infant abandonment in Italy; see pp. 76–7.

[51] Kertzer argues that the protection of family honour was the primary driver of Italy's culture of and institutional facilities for infant abandonment. See esp. pp. 25–6.

[52] ASR, TCPR, 1879, b. 3659, vol. 1B, ff. 133–4, interrogation of Pietro Cardinali, 13 November 1878.

If so, this detachment can be attributed to a range of factors, among which his gender and his sexual promiscuity loom large. But the customs of the day, which meant that giving up infants for adoption was common, and the emotional context of the circus family, must also figure in any interpretation of his attitude. Antonietta however, subject to the same customs and the same emotional regimes as Pietro, experienced and represented the conception, birth, and giving up of her children very differently. This is suggested, sadly, by the way she remembered, under questioning, the days of their births—17 March 1870 and 13 April 1871—without a moment's pause or reflection.[53] We can only speculate about what anguish she experienced, not just when she gave up the newborns, but each successive year as the anniversaries approached. Those days undoubtedly meant much more to Antonietta than they did to the infants' father.

How much love there might have been between the couple is similarly difficult to know, but certainly by the time the story came to light, emotions of that sort had been spent. Antonietta explained her willingness to enter into a sexual relationship with Pietro by reference to the familiar trope that he had promised to marry her.[54] Yet, at the time he made those promises, he already had an established relationship with Carolina, the woman who arrived with him in Cassano in the guise of his wife. Furthermore, at the point when Antonietta had fallen pregnant to Pietro, he had already had children with Carolina. Antonietta knew this at the time, and in retrospect acknowledged that the chances of Pietro marrying her were very slim. But she also claimed that she had been forced to submit to his sexual desires because he could be tyrannical and brutal and she feared him. In addition to Antonietta's own fears, she surmised that Carolina was jealous of Pietro's sexual interest in her. So behind the scenes, the circus ménage was fraught with emotional tensions: love, desire, fear, and jealousy. The women suffered in silence because their livelihoods depended on their membership of the company.[55]

Antonietta's account of life in the circus makes it clear that the emotional regime within the Cardinali community was a complex one, influenced by factors such as gender and occupational hierarchies. What may be more challenging to understand from a contemporary perspective is that, at least during their visit to Cassano in 1878, Cardinali resided with both his wife Carolina and Antonietta at the same time. Official investigators visiting their temporary abode reported that

---

[53] ASR. TCPR, 1879, b. 3659, vol. IB, ff. 131–2, interrogation of Antonietta Carozza, 12 November 1878.

[54] The perception that a promise of marriage legitimized illicit sexual relations had a long life in the Catholic world, from the Council of Trent well into the twentieth century. See Augusta Palombarini, 'Seduzione maschile con «promessa di matrimonio»', in *Amori e trasgressioni. Rapporti di coppia tra '800 e '900*, edited by Antonia Pasi and Paolo Sorcinelli (Bari: Edizioni Dedalo, 1995), pp. 53–82, here p. 64.

[55] ASR, TCPR, 1879, b. 3659, vol. IB, ff. 131–2, interrogation of Antonietta Carozza, 12 November 1878.

when they arrived asking for Pietro Cardinali, Carolina answered the door. She identified herself as Pietro's wife, and when Antonietta emerged too, she introduced herself as his sister. Apparently the women cohabited with Pietro under one roof in a relationship that displayed no obvious signs of tension to outside observers. Although the visitors noted the two women, the truth of the ménage did not come out until much later. In 1878 there was little sign that the people of Cassano were anxious about the familial or sexual arrangements among their colourful visitors, although they almost certainly found them intriguing.

This sense of intrigue is suggested by the town's eagerness to have the circus members as social company. Many of the local families particularly desired to host the alluring duo of Pietro and Antonietta in their homes after the evening's performances. The pair were fêted, and Pietro would later boast that he was friendly with the town's leading families, rattling off the names of local gentry, and even the parliamentary deputy, as proof of his social acceptance and high-level connections.[56] There is even some suggestion that these families vied among each other to entertain the glamorous pair they thought of as brother and sister. Gossip and hearsay collected after the circus had left Cassano tells of sparkling soirées in the town's leading families' large homes. Indeed several local eyebrows were caused to rise by the special intensity of the social links that sprang up between the circus's leading lights and the town's prominent families.[57]

For those with both a modern, and particularly a British-world perspective, members of a circus might be assumed to have an unshakably picaresque air about them that could have been a threat to local respectability if social boundaries were not well delineated. Brenda Assael's social history of the British circus confirms that in late nineteenth-century England there was a strong sense of distinction between the respectability of the audience and the disreputable air of the performers.[58] Conversely, earlier historiography on Continental circuses, particularly for France and Italy, stresses that high-ranking performers often had direct access to elite social circles. Their conduit was the horse, whose military, aristocratic, and royal associations functioned as a link that made equestrian artistes the natural friends of aristocrats and even royalty.[59] The social embrace afforded to Pietro and Antonietta Cardinali in Cassano suggests that the class distinction noted in Britain did not apply in Italy: far from being perceived as threatening, the stars of the circus had cultural capital and were highly desirable company.

---

[56] ASR, TCPR, 1879, b. 3659, vol. 1A, ff. 101–7, interrogation of Pietro Cardinali, 8 October 1878.
[57] ASR TCPR, 1879, b. 3659, vol. II, f. 226, witness statement by Vincenzo Fabiani, tax collector, 22 November 1878.
[58] Assael, *The Circus*, p. 17. See also Stoddart, *Rings of Desire*, pp. 24–6, who elaborates that the peripheral businesses around the circus, such as sideshows, were a particular source of moral anxiety. The Cardinali circus was too small to have such sideshows.
[59] Cervellati, *Questa sera grande spettacolo*, pp. 28–9 and pp. 58, 67; Jando, *Histoire mondiale du cirque*, p. 36.

In the competition to monopolize Pietro and Antonietta's company, one household in particular emerged as the clear leader: that of the Saraceni family. Consisting of Raffaella, her older brother Giuseppe, and their parents, with assorted servants present as well, the house became known as the circus stars' principal nocturnal haunt. The pair often went there to dine after the evening's performance, and the soirées continued into the small hours, to the envy of some observers. The social mingling was remarked upon by townsfolk, but it is difficult to tell what most preoccupied local observers: the intensity of the carousing, or something less legitimate. It is clear though that there was nothing surreptitious about this socializing. It had a proxy legitimacy in that the two pairs of siblings matched each other well, so while Raffaella was known to be friendly with Antonietta, Giuseppe was perceived as Pietro's *amico del cuore*, his bosom friend.[60]

Accounts of this socializing provide valuable insights into the culture of emotional bonds, under the broad category of friendship, in the historical context of a provincial southern town. Raffaella and Giuseppe had been among the young people who had formed friendships with members of the circus during their visit to Cassano many years earlier. Raffaella, who was then aged about eleven, had apparently formed a close friendship with Antonietta, who was the same age. During that sojourn too, the artiste often visited the Saraceni house, but after the circus's departure in the 1860s, they did not see each other again until the next visit, in 1878, somewhere between twelve and fourteen years later.[61] It is uncertain whether on that first occasion Giuseppe formed a friendship with Pietro, who would have been twenty-four years old then.

What is clear is that the friendships of 1878 between Raffaella and Giuseppe and Antonietta and Pietro developed in intensely familial contexts. The bonds were sponsored and supported by more senior members of their respective families, particularly in the Saraceni household. Raffaella and Giuseppe, although now young adults, still lived in their parents' large house, with several servants. During the 1878 visit the post-circus soirées took place in this home and involved the whole family and other friends too. Raffaella and Giuseppe's mother Carolina played a particularly prominent role in running the social life of the household, and was clearly eager to invite the circus artistes into her home. There are no signs that she feared tarnishing her family's honour by doing so.

Nor did the hospitality and largesse only flow from the well-off Saraceni family down to the Cardinalis. The circus members evidently did their part too. They seemed particularly keen to maintain the friendship, even after they departed

---

[60] ASR, TCPR, 1879, b. 3659, vol. II, ff. 176–9, interrogation of Maria Brunetti, former servant in the Saraceni household, 20 December 1878.
[61] ASR, TCPR, 1879, b. 3659, vol. IA, ff. 120–6, statement by Raffaella Saraceni to Michele Finizia, Rome, 10 October 1878.

from Cassano and moved on to Castrovillari, a larger town some 13 kilometres away. From there, Pietro sent a basket of culinary delicacies back to the Saraceni family in Cassano.[62] Then, before the circus left Castrovillari, Lorenzo Cardinali, Pietro's older brother and head of the circus family, commissioned a local hotelier to prepare a sumptuous lunch for a 'gentleman coming from Cassano'. The gentleman turned out to be Giuseppe Saraceni. He lunched with Lorenzo and Pietro Cardinali, and two other members of the circus whose names the hotelier did not know.[63] Clearly, the families had developed a sense of reciprocal obligation and hospitality that endured even when the circus was no longer in Cassano.

After the lunch, which consisted of five or six courses, Lorenzo Cardinali paid the hotelier and departed. Giuseppe and Pietro on the other hand, took a bedroom together, and lingered there for several hours. The hotelier reported that they ordered a bottle of wine and then withdrew behind closed doors, without him 'knowing what they did'.[64] The pair clearly were bosom buddies, but it is impossible to know whether their post-prandial hours together were simply a typical siesta (it was July, the height of the hot southern Italian summer), or the scene of something more conspiratorial. Either way, the bedroom hired by the hour must have had its own particular qualities as an intimately masculine arena. Soon afterwards, when the company finally departed Castrovillari, its members did so from the station at which they had originally arrived in the area to continue to their next port of call, Corigliano Calabro, 27 kilometres to the west. As they left, they were waved off by the company's most intimate and faithful local friends, Raffaella and Giuseppe Saraceni.[65]

Collectively, these tantalizing scenarios enrich our sense of the variety and intensity of southern Italian social life and its attendant emotional bonds. In some ways the images are reassuringly familiar: luncheons in restaurants, evenings in company at home, bidding farewell to friends at the station. The emotions surrounding each situation are all easily imaginable even a century and a half later. Yet, other aspects of the social dynamics of the period are much less historically and culturally decipherable. For example, two male friends retiring to a hotel room with a bottle of wine for several post-prandial hours together verges on the suspicious from today's standpoint, bespeaking a level of intimacy that well exceeds the usual bounds of modern male friendship.

---

[62] ASR, TCPR, 1879, b. 3659, vol. IA, ff. 120–6, statement by Raffaella Saraceni to Michele Finizia, Rome, 10 October 1878.
[63] ASR, TCPR, 1879, b. 3659, vol. II, f. 171, statement by Guglielmo Vigline, 43, hotel-keeper, Castrovillari, 18 November 1878.
[64] ASR, TCPR, 1879, b. 3659, vol. II, f. 171.
[65] ASR, TCPR, 1879, b. 3659, vol. IA, ff. 120–6, interrogation of Raffaella Saraceni by Michele Finizia, Rome, 10 October 1878. Raffaella did not mention that the farewell took place in the company of other townsfolk, reinforcing the sense that she and her brother had a special relationship with the circus company.

Similarly, over Cardinali's relationship with Raffaella, questions arise about what links there were between the horseman's regular presence in the Saraceni household and the sexual electricity observed between him and the married Raffaella while she watched the circus. How, it might be wondered, was this sexual energy managed in the private-yet-public arena of the Saraceni household—if at all? Were the Cardinalis invited to the Saraceni household because the daughter of the house desired him, and if so, what might her parents have thought about that? Or did Raffaella first get to know Cardinali at her parent's house, on the innocent basis of an old family friendship, and then pay him special attention at the circus as the result of an emerging attraction? Most pressingly, how did the perceived intimacy between Cardinali and Raffaella square with southern Italy's historical preoccupation, even obsession, as David Kertzer has put it, with female sexual virtue and fidelity?[66]

## *La Voce Pubblica*

It is not possible to answer these questions with certainty, but it is obvious that by the time the Cardinali Equestrian Company took their train to Corigliano Calabro, many residents of Cassano suspected that the arenas of the circus and the Saraceni household had overlapped with more intimacy than was socially acceptable. The town's views, often based on gossip and hearsay, were collected some time later, with witnesses providing their widely divergent interpretations to investigating officials. Public discussion of this type in nineteenth-century Italy was dignified with the identity almost of a persona, as *la voce pubblica*, the public voice. Although liberal legal codes were gradually reformed in an opposite direction, this form of public opinion still carried a surprising degree of authority in judicial discourse.[67]

According to the collective judgement of the region's *voce pubblica*, the Saraceni–Cardinali intimacy, witnessed in ways ranging from regular evening exchanges of hospitality to a post-prandial masculine colloquium between Pietro and Giuseppe, had culminated in the development of an illicit sexual relationship between Pietro Cardinali and Raffaella Saraceni. Amorphous gossip may still have been accepted as a reliable witness in Italy's law courts, but for historians its use lies less in establishing precise facts than as a guide to interpolating patterns

---

[66] Kertzer, *Sacrificed for Honor*, p. 25.
[67] See for example ASR, TCPR, 1879, b. 3659, vol. I, f. 262, a memorandum dated 19 October 1878 from the Carabiniere police, addressed to the 'Procuratore del Re presso il Tribunale Civile e Corrrezionale di Roma', which says that the *voce pubblica* 'confirms the existence of an intimate relationship between Saraceni and Cardinali'. On the notion of a neighbourhood's judgement, see Domenico Rizzo, 'Marriage on Trial: Adultery in Nineteenth-Century Rome', *Gender, Family and Sexuality: The Private Sphere in Italy, 1860–1945*, edited by Perry Willson (Basingstoke: Palgrave Macmillan, 2004), pp. 20–36, esp. pp. 25–6.

of thought and establishing outlines for a retrospective view of the historical context's cultural imagination. The *voce pubblica*'s interpretations of the growing intimacy between the circus company and the Cardinali family covered a broad spectrum. But broken down to constituent parts, each suggests possibilities about how contemporaries could visualize emotional intimacies in their particular historical context.

Exemplifying the town's level of 'soft suspicion', Vincenzo Fabiani, a state official resident in Cassano, expressed his view in general terms. He claimed that during the circus's visit, the public observed a 'too-advanced intimacy between the Saraceni family and Pietro Cardinali'. He added that Raffaella did not enjoy an 'advantageous' position in public opinion, because she was suspected of having affairs after the breakdown of her marriage.[68] Cassano's magistrate, Francesco de Cicco, expressed similarly generic notions, saying that even before the circus arrived, he had gathered that the Saraceni household was something of a magnet for young men. He even specified that he believed Raffaella herself was attracted to a young veterinary surgeon by the name of Gaetano Scorza. The magistrate reported that the common view was that the Saraceni family, including the parents, habitually showed 'troppa leggerezza'—they were morally lax.[69]

Already established, this view strengthened once the circus came to town and Pietro Cardinali became a frequent evening guest at the Saraceni household. Pressed on the question of an illicit relationship between Pietro and Raffaella, the magistrate replied that it was not out the question, but it was 'conjecture'.[70] Senior landowner Francesco Servidio held similar views. He had observed a 'great intimacy' between Pietro Cardinali and the Saraceni family, mentioning as an example frequent sightings of Pietro and Giuseppe striding about arm in arm. He was aware of 'murmurs' about a possible affair between Raffaella and the vet, Scorza, as well as conjecture about the same thing with Pietro. In his view such murmurs 'were not unfounded'.[71]

When approached directly, the vet Scorza confirmed that he had been a regular visitor at the Saraceni household, and this had been the case long before the circus came to town. He described frequent soirées dedicated to 'honest' entertainment such as playing cards, conversation, and playing the piano. The house did attract many young men, he admitted, but his account left it unclear whether the main attraction was Giuseppe, Raffaella, or simply convivial hospitality. Because Raffaella was married, the etiquette of the day would have frowned on

---

[68] ASR, TCPR, 1879, b. 3659, vol. II, f. 226, interrogation of Vincenzo Fabiani: 'si notò dal pubblico un'intimità troppo avanzata tra la famiglia Saraceni e Pietro Cardinali […].'

[69] ASR, TCPR, 1879, b. 3659, vol. II, ff. 325–6, interrogation of Francesco De Cicco, magistrate, Cassano, 20 December 1878.

[70] ASR, TCPR, 1879, b. 3659, vol. II, ff. 325–6, interrogation of Francesco De Cicco, magistrate, Cassano, 20 December 1878.

[71] ASR, TCPR, 1879, b. 3659, vol. II, f. 274, witness statement by Francesco Servidio, landowner, 25 November 1878.

her if she had enjoyed mingling too promiscuously with these young men, even if they were mostly her brother's friends. This might explain the town's supposed judgement of the family as morally 'light', an interpretation reinforced by the fact that Scorza himself had felt the need to reduce his level of attendance at the Saraceni's house to quell rumours about an affair between him and Raffaella. He flatly denied having had such an affair, or knowing anything of an alleged relationship between Raffaella and Pietro.[72]

Views such as those expressed by men from Cassano's professions and officialdom hover between benign tolerance and mild opprobrium, and they lie somewhere in the middle of the spectrum of views about the Saraceni family's morals. By contrast, at least some members of the Cassano community saw nothing at all immoral about the intimacy between members of the circus and this prominent family. In particular, several commentators explained the 'advanced intimacy' of the two families to themselves and others with reference to the 'antica amicizia', the long-standing friendship, between the Cardinalis and the Saracenis, referring to the circus's visit to Cassano many years earlier.[73] In their view, it seems, intimacy between young adults that had its roots in pre-pubescent friendships was nothing to worry about. Exemplifying those who expressed this view was a local church canon, Giuseppe Rago, one of the notably few religious figures to appear in the historical record in relation to the case. He said he had heard rumours of Pietro and Raffaella's illicit relationship, but he preferred to give them the benefit of the doubt and did not give such gossip too much credence.[74]

Others were also doubtful that a sexual relationship had developed between Pietro and Raffaella. Some of these were family servants, who might have been particularly well placed to witness anything of the type, but whose dependence on their employers may also have influenced their accounts. Maria Brunetti, a woman of twenty-three who had been a servant in the Saraceni household at the time of the circus's visit to Cassano, confirmed that Pietro Cardinali often came to the house socially, sometimes with others, sometimes by himself. On these occasions he chatted with the family, including Raffaella and her mother Carolina. Brunetti confirmed that the circus artists did stay the night on one occasion, once the circus had left Cassano, but she reported that Antonietta slept in the same bed as Raffaella, and Pietro slept in Giuseppe's room. She claimed to be unaware of an illicit relationship of any type, and put the visits down to 'a simple matter of friendship'. Curiously, Brunetti added that she had once asked Raffaella about the degree of intimacy between her and Cardinali. Raffaella answered that they had

---

[72] ASR, TCPR, 1879, b. 3659, vol. II, f. 207, witness statement by Gaetano Scorza, veterinary surgeon and landowner, 21 November 1878.
[73] For example, ASR, TCPR, 1879, b. 3659, vol. II, f. 205, witness statement by Alessandro Morelli, landowner, 21 November 1878; and ASR, TCPR, 1879, b. 3659, vol. II, ff. 194–6, witness statement by Giuseppe Rago, canon, 21 November 1878.
[74] Rago, ASR, TCPR, 1879, b. 3659, vol. II, ff. 194–6.

known each other for a long time—as if that excluded the possibility of overstepping the mark.[75]

Other female servants of the Saraceni household corroborated Brunetti's interpretation of the degree of involvement between the figures. As Raffaella would have wished, the servant Letizia Ravitti had the impression that the Cardinalis had been 'friends of the family' for a long time. She saw their many evenings together as 'innocent' entertainments. Ravitti also reported that when Antonietta stayed the night, she slept in Raffaella's room, but she did not specify on how many occasions this happened.[76] Another servant, Rosina Baia, confirmed that Pietro Cardinali was a frequent guest at the house. She said he only stayed the night after the circus had left Cassano, and on these occasions—in her view there was more than one—he 'slept with Sig. Giuseppe Saraceni'. She denied knowledge of an illicit affair between Cardinali and Raffaella.[77] Unsurprisingly, according to the servants, respectability was never breached in the Saraceni household.

Yet, the most strident elements of the *voce pubblica* had a way of marginalizing doubts or justifications and reifying the most scandalous conclusion, which was that Pietro and Raffaella were involved in an unrestrained and passionate sexual affair. This view strengthened notably once the circus had moved from Cassano to Castrovillari, about 13 kilometres to the north, because Pietro frequently returned to Cassano to visit the Saraceni household. These return visits made it hard for some people to continue to see the links between Cardinali and the Saracenis as an emotionally circumscribed family friendship. It becomes quite difficult to reconcile the accounts of those who insisted upon the essential innocence of the bonds between the Saracenis and Cardinalis, particularly that between Pietro and Raffaella, with the more unvarnished and even outlandish tales of the existence of an urgent erotic tryst between the pair.

An early account that tenaciously occupied the official investigators' minds and shaped subsequent enquiry was provided by a Castrovillari hairdresser, Rosina Garramone. Interviewed in her home town in October 1878, she reported that she had gone to Cassano to deliver letters from Pietro Cardinali to both Raffaella and Giuseppe Saraceni in mid-September. She did not know Raffaella at all, but she had heard that Pietro was engaged to a woman in Cassano and assumed Raffaella was the bride to be. Seeing an opportunity to drum up some business of her own, as she delivered the letter she offered to do Raffaella's hair for the wedding. Raffaella had replied that she was already married, but 'if the need should

---

[75] ASR, TCPR, 1879, b. 3659, vol. II, ff. 176–9, witness statement by Maria Brunetti, servant, 20 December 1878.
[76] ASR, TCPR, 1879, b. 3659, vol. II, ff. 267–9, statement by Letizia Ravitti, servant, 25 November 1878.
[77] ASR, TCPR, 1879, b. 3659, vol. II, ff. 293–4, statement by Rosina Baia, servant, 27 November 1878.

arise' she would take up Garramone's offer.[78] This was instantly interpreted by the authorities as a sign that Raffaella clearly envisioned her next wedding in the near future. But there was an even more damning story to come.

Rosina Garramone voluntarily made a second appearance before the authorities the next day, announcing that she had something to add to her previous statement. During the circus's stay in Castrovillari, she had become friendly with one of the circus performers, a young clown known only by his stage name, Carluccio. One evening in early August, Carluccio had visited her house, as he often did, and told her something alarming. While the circus had been resident in Cassano, he had been summoned by Raffaella Saraceni, who offered him the sum of 100 *piastre* (equivalent to about 500 lire, a princely sum for a clown) to go to Rome and assassinate her husband. Garramone reported that Carluccio was so mortified by the sense of being drawn into a murder plot that he decided to desert the circus and disappear from the area immediately.[79] The only thing we know to be true is that Carluccio did indeed disappear from the region in early August. Garramone's statement made an enormous impression on the investigators, who began a long search for the elusive clown all over Italy.[80]

Another very damning account came from Pietro's own form of servant, a stablehand by the name of Giuseppe De Luca. De Luca's view was that early in the circus's sojourn in Cassano, Raffaella had begun to *amoreggiare*, a verb probably closest to the older English phrase 'to make love', or flirt, with Pietro. In De Luca's account this soon led to an affair that took on 'proportions so marked that it was no mystery to anyone'. Moreover, De Luca said that Cardinali's 'so-called sister' Antonietta aided and abetted the love story and knew every detail. With a view to Antonietta's earlier relationship with Pietro, De Luca's allegation makes her own emotional life potentially even more complicated. De Luca stressed that Pietro's frequent returns to Cassano, not just from nearby Castrovillari, but also from the more distant town of Corigliano Calabro, were proof that there was much more to the story than an innocent family friendship.[81]

Pietro's insistence upon returning to Cassano on a regular basis despite the circus having departed the town was a key signal for many observers that intense emotions were at stake in whatever it was that was drawing him back. Some could not help but share the likes of De Luca's suspicions about an illicit love affair, and their accounts make the possibility of a merely innocent family connection increasingly less credible. An example was Cassano's mayor, Raffaele De Vincentis,

---

[78] ASR, TCPR, 1879, b. 3659, vol. II, ff. 167–8, statement by Rosina Garramone, hairdresser, Castrovillari, 14 October 1878.

[79] ASR, TCPR, 1879, b. 3659, vol. II, f. 166, further statement by Rosina Garramone, 15 October 1878.

[80] ASR, TCPR, 1879, b. 3659, vol. IB, ff. 253–78, and ff. 316–8 constitute a fascinating paper trail of official attempts to track down 'Carluccio', in a search stretching from Naples and Bari to Milan and Turin.

[81] ASR, TCPR, 1879, b. 3659, IA, ff. 94–100, interrogation of Giuseppe De Luca, Cardinali's stablehand, Rome, 8 October 1878.

a medical doctor and member of the same elite social circle as the Saraceni family themselves. Like others, he recalled that after the circus had left town, Pietro was known to make the journey back to Cassano in the late evening, so that he could spend time with Raffaella. He summed up his recollections in a memorable image, describing how one night at about 3.30 a.m. he saw Pietro Cardinali career past on his familiar buggy. The mayor said that he simply assumed that Cardinali was departing from the Saraceni house, 'since that is where he always went.'[82]

Nor did Pietro depart for Cassano only once his duties to the public in the arena were complete in the evening. According to Castrovillari's pharmacist, Vincenzo D'Atri, suspicion there about Cardinali's relationship with Raffaella reached a peak when one of the circus's shows was cancelled due to Pietro's absence. Everyone knew he was in Cassano. Giving a sense of how news was conveyed at the time, D'Atri recalled vividly that posters announcing the show's cancellation were hastily pasted up in the town square.[83] A different perspective on the cancellation was provided by the conductor of Castrovillari's orchestra, which provided the circus's music. Maestro Leonardo Rizzo recounted that on the day of Pietro's absence, his brother Lorenzo Cardinali had dismissed the orchestra as the circus could not perform without Pietro and the evening's entertainment was peremptorily cancelled. At the time, the conductor had glumly gathered simply that Cardinali was a guest of the Saraceni family, with whom 'he had a close friendship'.[84]

Cancelled performances would have been disappointing for the townsfolk and frustrating for the rest of the company, not to mention a threat to their economic well-being. On the occasion, standing next to the conductor, the pent-up resentment of the clown known as Carluccio finally overflowed. Fed up with what he obviously considered the tired euphemism of Pietro's 'friendship' with the 'Cardinali family', the young performer vehemently spat out words that made a deep impression on the maestro: 'Lovely friendship that one: it consists of eating, drinking, and fucking'.[85] Nor was such direct language restricted to the lower echelons of the circus. An usher at Castrovillari's town hall by the name of Luigi Musmano admitted to being amazed by the way Pietro Cardinali would set off for Cassano in his one-horse buggy, sometimes with Antonietta, after the show. These departures had prompted him to ask one of the other circus members if it was true that Cardinali 'went to fuck in the Saraceni house'. The circus artist

---

[82] ASR, TCPR, 1879, b. 3659, II, f. 210, witness statement by Raffaele De Vincentis, doctor and mayor of Cassano, 21 November 1878.

[83] ASR, TCPR, 1879, b. 3659, II ff. 174–5, witness statement by Vincenzo D'Atri, pharmacist, 18 November 1878.

[84] ASR, TCPR, 1879, b. 3659, vol. II, ff. 155–6, witness statement by Leonardo Rizzo, orchestral conductor, 17 November 1878.

[85] ASR, TCPR, 1879, b. 3659, vol. II, ff. 155–6. Rizzo quoted Carluccio as saying 'Bella amicizia è quella del Pietro: consiste nel mangiare, bevare [sic], e fottere'. The quotation was underlined in red, probably by the investigating magistrate.

concerned did not answer, but looked knowingly, which Musmano took to be an affirmative.[86] The artist concerned may or may not have been Carluccio.

## Conclusion: The Circus Departs

Whoever he was, the artist's ambiguous silence was sufficient to confirm the young Musmano's amazed conjectures, and the usher joined the ranks of many in the region who were convinced that Raffaella Saraceni had entered into an erotic relationship with Pietro Cardinali. If that was the case, it is unlikely to have been the first time that the emotions of desire generated by the circus resulted in an erotic fusion across two spaces: that of the circus itself, and that of the social world of a small Italian town. What is distinctive about the Cardinali Brothers' visit to Cassano allo Ionio in June 1878 is that ultimately it led to a chilling murder which placed the town at the centre of national attention. Investigation of the crime generated a rich repository of popular impressions on subjects that were part of daily life in nineteenth-century Italy: the private life of an itinerant extended family of circus people, the private life of a bourgeois couple and their family, and a provincial town's attitudes to the two spheres, especially when they were suspected of intimate overlap. But it is only through exceptional circumstances that these normal phenomena of the day became the central object of contemporary attention and later of historical records.

At the time, the revelations all generated substantial public reaction. Subsequently, they give historians the chance to glimpse emotional experiences that are often difficult to detect. First and foremost, the Cardinali circus, a descendent of ancient Rome's great extravaganzas, drew forth, like its predecessors, intense responses: most obviously, fear, joy, sadness, and surprise. In this way the circus epitomizes the idea of an emotional arena as a social space where particular feelings were elicited, played with, flirted with, and shared, but also contained. The public attended the circus hoping to experience a range of often intense feelings, within the safe boundary offered by the arena itself. Unlike the normally private arena of family life, the point of the circus was that the large audience amplified the emotional experience. A private viewing of the circus acts in an empty arena would have been a much less exciting affair.

As well as shining light on legitimate responses to satisfying entertainment, the circus arena also permits glimpses of a feeling that the emotional regimes of the day generally confined to private spaces: desire. From today's perspective the circus is an innocent thing, but in provincial Cassano the erotic overtones of Antonietta's and Pietro's daring and highly physical acts were considerable.

---

[86] ASR, TCPR, 1879, b. 3659, vol. II, f. 173, witness statement by Luigi Musmano, council usher, 18 November 1878. His words were 'andava a fottere'.

Though on a smaller scale, this element was no less intense for those in the audience than had been the more famous erotic currents generated by the likes of Adah Isaacs Menken or Jules Léotard in New York, Paris, or London. The emotions generated in the Cassano arena began as momentary sparks of desire, and usually that would have been sufficient. But in June 1878 those sparks appear to have ignited enduring lust, perhaps even love. These feelings were thought by officials and public alike to have escaped the arena's confines and to have entered more private realms.

The determined official investigation into whether those emotions found refuge in the Saraceni household fleetingly illuminated a very different emotional arena: a ménage within the Cardinali Brothers' circus. The triangular relationship between Pietro, his wife Carolina, and his adoptive sister Antonietta, reveals an intimate web marked by desire and lust, but also fear, shame, guilt, sadness, and jealousy. There may also have been happiness, but that is not what the officials were looking for. The emotions the officials did find, such as jealousy and resentment, are generated at times within all enduring intimate relationships. But they are not often seen, and even less recorded. The private life of Cardinali's harem was an emotional arena within an arena, in that it was visible within the circus group, but invisible to the townsfolk. It only came into the spotlight by chance.

Two final aspects come to light. One, quite straightforward but nevertheless worth dwelling on given the relatively little that has been written about the history of social life in the Italian provinces, is a sense of the dense texture and complexity of social connections in those small communities. The emotions that drove such connections come momentarily and unexpectedly to life through the papers of a dusty archive. The second aspect is that the emotions of desire generated by the circus's visit were not unique to that town or occasion. Desire had been sparked during the Cardinali's circus's visits to other places. But, rather than run amok as they seem to have done in Cassano, those desires and other emotions were carefully constrained within the virtual arenas of amorous correspondence that are examined in the next chapter.

# 3
# Virtual Arenas
## Illicit Love by Letter

### Hidden Emotions

After the Cardinali Circus moved on from Cassano and Castrovillari, its next stop was Corigliano Calabro, some 40 kilometres to the west. In those days that distance was sufficient to represent a definitive departure. We will never know what Raffaella's feelings were as she and her brother waved the train off at the station, but the mere fact that the siblings bade farewell to the troupe personally was later interpreted as evidence that special bonds had developed between certain members of the circus, and the young scions of the Saraceni family. The local *voce pubblica* became adamant in its conviction that Pietro had brought particular pleasure into Raffaella's life. That public voice did not represent everyone, but what began as murmurings of suspicion were eventually accepted as being very close to the truth. The *voce pubblica* was equally convinced that the illicit couple's pleasures did not dwindle after the circus's departure, but were instead transformed into a desire, and a determination, to be married.

The obstacle to these aspirations was Raffaella's estranged husband, Captain Giovanni Fadda. When the captain was murdered by Cardinali a few months after the circus's departure from Cassano, it seemed to prove local suspicions: Raffaella, unhappy with her husband, had fallen in love with someone else, whom she keenly wanted to marry. Easily put into words by witnesses, the scenario was nevertheless scandalous by the standards of prevailing expectations about marriage. Prompted by one or two key early witness statements, officials investigating the murder quickly fashioned an explanatory narrative for the murder. It featured a duplicitous, sexually hungry woman, in fatal concert with a caddish Casanova. After news of the crime broke, this story quickly took shape in both the official and popular minds of Italy, like a genie released from a bottle. Once out, it refused either to disappear into the ether, or to deflate and return whence it had come.

Nearly a century and a half later, the story of Raffaella's affair with Pietro Cardinali looks so like a plot from an operatic stage that it is difficult to interpret as anything but a colourful exception to a familiar historical rule: Italian women, descended from Eve but required to behave like the Virgin Mary, led emotionally

*Emotional Arenas: Life, Love, and Death in 1870s Italy*. Mark Seymour, Oxford University Press (2020). © Mark Seymour.
DOI: 10.1093/oso/9780198743590.001.0001

and sexually cloistered lives.¹ Sexually desiring women threatened society, and, particularly in the late nineteenth century, fear of appearing so became a common emotional denominator.² From infancy girls were taught that the merest hint of a sexual signal to a man could undermine a family's honour and bring its opposite: shame. Not just the menfolk, but an entire family were often involved in protecting the sexual purity of their unmarried females. It was 'unimaginable' for a bourgeois woman not to be a virgin at marriage, and 'vigilance over virgins' was one feature of Italian life that was quite uniform across Italy's regions and social classes for most of the nineteenth century.³

The received historical image of rigorous surveillance over women's sexual and emotional lives contrasts strongly with the way those lives were often portrayed in popular nineteenth-century art forms such as the opera or the novel.⁴ Recently scholars have begun to explore the elusive terrain that lies between everyday women's subjective experience and the richly emotional and sexually allusive literary and operatic models of the era.⁵ The mere cloistering of sexual and emotional desires could not have meant that ordinary women did not experience such feelings. As yet though, little is known of the subjective emotional experiences that made up the collective responses even in the major cities of France and Britain—to circus performers such as Léotard, for example—let alone in remoter parts of southern Italy. It is challenging historiographical ground, with few landmarks, but it begs patient exploration.

By chance, the investigation of Giovanni Fadda's murder unearthed further evidence of ordinary women's emotions of desire. It came in the form of highly secret letters written by women who were unable to express their desires openly for fear of terrible shame and dishonour.⁶ The writing of these and other love

---

¹ Antonia Pasi and Paolo Sorcinelli, 'Presentazione', in Pasi and Sorcinelli (eds), *Amori e trasgressioni. Rapporti di coppia tra '800 e '900* (Bari: Edizioni Dedalo, 1995), p. 8.

² Bruno P. F. Wanrooij, *Storia del pudore. La questione sessuale in Italia, 1860–1940* (Venice: Marsilio Editori, 1990), p. 171.

³ Michela De Giorgio, *Le Italiane dall'unità a oggi. Modelli culturali e comportamenti sociali* (Rome-Bari: Laterza, 1992), p. 274. De Giorgio's phrase 'vigilance over virgins' echoes Jane Schneider's pioneering research on such questions referenced in note 10 below.

⁴ For example, Sandra Corse, ' "Mi chiamano Mimì": The Role of Women in Puccini's Operas', *Opera Quarterly*, vol. 1, no. 1 (1983): 93–106; Emilio Sala, 'Women Crazed by Love: An Aspect of Romantic Opera', *Opera Quarterly*, 10 (1994): 19–41; Susan Rutherford, *Verdi, Opera, Women* (Cambridge: Cambridge University Press, 2013), p. 2 and Ch. 4; Katharine Mitchell, *Italian Women Writers: Gender and Everyday Life in Fiction and Journalism, 1870–1910* (Toronto: Toronto University Press, 2014).

⁵ For example, Valeria P. Babini, Chiara Beccalossi, and Lucy Riall (eds), *Italian Sexualities Uncovered, 1789–1914* (Basingstoke: Palgrave Macmillan, 2015), particularly Katharine Mitchell, 'Literary and Epistolary Figurations of Female Desire in Early Post-unification Italy, 1861–1914', pp. 125–42; and, Manola Ida Venzo (ed.), *Scrivere d'amore. Lettere di uomini e donne fra Cinque e Novecento* (Rome: Viella, 2015).

⁶ On secrecy as a strategy to avoid shame in a broader context, see Deborah Cohen, *Family Secrets: Living with Shame from the Victorians to the Present Day* (London: Viking Books, 2013), esp. pp. xii–xvi.

letters provided forms of emotional refuge, in William Reddy's sense of a space, real or imagined, where an emotional regime's norms were relaxed or reversed.[7] But the letters provided more than a refuge: within them women created and explored a different world from the one in which they lived. These letters represent virtual arenas, in which writers became prima donnas on their own operatic stages.

In the spaces of their imagination, writers explored, shaped, and staged feelings that had no socially acceptable outlet, and remained invisible to all except the correspondence's participants. The usual invisibility of such feelings earns those that do come to light a special place in any history of the emotions. They suggest that at least some women were able to fashion virtual emotional arenas in which the expressive norms were quite different from those of banal daily life.

## Detecting Feeling in Letters

The historiographical terrain of lived emotions is challenging because, unlike cultural texts, primary sources that preserve the personal feelings of ordinary people can be difficult to come by. This is particularly the case when the relationships concerned were illicit and the actors obscure.[8] In the context of a conservative, Catholic culture like Italy's, the miniature emotional arena represented by the confessional, designed for the expiation of guilt and regulating private life, particularly sexual life, is emblematic of the historical silence.[9] Women were especially strictly governed by an extensive cultural regime of shame in relation to their thoughts, feelings, and actions in the erotic sphere.

If confessional exchanges left written records, we would have a much more detailed picture of that emotional regime, its infringements, and their control, but it did not.[10] Intense taboos effectively limited the production of durable historical evidence of such feelings, especially those experienced outside the recognized emotional arena of marriage and the family. As Michela De Giorgio put it in her major history of Italian women, documentary evidence even of legitimate 'sentiments, expectations, and emotions is *scarna*'—literally, lacking in flesh, but

---

[7] William M. Reddy, *The Navigation of Feeling: A Framework for the History of Emotions* (Cambridge: Cambridge University Press, 2001), p. 128.

[8] On the special genre represented by 'adulterous letters', see Sally Holloway, '"You Know I am all on Fire": Writing the Adulterous Affair in England, c. 1740–1830', *Historical Research*, vol. 18, no. 244 (2016): 317–39.

[9] Pasi and Sorcinelli, 'Presentazione', p. 5; for more detailed studies of the ways confession and penitence shaped sexual experience for Catholics see Pino Lucà Trombetta, *La confessionione della lussuria. Definizione e controllo del piacere nel Cattolicesimo* (Genoa: Costa & Nolan, 1991); and Fernanda Alfieri, *Nella camera degli sposi. Tomás Sánchez, il matrimonio, la sessualità (secoli XVI–XVII)*, (Bologna: Il Mulino, 2010).

[10] Jane Schneider, 'Of Vigilance and Virgins: Honor, Shame and Access to Resources in Mediterranean Societies', *Ethnology*, vol. 10, no. 1 (1971): 1–24, esp. p. 20.

figuratively, scarce, or thin on the ground.[11] Sentiments, expectations, and emotions were either not committed to paper, or such material, carefully controlled by authors, families, and in some cases, archivists, rarely comes to light.

Nevertheless, over the last two decades, persistent historians have progressively unearthed rich archival lodes that have helped to flesh out understanding of such subjective feelings. Fascinating personal letters and diaries have been located, and have generally provided the most accessible insights into the emotional worlds of past lives. As mentioned in chapter 2 in relation to emotions in Raffaella and Giovanni Fadda's correspondence, since the 'emotive' turn pioneered by Reddy and others, scholars have been more willing to take personal writing as genuine evidence of emotions experienced in the past. In the last few years, a significant body of research has developed in this vein.[12]

The conscientious letters exchanged by Raffaella Saraceni and Giovanni Fadda have already helped to build a picture of the carefully regulated emotional arena of that couple's family life. Alas, no comparable evidence of the allegedly much more passionate relationship between Raffaella and Pietro Cardinali ever came to light. But, assuming that an illicit relationship between the two existed, the types of taboos mentioned above ensured that either they both resisted the temptation to express their passions on paper, or their communications were destroyed, lost, or for some other reason placed beyond the grasp of posterity.

Such a correspondence, it if ever existed, would certainly have provided a fascinating counterpoint to the dutiful letters exchanged between Fadda and his wife. And historians are not the first to wish they could get their hands on such a correspondence. On 7 October 1878, just one day after the murder of Captain Fadda, the mayor of the small town of Corigliano Calabro, acting on instructions telegraphed from Rome, took two officers of the carabinieri (a military police force) to search Pietro Cardinali's abode for 'anything that might have to do with an amorous relationship with Raffaella Fadda'.[13] The officials were received, perhaps with a sense of alarm, by a woman who said she was Cardinali's wife, Carolina Misuraca, and 'another woman who said she was his sister', Antonietta.[14] One of the carabinieri began the search by opening a locked trunk, where he soon found a cache of letters. He gave these to the mayor, who quickly read through

---

[11] De Giorgio, *Le Italiane*, p. 274.
[12] Sally Holloway's article mentioned in n. 8 above is a good example, as is her book *The Game of Love in Georgian England: Courtship, Emotions and Material Culture* (Oxford: Oxford University Press, 2019). In the Italian context, particularly on point are Manola Ida Venzo, 'Documenti del sé: usi e abusi', and Roberto Bizzocchi, 'Decodificare le emozioni', both in Manola Ida Venzo (ed.) *Scrivere d'amore*, pp. 11–18 and pp. 19–24 respectively; as well as Mark Seymour, 'Epistolary Emotions: Exploring Amorous Hinterlands in 1870s Southern Italy', *Social History*, vol. 35, no. 2 (2010): 148–64.
[13] Archivio di Stato di Roma, Tribunale Civile e Penale di Roma (henceforth ASR, TCPR), 1879, busta 3659, vol. IA, folios 264–5, Report by Luigi Garetti, mayor of Corigliano Calabro, 7 October 1878.
[14] ASR, TCPR, 1879, b. 3659, vol. IA, f. 264.

them, and decided to sequester a total of forty-four, whose contents he described tantalizingly as 'tutto amoroso'—all amorous.[15]

The letters were sent to Rome, where the chief investigating magistrate, Michele Finizia, sifted through them in search of proof of Cardinali's illicit relationship with Saraceni. Finizia was not interested in the cultural forms the letters took. He was an essentialist, seeking evidence of true feelings: of love, passion, and desire. His heart must have sunk as he realized that not one of the letters in Cardinali's possession had been written by Raffaella. Yet the provincial officials had not been wrong about the letters' contents in their initial appraisal. They were certainly 'all amorous', and the object of each letter's desire was indeed Cardinali. But their authors were a series of admirers and possibly lovers from Cardinali's previous ports of call, one dating as far back as 1866.

In the present, the letters are a rare collection of the sort of emotional outpouring that might have been received by Cardinali's more illustrious French counterparts. The letters turned out to be of little use to the investigating magistrate, except that they provided evidence that Cardinali was an inveterate womanizer. But for those interested in the emotional worlds of the past, the letters present an unusual opportunity to explore expressions of secret and intense feelings, written by the women whose hearts had been purloined by Cardinali. The letters constitute virtual emotional arenas where secret passions were rehearsed and staged for an audience of one man. By a quirk of fate, these written 'performances' were preserved and can now be witnessed by a wider audience.

Love letters are intriguing objects in themselves, exemplifying some of the many reasons for increased historical interest in personal correspondence over the last two decades.[16] If a reliable postal service provided Giovanni and Raffaella with a way to conduct a marriage whose members spent more time apart than together, the other side of the postal-culture coin was that it also allowed secret, illicit bonds to be established and conveyed materially over time and space. The collection of love letters preserved by Pietro Cardinali classically represents the microhistorical exceptional-normal: it was probably more normal to exchange secretive, amorous letters than we will ever know, because coming across them is the exception. The women who wrote love letters to Pietro Cardinali represent an unusual niche within a recognizably modern network of communication, and their pens and paper created material frameworks for secret emotional arenas.

For the letters' authors and recipients, no doubt their message was key, but hindsight has increased interest in the medium, and the materiality of these letters is fascinating even before their messages start to be deciphered. They present

---

[15] ASR, TCPR, 1879, b. 3659, vol. IA, f. 264.
[16] The 'adulterous letters' of Sally Holloway's article '"You know I am all on Fire"', present an even richer range of material variations, including a fascinating array of ink types, among them (invisible) lemon juice (p. 324).

a great variety of paper types, ink colours, and handwriting, as well as emotional tenors. However much letters are subject to cultural codes, the authors' individual characters shine through with as much colour variation as the ink and paper. Many were written in secrecy, for fear of the shame, even ruin, that could befall a woman known to have solicited amorous attention from a man.[17] Often, the letters refer to strategies of subterfuge to avoid discovery, such as the use of intermediary addressees. The identity of their authors will never come to light, but even so, attempts to tease out those authors' inner feelings and desires can make the scholarly reader feel like a voyeur. Such feelings of trespass are an occupational hazard that historians of epistolary culture happily live with.

Although it was common in the nineteenth century to hire scribes, the secret nature of these letters makes it unlikely that they were penned by anyone other than the enamoured women. There were about four or five authors in total, and the range of their personalities, linguistic, and orthographic skills is as wide as the variety of paper they used. In 1870s southern Italy, paper, pens and ink, envelopes, and postage, would have had significant costs when related to average incomes. The paper on which these letters were written ranged from an unremarkable coarse buff to decoratively embossed and obviously expensive bright white. The usual format was to fold one sheet in half, creating something like a blank four-page greeting card. The four small pages were then written on in sequence. Ink was generally a sepia colour, but it could also be blue or black.[18] In most cases sheer age has probably faded the ink and altered the letters' appearance, but the emotions they convey are as richly coloured as they were when they animated the hands of their writers.

As well as having the means to afford stationery and postage, the fact that their authors could write at all is sufficient to place these women in the upper echelons of southern Italian society. Literacy was far from the norm in 1870s Italy, with the national average standing at about 38 per cent of men and 24 per cent of women. Literacy levels in the south would have been significantly lower for both sexes.[19] Writing was also taught as a subject separate from reading, with the result that fewer people could write than read.[20] By today's standards, the written language in these love letters is colourful, even histrionic. Spelling had yet to be standardized in Italy, so orthographic variations should not be a surprise. But the letters

---

[17] It was considered 'dangerous' for a woman merely to write to a man even in the early twentieth century: De Giorgio, *Le italiane*, p. 316.
[18] The exact shade of the original ink is uncertain, but the three main colours of brownish, bluish, and blackish, remain distinctive.
[19] Ann Hallamore Caesar, 'Women Readers and the Novel in Nineteenth-Century Italy,' *Italian Studies*, vol. 56 (2001): 81–2. De Giorgio reports that in the rural mainland south at the time of unification (1861), only 3.05 per cent of women had elementary education. Nevertheless, about 15 per cent of southern women could read and write, suggesting much higher education levels in urban areas. De Giorgio, *Le Italiane*, p. 412.
[20] Caesar, 'Women Readers and the Novel', p. 82.

are further enriched and complicated with misspellings, local dialect, eccentric punctuation, and grammatical inconsistencies.

Even more striking is the fact that features of regional Italian accents, most commonly the pronunciation of 'P' as a 'B', 'C' as a 'G', and 'T' as 'D', are frequently evident in the spelling, echoing the key features of southern Italian speech.[21] Thus one admirer swore that her love was 'singero' rather than 'sincero'.[22] To get a sense of how this influenced the writing, non-Italian speaking Anglophones might imagine how the distinctive features of the speech of northern Britain, the southern United States, or Australian and New Zealand accents, for example, could be rendered on paper: New Zealand's favourite dinner, 'fush nd chups' (fish and chips), or the Australian exclamation of approval, 'Bewdy mite!' ('Beauty, mate'), come to mind. Moreover, a general lack of punctuation often makes the letters seem as if the writer were breathlessly hurried, uncannily compounding the sense of passion and secrecy they convey.

## Cardinali's Cache and Italian Amorous Culture

At the moment of the letters' discovery by officials, in the presence of Carolina and Antonietta, the mayor noted that only twenty-six were in their respective envelopes. Of these, fifteen were addressed to a certain Carmela Cannezzaro, ten were addressed to Cardinali's wife Carolina Misuraca, and just one directly to Pietro Cardinali. Asked why the addressees on the envelopes were different from the person for whom the letter was intended, Carolina is reported to have explained that 'she knew of various affairs [*diversi amori*] her husband had contracted in the towns where he had worked, and particularly remembered a certain Giulia Pachetta of Laino' and 'a certain Amalia, whose surname she had forgotten, of Città Sant'Angelo'. Carolina suggested helpfully that the letters probably came from these women, implying that such a correspondence would need its go-betweens.[23] Most of the letters were signed with a mysterious insignia, 'M. N. +' or some variation using those letters and the plus sign.

Also found in the trunk was a photograph of a soldier (see figure 3.1). Carolina told the men that the photograph was of a lieutenant whose name she did not know. The officials could not have known who the image represented, but it was Giovanni Fadda, and the only plausible way for the photograph to have come into Cardinali's possession was for Raffaella to have given it to him. The mayor simply noted his suspicion that the amorous cache related to 'Raffaella Fadda, who could

---

[21] There are of course many southern dialects and accents, though variations can be difficult to detect for the non-native speaker.

[22] ASR, TCPR, 1879, b. 3659, vol. IA, f. 310, undated letter from M. N. to Pietro Cardinali.

[23] ASR, TCPR, 1879, b. 3659, vol. IA, ff. 264–5, Report by Luigi Garetti, mayor of Corigliano Calabro, 7 October 1878.

**Figure 3.1** Photograph of Giovanni Fadda discovered in Pietro Cardinali's trunk (ASR, TCPR, 1879, b. 3659). Reproduced with permission from the Ministero dei Beni e Attività Culturali e del Turismo, ASRM 56/2015. Further reproduction prohibited.

easily have signed her name with those two initials followed by a cross as a pre-arranged sign'. He did not speculate further, but dutifully consigned the letters, envelopes, and the photograph, to Rome.[24] The mayor's hasty selection in those peculiar circumstances resulted in the creation of an unusual archive of love letters that was serendipitously preserved in the case's files.

But what of those peculiar circumstances in Cardinali's lodgings? It may not have been the first time that an officer of the law had seized epistolary evidence of an illicit love affair. But it must have been unusual to hear the recipient's wife explain, with apparent insouciance, that the letters were probably written by women with whom her husband had contracted 'diversi amori' in the course of his work.[25] We can only guess what this might say about the 'marginal' emotional community represented by Pietro's relationship with Carolina and the circus family more generally, but the possibilities range from a marriage where jealousy

[24] ASR, TCPR, 1879, b. 3659, vol. IA, ff. 264–5.
[25] ASR, TCPR, 1879, b. 3659, vol. IA, ff. 264–5.

played no role, to one in which it was sublimated, or perhaps even stimulating.[26] Later testimony from Antonietta about the relationships within the circus suggested that a certain amount of fear reigned between Pietro and his women, which may have eclipsed the jealousy. Perhaps Carolina derived a certain vengeful pleasure in sharing tales of her husband's infidelity with curious officials, but it is impossible to say anything with certainty.

More certain than the Cardinali marriage's emotional climate is its legal status. As part of the new Italian polity's effort to separate the spheres of Church and state and require greater engagement by citizens with the government, the new Italian civil law required couples to be married before a state official in order to obtain recognition of the marriage. From 1866, those who merely had a religious ceremony were not legally married in the eyes of the law.[27] Although it is not known when Pietro and Carolina were married, Pietro had mentioned that it was 'only a church wedding', and it is therefore unlikely to have had civil status.[28] This would explain why, despite living in a form of matrimony, Pietro was able to present himself as an eligible bachelor and pursue the possibility of a new marriage to Raffaella. And, as revealed by the letters Pietro had received from her predecessors, Raffaella was by no means the first woman to have found this a desirable possibility.

How did ideas about eligible bachelors take shape in the minds of Italian women who hoped to find one? Under a regime that carefully controlled unmarried women's contact with men, the joys of emotions like love and erotic desire could generally only be experienced vicariously through art and entertainments, or, through private discussions, imaginings, and fantasy. For the limited numbers of women who possessed literacy, leisure time, and means, literature and the opera probably provided the most tantalizing glimpses of the triumphs and tragedies of human intimacy. Hours alone with a serialized dramatic novel (or sharing one read aloud), or an evening out in company at the theatre, would have offered Italian women occasional refuge from the rigidities of the reigning emotional regime.[29] In such a culture, it becomes all the easier to envisage how a circus, with its engaging physical displays, its thinly veiled erotic elements, and its sheer physical energy, provided exciting opportunities to a large and varied audience for intense emotional engagement.

Is it any wonder then that women such as Raffaella, and others with limited opportunities to explore their amorous desires, were susceptible to the flirtatious

---

[26] Barbara H. Rosenwein, *Generations of Feeling: A History of Emotions, 600–1700* (Cambridge: Cambridge University Press, 2016), p. 3. I am grateful to Barbara Rosenwein for sharing her ideas about how to interpret this relationship.

[27] Mark Seymour, *Debating Divorce in Italy: Marriage and the Making of Modern Italians, 1860–1974* (New York: Palgrave Macmillan, 2006), pp. 19–20.

[28] ASR, TCPR, 1879, b. 3659, vol. II, ff. 71–2, statement by Nicola Ghenghi, coachman, and friend to Cardinali, Bari, 11 October 1878.

[29] Katharine Mitchell, in works mentioned in n. 4 and n. 5 above, has been at the forefront of research on the interface between cultural products and Italian women's lived experiences.

eye contact flashed about by Pietro Cardinali as he galloped around the arena? What is more surprising in the context of southern Italy is the way some of those yearnings, sparked in the circus arena, developed their own afterlives in the form of ongoing connections between Pietro and his admirers. These post-performance relationships, perhaps fuelled by meetings in, if not of, the flesh, were later nurtured in the secret hinterlands of certain women's imaginations and fantasies. These emotionally charged arenas of the mind were shaped and expressed in letters women sent to Pietro, and, by circumstance, they were preserved for posterity to pore over.

## Making Love by Letter: Three Women

Perhaps because Pietro's collection of love letters was soon discovered to be of little use to the contemporary investigators, since they had nothing to do with Raffaella, they were fixed into their final resting place by an archivist's binding threads in a disorderly fashion. So it is sheer coincidence that, of the torrent of epistolary passion that is to follow, the very first words to leap out of the file are from page two of a carelessly folded letter. They proclaim: 'Beloved Pietro I know that many women have loved you but it is impossible that any of them could have loved you more than I do [...]'.[30] The letter, undated, bore the signature of one 'Mariuccia Fiore'. Nothing is known of this woman beyond the obvious fact that she was in love with Pietro and had been sufficiently acquainted with him to have garnered some information about his amorous past.

It is impossible to know how many women Pietro had seduced, but there is no reason not to take Mariuccia at her word when she refers to the 'many' who have loved him. Far from feeling special or unique by virtue of having been singled out by Pietro, Mariuccia was quite aware that she was one of many in competition for the artiste's continued attention. As a starting point for historical analysis of this improbable collection, Mariuccia's declaration suggests that the phenomenon of educated, literate women falling in love with a circus horseman was not as outlandish or operatic as it might at first seem. In fact, by the time Pietro's cache of love letters was seized by the police in October 1878, the circus rider had been receiving such messages from women for over a decade.

The earliest, written in the 1860s, is also one of the most visually arresting. Its paper is thinner, more brittle, and more tissue-like than that of later correspondence. Unfortunately this also means it is more delicate, has more pieces missing, and is more difficult to read. Following a custom still used in Italy,

---

[30] ASR, TCPR, 1879, b. 3659, vol. IA, f. 266, undated letter to Pietro Cardinali signed Mariuccia Fiore. All translations are my own. I have not sought to reproduce the orthographical errors or southern accent, which are quite striking, but I have tried to preserve the sense of cadence created by the often irregular or absent punctuation.

the letter is headed with both a place and a date. It was written in Catanzaro, not far from Cassano and Corigliano, on 22 March 1866. In 1878, Raffaella Saraceni had recalled the Cardinali circus visiting Cassano 'about fourteen years ago'. It is probable that this letter dates from the tour the Cardinalis made of this region remembered by Raffaella. Pietro would have been about twenty-four years old at that point. It is the only letter preserved from his younger days, and the fact that Pietro kept it suggests that it was in some way emotionally significant.

The opening lines thank Pietro for his letter, indicating from the outset that the correspondence was reciprocal. His letter's arrival had been 'yearned for as is the sun by those who live at the pole after six months of darkness'. For the writer, the days, the months, and the years might pass in a flash, but what could never flee her mind was 'your name and the love that [paper missing]'. As if to provide the missing words about the love, probably that 'we shared', the writer immediately refers to her inclusion of a token of 'devotion', a small item of her own clothing, which she asks Pietro to wear or carry 'for the sake of my love and the love of the Madonna that lie within it'. Having announced the gift, the letter breaks off whimsically into a rhyming triplet:

Piccolo il dono
Grande é desio
Accetti questo per amor mio
(Small is the gift; great is the desire; accept this for my love).[31]

The intimate nature of the gift and the line about desire suggest that the unforgettable love shared between Pietro and the writer was tinged with erotic overtones, albeit purified by reference to the Madonna.

Yet, unlike many of the letters Pietro was later to receive from other women, no suffocating sense of secrecy permeates this writing. A second paragraph shifts away from the intimate tone of the first, announcing not only the writer's 'florid health', but also that of her sister. The letter conveyed the sister's kindest greetings to Pietro, as well as her good wishes for Easter, both to him and the entire circus company. These lines convey a sense of openness, of relationships shared in discussion and known about within a family setting. Put in mind of the circus, the writer adds that Pietro might like to know that another company had recently visited, but it had been second rate and had 'bored all and sundry'. Turning over the page, 'Enough', the writer suddenly announces, 'I'll finish by wishing you a good Easter and giving you thousands of hugs [paper missing] yours, forever, C [paper missing] lonidi.' This apparently hasty conclusion is belied by what looks to be an unsecretive signature consisting of a first name followed by a surname. In

---

[31] ASR, TCPR, 1879, b. 3659, vol. IA, f. 270, letter to 'Girolamo' dated Catanzaro, 22 March 1866. During the murder trial a member of the circus confirmed that Pietro Cardinali sometimes went by the name of Girolamo Francone. See ASR, TCPR, 1879, b. 3659, vol. IV, ff. 235–7, interview of Carlo Bartone, clown, 20 October 1878.

**Figure 3.2** The sacred heart near the signature on the letter of 22 March 1866 (ASR, TCPR, b. 3659, 1879). Reproduced with permission from the Ministero dei Beni e Attività Culturali e del Turismo, ASRM 56/2015. Further reproduction prohibited.

this respect it was different from the majority of letters Pietro received, which ended with a cryptic sign.

The letter's hurried conclusion is poetically embellished by a surprising postscript: a simple but carefully drawn wreath-framed heart, crowned with flames and pierced by an arrow, five drops of blood seeping from the wound (figure 3.2). A mixed visual metaphor, it is a Christian sacred heart pierced by the pagan Cupid's arrow of desire. The sacred heart, an image whose popularity had been increased by Pius IX's endorsement of the cult of veneration of this image over the course of his papacy, is pierced in a way that intensifies the message of love. But the image also purifies its message of loving desire by framing it within the mysticism of religion.[32] In simpler terms though, the image is a reminder of the heart's enduring history as an emotional symbol.[33]

---

[32] Fulvio De Giorgi, 'Forme spirituali, forme simboliche, forme politiche. La devozione al S. Cuore', *Rivista di storia della Chiesa in Italia*, 48 (1994): 365–459, here 371–7. See also Fulvio De Giorgi, 'Note sulla modernizzazione ecclesiale', *Rivista di storia contemporanea*, vol. 23, nn. 1-2 (1994-1995): 194–208, here 201–2; and Emily Jo Sargent, 'The Sacred Heart: Christian Symbolism', in *The Heart*, edited by James Peto (New Haven: Yale University Press, 2007), pp. 102–14.

[33] Fay Bound Alberti, *Matters of the Heart: History, Medicine, and Emotion* (Oxford: Oxford University Press, 2010), p. 15.

Much can be taken from this touching document. In several ways it is typical of the intimate letters of its time and culture, both in comparison to the sister-letters with which it was to share a journey to Rome twelve years later, and to letters analysed by historians working in other contexts. For example, 'abbracci'—embraces or hugs—regularly doled out by the thousands in nineteenth-century Italian personal letters, were a common, even debased currency that carried no special erotic charge.[34] Nevertheless the letter does carry a sense of intimacy, due to the gift, the request that the recipient wear it, and the pierced heart. This sits quite comfortably side by side with news of the writer's sister, Easter greetings, and mention of another circus. The letter's intriguing combination of intimacy and shared sociability subtly prefigures the social dynamics reproduced during the circus's sojourn in Cassano. There, the close relationships between the Saraceni siblings, Raffaella and Giuseppe, and their circus counterparts, Pietro and Antonietta, unfolded within the embrace of the wider household—and as we know, these were widely thought to have reached a level of intimacy that was 'too advanced'.

If in 1866 the local public had known about C.'s inclusion of a piece of her own clothing, it would probably also have been considered 'too advanced'. However, the inclusion of a personal gift in an intimate letter was not uncommon, especially something made of cloth. For example, Mariuccia Fiore, mentioned above, sent Pietro a small handkerchief, which she specifically said should not be washed, perhaps because it was perfumed. Another woman was later to mention gifts she sent to Pietro such as shirts. Other historians have written about Italian women sending items of embroidery to their beloved.[35] But C.'s inclusion of a small piece of her own clothing, perhaps even underclothing, and her request that Pietro wear it for the sake of their love, seems a more intimate gesture than usual. Is this an example of what Alain Corbin described, in the French context, as intimate articles of clothing becoming 'significant historical facts'?[36]

Ultimately, the letter projects a poetic ambiguity that makes it difficult to categorize the probable historical fact of Pietro and C.'s relationship. He clearly left an impression on her heart, as she may well have done on his. But there is no talk of a future, no mention of marriage, not even the hope of another round of correspondence or a future circus visit. The letter underlines the subtle complexity of emotional entanglements in the past, not to mention the challenges of deciphering their meanings. At the very least this single letter, by allowing a glimpse into heartfelt sentiments, suggests the need to develop more nuanced understandings of women's

---

[34] Martyn Lyons, '"Questo cor che tuo si rese": The Private and the Public in Italian Women's Love Letters in the Long Nineteenth Century', *Modern Italy*, vol. 19, no. 4 (2014): 355–68.

[35] Lyons, '"Questo cor che tuo si rese"', p. 355.

[36] Alain Corbin, 'Backstage' in *A History of Private Life. Vol. IV: From the Fires of Revolution to the Great War*, edited by Michelle Perrot (Cambridge, MA: Belknap Press of Harvard University Press, 1990), pp. 487–8.

quotidian emotional experiences. Certainly, the outwardly chaste, protective emotional arenas in which women lived had their complex interiors. Unfortunately, no more of this particular woman's letters, and no more clues about her emotional inner life, are to be found among Pietro's collection.

By contrast with C's restrained intensity, the other letters Pietro conserved in his collection were frequently laden with a sense of emotional storminess that was equal to any contemporary opera. Mariuccia Fiore, for example, who had declared that none could have loved Pietro as much as she did, admitted that she had been cold towards him after he announced 'this thing could not go on'. She tried to explain her coldness by saying she was overwhelmed with love and could not face the prospect of losing him. Her 'blood had run cold' and she had not said anything for fear of crying. She wrote that she had even thought of buying some poison, to hasten her exit to 'that other world'. Yet she begged Pietro to send his portrait 'as an eternal memento of our love', to be preserved 'like a sacred thing'. And although inflationary references had discounted the value of hugs and kisses in Italian scribal culture, Mariuccia outdid her competitors by sending 'a million kisses to your red lips', another million to 'your noble forehead', and a thousand to 'your rosy cheeks'. Having almost restored the erotic value of epistolary labial caresses by specifying their destinations, the letter ends with a touch of bathos: 'a thousand cordial embraces and a very heartfelt handshake from your unhappy Mariuccia Fiore'.[37]

Mariuccia's intense epistolary drama unfolded in two acts. She wrote the second letter in response to one she had received from Pietro. Addressing him with the charming though not unusual salutation, 'Light of my eyes', she exclaimed that he could not possibly imagine what a consolation it was to her 'poor afflicted heart' to receive his letter.[38] However, he had clearly insisted again that their relationship could not go on, so the pain had been re-inflicted. 'O Pietro', she responded, 'I would have preferred to be struck than to be told that.' She wanted him to know that she was 'the most unhappy woman on earth...her youth passed in mourning and weeping like a withered flower.' She became 'soaked in tears of blood' at the thought that their love would have to end. 'Destiny', she exclaims histrionically, 'how could you be so harsh to two hearts that loved each other so much?'[39]

At this point Mariuccia's strength fades and she swoons her way to the end of the letter: 'I want to say more but I can't I don't trust myself enough I know all I need to know to say adieux, adieux my dear and beloved Pietro adieux. Don't forget me and with my last breath I give you a heartfelt handshake and I declare

---

[37] ASR, TCPR, 1879, b. 3659, vol. IA, f. 266, undated letter to Pietro Cardinali from Mariuccia Fiore.
[38] ASR, TCPR, 1879, b. 3659, vol. IA, f. 268, undated letter to Pietro Cardinali from Mariuccia Fiore.
[39] ASR, TCPR, 1879, b. 3659, vol. IA, f. 268.

I will love you all the way to the tomb.'[40] If Mariuccia had been on stage, she would at that point have thrown the back of her hand to her forehead and fallen softly to the ground as the curtain came down, no doubt to enraptured applause. We cannot with any certainty connect her written emotional gestures with cultural examples, but the withered flower certainly recalls the camellia given by Violeta to Alfredo in Verdi's *La Traviata*. It would be surprising if this woman had never witnessed a performance by at least one prima donna. Although her orthography was rich with errors, faithfully reproducing the phonetics of her strong regional accent, she was clearly educated and literate, and somewhere she had learned the power of a dramatic exit.

Exit it was, for this was Mariuccia's last missive to Pietro. She had expressed desperate love for Pietro, and may well have seriously pinned her aspirations for the future upon him. It is only when he declares 'the thing cannot go on' that her blood runs cold, and the only way she could control her emotions was to project the chilliness back to Pietro himself. Mariuccia employs powerful images to express the pain of her disappointed love: a withered flower, tears of blood, the desire to end her own life. For her, this love was life's very essence: the sap of a flower, or her own lifeblood, expressed through sanguine tears, just as the Virgin Mary had done at Christ's crucifixion. Along with these evocative natural and religious metaphors, melodramatic influences also glimmer in the way Mariuccia expressed her emotional response to the prospect of lost love. Her letters, combined with that written by C. in 1866, provide telling peeks into mental universes. Their words reveal something of the way these women experienced and shaped the pleasures, complexities, and tribulations of their emotional lives.

One letter from C. and two from Mariuccia are sufficient to make it clear that cultural forms, whether religious or secular, reciprocally influenced the way women shaped and staged their most private emotions. But a fourth helps confirm the opposite notion, also evident in the first three: that virtual emotional arenas were as individual as the women who performed in them. A typically admiring letter by an unidentified woman written to Pietro on 17 July 1876 displays both similarities and differences in relation to those by C. and Mariuccia Fiore. The most obvious difference is that this one was written and mailed secretly. Unlike the others, it was not signed, not even with some cryptic mark.[41] An important element of this writer's inner world was fear, fear of the discovery of her attraction to Pietro and the shame that would follow its revelation. However, with the employment of some artful subterfuge, women such as she were able to

---

[40] ASR, TCPR, 1879, b. 3659, vol. IA, f. 268.
[41] ASR, TCPR, 1879, b. 3659, vol. IA, f. 375, letter sent to Pietro Cardinali by unknown author, perhaps 'Amalia', dated Città Sant'Angelo, 17 July 1876. Unusually, a single pale-blue sheet of paper, like twentieth-century airmail paper.

escape those confines, at least momentarily, and send smoke signals generated by the fires of their inner passion to the outside world.

The letter came from Città Sant'Angelo, many hundreds of kilometres north of Calabria. The small town is at about the same latitude as Rome, but on Italy's eastern, Adriatic coast. This was the place Cardinali's wife Carolina had mentioned to the mayor who came to retrieve the letters, saying she thought her husband had had a lover there by the name of Amalia. Although the letter bears no signature, its writer does mention that she had sent a gift to Cardinali, addressed to C. Misuraca. This was Carolina herself, so the claim about her husband having a lover in Città Sant'Angelo was not without foundation. It is impossible to know if the writer in Città Sant'Angelo was the 'Amalia' Carolina mentioned, but let us call her that for the sake of giving the author a name. The letter from 'Amalia' bears out Mariuccia Fiore's inkling of the many women who loved Pietro. It extends his territory, suggesting he was indeed a Casanova, holding the attention of a variety of women, in a variety of ways, over broad swathes of southern Italy.

'Amalia', weaving a certain no-nonsense practicality into her expressions of love, was different again from the winsome, dignified C., and the passionate, operatic Mariuccia Fiore. For example, her letter opens 'My dearest love',

> finally after thirteen days I've received your letter, I thought I'd been completely overlooked and that caused me intense pain. You know how much I love you and naturally you must know that withholding your news has the same effect on me as death so why then do you do it?[42]

Much of the letter concerns the practicalities of maintaining a secret correspondence and well as consigning gifts and money across the countryside. 'Amalia' seems to enjoy masterminding the operation. She asks Pietro to address his letters alternately to Luigi de Ceseris and then to Antonio (no surname), warning him, however, that Luigi was unaware that 'the letters are from you or even that the letters I write are to you'. Another sizeable section of the letter concerns the peregrinations of what appears to be a practical gift from her to Pietro, an object she calls a 'romanduca'. Probably a dialect word, its meaning is unclear, but it was clearly an object of some sort as 'Amalia', hoping Pietro would like it, mentioned that it had a six-month guarantee.[43]

Into these largely practical considerations 'Amalia' wove expressions of love whose tone recalls the more passionate and poetic notes of the previous writers. Her opening lines equate the yearning for love to a pain as terrible as death itself. Further on, she excuses the tone of an earlier letter, written five days before this

---

[42] ASR, TCPR, 1879, b. 3659, vol. IA, f. 375.   [43] ASR, TCPR, 1879, b. 3659, vol. IA, f. 375.

one, suspecting Pietro would not have liked it, but explaining that she had felt 'on the edge of desperation'. She may have been right about Pietro not liking the letter, for it did not figure among the letters he kept. Now, however, she states 'I am at peace because you say you love me.' The last few lines alternate between the dramas of love and the banalities of life:

> Pietro, love me as I love you, write to me soon, time is needed to restore my soul's tranquility because I am far away from you. Sorry to hear you have been unable to work for several days, here it has only rained for ten days so far. Adieux darling of my heart, love me well and take for yourself thousands of hugs and kisses from she who loves you so much and lives only for you.

The letter ends there abruptly, with no signature, no poem, no cryptic signs or symbolic icons.[44]

In all likelihood, despite Carolina's foregrounding of 'Amalia' as one of several lovers in her husband's life, the woman of Città Sant'Angelo's hope for continued association with Pietro Cardinali probably ended with this letter. She is the second woman to have sent Pietro a gift, but, unlike the first, this was not a small personal item already in the sender's possession. It was purchased with a six-month guarantee, and sent, apparently via one of the woman's intermediaries, first to a post office, and later, to Pietro, via his wife Carolina. 'Amalia' even mentioned sending him the sum of money necessary to pay the fees due to the post office for having held and forwarded the 'romanduca'. This letter from the third short-term epistolary admirer to have been preserved in Pietro's cache introduces two novelties: a woman's expenditure of money to give her emotions lasting material form, in the purchase of a gift and payment of fees; and resort to intermediaries, witting and unwitting, in order to keep the emotional bond a secret. In both these ways, 'Amalia' foreshadows themes for which the last woman to make love by letter to Pietro provides an unusually abundant source.

## Courting by Correspondence: M. N. +

In contrast to the staccato affairs represented by the exchanges considered so far, the most significant epistolary lover to figure among Pietro Cardinali's collection sent him fully thirty-eight letters. Enduring for more than a year, the correspondence was an extraordinary self-contained relationship that unfolds almost exclusively in writing. Reflecting contemporary cultural expectations of relationships between the sexes, the author's keenest aspiration was to marry the circus rider: her letters amount to a courtship by correspondence. Although we have no direct

---

[44] ASR, TCPR, 1879, b. 3659, vol. IA, f. 375.

access to Pietro's role in it, as with the previous letters his presence and attitudes can to some extent be discerned between the lines of his lover's letters. Although Pietro clearly initiated and then played an appropriately reciprocal role in the exchange, it is doubtful his ardour matched that of his correspondent.

What we are left with is a corpus of adoring letters that, with a degree of historical empathy, can be seen to constitute something well beyond their mere physical presence in an archive. The woman had an ordinary and not particularly gratifying life, from which she retreated into this correspondence as if it were a protective shell, a refuge from the banality of her daily life. But the collection amounts to more than just an emotional refuge. Because she wrote regular letters over the course of a year, ultimately the result was a full-scale virtual emotional arena of her own making, within which she gave passionate verbal shape to her strongest yearnings. She created a second existence for herself, which was emotionally much richer than her primary existence. Reading the letters closely, it is possible to go some way towards 'reconstituting', to use Lefebvre's word, this woman's emotional worlds.

Her letters had particularly caught the eye of the mayor when he first skimmed through Pietro's collection after they were retrieved from the locked trunk. The official had noted that the letters were all signed 'M. N. followed by a cross', and had speculated that this could easily have been a cryptic code prearranged between Pietro and Raffaella. That this was not the case must have quickly become clear to the investigating magistrate in Rome. M. N. was a different person altogether. The main clue was that these letters, unlike the others, mostly had their envelopes preserved, and almost all of them were posted in the town of Larino, in the province of Campobasso, some 400 kilometres from where Raffaella lived.[45] The mayor must have removed the letters from their envelopes to read them, and, although the envelopes were preserved, unfortunately they were not reunited with their original contents. Rather, these were sewn, empty, into a separate bundle, numbering twenty-six in total.

The envelopes themselves are nevertheless rich with forensic and historical interest. Postmarks, at the point of departure and sometimes the place of arrival, occasionally with an intermediate stopping place also marked, leave a trail not just of the letters' but also the circus's peregrinations across the southern half of the Italian peninsula.[46] This trail suggests that over the course of thirteen months, the circus visited about eleven different locations, giving an average sojourn in

---

[45] ASR, TCPR, 1879, b. 3659, vol. IA, ff. 274–83 and ff. 285–98, envelopes postmarked Larino. N.B. Neither envelopes nor letters were placed in the archival file in chronological order. The archival folio numbers are unrelated to the dates of envelopes and letters.

[46] For example, an envelope postmarked 3 November 1877, addressed to Carmela Cannezzaro at Matera di Puglia, had the original address crossed out and was redirected, probably by post office staff, to Laterza (22 km away). Several postmarks on the back of the envelope indicate the letter's arrival in Matera and later in Laterza. ASR, TCPR, 1879, b. 3659, vol. IA, f. 287.

each of about five weeks. The first letter from Larino was sent on 21 May 1877, and it travelled to Termoli, 27 kilometres away. Other destinations included Molfetta, Altamura, Matera, Brindisi, Francavilla Fontana (unfailingly written by M. N. in a southern accent as 'Frangavilla Fondana'), and Laterza, near Taranto, 235 kilometres from Larino. The last letter was posted on 18 June 1878. Its destination was Cassano allo Ionio. There, Pietro's liaison with Raffaella Saraceni had had the town talking since the circus's arrival. It was probably not a coincidence that M. N.'s correspondence with Pietro concluded at about the same time as new conquests were underway.

Of the twenty-six envelopes preserved, on the first ten, written between May and July 1877, the addressee was Carolina 'Masuraca' (a misspelling of Pietro's wife's surname), 'Cavallerizza' (horsewoman), followed by the name of the town the circus happened to be visiting. One envelope alone was straightforwardly addressed to Pietro Cardinali, but it came from Catanzaro on 29 August 1877, and is unlikely to have been sent by M. N., whose home was hundreds of kilometres from Catanzaro, with no evidence that she ever went there.[47] On the fifteen remaining envelopes, sent between October 1877 and June 1878, the addressee was one Carmela Cannezzaro. Who this woman was remains unknown, as her relationship to Pietro was not investigated. Since she must have moved with the circus, it is likely that she was either the wife of another Cardinali brother, or of one of the other circus members. In any case, M. N.'s persistent use of an intermediary underlines that she felt she could not afford to risk being observed sending mail addressed to a man on a regular basis by the staff at Larino's post office.

Conversely, M. N., as a woman, needed to be just as vigilant about mail addressed to her. In those days letters were not always delivered to individual houses, but instead collected by addressees at the post office. Having letters addressed to a trusted intermediary care of the post office was therefore a relatively easy way of maintaining a secret correspondence. M. N. instructed Pietro about whose name should appear on the envelopes containing his letters to her. Over the course of the thirteen-month correspondence, she provided him with the names of three different people. The first was Arcangelo Pecia, whose name she provided at the bottom of her second letter, in late May 1877.[48] The second name, provided only two weeks later, was that of Felippo (*sic*) Salvatore.[49] The third, provided twelve days later, was Andonia (*sic*) Parissa. Evidently 'Andonia'

---

[47] ASR, TCPR, 1879, b. 3659, vol. IA, f. 273, envelope addressed to Pietro Cardinali, postmarked Catanzaro, 29 August 1877. It is not possible to connect this specific envelope to a letter sent by one of Cardinali's female admirers, and may not in fact have been related to the 'amorous' letters at all.

[48] ASR, TCPR, 1879, b. 3659, vol. IA, f. 310, undated letter from M. N. to Pietro Cardinali, probably delivered in envelope f. 283 postmarked Larino, 26 May 1877.

[49] ASR, TCPR, 1879, b. 3659, vol. IA, f. 341, letter dated 13 June 1877.

was written the way the name Antonia rolled off the local tongue. Parissa's name appeared again in a letter dated 17 July 1877, but no further names appeared after that, suggesting that in 'Andonia', M. N. had found a trustworthy and enduring intermediary.

It would be interesting to know who these people were and what roles they played in M. N.'s life. In 1878, the investigating magistrate made concerted efforts to find out, heavily underlining the words 'Andonia Parissa' in striking red crayon in the letter of 3 August 1877 and instructing officials in Larino to track her down.[50] Ultimately he hoped to interview M. N. about Pietro Cardinali. The attempt to find Parissa led to nothing, since the name was not an exact match with any of the town's residents.[51] Fortunately for M. N. she escaped the shame of officials questioning her about her relationship with Cardinali. All we can ever know about her in the end is what Cardinali told the investigating magistrate: she was a woman of about forty years old, and she was a 'mantenuta', a woman maintained as the common-law wife of a man whose occupation was supplier to the local prison.[52] For Pietro, undoubtedly more glamorous than the prison supplier, it did not require great effort to ready this woman to be purloined away to genuine matrimony. On the other hand, until that actually happened, M. N. remained conscious of where her bread was buttered, and remained living with the prison supplier.

Gratifying as it would have been to know more about M. N. and her accomplices, the fact that her strategies to remain anonymous were successful underlines the point that it was crucial to her reputation and her relationship with the man she lived with that she remain undetected. It is worth noting that her two male intermediaries, Arcangelo and Felippo, played the role only briefly, whereas 'Andonia' probably held it for many months. The sense of community scrutiny conveyed by previous scholarly work on Italian women's lives and loves is certainly reinforced by M. N.'s story.[53] At one telling point the risks are even spelled out by M. N. herself, when the question arises of how she should sign her letters. She declares to Pietro 'you tell me that you want my signature...the reason I can't is that who knows what would happen if one of my letters went astray, I could find myself in great difficulty, you understand this, you shouldn't be annoyed

---

[50] ASR, TCPR, 1879, b. 3659, vol. IA, f. 345, letter from M. N. to Pietro Cardinali dated 3 August 1877, with the words Andonia Parissa heavily underlined in red. ASR, TCPR, 1879, b. 3659, vol. IB, ff. 135–6, Finizia's request to the Giudice Istruttore of Larino, asking him to find out what he can about M. + N., dated 13 November 1878.

[51] ASR, TCPR, 1879, b. 3659, vol. IB, f. 142, message from the mayor of Larino, saying that they had not found an Antonia Parissa, but an Antonia Parisi, dated 24 November 1878.

[52] ASR, TCPR, 1879, b. 3659, vol. IB/FF 133–4, interrogation of Cardinali by Finizia, 13 November 1878. These are Cardinali's explanations of his relationships with women.

[53] The sense of women's lives under constant scrutiny is effectively evoked by Schneider, De Giorgio, and Lyons.

about this, believe me, it's the truth.'[54] It turns out that she was wise to hide behind the signature 'M. N. +'.

The practicalities of conveying messages around the Italian peninsula and evading attention while doing so are certainly worthy of close attention, for they suggest much about little-known aspects of daily affairs in this historical context. But there is another practical aspect of M. N.'s letters that is even more intriguing, one that goes to the heart of the intimate relationship to which they bear witness: their appearance, and more particularly, the way this changed as the correspondence became established. The first letter was written on exquisite paper, texturally embossed and perforated in a snowflake pattern so that it resembles a doily, and bright white in colour.[55] At a time when paper itself was something of a luxury, this beautiful stationery must have been an impressive extravagance (figure 3.3).

M. N. was unsystematic about dating her letters, but fortunately for those interested in chronology, she provided some clues. The opening line on this luxurious paper announces that M. N. can barely express the joy she felt in reading 'your words for the first time, and the expressive and affectionate way they assured me with certainty of the sincere love you nourish for me...'. Towards the end she makes another reference to this, her own 'first letter', confirming its inaugural status. The paper's beauty matches the emotional tenor of the letter, which has overtones of an almost orgasmic joy: 'in the short time since I had the fortune to meet you...a new joy has flowed into me and seems to fill the void I felt in my soul until recently'.[56]

Such intense joy aside, scrutiny of the correspondence as a whole shows that a strategy may have been woven into M. N.'s choice of stationery. In response to Pietro's prompt reply to her first letter, M. N. wrote her second about six days later, using the same beautiful doily-like paper. The key line was M. N.'s hope that

> God will render us happy with a sacred knot so as never again to be divided unto death I will always be faithful tell me my love that you love me. That you will always be the same should I have faith in your promise for pity's sake tell me the truth?[57]

Despite only having known each other for a short time, the 'promise' of matrimony had quickly taken its place as the central subject of their correspondence. Such a promise was a very familiar trope in courting stages of the day, and became

---

[54] ASR, TCPR, 1879, b. 3659, vol. IA, f. 310, undated letter from M. N. to Pietro Cardinali.

[55] ASR, TCPR, 1879, b. 3659, vol. IA, f. 339, letter from 'Amante N. N.' to Pietro Cardinali, undated, but very likely to correspond with the envelope f. 277, dated 21 May 1877. On the first letter the writer signed her name N. N., but from the second letter onwards the signature was usually M. N., often followed by +.

[56] ASR, TCPR, 1879, b. 3659, vol. IA, f. 339.

[57] ASR, TCPR, 1879, b. 3659, vol. IA, f. 310, undated letter to Pietro Cardinali signed 'M. N. +'.

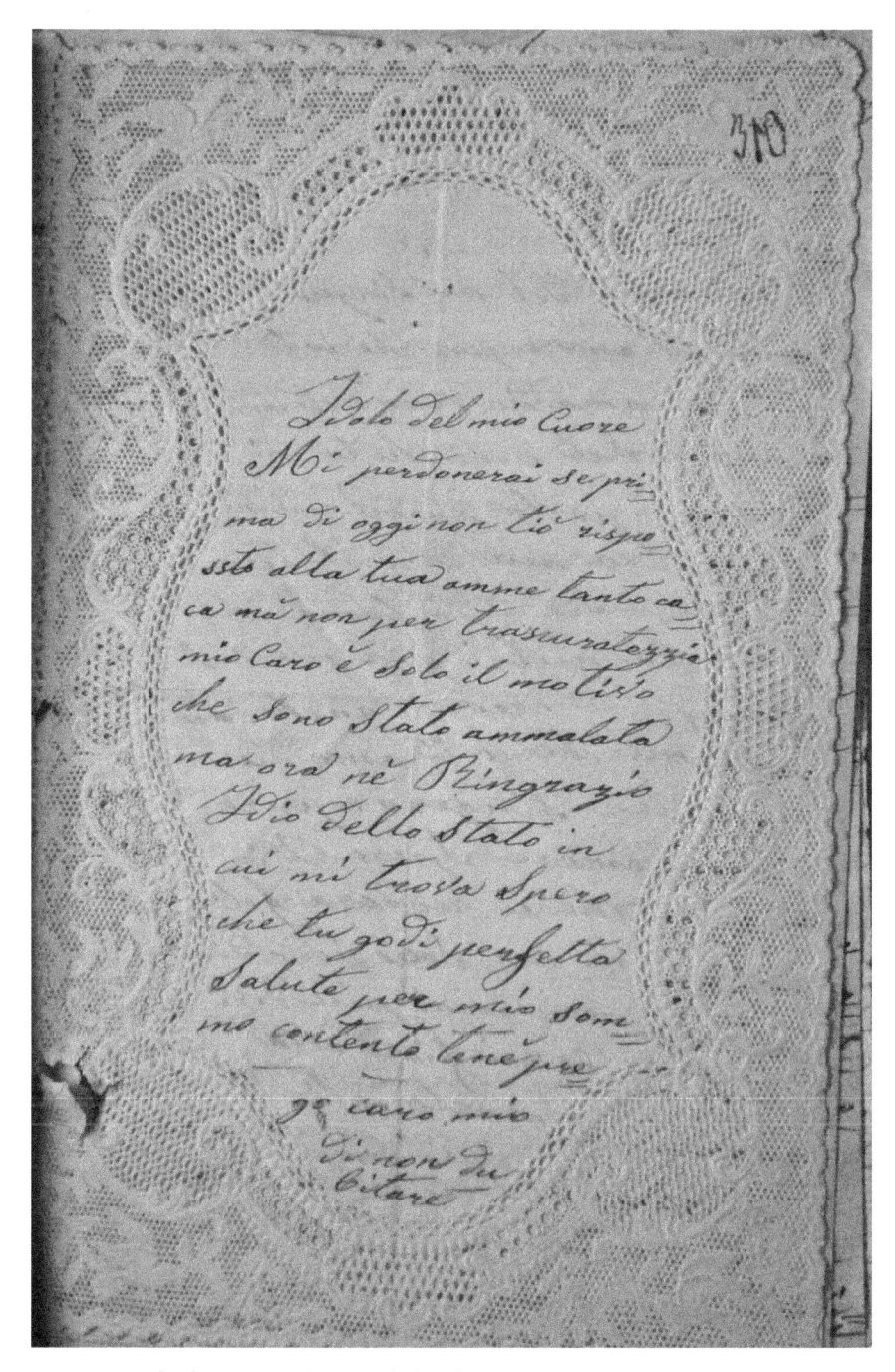

**Figure 3.3** The front page of M. N. +'s first letter to Cardinali (ASR, TCPR, 1879, b. 3659). Reproduced with permission from the Ministero dei Beni e Attività Culturali e del Turismo, ASRM 56/2015. Further reproduction prohibited.

infamous for the way it was used to legitimate premarital sexual relations.[58] Whether that had happened in this case we do not know, but M. N. was certainly very eager to do her part to keep Pietro true to his promise. Quite probably she wished to impress upon him that she was a woman of means, as if to underline that it would be well worth his while to keep his promise.

That the choice of paper suggests a strategy is confirmed by the fact that its quality subsequently declined in steps once the promise of matrimony had been established. After the first two letters on commensurately impressive-looking stationery, M. N. wrote her third and fourth letters to Pietro on paper that was a step down. It was still of high quality, attractively embossed with an appealing pattern, but it was sallow in colour and lacked the extravagant luxury of the first two.[59] From the fifth letter onwards, with one exception, M. N. settled on a dull, unremarkable paper that, although it varied in colour and style from time to time, displayed no decoration or embellishments. In comparison to the illustrious look of M. N.'s extravagant overtures, the remaining letters have a drab appearance.

It seems that once the relationship was established, M. N. felt no need for expensive paper. The one exception was a letter written to mark Pietro's onomastic name-day (usually the commemorative day of a saint of the same name, which even today has a similar status to a birthday in Italian culture). To mark this special day, M. N. chose an elegant, filmy paper, different from any of the other stationery she used, on which she wrote a relatively brief greeting.[60] Clearly, the woman had a strongly developed sense of occasion. But once that occasion had passed, M. N. reverted to ordinary paper.

The decline in stationery quality after the initial letters uncannily parallels a decline in the sense of harmony at the heart of this written relationship. Indeed it is difficult not to see the paper quality as a metaphor for the relationship itself, which began with the soaring ascent of M. N.'s hopes for marriage, buoyed up on paper that looks like a wedding dress. As it became clear that the couple had divergent aspirations, that exuberant opening gave way to drabber paper, and more time was taken up with the sort of negotiations and even bickering that might follow the heady early days of a love affair. In this paper courtship, the transition occurred at about the same time as the appearance of what was to become a key theme in the long correspondence: money. As the letters mount up, it seems even more plausible that M. N.'s flaunting of means through the stationery she used at first was less a reflection of her pure, soaring emotions, than it was her

---

[58] Augusta Palombarini, 'Seduzione maschile con «promessa di matrimonio»', in Pasi and Sorcinelli, eds, pp. 53–82, here p. 64.

[59] ASR, TCPR, 1879, b. 3659, IA, f. 325, undated letter on embossed stationery, but by logic of its contents, almost certainly the letter that followed f. 310, the second 'doily' letter, and almost certainly mailed in envelope f. 283 postmarked 27 May 1877; and f. 321, letter from M. N. +, dated Larino, 10 June 1877 (almost certainly contained in envelope f. 278 postmarked Larino, 10 June 1877).

[60] ASR, TCPR, 1879, b. 3659, vol. IA, f. 306, letter from M. N. +, dated Larino, 28 June 1877.

response to a canny intuition about which of her qualities was most likely to capture Pietro's attention.

## Romance and Reality

Pietro began to respond in a way that suggests M. N.'s intuition was correct. On 5 June 1877, in probably his third letter, he wrote to tell her that he had lost his wallet.[61] Reading between the lines of M. N.'s response, it is clear that Pietro expressed great anger and frustration about the alleged loss. He almost certainly asked her if she could send a little something to help him get by. Her reply would have been a disappointment. Perhaps as a way of avoiding the issue, M. N. at first made light of the loss, providing a little homespun advice about not wasting energy on anger: 'I tell you, my dear, that whatever might have happened, it is useless to be angry because as you well know 100 ducats of rage have never paid off one cent of debt.' She then admits that she is trying to cheer him up by making him laugh, but proceeds to show that true words are often spoken in jest: 'money can be made, but if you lose your health, it cannot be bought back.'[62] M. N.'s attempt to console Pietro is only likely to have irritated him more. It was the sort of advice easily given by a woman who could afford stationery like hers.

About half way through this letter though, M. N.'s tone and attitude suddenly changed, almost as if she had only read half of Pietro's letter when she began hers. She realized that he was so bitter about the loss that he wished he could die. The thought of what that would mean brings out her passion as she imagines life without him:

> if I had all the gold in the world without you who are the angel of my prayers for pity's sake don't say that because it kills me...I beg you write to me every day because I can't survive an hour without receiving your news I feel my soul is ripped when I see your beloved writing have compassion for a broken heart which dies of pain for you I won't tarry I send you a thousand kisses and hug you to my breast untiringly forever I declare myself for life your faithful
>
> Steadfast
>
> Lover M.
>
> N. +

This was much the most passionate conclusion of the four letters so far, and it now began to seem that M. N. was not the only correspondent who used a

---

[61] ASR, TCPR, 1879, b. 3659, vol. IA, f. 321, M. N.'s letter to Pietro dated 10 June 1877 refers to his letter of 5 June, received 8 June.
[62] ASR, TCPR, 1879, b. 3659, vol. IA, f. 321.

strategy to lure a lover beyond the point of no return: Pietro himself was a doyen of the arena, and he knew how to make women's hearts ache, whether in the circus ring, or in writing.[63]

Pietro's strategy was not to reply. This is clear because M. N. wrote an even more intense letter three days after the previous one. 'Mio caro Adoratore', she wrote,

> I would like to know the reason why you have not responded to my last letters. Was the cause... my having prayed to you that I could not endure not receiving your news [?] but why do you make me suffer what wrong have I ever done you that you treat me like this it isn't done when you truly love. The thing you have always promised me was to love me forever and never leave me for pity's sake have compassion on the misery of my heart... I cannot do anything but cry over my cruel fate.[64]

Now that M. N. thought of Pietro as the embodiment of her future, a sense of passion equal to that expressed by her amorous predecessor, Mariuccia Fiore, came dramatically to the fore. It remained a feature of M. N.'s writing as she sought to hold the relationship together. Just as Mariuccia had done, M. N. begged Pietro to respond immediately if he did not want her to die of pain. She outdid her previous greeting by offering a million 'scorching' kisses, squeezed him to her bosom 'Senza Stangarmi [*sic*] mai' (Without ever Tiring), and declared herself his '*fedelissima* and steadfast Lover'.[65]

Despite the rising mercury of M. N.'s passion, the cold theme of money did not go away. From the moment that Pietro had 'lost' his wallet, it seemed inevitable that he would prevail upon this apparently well-to-do woman for help. The question fell tactfully out of view for one cycle of letters, but it reappeared in M. N.'s letter of 25 June, just one month after the beginning of their correspondence. Having addressed him as 'Idol of my heart', she thanked him for his 'adorable note' of 22 June, but quickly launched into an expression of her dissatisfaction that he did 'not have faith' in her. Perhaps the problem was that he felt she was not putting her money where her mouth was, for she reassured him that she would have sent a person to 'make the purchase he wanted'. Further on, more starkly, she mentions that 'the money is ready.'[66]

At this stage there is no indication of the sum's scale, nor what it is for, but the idea that she might be asked for money, or to buy things for him, caused her no

---

[63] ASR, TCPR, 1879, b. 3659, vol. IA, f. 321.
[64] ASR, TCPR, 1879, b. 3659, vol. IA, f. 341, letter from M. N. to Pietro Cardinali, dated Larino, 13 June 1877.
[65] ASR, TCPR, 1879, b. 3659, vol. IA, f. 341. The initial capitals are original; the kisses were 'cucenti'.
[66] ASR, TCPR, 1879, b. 3659, vol. IA, f. 354, letter from M. N. to Pietro Cardinali, dated Larino, 25 June 1877.

irritation. That can quite safely be assumed because M. N. did not spare her ire on many other occasions when she did feel annoyed. The rest of the letter was a long and almost unpunctuated diatribe of several hundred words lamenting the fact that he had had the 'barbarous courage' to decide not to give her a portrait he had promised her. The picture was of a young lady, not Pietro himself, but M. N. seemed to want it desperately nonetheless. She was particularly vexed since, as she pointed out, it would have come back into his possession as soon as they were married. After many sentences of accusation and reprimand, M. N. excuses herself, and explains over and over that the problem is she loves him too much. The final greeting was just one kiss, but the lack of quantity was surely made up by its particular quality. This one was 'tenerissimo', extremely tender, and she swore that she was his forever.[67]

Hints about sums of money appear in the next letter, written one week later, but they are far from straightforward, and it may well be that, as well as using intermediaries to hide the writers' identities, M. N. veiled the would-be couple's emerging financial intrigues. What remained completely naked was the letter's overture, which was about love and adoration. 'My sweet treasure', wrote M. N., '... I am very pleased to hear about the affection you nourish for me and fully understand my dear that you love me and equally I love you with all the affections of my poor heart.' She then eases into business matters by saying, perhaps reprovingly, that he had taken it upon himself to make 'those purchases' but when the 'hour of our union comes' we must leave 'these places' because she 'absolutely does not approve of those purchases'. 'When we are married', she continued, 'I will be the one who thinks about what we do, and it's useless being annoyed if I am unable to send that sum you asked for because I simply don't have it.' The reason, it seems, was that any money she possessed was given to her, and at this point she simply could not send him that 'other 15'.[68]

The language is opaque, but it seems that if she sends him money, its source is probably a housekeeping allowance she receives from the man she lives with. Money was mentioned frequently during the correspondence, but only one letter referred concretely to the inclusion of a particular sum. On 11 February 1878 M. N. sent 30 lire by registered mail. It is possible that she sent smaller sums on other occasions, but mostly she wrote that she would send 'something soon', particularly if he wrote back quickly. Also in February M. N. acknowledged Pietro's request for her to send him some *taralli*, a biscuit still typical of southern Italy. She promised to do so as soon as she had time and opportunity to bake them, but she also reminded him that 'her position' did not make it easy.[69] The next letter

---

[67] ASR, TCPR, 1879, b. 3659, vol. IA, f. 354.
[68] ASR, TCPR, 1879, b. 3659, vol. IA, f. 358, letter from M. N. to Pietro Cardinali, dated Larino, 30 June 1877.
[69] ASR, TCPR, 1879, b. 3659, vol. IA, f. 333, letter from M. N. to Pietro Cardinali, dated Larino, 19 February 1878.

announced that the biscuits would be on their way within a few days.[70] Much later, Pietro recalled sharing them with the entire circus company.[71]

Biscuits are still biscuits, whether baked openly or in secret, but what sort of sum of money was 30 lire in 1878? There are probably several ways to translate the value into contemporary terms. One is to remain within the very sources used in this chapter, for example, the cost of the postage stamps M. N. used on her letters to Pietro. Regular delivery required 20 cents in stamps; the registered delivery letter she used in February 1878 cost 50 cents. So 30 lire would have covered the postage of 150 regular letters, or sixty registered letters. This indicates that the sums M. N. and Pietro wrote about settled down to relatively modest levels, but during the heated early stages of their relationship sums of 1,000 lire were mentioned. The pair may have had some grand plan, perhaps something related to those mysterious 'purchases' or even the dream of living together.

Whatever those plans were, they were so secret that they could only be discussed face-to-face. This would happen, M. N. declared in her letter of 30 June 1877, when she came to 'take the waters' (presumably at Termoli, a spa town mentioned in the correspondence). Then she would tell him everything: 'At that point', she wrote, 'you will know my Intention and my way of thinking because if it was a small amount then yes, but to tie up 1000 lire you know what that means and it can't be done.' She softened the blow with a thousand kisses and a bosomy embrace before signing off.[72] Certainly something more than kisses was being schemed—perhaps the dream of a jointly owned, economically viable way out of their lives' respective impasses—but alas we cannot know what it was. All we can do is try to interpret the cryptic traces that lie between the lines of this intriguing courtship.

A modern reader may have begun to feel a sense of distaste and suspicion in relation to Pietro Cardinali as soon as he started received gifts, particularly those that cost money. He seems to have held out the promise of emotional gratification via marriage, and then asked for something immediate and material in return. The sense of suspicion becomes stronger when the currency shifted from symbolic gifts to cash, and even more so when the sums were large. It should be remembered though that the ideal of love as an unalloyed and pure emotion, untainted by material interest, was a luxury that would only slowly encompass marriage itself.[73] In the context of nineteenth-century Italy, and no doubt many

---

[70] ASR, TCPR, 1879, b. 3659, vol. IA, f. 335, letter from M. N. to Pietro Cardinali, dated Larino, 1 March 1878.

[71] ASR, TCPR, 1879, b. 3659, vol. IB, ff. 133–4, interrogation of Pietro Cardinali, by Finizia about his relationships with women, having read this correspondence, 13 November 1878.

[72] ASR, TCPR, 1879, b. 3659, vol. IA, f. 358, letter from M. N. to Pietro Cardinali, dated Larino, 30 June 1877.

[73] On the Italian context for the transition of marriage from an economic transaction to one based on sentiment, see Paola Magnarelli, 'Amore romantico e amore coniugale in una vita piccolo borghese,' in Pasi and Sorcinelli (eds), pp. 83–110, here pp. 84–5.

others, questions of love, marriage, and material matters were woven together into an emotional tapestry whose threads cannot easily be disentangled, and perhaps ought not to be. This should temper any instinct to dismiss the emotional value of M. N's aspiration to marry Pietro just because money was involved.

Another aspect of the relationship that is unusual in this context is that a woman provided financial sustenance to a man. What we know about M. N. is sufficient to complicate assumptions about the gendered distribution of power in intimate relationships. Part of the complexity lies in the fact that documentary evidence created by M. N. shows her living in two relationships simultaneously. On the one hand, she was maintained by a man with whom she probably lived. She had to be extremely careful that no one knew of her liaison with Pietro, because she would certainly find herself 'in great difficulty'.[74] In her daily relationship, M. N. epitomized the vulnerability of a dependent woman. During the period of her correspondence with Pietro she probably lived with a degree of fear and guilt. Furthermore, though she was provided for in her visible relationship, quite possibly on generous terms, for some time she had felt a 'void in her soul', as she told Pietro in her first letter. The publicly visible side of her life's tapestry may have been rich in material comfort, but from within, she experienced it as an emotional void.

Conversely, M. N's position was very different in the relationship she built with Pietro. A short time after she met him, her heart exalted at the prospect that he had the potential to fill her soul's void. As the relationship took shape, M. N. found herself with more power than she was used to having in her other relationship, and she wielded it with a certain determination: she looked forward to telling him about *her* intention, and *her* way of seeing things. In an intriguing reversal of the other relationship, where she experienced traditional female vulnerability, with Pietro it was intoxicatingly different. She was emotionally vulnerable, and seemed to relish the intensity of those feelings, but she was materially strong. Her letters often alternate rapidly between one sensation and the other. Indeed, a reason her correspondence with Pietro may have lasted so long is that M. N. developed skill in expressing the intense and unaccustomed pain of emotional vulnerability, while also deploying, in measured doses, the power that her financial means gave her. Through her letters, we see M. N. inhabiting two arenas, one real and one virtual, with each requiring its own emotional tenor.

M. N. and Pietro continued their correspondence for many months, over the course of which it traversed much emotional terrain. For M. N. the high points were the sense of exaltation she felt whenever Pietro reassured her that he loved her. The low points, sadly more frequent, were largely to do with the tribulations of an insecure, long-distance love affair. The correspondence was also marked by

---

[74] As she put it in an undated letter, ASR, TCPR, 1879, b. 3659, vol. IA, f. 310.

other events, such as illness, the death of one of M. N.'s sisters, and the alleged death of Pietro's father. For example, M. N.'s envelope and letter dated 11 December 1877 were both ominously bordered in black, the classic and forbidding epistolary symbol of mourning. She announced gravely that one of her sisters had been taken gravely ill and had passed away. The letter braided M. N.'s deep sadness over this loss with the disappointment she felt when, upon returning to Larino, the one thing she had hoped might console her—a letter from Pietro—had not materialized.[75] M. N.'s letters and envelopes bore a black border for three months until March 1878, though the king of Italy had also died in January 1878, and the mourning may have been for him too. In any case, the sister was not mentioned in any of those letters—and nor was the king.

Within this period of mourning, the subject of death recurred in other guises. On 11 February 1878, M. N.'s letter to Pietro opened with passionate sympathy in response to news of his father's death. She said that all suffering is difficult, but that caused by death is the worst, and all he could do was resign himself to divine will.[76] Two days later, she found herself dispensing further words inspired by the prospect of death, this time Pietro's own. One of his letters had evidently mentioned, not for the first time, that he wished to take his own life. Possibly because it was at least the second time she had heard this, she was not taken in. She suggested that he was insufficiently strong to negotiate life's misfortunes, and that there were many other men who had far greater difficulties but never once thought about taking their own life. Then she asked him to pardon her for these words, explaining that they were prompted by the intense pain she felt to think that he might be capable of doing what only God had the right to do.[77]

Death as the high or low point of love's dramas appeared in the correspondence more figuratively and culturally too. Usually only inferences can be made about the way women like M. N. learned to inhabit the emotional cultures of their time and place, but on one occasion she refers specifically to having attended the theatre the night before she wrote the letter. The performance had been put on by a visiting company. Most likely an opera, the experience had not been a pleasure, but rather a continual torment, since it reminded her of Pietro's absence. Clearly she identified with whatever tragedy the stage heroine suffered, and she wrote the next day that she had been unable to hold back her sobbing: indeed, she felt as if she herself would die from the pain the spectacle caused her.[78]

---

[75] ASR, TCPR, 1879, b. 3659, vol. IA, f. 362, black-bordered letter from M. N. to Pietro Cardinali, dated Larino, 11 December 1877.

[76] ASR, TCPR, 1879, b. 3659, vol. IA, f. 308, black-bordered letter from M. N. to Pietro Cardinali, dated Larino, 11 February 1878.

[77] ASR, TCPR, 1879, b. 3659, vol. IA, f. 327, black-bordered letter from M. N. to Pietro Cardinali, dated Larino, 13 February 1878.

[78] ASR, TCPR, 1879, b. 3659, vol. IA, f. 351, black-bordered letter from M. N. to Pietro Cardinali, dated Larino, 29 March 1878.

## The End of M. N.'s Arena

The painful melodrama M. N. witnessed at the theatre in March 1878 uncannily foreshadowed the emotional climax and subsequent demise of her relationship with Pietro. The news exploded into the epistolary exchange in her letter of 1 April. This marked a return to plain paper after three months of black-bordered stationery. It was an ironic twist, because the letter is more burdened with mourning than any of the previous missives. M. N. had just found out that she was more than an April fool: she wrote that the previous day, she had discovered to her unspeakable horror that Pietro was already married. Even in a context already saturated with intense emotional outpouring, the depth of M. N.'s pain leaps out from the first lines:

> Mio caro
>
> With languishing heart and tears in my eyes I write you this tragic letter as I cannot hold back the sobbing and my hand trembles so I cannot write ho [sic] Heaven such a fatal blow has struck my heart that I will never find peace again I feel as if I am dying of pain...[79]

The cataclysm had come with a simple discussion the day before, 'with people who will remain nameless', who reported that Pietro was *married* to that woman he said was his 'mantenuta', his concubine. What was more, the young girl he had passed off as the woman's daughter was also *his* daughter. These horrific possibilities turned M. N.'s world upside down, and she hurled her new understanding back to Pietro, framing it with accusations of 'cruel trickery' and betrayal.[80]

The letter is an emotional outpouring, but some persistent themes stand out from the heartbroken onslaught. One is the difference between official and unofficial relationships of intimacy. Although M. N.'s letters had never mentioned anything of Pietro's love life, this letter reveals that she knew he had a concubine. Clearly, M. N. had not in any way seen his informal involvement with another woman as an obstacle to her own matrimonial aspirations—any more than her own informal relationship with the prison supplier might have been. But as soon as she understood Pietro's relationship to be one of marriage, of commitment rather than convenience, her careful courtship was emptied of meaning. 'How could you have denied being married when you are?', she asked.

> Why did you steal my heart,..., oh death don't delay I call you to me, oh wicked man, traitor who promised me love when you cannot, how can I live knowing

---

[79] ASR, TCPR, 1879, b. 3659, vol. IA, f. 370, letter from M. N. to Pietro Cardinali, dated Larino, 1 April 1878.
[80] ASR, TCPR, 1879, b. 3659, vol. IA, f. 370.

that all my affections for you were worthless, all my sighs thrown to the wind, what could possibly soothe my pain for pity's sake?[81]

M. N.'s dream of marriage had provided a structure for her dreams of love; without it, as she wrote herself, they were gone with the wind.

Yet M. N. wavered between a sense of total loss and trying to salvage something from the wreckage. As the letter proceeded, respite came as she wondered what might have been: 'if you had told me you were married I would have loved you all the same, not with the certainty that you would have married me, I would always have sent you a little something, but as a friend or a brother.'[82] Improbable as such a friendship must have been in the context, what had been the force that originally moved their relationship from friendship to something more? The answer must lie in physical intimacy, for, as soon as the idea of a more innocent bond was laid out, M. N. exclaimed powerfully, 'God, God, cursed be that instant which rendered me your lover, iniquitous, abominable man, I should have fled, rather than bind myself with this strong chain from which I can never release myself.'[83] Forty-year-old concubine that she was herself, it is difficult to dismiss the possibility that she had conceded sexual intercourse to Pietro and saw this as the 'instant' from which there had been no turning back. She had probably long lost her virginity, but sex with a new lover was still an immensely symbolic threshold. Pietro had promised the redemption of marriage, but had ultimately compounded her lack of honour, her disgrace, and her shame.

Pietro's entire collection of amorous letters is suffused with barely repressed expressions of physical desire, but sex itself was such a taboo that it left virtually no direct traces in his lovers' words. Even within their secret epistolary arenas, even at this climactic moment of M. N.'s affair, sexual intimacy can only be interpolated. Despite all, she thinks she might have given in regardless:

> Could you not have loved me without promising to make me yours forever, I certainly would never have denied you love, I would have made a thousand sacrifices to make you happy...I would have consented to your trembling desires to keep you content because I loved you too much, as I still do with a burning love that will never be erased from my poor unfortunate heart.

She begs him therefore to tell the truth and let her know whether she should die or not. She awaited his 'sentence', and signed off as his disgraced, hoodwinked lover.[84]

Over the course of four or five more letters M. N. stumbled around her emotional arena as it imploded upon her. Perhaps only the benefit of hindsight makes

---

[81] ASR, TCPR, 1879, b. 3659, vol. IA, f. 370.  [82] ASR, TCPR, 1879, b. 3659, vol. IA, f. 370.
[83] ASR, TCPR, 1879, b. 3659, vol. IA, f. 370.
[84] ASR, TCPR, 1879, b. 3659, vol. IA, f. 370. Her words were 'disgraziata, lusingata'.

it clear that Pietro was nothing but a knave, but he clearly reprised a range of tactics that had effectively rekindled M. N.'s failing love in the past. He strenuously denied that he was married, perhaps explaining that it had only been a church wedding. He counter-attacked by accusing M. N. of having fallen for someone else, a tactic reflected in her reply of 14 April 1878. Whatever he said, it was sufficient to reignite the flames of her passion and she responded by claiming to love him 'evisceratedly'. It was Easter, and she wished him all the happiness that his 'well-formed heart' could desire. She urged him not to eat everything his 'bride' was sending, but to save something for her to taste.[85] Pietro's next letter smacked of a tactic that had never failed to elicit a powerful effect on this woman: he announced that he was ill. In response, her heart 'spasmed with an ardent and pure love', and she noted intriguingly that he 'wished also for something from her piggy hands', her *mani di porci*. In response to this decidedly sexual reference she regretted being so 'constrained' that she could not even leave the house, but hoped that later she would be able to help him find 'contentment'.[86]

After the calamity of the letter of 1 April, M. N.'s faith that she was on the path to marriage had been quickly restored. More than once she made the claim that she was not among those silly women with 'long hair and a short brain', but the fact that she quickly fell back to believing what she so desperately wanted to believe only underlines the intensity of her desire to do so.[87] Her next letters reflect two more of Pietro's now very familiar strategies. The substance of the letter she wrote on 22 May was to try to turn him away from thoughts of suicide, claiming, as she had done on 13 February, that it was not for him but for God to decide who lives or dies. He had clearly asked her to send some money, for she said she would do so 'soon', and meanwhile he should keep the letters coming, even if she had to pay for the postage at her end because he was unable to buy stamps.[88] By 4 June, in response to the news that he was 'in continual unrest with his family', she prayed that heaven would soon bless their vows so that they would suffer no more.[89] M. N.'s faith in the unlimited redemptive powers of marriage to dissolve all other forms of emotional tribulation had been fully restored.

This faith, patched up improbably with M. N.s complicity over the last two months, did not have long to run. Two brief exchanges, one from Larino on 11 June, the second from Campobasso on 18 June, sought to keep the faith, even

---

[85] ASR, TCPR, 1879, b. 3659, vol. IA, f. 329, letter from M. N. to Pietro Cardinali, dated Larino, 14 April 1878.

[86] ASR, TCPR, 1879, b. 3659, vol. IA, f. 364, letter from M. N. to Pietro Cardinali, dated Larino, 27 April 1878. The envelope is F. 298, addressed to Ceglio di Ostino.

[87] ASR, TCPR, 1879, b. 3659, vol. IA, f. 303, letter of 15 September 1877 and f. 329, letter of 14 April 1878.

[88] ASR, TCPR, 1879, b. 3659, vol. IA, f. 368, letter from M. N. to Pietro Cardinali, dated Larino, 22 May 1878.

[89] ASR, TCPR, 1879, b. 3659, vol. IA, f. 366, letter from M. N. to Pietro Cardinali, dated Larino, 4 June 1878.

as M. N.'s elderly mother's declining health impinged on her time.⁹⁰ This was the reason for her trip to Campobasso, but it seems that she returned home to the news that it was finally all over with Pietro. Her last letter, shorter than usual, asked Pietro how a man who had sworn to be hers unto death could now, over 'such a trifle' (*una cosa da nulla*), so cruelly abandon her. She begged his 'compassion for a lacerated heart that still burned with ardent love' and asked him to write 'not as a lover, but at least as a brother', because if she at least had his news, she would be able to resign herself to not being his:

> Oh my fatal misadventure I wish I had never known you, tell me my love have you really the heart to leave me because I don't. I will always love you as long as my soul is mine, only death will make me forget you and even when I am up above I will pray for your happiness???
> +

The absence of M. N.'s usual initials, just the cross, represents a notable departure from her usual practice.⁹¹ These, it seems, were the last words M. N. ever wrote to Pietro. Undated, the letter must have been written in late June 1878, by which time Pietro was fully pursuing the new amorous possibilities offered by Raffaella Saraceni in Cassano allo Ionio.

## Conclusion

The privilege of historical perspective makes it easier to see that M. N.'s misadventure was bound to happen, that Pietro was a knave, and that M. N. was more gullible than she thought she was. But M. N. and her cohort of sisters deserve sensitive historical judgement. At the time, among cloistered women anxious to fulfil what they were taught was their destiny, the desire to find love and marry had also to be very carefully juggled against the sheer force of the need to survive. M. N. was caught on the horns of a dilemma that is recognizable well over a century later, between her secure but emotionally empty existence as concubine to a prison supplier, and the promise of deeper gratification held out by the more glamorous Pietro Cardinali. M. N.'s letters show that she preserved the one while aspiring desperately to the other, which she hoped would be apotheosized by 'real' marriage.

M. N. and her predecessors' letters reveal unfamiliar aspects of nineteenth-century Italian women's lives. They provide insight into the way they could create

---

⁹⁰ ASR, TCPR, 1879, b. 3659, vol. IA, f. 373, letter from M. N. to Pietro Cardinali, dated Larino, 11 June 1878 and f. 353, letter to Pietro Cardinali, dated Campobasso, 18 June 1878.

⁹¹ ASR, TCPR, 1879, b. 3659, vol. IA, f. 374, undated letter from M. N. to Pietro Cardinali.

virtual emotional arenas with themselves as the *prime donne*. More than just refuges where emotional rules were relaxed if not abandoned, such correspondences were parallel spaces in which the range of emotions both expressed and experienced could be very different from those offered by the sentimental palettes of everyday life. Such spaces were, in a way, virtual extensions built by the women themselves, conjuring the intense emotionalism normally only available through a serialized novel, a play, the opera, or indeed the circus. The preserved traces of their feelings help us bridge the gap between knowledge of the cultural arenas of the day, be they literary, theatrical, operatic, or circensian, and our understanding of the virtual emotional arenas created and inhabited personally by unknown, ordinary women. We have seen that the virtual emotional spaces created by the writers had much in common with cultural arenas and are likely to have been influenced by them, but they are not the same thing.

The love letters sent to Pietro Cardinali are conduits from the past to the present of normally evanescent features of the social environment and culture in which they were created. We know such arenas of the imagination must have existed, but they can be difficult for historians to find, let alone reconstruct. Pietro's letters allow the reconstitution of a revealing sample. Furthermore, because in these cases models of correspondence were secondary to the force of personality and sentiment, not the other way around, the idea that the emotional interiors of Italian women conformed to templates must give way before the evidence that, looked at closely, those interiors were vivid, varied, and highly personal. The letters have added much-needed 'flesh' to the often inscrutable 'sentiments, expectations, and emotions' of real though anonymous nineteenth-century Italian women. Moreover, by showing that other women ardently desired to be purloined away by Pietro Cardinali, the letters make Raffaella Saraceni's story seem less melodramatic, and more plausibly part of the emotional possibilities of her historical epoch.

Finally, while the letters allow a revealing tour of the virtual emotional arenas created by certain women in order to fill emotional voids after the departure of the circus, their discovery also reflects further light into the otherwise veiled emotional regime that prevailed backstage of the circus. Antonietta's account of her sexual and emotional relationship with Cardinali in chapter 2 had already pointed to the ways in which she and the woman identified as Cardinali's wife, Carolina, were forced to navigate fraught emotional cross-currents in the interests of their own material survival. Carolina's involvement as addressee of her husband's lovers' letters must also count as part of this navigation. And yet the only time Carolina's voice is heard in the record is when she tells the police, with apparent insouciance, that her husband had 'various lovers' and that they sent their letters to him in envelopes addressed to her.

Nothing more can ever be known about Carolina's feelings, but her plight prompts a broader view of the overlapping emotional arenas represented by the circus, its members, and their audience. Life on the road for a small provincial circus may well have been quite financially marginal. The letters indicate that if it rained, or if the performers were ill, the show could not take place, and revenue was lost. Let us think back to the first correspondent, C. of Catanzaro, who knew Pietro when he was twenty-four and sent him a gift (even if its value was only sentimental). It is possible to imagine that early on in his career, Pietro became quite used to receiving not just emotional, but material admiration from women such as C. It may well be that what began by chance as occasional emotional exchanges supported by material tokens gradually became woven in to the way Pietro conceived of his livelihood. The culmination was that he regularly asked M. N. for cash. There was a margin of material profit to be made from evoking emotions in women.

As time went on Pietro may have learned that making eyes at likely prospects, such as Amalia, M. N., or Raffaella, could lead to 'knowing' them profitably during the circus's extended sojourns in each town. An immediate benefit in some cases was rich hospitality for at least himself and his sister during that sojourn. In the longer term followed gifts such as a *devozione*, shirts, a 'romanduca' with a six-month guarantee, *taralli* biscuits, and ultimately, money. It may well be that, for the sake of acting as a recipient of letters that might contain gifts, Carolina was more than happy to play her part in helping these women build their virtual arenas, with her own husband playing the role of leading man. Whether this felt to her like an emotional sacrifice in return for material support we cannot know, but the question itself is a reminder that the division between matters of the heart and material existence was a luxury that had yet to delineate where emotions ended and material interest began.

It is too facile to see C. of Catanzaro, Amalia of Città Sant'Angelo, M. N. of Larino, and even Raffaella of Cassano, as short-brained dupes, over-eager to star in their own operatic plots. Rather, some of their deepest yearnings found protective space in the interstices of various emotional arenas—the real circus ring and the virtual versions they created, by mail, after the circus went on its way. Pietro's opportunities to instigate the creation of those virtual arenas, and their intensity, owed a great deal to a regime that strictly curtailed the emotional possibilities available to women in nineteenth-century Italy.

# 4
# Arenas of Mortality
## From Eros to Thanatos

### Death in the New Italy

The archival remains left by the trial for Captain Fadda's murder are rich with documents that testify to vivid emotions experienced by a wide range of people who lived, loved, and died long ago. As previous chapters show, feelings of attraction, desire, and love figure strongly in the narratives preserved by the official investigation. In addition to erotic themes, and in some cases their agonies and subterfuges, ultimately the story bequeathed by Fadda's life and death is a kind of judicial embalming: the archive is a collection of documents brought together as the result of an attempt to redress a terrible misdeed that caused an untimely end. It records a process that sought to contain and resolve the individual and social emotions evoked by the murder. Death easily competes with love for the intensity of feelings it generates, and the deep private and public emotions stimulated by the story that emerged out of Fadda's passing were responses to a striking conjuncture of Eros and Thanatos.

This chapter moves from arenas of attraction, intimacy, love, and lust, to those where the responses generated by death among those in the realm of the living were shaped and expressed. It explores the nature of these emotions, and how they were experienced within the ritualized social arenas where those left behind bade farewell to the departed and sought to come to terms with painful loss. The chapter thus explores specifically emotional aspects of 'death's social meaning', as Walter Laqueur has put it.[1] The emotional arenas of death are often public and quite concrete. Hospitals, mortuaries, churches, and cemeteries exemplify such physical spaces. But they can also be occasional. For example, funeral processions might be regarded as momentarily solid, distinctive emotional arenas. In addition to such tangible and visible locations, texts such as letters and newspapers also provided important venues for the expression and shaping of emotions generated by deaths.

The work of historians of death underlines that culture has a great deal to do with death's social meanings.[2] If, as Pat Jalland has argued, attitudes to death in

---

[1] Thomas W. Laqueur, *The Work of the Dead: A Cultural History of Mortal Remains* (Princeton: Princeton University Press, 2015), p. xiii.

[2] In addition to the work cited above, the following have broadly influenced the thinking behind this chapter: Philippe Ariès, *Western Attitudes toward Death: From the Middle Ages to the Present*, trans. Patricia M. Ranum (Baltimore: Johns Hopkins University Press, 1974); Ariès, *The Hour of our*

Britain were transformed in the 1870s and 1880s due to religious, demographic, and cultural forces, Italy also witnessed analogous transformations.[3] In the city of Rome in particular, the hegemony of a Catholic worldview was deeply challenged by liberal principles. The liberal ideology that guided Italian unification prized science and reason over religion and faith, though of course in daily life, belief systems coexisted and overlapped.[4] But the liberal challenge to a Catholic worldview made 1870s Italy a setting in which death's meanings and associated feelings were more fluid, and more contested, than they had been for centuries.

Rome, recently taken from the pope and hastily fashioned into Italy's national capital, was the urban nexus where the Catholic and liberal-secular worldviews most conspicuously coexisted. The story of Fadda's marriage, through which universal matters like love and death found such a prominent place in the public sphere, provides an exemplary microhistorical example for analysis of how such feelings were shaped, staged, and managed in a nation that was on the contested cusp of a more secular epoch.

## Deaths Great and Small

Several deaths mark the narrative framed by Giovanni and Raffaella's unhappy union. Unable to divorce, a contrived and violent death ended the marriage, and Fadda's demise is the focus of the chapter's second half. But before he died, two other deaths made heavy impressions on Fadda's world. The first, in August 1877, was that of his mother. Almost certainly the cause of intense suffering for Fadda as well as his father and brother, only indirect traces of their emotions remain accessible to posterity. By contrast, a few months after Fadda's mother's death, and nine months before his own murder, Italy's symbolic father and first king, Victor Emmanuel, died. The king, with Giuseppe Garibaldi and Camillo Benso di Cavour, had formed the triumvirate of Italy's Risorgimento. In the decades following Italy's unification, the king lived on as the most potent embodiment of a political union that was—like the human being himself—both glorious and fragile.

King Victor Emmanuel's death, after eighteen years as head of the new nation, gave Italians their first and most historically remarkable taste of grief on a national scale. Many worried that without its king, the nation might unravel into its constituent parts. Funerary arrangements gave state officials an opportunity to

---

*Death*, trans. Helen Weaver (London: Allen Lane, 1981); Pat Jalland, *Death in the Victorian Family* (Oxford: Oxford University Press, 1996); and Peter N. Stearns, *Revolutions in Sorrow: The American Experience of Death in Global Perspective* (Boulder, CO: Paradigm Publishers, 2007).

[3] Jalland, *Death in the Victorian Family*, p. 358.
[4] Hannah Malone, *Architecture, Death and Nationhood: Monumental Cemeteries of Nineteenth-Century Italy* (London and New York: Routledge, 2017), p. 129; Ariès, *Western Attitudes toward Death*, p. 81.

choreograph the Italians' collective grief on a secular national stage for the first time. As several scholars have shown, the ceremony was clearly designed to celebrate, and thus strengthen, the Risorgimento's political trajectory of Italian unity. An event of emotional choreography par excellence, the funeral took shape as a dramatic staging of death on a scale that had never before been witnessed by Italians. In terms of the paradigm permeating this book, state officials created an emotional arena of mourning in Rome shared by hundreds of thousands of people. Even more broadly, during the week of the funeral, all of Italy could be seen as an imagined community linked by common emotions, in which the fragile political bonds among Italians were to be reinforced by intense and consciously shared sentiments.

Victor Emmanuel, as ruler of Piedmont-Sardinia, had been Fadda's king for most of the soldier's life. In 1859, in his late teens, Fadda had left the island of Sardinia to follow the king into battles against the Austrian army that aimed to secure Italian independence. The loyal soldier had suffered grave wounds for that cause. After unification, Fadda, now a decorated veteran of the Risorgimento, continued to serve king and country as a military officer for nearly two decades. In January 1878, when the king died, Fadda witnessed and participated in the extraordinary theatre staged in Rome during the state funeral. In far-off Calabria, the king's death was the last in a string of delays affecting plans for Raffaella's brother's wedding, further postponing her move to Rome to live with Fadda. The emotional ramifications of the king's death played out not just on the nation's official stage, but at a capillary, provincial level, in the individual lives of his subjects. Ordinary people like Giovanni Fadda, Raffaella, her brother Giuseppe, and his wife-to-be, were deeply affected, in both emotional and practical ways.

By contrast, Fadda's own death nine months later, was that of just such an ordinary figure, one who would have remained unknown to most of the nation but for the drama of his murder and the ensuing trial. Once revealed, the story behind Fadda's life was of sufficient resonance to ensure that, like the king's, the soldier's death was an event that transfixed and moved the entire nation. Indeed, Fadda joined the phalanx of martyrs that were an important element of Risorgimento mythology and remain emblematic of the intertwining of Catholic and secular world views in Italy.[5] Moreover, because Fadda's death was quickly perceived as the result of disastrous emotional imbalance—too much lust and love, compounded by cold-blooded deliberation entirely lacking compassion—the feelings behind the murder were to become key elements in the trial's deliberations.

Even before the court case, which only commenced a year after the crime, Fadda's death caused emotional waves that rippled far and wide, in line with the notion that sudden deaths of adults in full flower are among the most shocking

---

[5] Lucy Riall, 'Martyr Cults in Nineteenth-Century Italy', *Journal of Modern History*, vol. 82, no. 2 (June 2010): 255–87.

and difficult to deal with in terms of the feelings they prompt.[6] In Fadda's case, those feelings, initially of shock, but soon of horror, and ultimately of compassion and grief, originated in the densely populated quarter of Rome where the murder took place. There, locals who witnessed Fadda's bloody body and saw the assassin try to flee, felt very strongly about the soldier's death. Those emotional shockwaves moved steadily outward from that central moment. They progressed from witnesses and officials, to Fadda's military colleagues, to his family, and, by word of mouth, telegraph, and the media, eventually to the whole nation and even beyond.[7]

Feelings about Fadda's death were eventually to reach a magnitude and intensity that was not far off the scale of that surrounding the death of the king he had followed into battle nearly twenty years earlier. In the king's case, the scale and form of the public spaces in which the death was mourned were carefully contrived by state officials. Those ceremonies established a new style of secular liturgy for Italians. In Fadda's case, the science of medical knowledge and the sagacity of forensic systems can also be seen to delineate a secular boundary around the feelings provoked by the soldier's demise. Through these three deaths in the late 1870s, the first of a virtually unknown woman, the second of an eminent personage, and the third of an Italian everyman, the citizens of the new nation participated in a range of emotional arenas, on the stages of which they expressed, shaped, and sought to come to terms with the feelings generated by the ultimate human loss.

## The Death of a Mother

More than a year before Fadda himself died, the first inkling of mortality in the story emerged from the archival collection by way of a small plain postcard. Written at the height of summer in August 1877 by Giovanni Fadda, it was addressed to his mother-in-law, Carolina. Fadda was stationed in the town of Chieti, in the Abruzzo region near the Adriatic coast. He sent the card to Carolina at her occasional residence in Naples, on the peninsula's opposite coast, about 200 kilometres to the west. Beginning 'Dear mother' as was his custom with her, he wrote that the latest news about his birth-mother's health was very grave. He had been called by telegram to her bedside in Sardinia, because it appeared that she was close to the end.[8] If he had arrived in time, he would have kept a vigil with his father and brother by her bedside as she passed away.

---

[6] Jalland, *Death in the Victorian Family*, pp. 66–7, and p. 313.

[7] Journalistic interest, particularly during the trial, went well beyond Italy, finding a place in English-language reportage all over the world, from Britain to the USA, and even Australia and New Zealand. Examples appear in chapter 5.

[8] Archivio di Stato di Roma, Tribunale Civile e Penale di Rome (henceforth ASR, TCPR), 1879, busta 3659, vol. IV, folio 172, postcard from Giovanni Fadda to Carolina Nola, dated Chieti, 9 August 1877.

Although undoubtedly the cause of some distress for Fadda, the brief postcard, its ink exposed to the elements and curious eyes as it made its way across Italy, gave off little in the way of sentiment. Fadda wrote that because of the 'great official projects about to get under way', it was proving difficult for him to obtain leave, partly because there was no one to replace him. Nevertheless, he reported seeking to persuade his colonel to let him go, and in the meantime he wanted to know what he should do with Raffaella. Would her parents come to collect her, and if not, would they let him know what he ought to do with her quickly, because he 'absolutely' had to get to Sardinia.[9] Time would tell that whatever her parents decided should be done with Raffaella, the death of Fadda's mother would indirectly mark a definitive rupture of the young couple's already spasmodic domestic arena.

From today's perspective the most striking thing about the card's message is not so much Fadda's lack of emotional expression about his mother as the implication that his wife completely lacked independence or agency. Fadda's concern about the etiquette of the day in relation to unaccompanied women outweighs, in the postcard at least, any anxiety about his mother's impending death. The thrust of his message was a question about how his wife would be taken care of by her parents in her husband's absence, given that he expected to depart for Sardinia at any moment. It is clear that Raffaella would not accompany him, but neither could she be left in Chieti alone. Nor did it seem that she could make the journey to the protection of her mother's abode without a chaperone. Would her parents come to collect their twenty-three-year-old married daughter?

As was nearly always the case in Giovanni Fadda's written communication, logistical problems and matters of form eclipsed sentiment, and his engagement in emotional expression was minimal. We cannot know whether anxiety about his mother's imminent death was actually his predominant feeling, but his emotions were unlikely to have been negligible. Other evidence shows that Fadda had the capacity to feel pain very deeply. The fact that he did not commit the slightest sign of such feeling to paper in this case indicates that Fadda carefully calibrated the way he expressed his feelings, even when they concerned something as momentous as his own mother's death. He laboured to produce a restrained emotional style that prioritized practicalities over the expression of emotion.

Equally striking is the way that, some three weeks after the postcard was written, symbolic markings on the next correspondence, a letter from Fadda to his wife, confirmed the fact of a death even before the letter had been read. The stationery was framed with a thick black border, darkly adumbrating his mother's passing. It is unlikely that this was the first letter Fadda sent to Raffaella after the death, as the postmark indicates that he had already returned from Sardinia to Chieti and the letter does not refer directly to the loss in any way. But the

---

[9] ASR, TCPR, 1879, b. 3659, vol. IV, f. 172.

emotional atmosphere left in the wake of the death is conveyed starkly by the stationery's black frame. So little emotion transpires from Fadda's writing that his heart seems to be an iron vessel as rigid as the paper's border. Contrasting with the grief presumably contained by Fadda's prodigious emotional self-control, the letter opened with the optimistic announcement that the time for the couple's move to Rome was fast approaching. Fadda hoped that Raffaella would be able to hurry her mother towards departure from Naples for Calabria, whence she was to join him once he settled in the capital.[10]

Further on, the letter poignantly recounts that, from afar, Fadda was doing his best to support his father after the 'grave misfortune'. He reported that he had sent him two 'lunghissime' letters and was waiting for a reply that would indicate the decisions his father would make (perhaps about whether he might come to live with them). But, 'out of delicacy', Fadda was trying to 'let things be initiated' by his father; 'he is my father, after all, and one must have respect and concern, and in my letters I am trying not to put any pressure on him.' Fadda closed the letter to Raffaella with a customary remark about his health. Within the phrase he chose, there is a hint that he was somewhat haunted by having witnessed what happens when a body altogether loses its life force. Using the imperative mood, he bade Raffaella to enjoy her good health and seek to maintain it always: 'that will be one of the best proofs of the esteem in which you hold me.'[11]

## A Wedding and a Funeral

Raffaella may not have held Giovanni in the high esteem he presumed. During the month following his mother's death, while he moved to Rome and made arrangements for his wife to join him, Raffaella's reluctance to return to his side became evident. While Fadda's stationery continued to carry the black borders of mourning, his prose made no further reference to his mother. Rather, Raffaella's resistance to his plans for their cohabitation in the capital was the chief source of his pain. Shortly after his own move to Rome, in early September 1877, Fadda wrote to her announcing that he had, with some difficulty, found an apartment whose rent was within his means. He hoped very much that she would like it. He also begged her to write to him more often, exclaiming with an uncharacteristic admission of feeling that 'if you don't you'll make me suffer.'[12] Raffaella still had not moved to Rome by mid-October, when a further letter from her forbearing husband acknowledged that the apartment was on the small side, but boasted a

---

[10] ASR, TCPR, 1879, b. 3659, vol. IV, ff. 173–4, letter from Giovanni Fadda to Raffaella Saraceni, dated Chieti, 30 August 1877.
[11] ASR, TCPR, 1879, b. 3659, vol. IV, ff. 173–4.
[12] ASR, TCPR, 1879, b. 3659, vol. IV, ff. 179–80, letter from Giovanni Fadda to Raffaella Saraceni, dated Rome, 10 September 1877.

location on one of Rome's main streets. He added enticingly that the building's staircase was lit by gas, and their fellow tenants were all 'very civil'.[13]

The correspondence preserved from this period is thin, but by late November 1877 an ostensible reason for Raffaella's tardiness became clear: she wanted to remain at her parents' home in Calabria until after her brother Giuseppe's wedding. The engagement had been announced more than four months earlier, in July, but for reasons that remained unclear, there had been delays and the wedding had not yet taken place.[14] In late November Raffaella wrote to an increasingly impatient Fadda in Rome, imploring him to permit her to remain in Calabria for another two weeks, by which time she thought the wedding was bound to have taken place. She assured him that this was not a mere 'caprice' on her part, but a necessity, adding that if it had been a matter of months, she would not have asked. Since it was a question of mere days, she was sure that she could rely on his 'sense of reason'.[15] Unusually, on this occasion Raffaella's brother Giuseppe himself also decided to write, in an effort to persuade Fadda, his-brother-in-law, to permit Raffaella to delay her departure from Calabria and share the joy of the imminent wedding.[16]

Faced with this mounting pressure from Raffaella and her family members, Fadda's patience wore thin and he began to express signs of frustration. His reply to Raffaella reported that he was trying to organize a leave of absence so that he could attend the wedding himself, but without an exact date it was difficult to finalize permission. He planned to join Raffaella's family on about 5 December, but would only have fifteen days of leave. He hoped that Giuseppe would be able 'to do what he needed to do' within that time as he would not be able to extend the stay. Fadda told Raffaella that every day his colonel asked him when he would need to leave. He did not think the colonel was being unduly harsh for pressing him, but rather, he indirectly reprimanded his wife, saying, 'it is we who are being capricious by asking for something and then delaying it.'[17] He was acutely conscious of the duty to behave correctly.

The wedding did not take place in December, despite Giuseppe Saraceni's assurance, due to a delay that may have been caused by legal difficulties of some sort. A marriage was just as much a property settlement as it was the official blessing of

---

[13] ASR, TCPR, 1879, b. 3659, vol. IV, ff. 177–8, letter from Giovanni Fadda to Raffaella Saraceni, dated Rome, 17 October 1877.

[14] ASR, TCPR, 1879, b. 3659, vol. IV, f. 171, letter from Giovanni Fadda to his father-in-law, Domenico Saraceni, dated Chieti 14 July 1877.

[15] ASR, TCPR, 1879, b. 3659, vol. IA, f. 15, letter from Raffaella Saraceni to Giovanni Fadda, undated but probably 25 November as the letter from her brother Giuseppe, saying he wanted to add his voice to that of his sister and persuade Fadda to permit her to stay, was dated 25 November 1877 (see next note).

[16] ASR, TCPR, 1879, b. 3659, vol. IA, f. 42, letter from Giuseppe Saraceni to Giovanni Fadda, dated 25 November 1877.

[17] ASR, TCPR, 1879, b. 3659, vol. IV, f. 181, letter from Giovanni Fadda to Raffaella Saraceni, dated Rome, 27 November 1877.

an emotional bond, but, as mentioned in chapter 3, under Italian law since 1866 marriage was a secular, rather than a religious matter, and the blessing, as it were, had to be given by a state official. On new year's day 1878, Carolina Nola sent Fadda a postcard, reporting that she had contacted both the notary and the mayor, so the wedding could now be planned.[18] On Thursday 10 January Carolina and Raffaella wrote a joint invitation to Fadda's brother Cesare, who lived relatively nearby in Castrovillari, announcing that finally a date had been set for Giuseppe's much-delayed wedding. 'God-willing', they wrote superstitiously, the wedding would take place on Sunday 13 January, and they warmly invited Cesare to attend.[19] The tone of the letter was a peculiar mixture of both joy at the prospect of the wedding, and anxiety that something would intervene to cause yet another delay.

God, as it turned out, was not willing. Although Carolina and Raffaella did not know this when they wrote to Cesare, the day before they penned the wedding invitation, on 9 January 1878, King Victor Emmanuel II had died. Despite being a state official himself, Cesare Fadda did not seem to know this either when he replied to the invitation. He wrote back on the same sheet of paper, stating in elaborately polite prose that he would not be able to attend the wedding due to 'work commitments'.[20] If the invitation had arrived a day later he would not have needed to excuse himself: the wedding was cancelled as the nation plunged into official mourning and collective grief. The king's death shocked Italians deeply and brought the country to a standstill; some even feared that the nation's fabric might unravel.[21] Weddings, and any other joyous occasions, would have to wait, while all of Italy's emotional energies were channelled into grieving for the nation's first king.

Victor Emmanuel II's death on 9 January 1878 was a turning point both for Italy, and, as it turned out, for Fadda and Raffaella's marriage. In the short-term the pair's personal tribulations were dwarfed by a wave of feeling that made their own concerns insignificant against the background of national mourning. They, and all Italians, suddenly inhabited a nation that was united into an imagined community by a momentarily unanimous press.[22] While the king's death required the postponement of Giuseppe Saraceni's wedding and can ultimately be seen as precipitating the painful breakdown of Fadda's own marriage, Italy held itself together as a political entity. In fact, a strong interpretive current among contemporary

---

[18] ASR, TCPR, 1879, b. 3659, vol. IA, f. 33, postcard from Carolina Nola to Giovanni Fadda, postmarked 1 January 1878.

[19] ASR, TCPR, 1879, b. 3659, vol. IA, f. 31, wedding invitation from Carolina Nola and Raffaella Saraceni to Cesare Fadda, dated 10 January 1878.

[20] ASR, TCPR, 1879, b. 3659, vol. IA, f. 31. Cesare replied on the reverse side of the invitation.

[21] Umberto Levra, *Fare gli italiani. Memoria e celebrazione del Risorgimento* (Turin: Comitato di Torino dell'Istituto per la Storia del Risorgimento, 1992), pp. 3–4. Levra's detailed reconstruction of the main funeral, held in Rome on 17 January 1878, has become the canonical study of the event's successful mobilization of national sentiment and memory.

[22] Levra, *Fare gli italiani*, p. 8.

observers was that the collective shock experienced by Italians at the beginning of 1878 created new national bonds that were reinforced by shared emotions.

The king's death, such observers claimed, encouraged Italians to perceive themselves as one people united by fellow feeling. The Rome newspaper *Il Bersagliere*'s reports exemplified this stance, for example with the assertion on 18 January that the king's death was a 'triumph greater than a thousand triumphs', because the emotional unity it revealed 'demonstrates *that Italy is*'.[23] In a similar vein, another Roman newspaper, *L'Opinione*, famously caught the mood when it claimed that the collective expression of emotion amounted to a 'new plebiscite' affirming Italian nationhood.[24] As we will see, modern historical interpretations, critically analysing initial impressions that Victor Emmanuel's death generated a sense of national togetherness rather than disarray, tend to affirm the positive contemporary claims.

Across a territory whose only shared rituals had been those of the Church, the king's death offered an unprecedented opportunity to orchestrate the type of national ceremony that nations such as England and France already had great experience in staging.[25] In the French context, Avner Ben-Amos has shown that from the advent of modern French nationhood in 1789, the state funeral held a special position among the nation's armoury of civic ceremonies.[26] Spurred by fear of national disaggregation, anxious Italian politicians spared no effort to ensure that their newly fledged polity witnessed the invention of a tradition of state funerals that rivalled those of older nations.[27]

As historians of Italy have revealed, while the outpouring of emotion over their first king's death may have been spontaneous, officials successfully harnessed that expression in a way that exalted its unexpected breadth and uniformity.[28] Francesco Crispi, Minister of the Interior, insisted that the burial should take place in Rome, rather than the Savoy dynasty's home city of Turin, to reinforce the national role of the recently established capital. The choice of Rome's famous Pantheon as the ceremony's focus made Crispi's motives even clearer: it was part of a desire to wrest the potently symbolic building from Vatican control, convert

---

[23] *Il Bersagliere* (Rome), 18 January 1878, p. 1 (emphasis original).

[24] 'Il nuovo plebiscito', *L'Opinione* (Rome), 12 January 1878, p. 1.

[25] See for example E. P. Thompson, *Customs in Common* (London: The Merlin Press, 1991), pp. 43–5. More recently, and for a slightly later period, Charles Sowerwine gives a convincing emotions-centred account of the most remarkable French example of death rituals, in 'Channelling Grief, Building the French Republic: The Death and Ritual Afterlife of Léon Gambetta, 1883–1920', in *Emotion, Ritual and Power in Europe, 1200–1920: Family, State and Church*, edited by Merridee L. Bailey and Katie Barclay (Basingstoke: Palgrave Macmillan, 2017), pp. 145–67.

[26] Avner Ben-Amos, *Funerals, Politics, and Memory in Modern France, 1789–1996* (Oxford: Oxford University Press, 2000), p. 6.

[27] Levra, *Fare gli italiani*, pp. 3–23.

[28] For example, Alberto Mario Banti, 'The Remembrance of Heroes', in *The Risorgimento Revisited: Nationalism and Culture in Nineteenth-Century Italy*, edited by Silvana Patriarca and Lucy Riall (Basingstoke: Palgrave Macmillan, 2012), pp. 171–90, here p. 177, as well as the work cited below.

it into a national rather than religious monument, and claim Victor Emmanuel, not the pope, as the modern heir of ancient Rome's glory.[29]

Crispi took the lead in orchestrating an extraordinary funeral that was to be a powerful ceremonial debut for the nation, as well as the king's last rite of passage.[30] For a month in early 1878, Rome became the focal point of a nationally scaled emotional arena the likes of which had never been witnessed in Italy.[31] Encouraged by 75 per cent discounts on railway tickets, more than 200,000 citizens are thought to have made the pilgrimage to Rome to pay their respects at the funeral. This represented a doubling of the city's usual population, and the crowds, coordinated by Crispi's ingenious choreography, ensured that the farewell ceremony was an immense and memorable spectacle.[32]

During the day of the funeral, a cannon was fired once every minute from dawn to dusk, its insistent boom creating a lugubrious and distinctively secular soundscape, reminding those whose thoughts might have wandered about the gravity of the day.[33] The funeral carriage was drawn by eight horses through crowds that lined the streets from the Quirinal Palace to the Pantheon. Behind it walked the great white stallion ridden by the king during the battle of San Martino. It was followed by a vast procession that included representatives of virtually every stratum of the Italian state and civil society.[34] In short, the funeral created an emotional space which corralled and shaped citizens' emotions in a new and distinctive way. It used sight and sound to pay homage to an old dynastic regime, but showcased the modern parliamentary nation of which the king had been the first head.[35] Umberto Levra affirms that newspapers and all manner of private correspondence vividly attest to the event's key features: a stunning spectacle, high levels of emotion, and a vast crowd, 'all perfectly controlled'.[36] Crispi's efforts had turned Rome, and all of Italy, into a carefully contrived emotional arena.

Within this grand spectacle, the king's death affected his subjects in specific ways. Giovanni Fadda was one of the many men of his generation whose personal history was deeply entwined with the king's reign. He had suffered serious

---

[29] Malone, *Architecture, Death and Nationhood*, p. 162.

[30] Christopher Duggan, *Francesco Crispi 1818–1901: From Nation to Nationalism* (Oxford: Oxford University Press, 2002), pp. 376–81.

[31] Cecilia Dau Novelli, *La città nazionale. Roma capitale di una nuova élite (1870–1915)*, (Rome: Carocci editore, 2011), pp. 293–4.

[32] Duggan, *Francesco Crispi*, pp. 379–80.

[33] The cannon would have contrasted with the more familiar soundscape of church bells, on which the 'canonical' work is Alain Corbin, *Village Bells: Sound and Meaning in the Nineteenth-Century French Countryside* (New York: Columbia University Press, 1998). More recent emotions-history work has tended to focus on music, but on sound and emotion see Dolly McKinnon, '"The Ceremony of Tolling the Bell at the Time of Death": Bell-ringing and Mourning in England c.1500-c1700', in *Music and Mourning: Interdisciplinary Perspectives*, edited by Jane W. Davidson and Sandra Garrido (Abingdon: Ashgate Publishing, 2016), pp. 31–9.

[34] Christopher Duggan, *The Force of Destiny: A History of Italy since 1796* (London: Allen Lane, 2007), p. 306.

[35] Levra, *Fare gli italiani*, p. 21.   [36] Levra, *Fare gli italiani*, p. 20.

wounds on the symbolic battlefield at San Martino, perhaps even within sight of the king and his famous charger. After unification, Fadda had loyally served king and country as an army officer. For men like Fadda, the king's passing was effectively the death of part of their own history, a history they had helped to shape. It is easy to imagine that their feelings of loss would have been intense, perhaps even to the point of disorientation. Already suffering over a marital situation that caused him deep unhappiness, it must have been particularly significant for Fadda to witness and participate in the extraordinary days of ceremony choreographed around the king's funeral.

Posterity possesses no direct testimony of Fadda's feelings about the king's death, but a letter from Raffaella suggests that he recounted how affected he was. She wrote saying that she 'too' was much saddened, adding, perhaps in an attempt to console her husband, that 'there is nothing to be done, we are all mortal and, some sooner, some later, we all have to go.'[37] Instead, having delivered her homespun philosophy on the inevitability of death, Raffaella's ongoing concerns were very much those of daily life. She empathetically acknowledged how busy her husband must have been in the days prior to the official funeral, then fatefully proceeded with the announcement that her brother Giuseppe's wedding, intended for 13 January, had of course been cancelled because of the king's death. Once the period of mourning was over, she added, the family hoped the wedding would finally take place.[38]

Until this point Fadda had shown only restrained signs of impatience over his wife's reluctance to move to Rome. But the news that Giuseppe's wedding was to be put off again, for a period that Fadda interpreted as the official national mourning period of six months, precipitated a profound reaction. He had behaved like a patient beast of burden, but this entanglement of the royal death with his brother-in-law's wedding and his own marriage seems to have been the straw that broke his emotional back. The royal funeral took place on 17 January. The following day Fadda wrote a very brief and notably cool letter to Raffaella, on black-bordered stationery. He also included some money, described as the 'instalments for November and December'.[39] On the same piece of paper, Fadda wrote a note to his mother-in-law Carolina, saying Raffaella's pianoforte was too large for the apartment in Rome and that he wished to send it back to them. The message concluded with a graphic account of the imposing spectacle of the king's funeral in Rome and the influx of crowds to the city. The ceremony may have been carried

---

[37] ASR, TCPR, 1879, b. 3659, vol. IA, f. 15, undated letter from Raffaella to Giovanni, but probably after 13 January and before the king's funeral on 18 January 1878.
[38] ASR, TCPR, 1879, b. 3659, vol. I, f. 15.
[39] Although no previous letters had referred to such payments, these are likely to have been the interest generated by Raffaella's dowry. See Michela De Giorgio, in *Le Italiane dall'unità a oggi. Modelli culturali e comportamenti sociali* (Rome-Bari: Laterza, 1992), p. 312, on the arrangements for the dowries of women married to army officers.

off with perfect order, as Levra wrote, but in Fadda's view, there was 'great confusion, and even women are sleeping in cafes'.[40]

It is difficult to pinpoint what happened in Fadda's mind, but the few days around the king's death clearly mark the beginning of the end of his and Raffaella's relationship. Fadda appears to have assumed that Raffaella did not intend to join him in Rome until after her brother's wedding had taken place, at the conclusion of national mourning many months hence. Faced with this prospect, he gave up hope on his marriage. His request to return the pianoforte, although couched among interesting but seemingly innocuous news about the funeral crowds in Rome, was in turn interpreted by Raffaella and her mother as a signal that Fadda wished to repudiate his wife—to break off relations and excise Raffaella from his life by cutting their ties and returning her belongings.

What Raffaella found herself contemplating in the wake of the rupture represented by the king's death was a primitive form of divorce, even though the absence of a divorce law meant the couple would have remained legally married until one of them died. Given their relative youth, the prospect of one of their deaths was not yet within view for any of the subjects concerned. But for the historian, whose means allow a peek over his subjects' horizons, the momentous week of the Italian king's death in 1878 foreshadowed that before long Fadda would once again follow in the king's footsteps—not into battle, but to a premature death.

## Death Throes of a Marriage

Raffaella and Carolina may well have been correct to take Fadda's request to unburden himself of the pianoforte as a signal that he had lost patience and was about to take drastic action. Something certainly snapped in Fadda's mind that week. He left remarkable evidence both of the feverish atmosphere of Rome in those days, and, more subtly, of his own overwrought emotions. One poignant signal of his torment took the form of a letter addressed to Raffaella, very vividly written and quite out of character for the usually self-controlled soldier. Dated 23 January 1878, one week after the king's funeral, the letter opened with an expression of relief that 'Finally, we can breathe again and Rome has returned to normal.' This relief followed days of madness described almost comically: 'one couldn't eat because in restaurants people snatched each others' meals, cafes were taken over for eating and sleeping, and anyone who had a seat did not give it up on any account.' Such impressions provide eccentric perspectives on the arguments of subsequent historians about the way the king's funeral brought Italians closer together, but ultimately, Fadda's view accords with the later interpretations. As he

---

[40] ASR, TCPR, 1879, b. 3659, vol. IV, ff. 186–7, letter from Giovanni Fadda to Raffaella Saraceni and Carolina Nola, dated Rome, 18 January 1878.

put it, during those days, 'Rome could be said to represent all of Italy', united by the same feelings.[41]

Fadda elaborated the point, reporting that visitors had come from every city and town: 'from Cosenza, from Milan, even from Chieti'. These towns neatly represented the south, north, and centre of Italy respectively, but Fadda's choice of the minor town of Chieti, where he and Raffaella had last lived together, was more strategic than representative. Fadda's letter proceeded with affected insouciance:

> ...in relation to that last place [Chieti], I was greeted by one Signor **Edoardo** Donzelli, greetings he extended to you and your servant Maria. He is clearly a gentleman because even though I have never met him, he knew who I was...He also told me about Signora Lombardi, who is crazed with jealousy about her husband who gets up early to chase servant girls around the market-place, even though this sort of jealousy is quite out of fashion. Others tell me that Signor **Edoardo** is conquering all of Chieti (that is to say, he is conquering all the conquerable ladies)—it seems impossible that a man so ugly could be so fortunate with women.[42]

From someone whose letters had never contained so much as one word of gossip, this account is remarkable, even outlandish. As Roberto Bizzocchi has shown, the age of the *cicisbeo*, a married woman's officially sanctioned male companion, had ended long ago. By the 1870s, Italian gentlemen such as this Signor Edoardo, whose name Fadda emphasized with heavy pen strokes, would not have had independent friendships with married women and their servants, let alone pass their greetings on to them via their husbands.[43]

Outlandish is in fact just what the letter was. It was fantasy, the restrained expression of a mind that had been consumed by jealousy. Fadda did not send the letter and probably never intended to. It was recovered from the desk in his apartment nine months after it was written, shortly after he was murdered. It only made sense to anyone when his brother, Cesare, told the police that Fadda had harboured grave suspicions about Raffaella's fidelity. Fadda had once intimated to Cesare his painful suspicion she was having an affair with a man named Edoardo, and felt that she was also attracted to Chieti's local bank manager, one Signor

---

[41] ASR, TCPR, 1879, b. 3659, vol. IV, f. 43, letter from Giovanni Fadda to Raffaella, dated Rome, 23 January 1878.
[42] ASR, TCPR, 1879, b. 3659, vol. IV, f. 43, letter from Giovanni Fadda to Raffaella dated 23 January 1878. Each instance of the word Edoardo was written in slightly larger and bolder hand than the other words.
[43] Roberto Bizzocchi, in *A Lady's Man: The Cicisbei, Private Morals and National Identity in Italy* (Basingstoke: Palgrave Macmillan, 2014), argues that the emergence of Italian nationhood brought with it a displacement of aristocratic morals and a renewed emphasis on the hermetically faithful married couple. See especially pp. 241–8.

Lombardi.[44] In January 1878, when Fadda had written the letter, it must have served as a vent for his jealousy, and it provides a rare glimpse into this very private man's most intimate feelings. Indeed, Fadda concluded the fantasy letter with the line 'For the last couple of days I've had a bit of a fever today I feel a bit better it must all be the effect of emotions.'[45] Clearly, the week of the king's death forced Fadda's emotions to overflow the boundaries of his self-control, even if they only spilled onto paper that never left his desk.

Fadda's term *emozioni* in nineteenth-century Italy may well have had different connotations from 'emotions' in modern English, the link to his fever echoing earlier ideas about sentiment and bodily tempers.[46] Nevertheless his use of the word bears personal witness to some of the ways the king's funeral left Roman citizens more than simply physically enervated. In his own case, Fadda mused, *emozioni* had made him ill. Ensuing letters strongly suggest in fact that Fadda's normal self-control had finally given way, and that he had become prey to unfettered emotions (as we understand them now) that seemed to poison him from within. He precipitately concluded that Raffaella planned to use the period of national mourning to postpone her departure for Rome indefinitely. To him this indicated that the marriage, which had never flourished, was as good as dead. In the context of nineteenth-century Italy, a dead marriage with living members would have been cause for intense personal shame. The civil law under which Fadda and Raffaella had married offered no feasible form of dissolution, such as divorce. Instead, Fadda improvised a proxy, a unilateral exit from this now unbearable emotional arena.

Fadda signalled his abandonment of the marriage to his wife and mother-in-law by sending Raffaella's belongings to Calabria. This began with the pianoforte, a gesture that resulted from Fadda's decision to quit the home he had found for the couple and move into a smaller one. His quitting of the conjugal arena he had physically created was also a clear symbolic gesture. He proposed that the two sides meet on the neutral ground of a hotel in Taranto (in Puglia, about 140 kilometres from Cassano) to discuss an official separation. That proposal was met with horror and refusal by both Carolina and Raffaella. In February and March 1878, the two women both wrote letters to Fadda imploring him to come to his senses. Carolina even explicitly accused him of making decisions 'irrationally' and 'emotionally'.[47]

---

[44] ASR, TCPR, 1879, b. 3659, vol. IA, ff. 136–42, statement by Cesare Fadda to Michele Finizia, Rome, 11 October 78.

[45] ASR, TCPR, 1879, b. 3659, vol. IV, f. 43, letter from Giovanni Fadda to Raffaella, dated Rome, 23 January 1878. The final phrase reads 'oggi vado un pò meglio sarà effetto di emozioni'.

[46] On the evolution of emotion as a category of feeling, see Thomas Dixon, *From Passions to Emotions: The Creation of a Secular Psychological Category* (Cambridge: Cambridge University Press, 2003), esp. pp. 1–5 and pp. 99–104.

[47] ASR, TCPR, 1879, b. 3659, vol. IA, ff. 34–6, letter from Carolina Nola to Giovanni Fadda, dated 20 February 1878.

She was perfectly correct, but it is unlikely that she understood the full extent of her son-in-law's torment.

The lack of a divorce law in Italy's civil code meant that a marriage could only legally come to an end with the death of a spouse. In this way, the law of the land tied Eros to Thanatos indissolubly, and the de facto failure of a marriage for most Italians in the nineteenth century represented a very awkward limbo. Indeed, it may not have seemed far off the horror of death itself. Fadda, convinced that his wife would never come to live with him, became riddled with poisonous emotions that convinced him his marriage could no longer subsist. His health suffered as a result. At one point he must have told Raffaella that he felt he would die of his emotional pain, because she reprimanded him for what she saw as a melodramatic misinterpretation of her reluctance to come to Rome, accusing him of having 'created an impossible situation'.[48] There ensued a painful correspondence over what was a family tragedy: the death of a marriage.

Fadda, motivated by what was clearly a deep emotional crisis precipitated at the time of the king's death, effectively left Raffaella 'neither married nor a spinster at twenty-five years old', to use her mother's words.[49] The couple's correspondence continued sporadically through the summer of 1878, but it was almost entirely concerned with settling questions of property. The letters came to an end around August 1878, by which time Fadda had consigned all items of value to his wife, complete with punctiliously itemized lists that he requested her to sign. By this time the couple's feelings for each other were exhausted. Their communications expressed no anger, no love, no bitterness; just the desire to scrape some sense of resolution from the limbo of a marriage that had lost the will to live but which the law would not allow to die.

## A Murderous Mission

Because Italians knew so well that the law offered no legal possibility of escape for individuals whose fate it was to suffer irretrievable marital breakdown, there was a certain brutal logic in the fact that an assassin should eventually have turned up at Giovanni Fadda's doorstep, even if the result was also shocking. The assassin was the professional equestrian, Pietro Cardinali. Cardinali and his circus had spent the early summer of 1878 in Calabria. At about the time Raffaella and Giovanni Fadda resolved to live apart, the circus arrived for a sojourn in Cassano allo Ionio, Raffaella's town. Here, as in other such towns, the troupe had given

---

[48] ASR, TCPR, 1879, b. 3659, vol. IA, f. 22, undated letter from Raffaella Saraceni to Giovanni Fadda, probably February 1878.
[49] ASR, TCPR, 1879, b. 3659, vol. IA, ff. 37–9, letter from Carolina Nola to Giovanni Fadda, dated 30 March 1878.

regular performances for several weeks. What made their stay in Cassano distinctive, as shown in chapter 2 is that the circus and the private lives of some of the town's citizens became enmeshed.

According to any number of Cassano's townsfolk, Raffaella had willingly been drawn into the exciting arena of Cardinali's circus, just as Cardinali had eagerly and notoriously insinuated himself into the vacuum of Raffaella Saraceni's postmarital emotional landscape. As many townsfolk saw it, the offspring of this liaison was a plot to murder Giovanni Fadda. It would be for a court of law to decide whether Raffaella had gone so far as to put Cardinali up to helping her end her marriage in the only way possible. What quickly became unarguable is that, in the early morning of Sunday 6 October 1878, Cardinali, a grim reaper in riding boots, knocked at Fadda's door in Rome. On being admitted, he enacted a cold-blooded plan to kill Raffaella's long-suffering husband. Taking Fadda by surprise, he thrust a knife into his body over twenty times, before bolting down the stairway and attempting to flee the scene.

To witnesses whose Sunday morning was rent by Fadda's calls for help as he staggered onto the street a few seconds later, wearing only his blood-soaked undergarments, the event immediately smacked of the explosive emotions that fuelled vendettas. Cardinali knew he could rely on such cultural tropes to suggest that the assassin had been a man driven by jealousy. Indeed, he took the trouble to prepare a letter that pointed to such a conclusion, and he brought it to Fadda's apartment. Found on the floor by an eager police officer soon after the murder, the letter began: 'My dear D Giovanni, I beg you, do not come tonight, my husband knows you have been to my house and has threatened to take your life and mine.' The letter was signed in the style of the love letters Cardinali himself knew so well: 'I clasp you to my bosom, and swear I will love you until death, your dear Teresina Panzi.' The officer, naturally assuming the letter explained everything, scooped it up and put it into an envelope marked 'LETTER FOUND ON CAPTAIN FADDA'S FLOOR. IMPORTANTISSIMA.'[50] Emblematic of the letter's presumed forensic significance, the official envelope it was wrapped in was closed with no fewer than five seals of dark red wax. These, even well over a century later, alarmingly resemble heavy clots of dried blood (figure 4.1).

As Cardinali's carefully contrived decoy ironically makes clear, Fadda's murder was anything but a crime of passion. It was a death almost foretold, the result of a plan conceived in Calabria, gestated during a railway journey to Rome, and adapted over the course of several days' reconnaissance in the eternal city itself. Cardinali had departed Calabria by train in the company of his stablehand, Giuseppe De Luca, in late September 1878. Cardinali initially told De Luca that they were going to Naples to look for new work in another circus. Their first train

---

[50] ASR, TCPR, 1879, b. 3659, vol. IV, unnumbered folio, bound immediately after the initial 'Compendio', undated letter found on the floor of Fadda's apartment on 6 October 1878.

ARENAS OF MORTALITY: FROM EROS TO THANATOS    129

**Figure 4.1** The letter found on Fadda's floor after the murder, and the official envelope in which it was stored (ASR, TCPR, 1879 b. 3659). Reproduced with permission from the Ministero dei Beni e Attività Culturali e del Turismo, ASRM 56/2015. Further reproduction prohibited.

took them as far as Bari, the main port city in Puglia, on Italy's Adriatic coast. The pair stopped for lunch at a wine cellar run by a young man named Michele Forleo. Some six or seven years earlier, when Forleo was in his early teens, he had formed such a close friendship with Cardinali while the circus was in Bari that the pair had 'always been together'.

When the circus departed, Cardinali gave his young friend a signed photograph of himself as a memento (see figure 2.1).[51]

Forleo was surprised and pleased to see Cardinali again in 1878, and, with De Luca hovering outside, he, his uncle Nicola Ghenghi, and the celebrated equestrian artist sat down to a leisurely luncheon in the cool penumbra of the wine cellar (figure 4.2).[52] Naturally the conversation began with a question about Cardinali's business in Bari. He told his hosts that he was on his way to Rome to

**Figure 4.2** Pietro Cardinali having lunch with old friends in Bari, on his way to Rome.
Source: *L'Epoca* (Genoa), 9–10 October 1879, p. 1, reproduced with permission from the Biblioteca di Storia Moderna e Contemporanea, Roma.

---

[51] ASR, TCPR, 1879, b. 3659, vol. II, ff. 69–73, statement by Michele Forleo to prosecutor Paolo Aquila, Bari, 11 October 1878.
[52] ASR, TCPR, 1879, b. 3659, vol. II, ff. 69–73, Forleo's statement, Bari, 11 October 1878.

buy new horses. Forleo joshed him, saying 'Who knows what you're really up to, you were always a bit of a trickster.' Perhaps Cardinali's tongue was loosened by the local wine, for he soon became expansive, and revealed that he was in love with a beautiful, rich, married woman from Calabria. This woman, he claimed, had charged him with the task of 'unburdening' her of her husband, so that she and Cardinali could marry. She had given him 120 piastres to find an assassin who would take on the job of killing her husband.[53]

Cardinali asked Forleo and his uncle if they knew such a man, adding that if he failed to find one, he would have to do the deed himself. Forleo and his uncle both claimed to have been horrified and sought to dissuade Cardinali from this awful mission. They asked what would become of the woman and children he had lived with when he first visited Bari. His answer was that he would keep the children and give the woman enough money to 'go away'. Clearly morally untroubled by his grand plan, Cardinali even playfully menaced Forleo with a frightening knife, before departing on the 3 p.m. train to Naples.[54] The uncle noted that Cardinali did not kiss Forleo goodbye, as would have been the custom. Instead, he said he would see to that duty, as well as paying the money he owed them for lunch, on his return journey.[55]

Cardinali and De Luca did go to Naples as originally planned, but after staying there for two nights, they caught the train to Rome. Their journey involved a change at Caserta station, about 50 kilometres north of Naples. During the wait, Cardinali offered a cigar to a young station attendant named Michele Belli. He then asked Belli if he would write a letter for him. The railway attendant agreed, and, using the windowsill of the third-class waiting room to lean on, he wrote as Cardinali dictated. As far as he could recall, the letter went as follows: 'My dear sir, I beg you, do not come to my house any more as my husband knows, and says that if he finds you, he'll introduce you to his Sicilian dagger...'. Intrigued, Belli asked what the letter was for. Cardinali said it was part of a practical joke. Belli even recalled constructing an envelope out of a second piece of paper, and addressing it to a captain in the '23rd Infantry regiment' in Rome. According to Belli's statement, Cardinali then took the letter, rejoined his shady-looking companion, and boarded the 10.16 train for Rome.[56] The letter was to be delivered by Cardinali personally at Captain Fadda's lodgings some days later.

For Cardinali, recipient of many a letter from women in love, it did not require much imagination to dictate a letter that feigned the emotions of an amorous

---

[53] ASR, TCPR, 1879, b. 3659, vol. II, ff. 69–73, Forleo's statement, Bari, 11 October 1878. Forleo's words were 'Chi sa che vai facendo, tu sei sempre stato un imbroglione'. 120 piastres was a significant sum equivalent to several hundred Italian lire.

[54] ASR, TCPR, 1879, b. 3659, vol. II, ff. 69–73, Forleo statement, Bari, 11 October 1878.

[55] ASR, TCPR, 1879, b. 3659, vol. II, ff. 71–2, statement by Nicola Ghenghi (coachman and Forleo's uncle), Bari, 11 October 1878.

[56] ASR, TCPR, 1879, b. 3659, vol. II, ff. 104–105, witness statement by Michele Belli (station attendant), Caserta, 9 October 1878. Belli did not quite get the regiment number correct—it was the 32nd.

woman. Although the letter sounds histrionic now, it was uncannily similar in style to those Cardinali had regularly received from various past admirers. The letter also convinced the first police officer who read it that it was *importantissima*. Whether Cardinali hit upon this ruse because of the common trope of the murderously jealous husband, or because it was easy for him to take a leaf out of his own life experience, is difficult to say. Both interpretations are suggested by the existence of the letter. Equally, it is clear that Cardinali was unable to look far enough ahead to foresee men he had befriended such as Forleo and Belli, or the station attendant, becoming witnesses. He was completely taken in by the drama of which he was playwright, ringmaster, and leading man.

Although in Bari Cardinali's original plan may still have been to commission someone else to murder Fadda, it is unlikely that he would have gone to the trouble to provide such a person with a letter designed as a red herring. Two days' searching in Naples apparently did not yield a suitable assassin, and it seems clear that by the time the pair set off for Rome, Cardinali had resigned himself to the fact that he personally would be the one to 'unburden' Raffaella of her husband. De Luca accompanied him throughout the journey. Although the stablehand clearly looked the part of accomplice, he played a very secondary role, waiting outside while his master ate lunch in Bari, and remaining in the background while Michele Belli wrote the last letter Fadda would ever read. De Luca claimed that it was only when they arrived in Rome that Cardinali revealed their main task as 'a great act of vendetta' upon Captain Giovanni Fadda.[57]

Despite the main purpose of the journey to Rome, Cardinali spent his first few days in the city making inquiries about circus work there. On Sunday 29 September, he attended a performance at the circus run by the famous impresario Emilio Guillaume, at the great Teatro Politeama, on the Trastevere side of the Tiber River. After the public had left, Cardinali approached Guillaume and asked if he needed an artist who rode bareback, boasting that he was one of the best. Cardinali seems to have visited the circus a few days running, and although he had not brought a riding costume, eventually he gave a demonstration in the arena on Saturday 5 October, the day before he was to murder Fadda. Guillaume was impressed, assessing Cardinali as an artist who could earn 'about 400 francs a month'. But the impresario was put off by the rider's 'slightly sinister look', and decided not to hire him. Later the same day, Guillaume recalled, while he was having a shave at his barber's, the equestrian artist also came in, and asked the barber to remove his goatee. Once this was done, Cardinali departed, according to Guillaume, in the company of a man 'even more sinister looking, dressed like a Calabrian'.[58]

---

[57] ASR, TCPR, 1879, b. 3659, vol. 1A ff. 84–7, De Luca's first statement, made to the police on 6 October 1878.

[58] ASR, TCPR, 1879, b. 3659, vol. II, ff. 42–3, statement by Emilio Guillaume, 45, circus impresario, 11 October 1878.

Where Cardinali and De Luca lodged for their first few nights in Rome is not recorded, but on Wednesday 2 October, they took a room in a hotel at number 4 Via delle Marmorelle, in the densely populated area of Rome then known as the Quartiere Alessandrino (see the map provided in figure 0.1). Its buildings lay over parts of the ancient Roman Forum, between Trajan's Column and the Colosseum. The area was cleared with great fanfare in the early 1930s to make way for the construction of Mussolini's monumental Via dell'Impero.[59] The hotel Cardinali chose was located very close to Via dei Carbonari, the location of the small apartment to which Fadda had moved in March 1878 after losing hope that Raffaella would ever join him.[60] Cardinali evidently planned to shadow Fadda and learn about his movements. For his first approach to Fadda's house, he posed as a messenger on an errand from the soldier's previous abode in Chieti, and spoke to Fadda's orderly.[61] Cardinali was dismayed to learn that his target was not in Rome: he had gone to Calabria to visit his brother Cesare.

Not knowing quite what to do, Cardinali exchanged several telegrams with his adoptive sister and sometime lover, Antonietta, who remained with the circus in Calabria. These mysterious missives, each of about twenty-five or thirty words, contained odd phrases whose meanings were not immediately clear, though the essence was decipherable. The first, from Pietro to Antonietta, reported 'NOT FOUND, WILL ARRIVE NEXT WEEK, GET MOTHER MILK TO GIVE THE TELEGRAM. I DON'T KNOW IF I WILL COME BACK. IF THE CIRCUS WANTS TO DEPART SO BE IT.'[62] The second, also from Pietro to Antonietta, said 'TELL VASCA HE IS IN CASTROVILLARI WITH HIS BROTHER. WOULD LIKE TO KNOW IF HE GOES TO SEE HER AND IF SHE HAS CHANGED HER MIND ABOUT ME. REPLY. PIETRO.'[63] And the third, a reply from Antonietta to Pietro, said 'MOTHER MILK TOLD EVERYTHING. VASCO DIDN'T GO VASCA. VASCA THE SAME [...].'[64] The telegrams incorporated cryptic elements, and the words 'Vasco' and 'Vasca' in particular successfully flummoxed the investigators. These turned out to be circus jargon meaning a gentleman and his wife, in this case indicating Fadda and Raffaella. Cardinali was anxious to know whether Raffaella still felt the same about him, and if Fadda had visited her while he was in Calabria.

The telegrams give chilling insight into the murder plot's full extent, incriminating Antonietta Cardinali, and to a lesser extent the character known in the early stages only as 'Mother Milk', as accessories. Moreover, because very little concrete

---

[59] Borden W. Painter Jr, *Mussolini's Rome: Rebuilding the Eternal City* (New York: Palgrave Macmillan, 2005), pp. 22–3.
[60] ASR, TCPR, 1879, b. 3659, vol. II, ff. 38–9, statement by Rosa Zaccari, Fadda's landlady, 11 October 1878.
[61] ASR, TCPR, 1879, b. 3659, vol. II, ff. 1–4, statement by Fadda's orderly, Matteo Angelo, 21, 9 October 1878.
[62] ASR, TCPR, 1879, b. 3659, vol. IA, f. 176, telegram dated 2 October 1878 from Pietro to Antonietta.
[63] ASR, TCPR, 1879, b. 3659, vol. IA, f. 177, telegram dated 3 October 1878 from Pietro to Antonietta.
[64] ASR, TCPR, 1879, b. 3659, vol. IA, f. 178, telegram dated 4 October 1878 from Antonietta to Pietro.

evidence about Raffaella's and Cardinali's relationship ever came to light, it was particularly significant that the second of the telegrams left little doubt that Cardinali's plan was motivated by his perception of Raffaella's feelings for him. Without Antonietta's reassuring response, 'Vasca the same', it is quite possible that Cardinali would not have proceeded with the plan to murder Fadda. Suitably buoyed up, he did proceed, biding his time until Fadda returned to Rome. Although Rome was a fairly large city, with a long history of comings and goings related to pilgrimage and tourism, it was not so impersonal that two newcomers, particularly those of distinctive appearance, could take up residence in a densely populated area without being noted. And so, for the next few days, while Cardinali and De Luca waited for Fadda, they unwittingly made impressions on the people around them that would soon become evidence for the police, and ultimately, for historians.

## A Death Foretold?

Cardinali and De Luca made a regular haunt of a particular trattoria, a modest eating house on the Piazza delle Chiavi d'Oro (Golden Keys) run by Vincenzo Farghi and his wife Maria Paladini. A table in the window afforded a view of Fadda's apartment windows. The two men, one described by Farghi as 'tall, all dressed in black velvet with a wide brimmed hat', and the other, 'well built, with black hair, moustache and goatee, dressed like a local artisan', would order a carafe of wine and settle in, gazing up at the windows of Via dei Carbonari 2. According to Farghi, the pair seemed restless. One would leave, shortly to return, and then the other would do the same. They kept asking each other sotto voce 'Did you see him? Did you see him?' On Thursday 3 October, Fadda himself, having returned early from Calabria, walked past the restaurant with his orderly, who, seeing Cardinali through the window, recognized him as the man who had asked after Fadda the day before.[65] The restaurant owner's suspicions were naturally aroused by his customers' peculiar behaviour. He told himself they might be police officers disguised as civilians, since one had a revolver and the other a knife, and he chose not to interfere.[66]

At night Cardinali and De Luca repaired to their hotel, where they shared a room with a photographer named Albino Albanesi, aged twenty-nine, from the southern city of Avellino, near Naples. Albanesi did not like the look of his fellow guests, and felt uncomfortable about sharing a room with them. His descriptions

---

[65] ASR, TCPR, 1879, b. 3659, vol. II, ff. 1–4, statement by Fadda's orderly, Matteo Angelo, 9 October 1878.
[66] ASR, TCPR, 1879, b. 3659, vol. II, ff. 44–5, statement by Vincenzo Farghi, 48, innkeeper, 12 October 1878; exactly the same story was told by Farghi's wife, Maria Paladini: vol. II, ff. 46–7, 12 October 1878.

of the men, one 'well proportioned, muscular, wearing riding boots', and the other, 'tall, all in black, with a soft broad hat', closely matched those of other witnesses. Albanesi felt they had a 'sinister appearance' and was concerned that they had not signed the hotel's register. He asked the landlady to make sure they did so.[67] The innkeeper, Veronica Santi, told much the same story about her dubious guests.[68]

In response to Albanesi's insistence that they sign the hotel register, the one in boots said he never revealed his handwriting to anyone, so the photographer offered to write it for him. Cardinali provided the name 'Michele Solie', saying he was from the Abruzzo region, and had come to Rome to buy horses. Albanesi reported that on Thursday 3 October, 'Solie' left for safekeeping with the innkeeper a revolver and a 'fearsome-looking' knife. On Saturday 5 October, Cardinali and De Luca came to bed at 11 p.m. Albanesi pretended to be asleep, but he listened as Cardinali whispered to De Luca that they would create less suspicion if they were to strike early in the morning. The whispering reportedly concluded 'Damn women, look at the lengths we go to for them. Enough, tomorrow we must get up early'.[69]

During their few days in the area, on several occasions De Luca bought a small bottle of brandy from Carlo Marini, who ran a shop in the forebodingly named Via della Testa Spaccata (Split Head). Marini later described his customer as 'a tall, thin-bearded fellow of sinister aspect', and reported that very early on the morning of Sunday 6 October 1878, this fellow came in to the shop with a second man, whose 'riding boots over his trousers' later identified him as Cardinali. The man dressed in velvet asked if he could deposit a knife, while the one in boots left a cloak. Marini noted that the man in boots seemed to be in a great hurry and rushed his companion. About a quarter of an hour later, the pair returned and retrieved their belongings. Once again the man in boots exuded a sense of urgency, hissing to his companion 'Quick, we must hurry, things are ready'.[70]

The sense of theatricality conveyed by the eyewitness accounts of Cardinali and De Luca both before and after the murder is a prominent feature of the way observers recalled the pair. If Cardinali had been directing a work for the stage, he could hardly have invented a more appropriate series of set pieces to dramatize a plan that would end in murder. It seems not as if his main aim was to escape notice, but to write a libretto for the most melodramatic of operas, complete with 'sinister' looks and cloak-and-dagger antics. Why was this so? One reason could

---

[67] ASR, TCPR, 1879, b. 3659, vol. II, ff. 30–2, statement by Albino Albanesi, 29, photographer, 11 October 1878.
[68] ASR, TCPR, 1879, b. 3659, vol. II, ff. 36–7, statement by Veronica Santi, 68, innkeeper.
[69] ASR, TCPR, 1879, b. 3659, vol. II, ff. 30–2, statement by Albino Albanesi, photographer, 11 October 1878.
[70] ASR, TCPR, 1879, b. 3659, vol. II, ff. 62–3, statement by Carlo Marini, 36, shopkeeper, 14 October 1878. Cardinali is alleged to have said 'Presto, sbrighiamoci, perchè i cacagli sono pronti'. The word 'cacagli' is likely to be nineteenth-century dialect as its meaning is now completely lost, but in the context it clearly means something like 'we are ready to roll' or 'the goose is cooked'.

have been Cardinali's profession, as the star of a kind of make-believe arena. He may have been a larger-than-life persona whose sense of the boundaries between circus ring and daily life was more than semi-permeable. Certainly, his approach to planning Fadda's murder possessed the hallmarks of a story conceived for a theatrical stage.

But allowance must also be made for the fact that the impressions permitting historical reconstruction—provided by the circus impresario, the restaurateur, the hotel guest, the hoteliers, and the shopkeeper—were recollections expressed after it became clear that they had all witnessed, and even unwittingly played their parts in, a scheme to commit murder. It is quite possible that De Luca's and Cardinali's 'sinister' appearance, noted independently but uniformly by those who had dealings with the pair, accurately described the way they looked to their observers. But it is also possible that the witnesses' memories were retrospectively coloured by the news of Fadda's ghastly death at Cardinali's hands. It was, after all, news that spread around Rome very quickly in the immediate aftermath of the event itself.

On the morning of Sunday 6 October, an anxious Cardinali was clearly ready to bring his drama to a conclusion. Activity evidently started extremely early on a Sunday in 1870s Rome. Thanks to their fellow guest, we know that Cardinali and De Luca rose at about 5 a.m.[71] By 7 a.m. Cardinali had managed to lure Fadda's orderly, Matteo Angelo, to a shop in the Piazza Montecitorio, which happened also to be the site of Italy's parliament. Cardinali claimed to have deposited a parcel there, brought from Chieti and addressed to Captain Fadda. Finding the shop closed, as he knew it would be, Cardinali asked Angelo to wait in the piazza while he went to find the shop owner so they could retrieve the parcel. Instead, having drawn Angelo out of his master's house and left him waiting for an unspecified period, Cardinali rushed back to Fadda's house and knocked on the door.[72]

With the orderly absent, the captain himself responded to the knock, even though he was dressed only in his long undergarments. Cardinali proffered a letter, almost certainly that written by 'Teresina Panzi'.[73] Having gained entry, and while Fadda was trying to make sense of the letter, Cardinali plunged the fearsome knife into his unsuspecting, distracted target, with all the force that a well-built, adrenalin-fuelled equestrian acrobat could muster. The only eye witnesses to the fateful skirmish in Fadda's apartment were the men themselves, both driven

---

[71] ASR, TCPR, 1879, b. 3659, vol. II, ff. 30–2, statement by Albino Albanesi, 11 October 1878.

[72] This account of Cardinali's movements immediately prior to the murder draws from the synthetic 'Compendio' compiled by chief prosecutor Michele Finizia bound in ASR, TCPR, 1879, b. 3659, vol. IA, folios unnumbered.

[73] ASR, TCPR, 1879, b. 3659, vol. II, ff. 78–81, statement by Gaetano Rossi, Cardinali's police-cell companion, 20 October, 1878. Cardinali reported that he had given Fadda a letter and attacked him while he was reading it.

by a mortal fear: Fadda, a hair's breadth from the jaws of death; Cardinali, well beyond the point of no return in a tragedy of his own making.

Adrenalin would have made the blood rush in each man's arteries. The pair seem to have lurched about the apartment in combat, but the event was over in the time it took Cardinali to stab Fadda's body twenty-three times, probably less than twenty seconds. Forensic reconstructions, following a trail of blood, suggested that in the confusion, Fadda fell back onto an ottoman.[74] A witness in a neighbouring building later said she thought she heard muffled cries from Fadda that made it sound as if someone had covered his mouth.[75] Rushing from the scene, Cardinali dropped the knife on the stairway of the building, where it skittered to a standstill, to be found by a neighbour 'all drenched with blood' a few minutes later.[76]

As he exited the building Cardinali tried to slow to a normal pace, but Fadda's unexpected cries for help at the doorway, as he sought to pursue his assailant, impelled the assassin back into a run. The fugitive's dash was quickly foiled as he was caught by the policemen who happened to be at the nearby barbershop and had heard Fadda's cries for help. As the two officers struggled to restrain Cardinali, they looked up to see Fadda falling to the ground, pointing as he did so to the writhing, red-handed man they had caught.[77] The eloquence of Fadda's final gesture, reported by witnesses, was to be captured in both the chief investigating magistrate's written report, and by newspaper illustrators who reconstructed the events for the public in vivid engravings (see figure 0.2).[78]

Cardinali was escorted away, loudly protesting his innocence, while locals gathered around Fadda's body, inert on a baker's doorstep. One of the first to arrive at Fadda's side was Benigno Menni, who lived nearby and had heard the calls for help. He was a member of Fadda's regiment, and as he reached the wounded man he was distressed to recognize his fellow soldier.[79] Later, testifying in court, Menni remembered feeling greatly pained to see that Fadda was 'moribund'.[80] Though inert, Fadda was in fact still breathing. Menni quickly arranged for his comrade to be transported across the Roman Forum to the Ospedale della Consolazione, a

---

[74] ASR, TCPR, 1879, b. 3659, vol. IA, ff. 3–4, 'Visit and description of locality' recorded by prosecutor Michele Finizia, 11 a.m., 6 October 1878.
[75] ASR, TCPR, 1879, b. 3659, vol. IA, noted in Finizia's 'Compendio'.
[76] ASR, TCPR, 1879, b. 3659, vol. II, ff. 24–6, statement by Filippo De Giovanni, 40, servant, who lived at Via dei Carbonari no. 5. He described the dagger as 'tutto intriso di sangue'.
[77] ASR, TCPR, 1879, b. 3659, vol. IA, from Finizia's 'Compendio' but corroborated by various witness accounts, including the officers' testimony at the trial, recorded in *Processo Fadda illustrato. Dibattimento alla Corte d'Assise di Roma dal 20 settembre al 31 ottobre 1879* (Rome: Giovanni Bracco Editore, 1879), pp. 58–63.
[78] For example, *Processo Fadda illustrato*, pp. 116–17. A similar rendition of Fadda's famous gesture was published on the front page of the Genoa newspaper, *L'Epoca*, 14–15 October 1879.
[79] ASR, TCPR, 1879, b. 3659, vol. II, ff. 7–8, statement by Lieut. Benigno Menni, 30, of the 32nd Infantry, 9 October 1878.
[80] *Processo Fadda illustrato*, pp. 69–70.

few hundred metres distant. Menni followed the cart to the hospital then kept watch at Fadda's bedside, waiting for his ineluctable death.[81]

Meanwhile, the authorities had started to respond. The first on-duty official to arrive at the crime scene was Vittorio Belmonte, head of the police station to which the guards had delivered Cardinali. As soon as the suspect was securely locked in a cell, Belmonte hastily made his way to Via dei Carbonari, where he surveyed the scene of the crime. While there, he took custody of the bloody knife and the suspicious letter from 'Teresina Panzi', both of which had been recovered by an eager underling.[82] Belmonte then made his own way to the victim's bedside to see if he could capture any evidence before the man's soul departed. He asked Fadda who his assassin might have been. The dying man moved his lips, but no sound was audible.[83] The hospital's medical report said that Fadda had arrived at the hospital at about 7.45 a.m., and had 'ceased to live' about half an hour later, due to loss of blood.[84] The comrade, Menni, later poignantly described Fadda's passing: 'In the last moments of life, he looked at me, but was unable to say a single word.'[85] The tragedy of Fadda's untimely death hovers ineffably in Menni's simple description of watching a life slip away.

## Hot Blood, or Cold?

Over the next few hours and days, the disturbing news of the attack emanated from the narrow streets of the Quartiere Alessandrino, out into the wider city. Fadda's death, its violence, and the fact that many people had seen and even had contact with the chief suspect, left in its wake a sense of shocked disorientation but also wonderment and fascination. Violent deaths were not rare in Rome, but premeditated murders were far outnumbered by those that took place in the heat of the moment.[86] As murders went, Fadda's death reportedly struck a chord in people's hearts more than others had done. Indeed, as studies by Angela Groppi and Thomas Simpson have shown, especially in relation to the trial, the murder was taken up by the media with almost unprecedented interest, such that Simpson argued it was a key moment in the history of Rome's newspapers.[87]

[81] ASR, TCPR, 1879, b. 3659, vol II, ff. 7–8, statement by Lieut. Benigno Menni.
[82] ASR, TCPR, 1879, b. 3659, vol. IA, f. 76, report by Vittorio Belmonte, 6 October 1878.
[83] ASR, TCPR, 1879, b. 3659, vol. IA, f. 76, report by Vittorio Belmonte.
[84] ASR, TCPR, 1879, b. 3659, vol. 1A, f. 2, 'Relazione chirurgica' issued by the Veneranda Arcispedale di S. Maria della Consolazione, 6 October 1878.
[85] *Processo Fadda illustrato*, p. 70.
[86] Daniele Boschi, 'Homicide and Knife-Fighting in Rome, 1845-1914', in *Men and Violence: Gender, Honor and Rituals in Modern Europe and America*, edited by Pieter Spierenburg (Columbus: Ohio State University Press, 1998), pp. 128–58, here p. 133.
[87] Angela Groppi, 'Il teatro della giustizia. Donne colpevoli e opinione pubblica nell'Italia Liberale', *Quaderni Storici*, vol. 37, no. 111 (2002): 649–80; Thomas Simpson, *Murder and Media in the New Rome: The Fadda Affair* (New York: Palgrave Macmillan, 2010).

Printed evidence that journalists sensed something deeply resonant in the events at Via dei Carbonari that Sunday appeared the next day. The lively *Gazzetta della Capitale* reported that the city was 'funestata'—distressed, or afflicted—by an extremely mournful event, a 'sad and brutal tragedy'.[88] On Tuesday, *Il Bersagliere* reported that the murder had made a 'profound impression' on the citizens of the city.[89] Even the notably serious *L'Opinione*, which cost twice as much as the other newspapers, provided a vivid and detailed story of the murder. Although it was the least speculative and most accurate report, it was nevertheless dramatic, peppered with exciting phrases such as 'at that very moment…'.[90] The high levels of media interest are best explained by the story that quickly emerged out of the murder investigation, for it was an unusual and beguiling blend of hot-blooded passion and cold-blooded premeditation.

The intensity of the public response to the murder was sufficient to ensure that it did not remain merely provincial, or even national news. On Tuesday 8 October the 'Italy' section of *The Times* of London's international page began with the usual political and diplomatic matters, but a substantial section of twenty-three lines announced that 'A dreadful murder committed yesterday in the Via dei Carbonari […] has created an intense excitement throughout the city.' The correspondent claimed that such high levels of interest had not been seen since the murder of the editor of the newspaper *Il Capitale*, Edoardo Sonzongno, in 1875. Providing a few rudimentary facts about Fadda's status as paymaster of the infantry, and noting that the suspected murderer had been seen hovering about for some days, the report concluded that the assassin was not known to Captain Fadda and 'would seem to have been an instrument employed to carry out a vendetta'.[91]

*The Times*' report of Fadda's murder was already well out of date by the time the British public read it two days after the event. The 'vendetta' theory, sparked momentarily by the letter found on Fadda's floor, may well have fitted British stereotypes of Italian hot-bloodedness, but in Italy itself the theory did not even survive Sunday morning. This was because the story of the assassin's relationship with the victim's wife, and their alleged plan to be rid of Fadda so that they could marry, was revealed to Italian investigators within hours of the murder. It was not the first time in history that an apparently torrid passion had gone hand in hand with a coldly planned and mercilessly executed killing. But on this occasion the flesh-and-blood subjects of the story evoked particular fascination, as it became possible to visualize the way Cardinali's and Raffaella's relationship represented an extraordinary overlap between two very different emotional domains: an unruly but exciting circus love affair, and a dutiful but emotionally and physically moribund marriage.

---

[88] 'Cronaca cittadina', *Gazetta della Capitale* (Rome), 7 October 1878, p. 3.
[89] 'L'assassinio del capitano Fadda', *Il Bersagliere* (Rome), 8 October 1878, p. 3.
[90] 'L'assassinio del capitano Fadda', *L'Opinione* (Rome), 7 October 1878, p. 3.
[91] 'Italy', *The Times* (London), 8 October 1878, p. 3.

140   EMOTIONAL ARENAS

The story took shape quickly because, thanks to a tip-off from fellow hotel guest Albino Albanesi, Cardinali's accomplice De Luca had been caught soon after the murder. He was arrested at Rome's Termini station, attempting to escape the city by the same means he had used to arrive.[92] Clearly anxious to distance himself from the crime, De Luca recounted the entire plot succinctly as soon as he was asked. His questioner was Michele Finizia, the magistrate who took charge of the case. De Luca told him that Fadda had been separated from his wife Raffaella for some time; that she was rich, and that, 'as the whole town knows' (meaning Cassano allo Ionio), she and the equestrian artist Pietro Cardinali were lovers. The murder, De Luca concluded, 'was a crime that could be seen coming, because the wife of the captain, as the public voice put it, was bored with him, and she arranged with Cardinali to have him killed'. De Luca provided many useful details, including the fact that Cardinali had himself dictated, at Caserta station, the letter found on Fadda's floor.[93]

A sceptical investigator might have thought this was all a tale designed to make sure the witness's own role in the murder was minimized, but more detailed investigation tended to confirm, rather than undermine, De Luca's allegations. Furthermore, while De Luca was detained under the charge of accomplice to the murder, his own death, from tuberculosis, was not far off. On his deathbed, still in prison two months after the murder, De Luca called for the investigating magistrate to visit him. He then confirmed that everything he had said was the absolute truth. This last 'confession' was taken as a sign of the ultimate veracity of all De Luca had claimed.[94] On the morning of the murder, those claims led to the quick elimination of the vendetta theory. It was replaced with the notion of an illicit love affair leading to an attempt to end one marriage, through murder, to make way for another. Word of mouth and the newspapers quickly conveyed the story's astonishing combination of lustful emotions and ambitious calculations to the public. All of this helps explain the unprecedentedly intense 'excitement' conveyed by the Italian press, and reported to British readers by *The Times*.

In those early days though, the excitement generated as the story emerged did not eclipse the sense of shock and sorrow surrounding Fadda's death. The still point around which the emotions swirled was Fadda's corpse, laid out on a marble slab, covered by a sheet, awaiting its post-mortem examination.[95] It was the body of man who had been wounded in the cause of liberating Italy from Austrian domination, and who had served the state loyally ever since he had helped create

---

[92] ASR, TCPR, 1879, b. 3659, vol. IA, ff. 60–2, report by Brigadier Mattia De Carolis, 6 October 1878.
[93] ASR, TCPR, 1879, b. 3659, vol. IA, ff. 84–7, first statement by Giuseppe De Luca, Cardinali's stable-hand and accomplice, 6 October 1878.
[94] ASR, TCPR, 1879, b. 3659, vol. IA, magistrate Finizia's 'Compendio'; vol. IB, f. 331, note from the Direzione delle Carceri Giudiziarie [judicial prison] dated 13 January 1879, recording that De Luca died that day at 8.30 p.m., of tuberculosis.
[95] 'La sezione del capitano Fadda', *Gazzetta della Capitale*, 8 October 1878, p. 3.

it. Although the quest to explain and redeem the injustice of Fadda's death quickly became fascinating and diverting, the days between his murder and burial, in terms of emotional tenor, were marked by the doleful sobriety of the public authorities whose duty it was to bring proper closure to the life of a faithful fellow servant of the state and Italian patriot.

## Death in Forensic Arenas

There were two main aspects to these sad duties. The first was to carry out the elementary forensic groundwork for what would undoubtedly be a major trial: who was the victim, and what could the corpse reveal about his life and death? The second task was to give Fadda an appropriately dignified funeral. Although the funeral was the more obviously emotional arena, both these processes involved the shaping and staging of intense emotional reactions to the fact of death. And although the word 'forensic' now connotes the detached scientific study of legal evidence, the word's etymology goes back to the very ground over which the mortally injured Fadda was carried to hospital: the *Foro*, or Forum, of Republican Rome, the centre of civic and legal activity in the ancient city.[96] The modern ideal of a court of law that privileges reason over emotion ought not to eclipse the undoubtedly emotional elements of the rhetorical processes that have been part of forensic arenas from the earliest days.[97]

In Liberal Italy, the figure who dominated the forensic aspects of criminal cases was the *giudice istruttore*, the examining magistrate. A state functionary, this person's primary task was to investigate the crime and prepare a case for prosecution. The official's mission can also be seen as an application of the meticulous procedures of the law, with its ordered reasoning, to the emotionally ragged events surrounding the murder. A particularly poignant task when the victim was a fellow state functionary with claims to self-sacrificial heroism, it was a process designed to contain and manage the strong emotions generated by such an event. Ideally these pressures and pains would be regulated and ultimately dissipated. The man appointed to head the forensic investigation, Michele Finizia, spent several months preparing the case for trial. He interviewed suspects, collected evidence locally in Rome, and directed state functionaries in the provinces to undertake analogous tasks.

Reading Finizia's deliberations, a sense of emotional management is immediately evident. While the tone of his writing is sober and objective, between the lines of his careful reports glimmer both professional pride and a certain zeal for

---

[96] Leanne Bablitz, *Actors and Audience in the Roman Courtroom* (London: Routledge, 2007), p. 50.
[97] The next chapter elaborates on this idea, but on performance and emotion in Roman legal culture see also Sophia Pappaioannou, Andreas Serafim, and Beatrice Da Vela (eds), *The Theatre of Justice: Aspects of Performance in Greco-Roman Oratory and Rhetoric* (Leiden: Brill, 2017).

ensuring justice was done. This is not surprising, because Finizia personally witnessed the crime scene and Fadda's post-mortem. He arrived at the location of the murder soon after it happened. He wrote his first report at 11 a.m. on the day of the crime, recording the observations of his first visit to Fadda's abode. He noted that in the entrance hall, both on the walls and on the ground, there were bloodstains. Though they had been generated in the opposite direction, from Finizia's perspective these continued up the stairs to the first floor. At the top of the steps down which Cardinali had recently run and Fadda had lurched, there was a landing. On the right was the door to Fadda's apartment. There the magistrate met the landlady, Signora Rosa Zaccari, and Fadda's orderly, Matteo Angelo, who showed him the apartment.[98]

Describing a modest living room with two windows facing the street, Finizia noted that there was much blood near an ottoman, with splatters leading to the front door. Finizia looked at the bedroom, which gave him the impression of a space where someone had recently woken up. A damp towel suggested that the captain had washed not long before. Back in the living room, there were newspapers on the table. Finizia noted the dates and titles, and the fact that they all had blood on them. He formed the view that Fadda was attacked near the ottoman, well out of reach of his sword and revolver.[99] The magistrate collected various documents from Fadda's desk, as well as a photograph of the captain, and another of his wife.[100] He also went through all Fadda's belongings, listing two gold rings (one of which was a wedding band that Fadda must have ceased wearing) and all other items, right down to six handkerchiefs.[101] It must have been a chilling scene, though perhaps a regular Sunday morning's work for the magistrate.

As yet Finizia knew nothing whatever of Fadda's marriage, and his report is mostly factual, though he was no doubt affected by the bloody scene and the knowledge of the murder. Perhaps in his office later on, Finizia did make value judgements about each item of Fadda's belongings, and their possible relationship to the crime. As a result of these deliberations, he sent the clothing and the rings back to the army to be returned to Fadda's relatives, but he retained the letters, the photographs, a handwritten poem, and other documents. Though striving to be objective, he could not resist some speculation: of the letters he wrote in his first summary, 'there is something indistinct and mysterious to be read between the lines of that correspondence.'[102]

---

[98] ASR, TCPR, 1879, b. 3659, vol. IA, f. 3, 'Visit and description of locality', Michele Finizia, 6 October 1879.
[99] ASR, TCPR, 1879, b. 3659, vol. IA, f. 3, 'Visit and description of locality', Michele Finizia, 6 October 1879.
[100] ASR, TCPR, 1879, b. 3659, vol. IA, Finizia's 'Compendio'.
[101] ASR, TCPR, 1879, b. 3659, vol. IA, f. 45, a detailed list of Fadda's belongings.
[102] ASR, TCPR, 1879, b. 3659, vol. IA, Finizia's 'Compendio'.

Another of the documents that must have piqued Finizia's imagination was an official certificate, produced at Fadda's request, in Cagliari in October 1871. This was five months after his marriage to Saraceni. The certificate attested to the fact that twelve years earlier, during 1859's battle of San Martino, a key moment in Italy's wars of independence, Fadda had been hit in the groin by a bullet. This had wounded him seriously in the left testicle and thigh.[103] As Finizia walked away from the scene of the crime with his clutch of documents, he might well have aspired to keep his emotional reactions separate from his reasoning, and to keep fact from fiction. But he must also have been deeply affected, and his report indicates that at the very least he was intrigued by what was yet to be discovered between the lines of Fadda's life story.

The next day Finizia had to attend to a more dolorous and concrete task than pondering ideas about the victim's life. It was the matter of identifying Fadda's body and witnessing a post-mortem to determine the exact cause of death.[104] These procedures began at 9 a.m. on Monday 7 October, in the mortuary of the hospital where Fadda had died. Few spaces could be as emotionally distinctive an arena as the morgue, but historians, even those interested in death, have rarely lingered in them.[105] There, the stark finality of Fadda's death was laid out for those who needed to see it, whether for legal or personal reasons. The cadaver lay on a slab of marble, under a sheet which, when lifted, revealed a 'piteous spectacle'.[106] But the autopsy was not the occasion for those present to release their sorrow. The space imposed restraint, its function above all forensic in the modern sense. It was designed for the gathering of information that would underpin the judicial, rhetorical, or merely bureaucratic processes that were to follow. It entailed not, as would unfold in court later, the reconstruction of a human narrative, but rather, the systematic analysis of Fadda's corpse, to compile a body of scientific evidence.

Finizia, various officials from Fadda's regiment, hospital officials, and others—perhaps a journalist or two—observed the process.[107] If members of Fadda's family had been there to identify the body, perhaps there would have been displays of grief such as tears and touching farewell kisses. For unknown reasons, however,

---

[103] ASR, TCPR, 1879, b. 3659, vol. IA, f. 14, certificate attesting to Fadda's war injuries (inflicted 24 June 1859), dated Cagliari, 2 October 1871.

[104] Ariès, in *The Hour of our Death* (1974), stresses the medicalization of death from the eighteenth century, pp. 353–68; in *The Work of the Dead*, Laqueur vividly describes the autopsy's rising prestige late in the eighteenth century (pp. 337–58), as well as recalling his own fascination when his pathologist father was called during dinner to go and do 'a post' (p. ix).

[105] Ariès stressed the profound impact that pre-modern anatomy rooms, often attached to a chapel, had on the popular imagination of the period (*The Hour of our Death*, p. 367); Stearns (in *Revolutions in Sorrow*) and Laqueur (in *The Work of the Dead*) have surprisingly little to say about the modern morgue.

[106] 'La sezione del capitano Fadda', *Gazetta della Capitale*, 8 October 1878, p. 3.

[107] 'Piccolo Corriere di Roma', *L'Opinione*, 8 October 1878, p. 2. Various journalistic accounts described the post-mortem as if the authors were eye witnesses, but the official report, ASR, TCPR, 1879, b. 3659, vol. IA, ff. 47–55, 'Verbale di visita, descrizione, ricognizione, e perizia di cadavere', noted those present without mentioning journalists.

no family members were present, and it is unlikely that any intimate gestures were made. The post-mortem report described the body as appearing to be about thirty-five years old (Fadda was in fact thirty-seven), of 1.6 metres in stature, covered in blood, with brown eyes still open, black hair 'a little thin on the top', and a black moustache. The task of formal recognition fell to two of Fadda's military comrades. One was Benigno Menni, who had been by Fadda's side throughout his final hour of life. The two soldiers declared that the cadaver 'had belonged when alive' to Captain Giovanni Fadda. Their recognition was 'based on cordial relations of friendship for some years'. That the corpse 'had belonged' was printed on the bureaucratic form, only the variable parts of which were filled in by hand.[108] The phraseology drew attention to the notion that the soulless cadaver and Giovanni Fadda were now separate entities: the body was, as Thomas Laqueur put it memorably, 'the lifeless matter from which a human had fled'.[109]

The autopsy itself sought answers to the question of how, and perhaps even why, Giovanni Fadda had been forced to flee his body in such an untimely and brutal fashion. After the cadaver's identity was confirmed, one of the three medical doctors attending proceeded to inspect the body's wounds, carefully measuring each one and recording the details. He counted a total of twenty-three, listing and describing each one individually. Wounds '1, 2, and 3', on the face, were judged to have been made by a human hand, consonant with an attempt to stifle the victim's cries during the attack. Eighteen were made by a 'knife, dagger, or similar'. The final two did not merit detailed description.[110] In fact only three of the wounds were judged to have been fatal: two to the chest that perforated a lung; and one to the thigh that severed an artery.[111] Nevertheless, the sum total of twenty-three wounds became a byword, in official rhetoric and the public imagination, for the assassin's brutal determination to force Fadda to flee from his body.

After the wounds had been carefully recorded and the cause of death discussed, the autopsy took an unusual turn. The investigating magistrate, no doubt alerted by the medical certificate he had found on Fadda's desk, asked the doctor to examine the cadaver's sexual organs. Confirming the certificate's claim about Fadda's war wounds, a jagged scar five millimetres in length was noted on the scrotum. The surgeon also remarked that one testicle appeared to be very small. He then slit open the scrotum and pulled it aside, revealing that the left testicle was indeed atrophied, to the size of 'half a hazelnut', while the other was normal. The doctor then took a further step. With a 'circular incision near the pubic bone', he 'separated the penis from the body and removed it, together with the bladder

---

[108] ASR, TCPR, 1879, b. 3659, vol. IA, ff. 47–55, autopsy report.
[109] Laqueur, *The Work of the Dead*, p. 1.
[110] ASR, TCPR, 1879, b. 3659, vol. IA, ff. 47–55, autopsy report.
[111] 'Piccolo Corriere di Roma', *L'Opinione*, 8 October 1878, p. 2.

to which it was attached'. Making a long cut down to the very centreline of the penis, the doctor 'explored the urethra along its full length'.[112]

This procedure revealed a 'marked organic restriction' at the crucial point where the spermatozoa produced by Fadda's one functional testicle should have entered his urethra, at the 'verumontanum' (now known as the seminal colliculus).[113] Having asked the doctors to investigate this area of Fadda's body, it is almost certain that the magistrate inquired about the implications for Fadda's sexual potency and reproductive ability. Both would have been compromised at the very least: a bullet in the groin could easily have caused nerve damage, resulting in erectile problems. And even if Fadda had not been impotent, it is likely that his spermatozoa would have been thwarted by the 'organic restriction' they encountered as they sought to enter his seminal fluid, resulting in sterility.[114] But if such a conversation took place, it was not recorded. More likely, Finizia filed this delicate information away mentally, to be drawn upon later, and only if strictly necessary.

If the several male officials observing the dissection of Fadda's sexual organs experienced aversion or horror, such feelings did not leave impressions in the autopsy report or travel beyond the mortuary. The men observed the process in the cool emotional arena of the morgue, apparently detached from feeling. If any emotions left archival traces, there is a certain pride to be discerned in the neatness of the 'circular incision' and the intactness of the anatomical assemblage as it was extracted. But as a professional space, the hospital's mortuary imposed the same genre of emotional self-control that Fadda himself had embodied in life. The report remains factual, the scientific tone oblivious to the dramatic potential of a murdered corpse. There is certainly pathos in the description of the cadaver, with its open unseeing eyes, and a touch of tenderness might even be conveyed in the comment that the corpse's hair was a little thin on top. But these are most likely to have been straightforward observations, ultimately reinforcing the sense of professional neutrality that pervades the entire report.

By contrast to the emotionally restrained atmosphere of the morgue, in the much more public forum represented by the newspapers, every drop of dramatic potential was squeezed from Fadda's post-mortem procedure. The *Gazzetta della Capitale*'s article, longer than those of other newspapers at seventy-three lines, is the most notable example. It vividly described the 'piteous spectacle of a body that was young, beautiful, at the peak of its strength, riddled with wounds'. The corpse epitomized the tragically truncated life of a martyr. Not content with a still-life portrait, the journalist asserted that on Fadda's body could be 'read, lesion by lesion…the details of the horrible tragedy'. In a way that the post-mortem report itself carefully eschewed, the journalist brought out the emotional potential

---

[112] ASR, TCPR, 1879, b. 3659, vol. IA, ff. 47–55, autopsy report.
[113] ASR, TCPR, 1879, b. 3659, vol. IA, ff. 47–55, autopsy report.
[114] I am grateful to Dr Yusuf Cakmak, of the University of Otago's Department of Anatomy, for helping me decipher this section of the autopsy report and clarifying the implications of Fadda's wounds.

of Fadda's corpse by presenting it as a narrative, even a text. But the article stopped short of describing the post-mortem's final exploration.[115]

If the essence of narrative drama lies in the careful trickling out of detail, a few days later the *Gazzetta della Capitale* took matters a step further in relation to the autopsy. A brief report, appearing at the end of the day's news on the Fadda case on Friday 11 October, added a tantalizing 'last particular' not noted by any other newspapers: the investigation of a wound in Fadda's genital area that 'had certainly offended the Potency of the captain.'[116] The journalist surmised that Fadda's wounded genitals were the 'origin of the *freddezza* [coldness] between husband and wife' and concluded confidently that 'This particularity will exercise more than a little influence over the trial.'[117] Even in death, questions of eros would not go away. The *Gazzetta della Capitale* was correct to predict that ultimately the question of whether Captain Fadda was sexually potent would influence the trial.

A few days after the murder, Fadda's sexual capacity was not yet a matter that had made its way to the forefront of official or public concern. The emergence of the word *freddezza* may have been a conscious echo of news or even just gossip about how Raffaella herself reacted to her husband's death. Contemporary details are scant, but early in the investigation, Michele Finizia ordered Raffaella's arrest in far-off Calabria. On Wednesday 9 October, two officers stationed in Cassano went to the Saraceni household, where they found 'la Fadda', in company with her father, mother, and brother. The family must surely have known by this stage that Fadda had been murdered, but the report of arrest does not mention that. It only says that Raffaella seemed 'serene' and asked where she would be taken.[118] Later, the 'serenity' demonstrated by Raffaella was interpreted as coldness, and the guard who had arrested her elaborated on her surprising lack of emotional expression upon hearing that her husband was dead.[119] Her serenity in the face of his death was later to be interpreted as a chilling emotional deficit.

## Fadda's Funeral

Fadda's life had been brought to a violent end in a way that provoked a welter of emotional responses that were more complex, and more publicized, than most deaths due to age or illness. Arguably, those responses were commensurate with the untimely death of a still-promising Italian state official who had clearly sacrificed much for the sake of the nation on the battlefield. After the necessary

---

[115] 'La sezione del capitano Fadda', *Gazzetta della Capitale*, 8 October 1878, p. 3.
[116] 'Cronaca cittadina', *Gazzetta della Capitale*, 11 October 1878, p. 2.
[117] 'Cronaca cittadina', *Gazzetta della Capitale*, 11 October 1878, p. 2.
[118] ASR, TCPR, 1879, b. 3659, vol. IA, f. 113, report of arrest of Raffaella Saraceni, 9 October 1878. A more elaborate and somewhat different account was provided by one of the guards some two months later, as indicated in the next note.
[119] ASR, TCPR, 1879, b. 3659, vol. II, ff. 327–8, statement by Michelangelo Chiodi, the guard in charge of the arrest of Raffaella Saraceni, provided on 26 December 1878.

forensic evidence had been gathered through the careful examination of his corpse, the grief of friends, colleagues, and the general public found an arena of concerted expression in Fadda's funeral. Several newspapers announced that the procession would depart from the hospital at 9 a.m. on Tuesday 8 October 1878, and would proceed along the Roman Forum, down the Via Alessandrina through Fadda's old neighbourhood, to Trajan's Forum, then up the Via Nazionale—the splendid new street built to mark the unification of Italy—and along Via San Lorenzo to Rome's main cemetery, Campo Verano, on the outskirts of the city.[120]

In a sense, Fadda's funeral ceremony was a miniature replay of the great procession that had taken place nine months earlier for King Victor Emmanuel II. It was heavily inflected with a sense of ritual that was a combination of both secular and Catholic liturgies. Before the procession departed, a mass was said, and priests carrying a cross headed the subsequent procession. On a carriage pulled by two horses, four soldiers of the same rank as Fadda kept watch over his coffin. On it had been placed Fadda's tunic, his kepi, and his sword. Observers could clearly see Fadda's three medals of military valour, attached to the breast of the dark blue tunic.[121] The newspaper *Il Bersagliere* reported that the coffin was also decorated with an evergreen wreath, which carried the words 'To Giovanni Fadda. His Fellow Citizens', in this case meaning his compatriot Sardinians.[122] The paper mentioned that the bands of various regiments accompanied the procession with suitably military marches, and the streets were densely crowded with onlookers.[123]

The procession was slow, burdened with shared sentiment. Newspapers reported that the procession consisted of an 'imposing number' of military officials, but also a crowd of citizens of all types.[124] They came together to form a distinctive emotional arena that exhibited a strange mixture of grief, indignation, military precision, and musical exuberance. Such processions, albeit with cultural variations, remain recognizable and powerful in a wide variety of cultures today. The marchers did not necessarily all know Fadda, but there was 'universal expression of intense sorrow' over 'the tragic, wretched death of a soldier who had served the nation and risked his life in nearly all the battles for Italian independence'.[125] The rhetorical key was clearly that of both the Catholic and patriotic notion of the 'sacrificial death'.[126]

A sense of bitterness about Fadda's death and the waste of life it represented were also very much to the fore. The *Gazzetta*, nearly always a touch more emotive in its reporting than other newspapers, commented on the number of notable

---

[120] 'L'assassinio del capitano Fadda', *Il Bersagliere*, 8 October 1878, p. 3.
[121] 'Piccolo corriere', *L'Opinione*, 9 October 1878, p. 2.
[122] 'Ancora dei funerali del capitano Fadda', *Il Bersagliere*, 10 October 1878, p. 2. The previous day this and other newspapers claimed the wreath was from his immediate colleagues. This report corrected that mis-attribution.
[123] 'Funerali del capitano Fadda', *Il Bersagliere*, 9 October 1878, p. 2.
[124] 'Funerali del capitano Fadda', *Il Bersagliere*, 9 October 1878, p. 2.
[125] 'Piccolo corriere', *L'Opinione*, 9 October 1878, p. 2.
[126] Malone, *Architecture, Death and Nationhood*, p. 128.

citizens who took part in the procession. It reported that 'everyone took off their hats, showing visible signs of commiseration and indignation about the assassination.'[127] Perhaps they would have done this for any funeral, but there is good reason to believe that the distressing circumstances of Fadda's death had particularly touched everyone who witnessed the procession in a particular way, as a tragic event rather than an inevitable one.

The funeral may have begun with a mass, but it culminated with a secular and poignant speech at the cemetery gates, delivered by one of Fadda's close friends, fellow Sardinian Girolamo Carta. His words acknowledge that Fadda's surviving relatives did not attend the funeral (for reasons unknown), but they also capture the sense of loss, both personal and to the nation, represented by his premature death:

> If silence is a potent manifestation of the pain of great misfortune, often a word is necessary to ease the pain from the souls of those afflicted.
>
> The word I have to say today is *addio, addio* to you, our *amatissimo*. It is a great comfort to say *addio* to your body, but this comfort is not to be had by his nearest and dearest.
>
> A few days ago he was alive and among us, and now he is no longer. He was so young in years yet so old in experience of life.
>
> A man who exposes his life in battle does not need a eulogy. His wounds at San Martino earned him promotion, an honourable mention of his valour, and a French medal. Justice must be done, even though we're not the type to claim vendetta.
>
> He is missed terribly by his family, his colleagues, his dear father.
>
> To the disconsolate family, let there be some comfort in the distant echo that will come from the immense pain that has been inflicted on the entire citizenry, a pain even more sharply felt by those who were colleagues and friends.
>
> Poor Fadda, we who so often spent time together easing life's bitter moments, may your lovely soul find peace.[128]

Carta's words gave shape to the tragedy of the moment, and they held out hope for the secular redemption offered by justice. After this 'moving salute', as a newspaper reporter put it, 'the ceremony dissolved.'[129] With this the funeral had done its work, providing a finite structure for the acute emotions generated by Fadda's death, and laying to rest the 'lifeless matter from which a human had fled'.

---

[127] 'Cronaca cittadina', *Gazzetta della Capitale*, 9 October 1878, p. 3.
[128] This is an abbreviated account of Carta's speech, reported in full by *Il Bersagliere*, 'Ancora dei funerali del capitano Fadda', 10 October 1878, p. 2.
[129] 'Ancora dei funerali del capitano Fadda', *Il Bersagliere*, 10 October 1878, p. 2.

## Conclusion

Scholars have shown how the rituals that develop around death provide culturally specific frameworks for grief. In terms of the paradigm that informs this book, those rituals involve a variety of emotional arenas, each with a particular tenor. The deaths of three very different figures in Italy in 1877 and 1878 allow us not only to visualize emotional arenas in action, but in two cases to discern political and cultural tides moulding the boundaries of these arenas. This probably applied least in the case of Fadda's mother's death, which is likely to have been marked quite traditionally. It is possible to envisage the intense and intimate suffering of her husband and two sons while they kept vigil during her final hours, but of the funeral itself we know nothing.

The emotional arenas of Signora Fadda's death are likely to have represented tradition rather than cultural change, but this we certainly begin to see in the deaths of King Victor Emmanuel II and Giovanni Fadda himself. The imposing spectacle of the king's funeral has attracted so much scholarly attention partly because it was perceived as remarkable by contemporaries. The city of Rome was consciously converted into a distinctive emotional arena by features such as the boom of a cannon every sixty seconds, the endless procession, the horses, the intense emotion, 'all perfectly controlled', as Levra put it. This was a new state using the death of a great figure to occupy emotional territory that was previously the exclusive domain of the Catholic Church. The funeral's organizers carefully studied the 'emotional arenas' wrought previously by such events in France and elsewhere in their quest to do the same in Italy.

Nine months later, Fadda's own funeral was a miniature replay of the king's ceremonial pageant. Though a mass was said at the beginning, the religious element was balanced if not eclipsed by the military notes of the marching band, and the essentially secular tenor of Carta's final farewell. Prior to that, the disciplined emotional style of professional men of science—whether instructing magistrates gathering evidence or doctors dissecting Fadda's corpse in the morgue—signalled that liberal Italy's emotional values were on their way to supplanting those of the Catholic regime it had supplanted.

For Fadda's predecessors in death—his own mother, the king of Italy, or anyone else who died of natural causes—the funeral was the final distinctly discernible emotional arena staged around a particular life. Commemorative echoes might continue, but their emotional intensity was softened by the course of time. In Fadda's case though, as Carta had noted, the redemption of justice had yet to be found. Important as the funeral undoubtedly was in marking the conclusion of his life, Fadda's soul would not truly be laid to rest until after he had been resurrected in a final arena of distinctive emotional tenor: the court of law.

# 5
# Arena or Temple?
## The Trial in Rome's Court of Assizes

Murder trials, if held to the light at the proper angle, are an almost unexcelled mirror of an epoch's mores.[1]

King Victor Emmanuel II's death marked a key stage for a national cult of heroes in whose pantheon even the unfortunate martyr Giovanni Fadda found a momentary place. As shown in chapter 4, historians have interpreted the energy invested by governing elites in commemorating such figures as an expression of the need to foster emotional allegiance to the new polity of Liberal Italy. In short, once the poetry of the Risorgimento gave way to the prosaic politics of unified Italy, the governing classes felt the need for ongoing commitment from the public more urgently than ever. The famous phrase 'We have made Italy, now we must make Italians', apocryphally attributed to Risorgimento patriot Massimo D'Azeglio in the 1860s,[2] endured because it captured the need to bond Italians by sentiment as well as by geopolitical formalities. Ritualistic commemorations of heroes and martyrs were one notable strategy for conjuring national feeling.[3] But more regular rituals for making Italians were also needed.

Beyond the occasional liturgy of state funerals, Italy was slow to develop a repertoire of 'spectacle, imagery and display', as Christopher Duggan put it, designed to conquer a public whose emotional loyalties were unevenly divided between local, spiritual, and national claims. The tardiness can partly be explained by the state's peculiar coexistence with a Church that continued to hold a monopoly over the sort of ritualistic traditions that generate feelings of social cohesion and mutual belonging. Long after unification the Church continued to dominate the spectacles and pageantry that were proven tools for sustaining popular allegiance, from weekly Mass to saints' days and processions. By the 1870s, some Risorgimento patriots were losing hope that Mazzini's dream of a secular religion founded on

---

[1] Eleanor Gordon and Gwyneth Nair, *Murder and Morality in Victorian Britain: The Story of Madeleine Smith* (Manchester: Manchester University Press, 2009), p. 5.

[2] Silvana Patriarca, *Italian Vices: Nation and Character from the Risorgimento to the Republic* (Cambridge: Cambridge University Press, 2010), p. 51.

[3] Merridee L. Bailey and Katie Barclay, 'Emotion, Ritual and Power: From Family to Nation', in *Emotion, Ritual and Power in Europe, 1200–1920: Family, State and Church*, edited by Merridee L. Bailey and Katie Barclay (Basingstoke: Palgrave Macmillan, 2017), p. 4.

the nation would ever displace the Church's influence.⁴ As for the physical staging of nationally inflected occasions, Liberal Italy had few if any arenas that it could claim as its own. This was particularly the case in Rome, the capital from late 1870, where the Catholic Church enjoyed a symbolic hegemony established over more than a thousand years.

This chapter portrays Rome's Court of Assizes during the trial for Giovanni Fadda's murder as an emotional arena par excellence, and one whose ownership could be claimed by Liberal Italy. After unification, courts all over the emerging nation were opened to the public, in some cases for the first time. The public audience in legal hearings, especially in criminal cases, was a fundamental tenet of Italy's liberal ideology, a symbol of its achievement of modern civilization.⁵ My analysis examines public participation in the Fadda trial against the background of a state's need to engage its citizens in rituals that were unmistakably identified with the nation. Exciting trials shot through with human drama offered particular potential in this area, even if, in contrast to state funerals, engagement with the state at an emotional level was not the ostensible aim of the proceedings.

The Fadda trial offered the state an opportunity to engage the public in its processes that it did not intend to miss. Official enthusiasm for wide public participation is underlined by work undertaken to install a large amount of extra seating in Rome's already capacious Court of Assizes prior to the trial's commencement.⁶ Clearly, the state expected, and tacitly encouraged, participation by a large crowd. On the other hand, there was tension between such trials' potential to generate this precious 'collective effervescence'—posited by Emile Durkheim in 1912 as the basis of social cohesion⁷—and the quasi-sacred role of law in a regime based on liberal ideology. These tensions were very evident during the trial for Fadda's murder, which, along with similar examples, gave rise to intense debates about the public's place in criminal justice that continued for decades.⁸ Sacrosanct as the principle of wide participation was, many felt that the public's very presence could threaten the sacred dignity of the law itself.

The law became particularly sacred in states that consciously untethered themselves from the Church and sought a secular basis for their legitimacy. In France

---

⁴ Christopher Duggan, *The Force of Destiny: A History of Italy since 1796* (London: Allen Lane, 2007), pp. 292–3.
⁵ Gian Marco Vidor, 'The Press, the Audience, and Emotions in Italian Courtrooms (1860s–1910s)', *Journal of Social History*, vol. 51 no. 2 (2017): 231–54, here p. 247.
⁶ 'Processo Fadda', *Corriere della Sera* (Milan), 30 September 1879, p. 2; *Gazzetta Piemontese* (Turin), 28 September 1879, p. 1, col. 5, refers to 'great preparations' in the court to accommodate public and journalists; 'Il processo Fadda', *Gazzetta Piemontese*, 1 October 1879, p. 3, claims the court 'had to be transformed', with the construction of new seating to accommodate the public. Such arrangements were mentioned in several other newspapers. I thank Cristina Bon for prompting me to think about the significance of these arrangements.
⁷ Emile Durkheim, *The Elementary Forms of Religious Life*, trans. Karen E. Fields (New York: The Free Press, 1995[1912]), pp. 217–20.
⁸ Vidor, 'The Press, the Audience, and Emotions', 231–54.

after the Revolution of 1789, for example, the law's importance was reflected in the fact that courts were styled as *temples de la loi*.⁹ Similarly, for Italians after unification, a court was often referred to as a *tempio della legge* (a temple of law). But in all places where criminal trials were public affairs, there was a risk that the law could be desecrated by the banal theatrical drama of trial narratives. The degree of emotional arousal generated by a trial could determine whether a court of law was perceived as a rowdy arena or a sacred temple. As we will see, in the 1870s, the neophyte Italian state was still in the process of establishing a suitable balance between these elements. The Fadda trial oscillated between the politically tempting appeal of a court as a popular arena, and protection of the law's dignity through rules of emotional expression more akin to those of a religious temple.

Many perceived from the outset that the trial for Captain Fadda's murder had unusual potential to elicit strong public sentiment. As well as the story behind the crime, other aspects compounded the public's engagement. Most obviously, criminal trials open to the public were still a novelty in Rome. They had only replaced the closed inquisitorial system of the papal regime in 1871, after the city was taken over by the Italian state. The courtroom was thus still a relatively new public space in the ancient city. Its freshness offered valuable opportunities for the staging of Duggan's triad of 'spectacle, imagery, and display' in a way that was exclusively associated with the city's new government.

In a context where the local audience was still somewhat unfamiliar with sensational trials, the state's challenge in causes célèbres such as the hearing for Fadda's murder was to temper the rousing draw of sensationalism with the imposition of procedural sobriety. Rome's Court of Assizes in October 1879 exemplified a novel social space where questions about whether the emotional relationship between the state and the people should be staged in a sacred temple, or a bread-and-circuses arena, were themselves explored and tested. Such questions formed a subtext to the narrative of the hearing. The self-conscious new state used the mirror of the murder trial not only to explore and adjudicate the epoch's mores, but to reflect its own existence out into the world, and to draw the public to participate emotionally in a prestigious arena of liberal ideology.

## Arena for Liberalism, or Colosseum Revisited?

The courtroom may have been a new arena in Roma *capitale*, but its gravitas was nourished by ancient symbolic roots. The Roman public, excluded from participation in the justice system for well over fifteen centuries, could nevertheless draw on memories of their city's great tradition of open trials. Many of those trials had taken place on the very stones of the Forum over which Fadda's dying body had been

---

⁹ Robert Badinter, 'Preface', in *La justice en ses temples. Regards sur l'architecture judiciare en France* (Paris: Editions Errance, 1992), p. 11.

carried in October 1878. The reintroduction of public trials in the new capital in 1871 could be seen as the revival of a venerable form of Roman theatre.[10] In the 1870s as in ancient times, trials offered women, who continued to be largely excluded from the Italian public sphere after unification, one of the few forms of participation available to them in the nation's official life.[11] Women and men of all classes, whose collective responses constituted a newly prestigious 'public opinion', welcomed trials as an opportunity to participate in the procedures of the nation-state.[12]

The trial for Fadda murder began in Rome's Court of Assizes on the last day of September 1879, after months of painstaking enquiry and several false starts. Members of the public were transfixed by the elements of the story they already knew, and many were intent upon witnessing its protagonists in the flesh. While public demand to participate in the trial far exceeded the space available (even after the increase in seating), how members of the public gained admission is less certain. Some newspaper reporters made passing references to the way the public, particularly Rome's women, 'exercised every shred of influence they possessed in order to obtain a ticket', suggesting that there was some sort of ticketing system.[13] And after the trial, the Minister of Justice himself was angered by rumours of 'first and second class tickets' being sold for the extra seats constructed.[14] Unfortunately, no hints of how those tickets might have been distributed has come to light. What is beyond doubt though, is that the trial generated a great desire to be part of it among the public.

For those who were not fortunate enough to witness the proceedings in person, newspapers, both national and international, provided regular and rousing accounts. Though the trial represented an excellent opportunity for public engagement with the state, and for newspapers an opportunity to increase sales, many observers were discomfited by the whole affair. It would not be going too far to say that the trial represented a moment of cultural panic. Pessimistic observers quickly interpreted the sensational spectacle as a modern version of the corrupt extravaganzas of the city's famous arenas at the peak of imperial Roman decadence. The view is exemplified by the 'national poet', Giosuè Carducci. At the height of the trial, his poem, *A proposito del caso Fadda* (*About the Fadda Case*), was published on the front page of the *Fanfulla della domenica*, a prestigious cultural newspaper.

---

[10] Leanne Bablitz, in *Actors and Audience in the Roman Courtroom* (Routledge: London, 2007), p. 1, stresses that trials in ancient Rome were public gatherings with strong elements of performance and spectacle. See also Sophia Papaioannou, Andreas Serafim, and Beatrice Da Vela (eds), *The Theatre of Justice: Aspects of Performance in Greco-Roman Oratory and Rhetoric* (Leiden: Brill, 2017), esp. Jon Hall, 'Roman Judges and their participation in the "Theatre of Justice"', pp. 243–62. Thanks to Jon Hall for sharing this source prior to publication.

[11] Valeria P. Babini, *Il caso Murri. Una storia italiana* (Bologna: Il Mulino, 2004), p. 150.

[12] Angela Groppi, 'Il teatro della giustizia. Donne colpevoli e opinione pubblica nell'Italia Liberale', *Quaderni Storici*, vol. 37, no. 111 (2002): 649–79, here p. 652.

[13] 'Il processo Fadda', *Gazzetta Piemontese*, 1 October 1879, p. 1; 2 October 1879, p. 1; 17 October 1879, p. 1.

[14] Giovanni Battista Varè, 'Circolare 3 Novembre 1879. Giudizi innanzi alle Corti d'Assise', *Raccolta circolari emanate dal Ministero di Grazia e Giustizia e dei Culti, anni 1871 al 1880*, vol. 2 (Rome: Regia Tipografia, 1881), pp. 1172–4, here p. 1174.

It particularly apostrophized the female audience, whom the grand poet likened to the bloodthirsty Roman matrons of antiquity:[15]

I.
Da i gradi alti del circo ammantellati
    di porpora, esse ritte
ne i lunghi bissi, gli occhi dilatati,
    le pupille in giù fitte,
abbassavano il pollice nervoso
    de la mano gentile.
Ardea tra bianche nuvole estuoso
    il sol primaverile
su le superbe, e ne la nera chioma
    Mettea lampeggiamenti.
Fremea la lupa nutrice di Roma
    Da i lor piccoli denti,
bianchi, affilati, tra le labbra rosse
    contratte in fiero ghigno.
Un selvatico odor su da le fosse
    vaporava maligno.
Era il sangue del mondo che fervea
    con lievito mortale,
su cui provava già Nemesi dea
    al vol prossimo l'ale.
E le nipoti di Camilla, pria
    di cedere le mani
ai ferri, assaporavan l'agonia
    de' cerulei Germani.

II.
Voi sgretolate, o belle, i pasticcini
    fra il palco e la galera;
ed intente a fornir di cittadini
    la nuova italica èra,
studiate (o professor Giovanni Rizzi,
    anche questo è ideale)

I.
From their prime seats in the circus
    wide-eyed women, draped in purple,
sitting stiffly upright in their long robes,
    and gazing at the scene below,
nervously turned down the thumbs
    of their fine hands.
Blazing through white clouds
    the spring sun
glared down on the proud women,
    flashing like lightning in their black hair.
Rome's she-wolf raged
    through their fine white teeth,
sharp between red lips
    taught in a proud sneer.
From the pit rose
    a savage, malicious smell.
It was the blood of the world, seething
    with deadly ferment,
over which the goddess Nemesis
    had already beat her wings.
And Camilla's nieces, prior
    to giving their hands to the chains,
savoured the agony
    of the blue-eyed Huns.

II.
You crumble, o beauties, your pastries
    between stage and prison;
and, intent on providing
    the new Italic age with citizens,
you study (oh Professor Giovanni Rizzi,
    this too is the Ideal)

---

[15] Giosuè Carducci, 'A proposito del caso Fadda', *Il Fanfulla della domenica* (Rome), 19 October 1879, p. 1. This was the weekly cultural supplement to Rome's widely read daily, *Fanfulla*, also owned by E. E. Oblieght. Carducci, hailed as the 'Poet of the Third Italy', was appointed to a chair in Italian literature at the University of Bologna in 1860, aged twenty-five. See Paul Arpaia, 'Constructing a National Identity from a Created Literary Past: Giosuè Carducci and the Development of a National Literature', *Journal of Modern Italian Studies*, vol. 7, no. 2 (2002): 192–214.

| | |
|---|---|
| gli abbracciamenti de' cavallerizzi | the embraces of circus horsemen |
|    fra i colpi di pugnale; |    between the thrusts of the dagger; |
| e palpate con gli occhi abbracciatori | and fondle with caressing gazes |
|    le schiene ed i toraci, |    their backs and torsos, |
| mentre rei gerghi tra sucidi odori | while guilty tongues and lurid odours |
|    testimonian su i baci. |    testify to their kisses. |
| Poi, se un puttin di marmo avvien che mostri | Then, if a marble angel happens to bare |
|    qualcosellina al sole, |    a little something to the light of day |
| protesterete con furor d'inchiostri, | you'd protest with storms of ink, |
|    con fulmin di parole; |    with thunderbolts of words; |
| e pur ieri cullaste il figliuoletto | though yesterday, amid nocturnal spectres |
|    tra i notturni fantasmi |    you rocked your little baby |
| co'l piè male proteso fuor del letto | with foot wickedly stretched from the bed |
|    ne gli adulteri spasmi. |    in adulterous spasms. |
| Ma voi siete cristiane, o Maddalene! | But you are Christians, oh Magdalenes! |
|    Foste dai preti a scuola. |    You were schooled by priests. |
| Siete moderne! avete ne le vene | You are modern! You have in your veins |
|    L'Aretino e il Loiola.[16] |    Aretino and Loyola. |

What chagrined Carducci and his ilk was the irony that even educated Italians, conscious of the liberal advances represented by the unification, were so easily seduced by spectacles reminiscent of ancient times. Emotional gratification, Carducci felt, too easily eclipsed reason, restraint, and decorum. Furthermore, the influx of women to the public had, in his view, only exacerbated the tendency. He thought women's attraction to the trial demonstrated their appetite for intense emotions and thus their unfitness for the public sphere. Carducci conveniently overlooked the fact that men, including many notables, were just as fascinated. The poem is one of many historic traces of a certain disorientation about the appropriate emotional tone for such an event. The confusion was epitomized more prosaically by a journalist for Naples' *Il Piccolo*, an established conservative-liberal newspaper. Having himself reported enthusiastically on the trial for nearly a month, the journalist summed up the event as having debased the 'temple of justice' to the level of a circus.[17]

The spectacle of the trial, and the excitement it prompted, have attracted keen analyses by modern scholars, most notably Angela Groppi and Thomas Simpson. Both foreground Carducci's poem for the way it crystallized elements of anxiety

---

[16] The poem appears with a slight variation of wording and layout in subsequent published versions. I have referred to both the original in the *Fanfulla della Domenica* and the version reproduced in *Processo Fadda illustrato. Dibattimento alla Corte d'Assise di Roma dal 30 settembre al 31 ottobre 1879* (Rome: Giovanni Bracco Editore, 1879), p. 144. I thank Virginia Jewiss and Jon Hall for assistance with the translation and classical references.

[17] 'Le ultime ore del processo Fadda', *Il Piccolo. Giornale politico della sera* (Naples), 31 October 1879, p. 1. Grateful thanks to Teresa Volpe of Rome's Biblioteca Nazionale Centrale for arranging special access to this very fragile volume.

about the event, particularly in relation to the highly feminized audience. Groppi emphasizes the gender questions thrown into relief by the new legal procedures of unified Italy. Central to her analysis are the complex relationships between women on trial and the novel role of women in the formation of 'public opinion'.[18] Simpson's account, on the other hand, focuses on the role of a new capital's nascent media, only recently able to claim limelight on the national stage. In order to boost sales and gain national profile among as broad a reading public as possible, Rome's newspapers fanned the already strong flames of public curiosity about the Fadda trial.[19] The result, according to Simpson, was a 'spectacle of distortion' that became a prototype for later 'media circus trials' in Italy.[20]

The month-long trial, its local allure, and its national reverberations, still deserve further analysis and evaluation: there is more to be discerned about the epoch's mores—and its emotional values—in the mirror of the murder trial. Like Carducci himself, previous analyses tend to take for granted that the hearing quickly fell into bacchanalian excesses. The trial has been portrayed as an event barely contained within the bounds of civility by a neophyte, almost inept state. It is true that unlike Britain or France, for example, Italy did not yet have great experience in conducting such events. It may also be true that in some respects this lack of state and public experience became evident during the Fadda case. However, the trial was conducted without serious mishap or miscarriage, even if its duration, complexity, and cost left it open to critique. Viewed symbolically, it could even be regarded as a spectacle of success for a neophyte state in search of a public.

Moreover, as research on trials in Britain, France, and the United States has shown, the enormous surges of public emotion thrown up from time to time by criminal trials could prove challenging even in more mature political contexts.[21] Without denying the Fadda trial's problematic elements, an eye on the broader historical background and a focus on the emotions generated locally by the Fadda trial support a more positive interpretation of the way the new state conducted the process. It is perhaps too easy to be critical of the sensation sparked by a trial that exposed to public gaze a slain Risorgimento hero of sadly compromised virility, a sexually desirous wife for whom merely thinking of Italy was not enough, and a virile horseman who came to her rescue with his adopted sister-lover in tow. It may have seemed a plot from an Italian opera, but such a story would have sparked a media circus anywhere in the world.

---

[18] Groppi, 'Il teatro della giustizia,' pp. 651–2.

[19] Thomas Simpson, *Murder and Media in the New Rome: The Fadda Affair* (New York: Palgrave Macmillan, 2010), throughout but for example. p. 32, p. 206.

[20] Simpson, *Murder and Media in the New Rome*, p. 2.

[21] See for example Gordon and Nair, *Murder and Morality in Victorian Britain*; Thomas Cragin, *Murder in Parisian Streets: Manufacturing Crime and Justice in the Popular Press, 1830–1890* (Lewisburg, PA: Bucknell University Press, 2006); and Patricia Cline Cohen, *The Murder of Helen Jewett: The Life and Death of a Prostitute in Nineteenth-Century New York* (New York: Alfred Knopf, 1999).

Rome's Court of Assizes in October 1879 was as an arena that the public quite understandably perceived as a thrilling and perhaps confusing kaleidoscope of earlier emotionally charged spaces: an opera theatre; a circus arena; a confessional box turned inside out; all within the new sacred temple of law. The state, eager to 'make Italians', had something to gain from the public's interest, even as it sought to maintain the decorum required by one of its most prestigious institutions. The courtroom which staged the trial for Fadda's murder was both a temple of liberal principles and an emotional arena that resounded with cultural echoes—of ancient Roman extravaganzas, of lofty Catholic churches, of dramatic operas, and even of contemporary circuses. Contextualizing the Fadda trial against the Italian public's emotional expectations, it becomes less anomalous than previous accounts have made it seem, and more interpretively useful.

More soberly, just as important is the international context for Liberal Italy's legal setting. The new state's regime and the rituals of its courts of law owed much to those of more northern countries, particularly France. For that reason, before raising the curtain on the spectacle of the trial for Captain Fadda's murder, an excursus that places Italy's new public courts into a broader European context is called for. Viewed against this background, the Fadda trial suggests that the judicial procedures of the new state sought not so much to contain the spectacle as to harness the 'effervescence' it generated, in an arena that the liberal state could confidently claim as its own.

## Italy's Legal System in Context

Prior to unification, Italy's diverse polities had their own independent legal systems. Some, notably the Kingdom of the Two Sicilies and Tuscany (and later, Piedmont-Sardinia), had emergent traditions of public participation in criminal trials, while others, particularly the Papal States and the areas dominated by Austria (Lombardy and the Veneto), did not.[22] Broadly, the legal system imposed across the unified nation from Turin after unification had evolved from the Napoleonic template of 1808, which had been retained in Piedmont after the revolutions of 1848. From the mid-1860s onwards, criminal trials were open to the public across the nation except in Rome, where the principle only applied about one year after the city was taken from the pope in September 1870.[23] By this stage too, as others have argued, developments in the Italian press gave trials a far wider audience than they would have had early in the century.[24]

---

[22] Franco Arato, *Parola di avvocato. L'eloquenza forense in Italia tra Cinque e Ottocento* (Turin: G. Giappichelli editore, 2015), pp. 11–12.
[23] Georgia Alessi, *Il processo penale. Profilo storico* (Bari: Laterza, 2001), p. 159.
[24] See Simpson, *Murder and Media*, throughout.

Legal scholars describe Italy's post-unification criminal law system as 'mixed': it involved both a confidential 'inquisitorial' stage, in which the state's judicial officers investigated a crime, and a public adversarial stage, in which the prosecution and the defence fought the trial in court before judges, jury, and public.[25] Rules governing the twelve-man jury were, in the view of some Italian scholars, far from the canonical ideals of English law. The pool from which jurors could be selected was restricted to the small percentage of the population who, by dint of education and taxable income, had voting rights.[26] Moreover, local prefects had strong influence on the choice of jurists, and the jury's verdict was based on majority, rather than unanimous, opinion.[27] Nevertheless, the system as a whole represented an undoubted advance, and, when it was adopted in Rome from September 1871, the fact was welcomed, albeit with a touch of condescension, by the likes of London's *Times* correspondent.[28]

Commentators on the role of public opinion in Italy's criminal justice observe a tension between the new ideological centrality of individual rights on the one hand, and the inquisitorial secrecy that remained a hallmark of the pre-trial investigation on the other. The confidential nature of the investigative phase could imbue the public trial with the sense that it was a brief but momentous opportunity to compensate for the inevitable distortions of the judicial investigation. Having had little to do during that first phase, the defence often burst onto the stage at the trial as the key protagonists. Lawyers sometimes employed spectacular psychological strategies in their attempts to win over public opinion both within and outside the court. Such techniques, particularly in sensational cases, have led to assessments of the Italian courtroom as a place of 'excessive and distracting theatricality'.[29] Though these are the observations of a group of modern legal scholars, they echo contemporary concerns expressed by Carducci and others who felt the sacred 'temple of justice' could too easily become a circus in Italy.

The fears of contemporary observers and perceptions of modern scholars might be put down to the shock of the new represented by the sudden appearance of the public at Italian criminal trials in Rome in 1871. More broadly, the Risorgimento and unification had given rise to a much more dynamic press than in earlier decades, which greatly amplified the sense of 'publicness' of criminal trials.[30] Italian officials were caught between the desire for the nation to attract public emotional investment and a consciousness that the state needed to establish the legitimacy that would warrant such investment. More pessimistic observers,

---

[25] Floriana Colao, Luigi Lacchè, and Claudia Storti, 'Premessa', in *Processo penale e opinione pubblica in Italia tra Otto e Novecento*, edited by Colao, Lacchè, and Storti (Bologna: Il Mulino, 2008), p. 8.
[26] *Gazzetta Ufficiale del Regno d'Italia*, no. 320, 12 December 1865, p. 2.
[27] Alessi, *Il processo penale*, p. 161.
[28] 'Trial by Jury at Rome', *The Times*, 26 September 1871, p. 8, reports that public trials had commenced 'a few weeks earlier'.
[29] Colao et al, 'Premessa', in *Processo penale e opinione pubblica*, p. 9.
[30] Groppi, 'Il teatro della giustizia', p. 652.

like Carducci, worried that emotionally arousing displays and excessive theatricality would undermine the seriousness of court proceedings. But those fears might also betray contemporary Italian critics' lack of awareness of the theatricality of courts elsewhere. New regimes like Italy's were by no means the only ones where tensions between the alleged rationality of the law and unpredictable human emotions could result in theatrical episodes.[31]

As scholars of antiquity know well, the sense that trials were a form of drama is as old as the law itself.[32] In more modern times, such as nineteenth-century England—the legal ideal to which progressive Italians tended to look—prominent novelists such as Charles Dickens made much of the dramatic potential of trials. His most famous case was 'Jarndyce and Jarndyce' in *Bleak House* (1852–53), after whose long and anti-climactic conclusion the audience exited looking 'flushed and hot' but 'exceedingly amused...more like people coming out from a Farce or a Juggler than from a court of Justice'.[33] Some years later, Gilbert and Sullivan's comic operetta *Trial by Jury*, first staged in London in 1875, played on the theatrical potential of the courtroom, particularly when the hearing examined intimate matters such as a breach of promise of marriage. And for more recent observers, the notion of theatricality has been built in to potentially all social processes since at least as far back as Erving Goffman's influential 'dramaturgical' analyses of contemporary life in the 1950s.[34]

In the 1970s, an early generation of British social historians, notably Douglas Hay and E. P. Thompson, were at the vanguard of exploration of legal proceedings 'from below'. They stressed the symbolic, performative, and theatrical nature of British justice and its reception by the public.[35] More recently, historians of Britain, the United States, and France, as well as Italy, have shown that trials of crimes motivated by intense human emotions (particularly love, resentment, or jealousy) often became irresistibly attractive to the public.[36] Ruth Harris's pioneering 1980s work on women in *fin-de-siècle* French courts persuasively revealed the way female defendants played 'roles' that influenced both public and judges.

---

[31] A recent study where this tension is prominent, and with a similar focus on the link between courts and national identity, is Katie Barclay, *Men in Court: Performing Emotions, Embodiment and Idenity in Ireland, 1800–45* (Manchester: Manchester University Press, 2019). I am grateful to Katie Barclay for providing a preview of this work.

[32] See, for example, Bablitz, *Actors and Audience*, and Papaioannu et al., *The Theatre of Justice*.

[33] Quoted in Clare Graham, *Ordering Law: The Architectural and Social History of the English Law Court to 1914* (Aldershot: Ashgate, 2003), p. 127.

[34] Erving Goffman, *The Presentation of Self in Everyday Life* (Woodstock, NY: The Overlook Press, 1973 [1956]), esp. p. 240.

[35] See, for example, Douglas Hay, 'Property, Authority and the Criminal Law', in *Albion's Fatal Tree: Crime and Society in Eighteenth-Century England*, edited by Douglas Hay et al. (London: Allen Lane, 1975), pp. 17–63; E. P. Thompson, *Customs in Common* (London: The Merlin Press, 1991), esp. pp. 43–5.

[36] Works whose reconstructions of sensational trials have been particularly helpful are (in order of original publication), Patrizia Guarnieri, *L'ammazzabambini. Legge e scienza in un processo di fine Ottocento* (Rome-Bari: Laterza, 2006 [1988]); Ruth Harris, *Murders and Madness: Medicine, Law and Society in the fin de siècle* (Oxford: Oxford University Press, 1989); Edward Berenson, *The Trial of*

Many others have followed suit, several scholars focusing on the way sensational trials were disseminated as forms of entertainment by nascent popular presses.[37] All of this is to say that 1870s Italy did not so much fail to shake off antiquity's susceptibility to the court's dramatic allure, as simply to join the liberal cultures that had already accepted it as a norm.

The court thus emerged, slowly in places like Britain, and relatively quickly in places like Italy, as a theatrical stage where elements of the modern state's relationship with its citizens were acted out. Indeed the word 'theatre' derives from the Greek 'to behold', and since trials were a process that states invited and required citizens to behold, theatrical elements were built in to the choreography of legal procedures as a matter of course. Ultimately, theatrical features were also built into the architecture of western courts of law. In England, where the criminal law developed slowly over centuries, the notion of a dedicated courthouse emerged only relatively recently, as Linda Mulcahy has underlined. Gradually, such improvised locations as church doorways or even particular trees gave way first to 'buildings that happened to house courts', then finally to purpose-built courthouses. Even as late as 1914, English assize courts were held in range of shire-, county-, and guildhalls, as well as other suitable buildings.[38]

Before the advent of dedicated courthouses, the atmosphere of stability, power, and gravitas required to underpin a court's legitimacy was conjured mainly through ritual, pageantry, and spectacle.[39] Unsurprisingly, these closely mirrored ecclesiastical rituals. Religious liturgy ought in fact to vie with theatrical metaphors in analyses of court proceedings, but has been less frequently invoked, perhaps for the very reason that secular law was an instrument of states that, from the Enlightenment onwards, were increasingly keen to establish identities separate from 'the church'. Nevertheless, much of the ritual and spectacle of legal courts was derived from religious patterns. As Hay argued persuasively in 1975, the criminal law echoed 'many of the most powerful psychic components of religion', particularly 'its rituals, its judgements, and its channelling of emotion'.[40] One of those emotions was fear, for religion embodies a disciplinary element that theatre

---

*Madame Caillaux* (Berkeley: University of California Press, 1992); Cohen, *The Murder of Helen Jewett*; Valeria P. Babini, *Il caso Murri. Una storia italiana* (Bologna: Il Mulino, 2004); Gordon and Nair, *Murder and Morality in Victorian Britain*; Simpson, *Murder and Media*; and Arianna Arisi Rota, *1869: il Risorgimento alla deriva. Affari e politica nel caso Lobbia* (Bologna: Il Mulino, 2015).

[37] In addition to Simpson on Italy, on France see Cragin, *Murder in Parisian Streets*; Cohen makes a similar argument in the context of 1830s USA in *The Murder of Helen Jewett*, pp. 23–31; see also Rosalind Crone, 'Publishing Courtroom Drama for the Masses, 1820–1855, in *Crime, Courtrooms and the Public Sphere in Britain, 1700–1850*, edited by David Lemmings (Farnham: Ashgate, 2012), pp. 193–216. Architectural historians have also stressed the role of the press in mediating the relationship between the interior of the courthouse and the broader public beyond, for example, Graham, *Ordering Law*, p. 296; and Linda Mulcahy, *Legal Architecture: Justice, Due Process and the Place of Law* (Oxford: Routledge, 2011), pp. 10–11 and 97–100.

[38] Mulcahy, *Legal Architecture*, p. 24.   [39] Mulcahy, *Legal Architecture*, pp. 24–8.
[40] Hay, 'Property, Authority and the Criminal Law', p. 29.

does not. A judge, as Hay put it, could play the role of priest and deity, 'both the god of wrath and the merciful arbiter of men's fates'.[41] An actor might play those roles too, but real fates were not at stake in the theatre, whereas they were in court, which could therefore be even more deeply affecting.[42]

The potential of Hay's insightful analysis of the interweaving of law and religion in the *mentalités* of ordinary folk tends to have been eclipsed by historians' assumptions about the decline of religious influence in modern life. For example, in the 1980s, J. A. Sharpe argued that by the end of the eighteenth century, the law 'had come to replace religion as the main ideological cement of society'. In retrospect that seems too sweeping a statement, but the implication of competition as well as cooperation between religion and law is useful. Clare Graham's exhaustive 2003 study of the architecture of English courts interprets the increasing 'dignification' and specialization of court buildings very much in the vein of the law's rising importance as an ideological foundation of modern society.[43] Ultimately, it might be said that in polities under the rule of law, the courthouse was designed to embody the state much as church buildings embodied religion.

But if, as Hay argued, fear was an ingredient in the ideological structures such buildings represented, more recent research has suggested that it was an emotion that motivated the powerful as well as the vulnerable. Mulcahy argues that officialdom's fear of the public played a very significant role in influencing court architecture.[44] Similarly, David Lemmings has suggested that over the *longue durée*, British courts grew more formal and distant from the masses in order to protect the formality of the dialogue between prosecution and defence, however vital the public's presence was in theory.[45] Anxieties over the sullying potential of the masses, as well as straightforward fear of public anger, were clearly a challenge shared by all states adopting the principle that justice required popular participation. Recognizing this gives insight into the ways emotional considerations shaped legal regimes from both above and below. In turn, it helps to explain the physical form of the social spaces in which they were enacted.

## The Court as a Temple

Although progressive Italians might have looked to England as an ideal, unified Italy's legal system bore a closer family resemblance to that of France, which in

---

[41] Hay, 'Property, Authority and the Criminal Law', p. 29.
[42] Simon Devereaux provides a lively account of the early overlap between courts and theatres, acting and legal advocates, in 'Arts of Public Performance: Barristers and Actors in Georgian England', in Lemmings, *Crime, Courtrooms and the Public Sphere*, pp. 93–117.
[43] Graham, *Ordering Law*, pp. 74–8. The quotation from J. A. Sharpe's *Crime in Early Modern England* (1984) is taken from Graham (p. 74).
[44] Mulcahy, *Legal Architecture*, p. 9.
[45] David Lemmings, 'Introduction: Criminal Courts, Lawyers and the Public Sphere', in Lemmings, *Crime, Courtrooms and the Public Sphere*, pp. 1–21, here pp. 2–4.

turn drew much symbolic inspiration from Greek and Roman antiquity. Modern French notions of justice, born during the Enlightenment, took shape at the time of the Grand Tour, through which elite French travellers discovered Herculaneum, Pompeii, Rome's Pantheon, and the like. In their own way French courts exemplified both religious influence and classical spectacle, but the Revolution of 1789 created a rupture that ensured their evolution took a distinctive turn. If 'the law' in England emerged slowly as an alternative to religious and royal authority, in France it did so peremptorily. Classical inspiration may have provided the sacred foundations necessary for early modern French justice, but the tendency was much reinforced by the Revolution. While the English gradually dignified their early itinerant courts with dedicated buildings as the law gained prestige, after the Revolution, the French overtly dignified their purpose-built legal edifices as *temples de la loi*.[46]

As architectural historian Katherine Fischer Taylor's research underlines, the French sense of sacred ideological mission connoted by referring to courts as 'temples' coexisted with popular, theatrical elements. During the revolutionary decade, novel circular court design reduced to a minimum the distance between judges and audience, emphasizing that judicial power was authorized by the will of the people.[47] As Napoleon moved France away from radical democracy, courts too returned to a less intimate and more formal rectangular model, reviving hierarchies of the *ancien régime* while still retaining some theatrical elements acquired during the Revolution. Taylor interprets the newly rectangular early nineteenth-century designs as a return to church-like layouts. Though unable to find an explicit contemporary claim that it was deliberate, she suggests 'It cannot be accidental that this courtroom layout situates the judges like clergy in the chancel of a church, facing a congregation in the nave.'[48] Over several decades of ideological tumult in France, courts can be seen as both temples and theatres contemporaneously, alternately reflecting one tendency more than the other, according to prevailing ideological currents.

Temples and theatres are both intended for audiences, but each frames and prompts public response in a different way. A key variable is the emotional register a space conveys, signalling how expressive or even rowdy the public might be. Buildings and spaces exert emotional rules, or at the very least, strong cues. In the early 1990s, well prior to the boom in interest in the history of emotions, Taylor was drawn to related questions by the first sensational murder trial to attract a mass audience to the newly opened Court of Assizes in Paris's Palais de Justice in 1869. The building was part of Baron Haussman's ambitious reshaping of the

---

[46] Badinter, 'Preface', *La justice en ses temples*, p. 11.
[47] Katherine Fischer Taylor, 'Geometries of Power: Royal, Revolutionary and Postrevolutionary French Courtrooms', *Journal of the Society of Architectural Historians*, vol. 72, no. 4 (2013): 434–74; here 446.
[48] Taylor, 'Geometries of Power', p. 436.

French capital in the mid-1800s. Key protagonist of the trial was a twenty-year-old Alsatian mechanic, Jean-Baptiste Troppmann, accused and ultimately found guilty of murdering a family of eight, including six children.[49] Taylor's analysis, paying specific attention to the architectural space in which it took place, deconstructed Troppmann's trial as a staged and emotional spectacle. It brings Hay's insights on England to a Continental court.

In many ways, the Troppmann trial foreshadowed concerns that would surface at the Fadda trial in Rome a decade later. A key question in 1869 Paris was how successfully the new building helped the court balance the inevitable sensation and the required tenor of sobriety. The local audience may have been quite familiar with sensational trials, but the French could still perceive such encounters as new, exciting, and risky.[50] Troppmann's trial clearly fascinated both men and women in equal measure, but, just as Carducci was to do ten years later, some Parisian commentators found it convenient to condemn female zeal as a key factor in undermining the dignity of proceedings. The alleged introduction of picnic hampers and even champagne to the court would certainly have made it more an entertaining arena than a sacred temple, but what worried critics in a more general sense was the atmosphere of 'garish sensationalism' that surrounded the trial and permeated the city while it was heard.[51] The Troppmann trial epitomized what Italian scholars would soon criticize in their own system as 'excessive theatricality'.

Some commentators blamed the new Palais de Justice itself. They were critical of the court's rich gold décor, regarding it as too much of a proscenium for the elegant female audience that crowded into it. This portended a broader concern that the space was altogether emasculated. The design and décor were seen as undermining the 'masculine duty of repression' that such commentators thought so necessary for the independent self-government of both states and individuals.[52] In short, for some the building encouraged a 'feminized' emotional style that was insufficiently restrained. For Carducci's French predecessors, the sobriety of the prestigious *temple de la loi* and the role of reason within it were threatened with desecration by explosive sentiments that women, like stowaways from some emotions-laden Trojan Horse, were accused of smuggling into the court.

As we know, in 1870s Rome, analogous anxieties were expressed over the Fadda trial. But while Paris's grand and luxurious court was part of a thorough reshaping of the French capital from the mid-1800s, the Italian government of the 1870s had far less margin for reshaping Rome as an expression of Italy's new regime. The cultural accretions of the eternal city were more sacred, more calcified, and

---

[49] Katherine Fischer Taylor, *In the Theater of Criminal Justice: The Palais de Justice in Second Empire Paris* (Princeton, NJ: Princeton University Press, 1993).
[50] Taylor, *In the Theater of Criminal Justice*, p. 10.
[51] Taylor, *In the Theater of Criminal Justice*, pp. 27–8.
[52] Taylor, *In the Theater of Criminal Justice*, pp. 66–7. Barclay's *Men in Court* develops further the sense of courts as gendered spaces.

had deeper roots than those of any other place in the world. Effacing or overlaying them would be an enormous task that was only really to gain any momentum in the following century. With the notable exception of the imposing monument to Victor Emmanuel II, begun in the early 1880s, the Italian government, instead of raising new buildings that embodied the liberal tenets of unified Italy, tended to take over the great buildings wrested from its predecessor, the papal regime.[53] Like a hermit crab, the state inhabited the shells it found, and, in contrast to Second-Empire France, it was initially timid about asserting its own identity through architecture.

Rome's new Court of Assizes from 1871 is a telling example of the way the Italian state repurposed existing buildings. The edifice chosen to house the court began its life as a religious centre. It was designed and built in the seventeenth century for the Congregation of the Oratory, a confraternity founded by Saint Filippo Neri in 1575, during the early stages of the Counter Reformation. The congregation was unusual in that it was governed by consensus and dedicated to new ways of expressing faith and devotion. These expressions were mainly based on collective reading, discussion, and musical performance. Informal and unscholastic, the 'oratorians', as they became known, might well be considered direct descendants of the types of religious emotional communities of a much earlier period so persuasively characterized by Barbara Rosenwein.[54] Like their medieval predecessors, the oratorians shared similar 'norms of emotional expression', and their sense of community was reinforced by shared emotional 'values', regularly expressed in their communal rituals.[55]

By the late 1500s, Rome's oratorian congregation had gained a notable public following, such that its members decided to build a devotional space appropriate to the community's activities. The result was a large oratory, designed by the celebrated Baroque architect Francesco Borromini. It was situated next to the church of Santa Maria in Vallicella in the centre of Rome, on what is now one of the city's main thoroughfares, the Corso Vittorio Emanuele. Begun in 1637, the oratory was to become the centre of the congregation's communal life. Their Sunday oratory increasingly dedicated time to performing music of particular emotional force, later giving rise to the oratorio as a musical genre.[56] The Oratory of the Filippini was a temple, but one that distinguished itself by resounding more and more regularly with stirringly emotional performances of vocal music.

It was this building, imposing in scale but by Baroque standards aesthetically restrained, that the Italian state confiscated in 1871 to convert into Rome's Court

---

[53] Vittorio Vidotto, *Roma contemporanea* (Rome-Bari: Laterza, 2001), p. 56.
[54] Joseph Connors, *Borromini and the Roman Oratory: Style and Society* (New York: Architectural History Foundation, 1980), pp. 1–7.
[55] Barbara Rosenwein, *Emotional Communities in the Early Middle Ages* (Ithaca, NY: Cornell University Press, 2006), p. 2.
[56] Connors, *Borromini*, pp. 69–70. See also Emanuela Chiavoni, *Il disegno di oratori romani. Rilievo e analisi di alcuni tra i più significativi di Roma* (Rome: Gangemi Editore, 2008), pp. 152–66.

of Assizes. The building was to remain a temple, but dedicated to the law, and it was chosen partly for its capacity to hold a large public. How much the rich emotions expressed in the space's past might echo in the new court of justice remained to be seen. Meanwhile, the sheer scale of the interior certainly impressed the Rome correspondent of London's *Times*, who reported on one of the court's first hearings in September 1871. He described the space as a 'splendid hall of great size', providing 'an enormous amount of accommodation to those desirous of witnessing the trials'. Furniture suitable for the court had been installed, but the architectural features remained unchanged since Borromini's day: 'four magnificent Oriental alabaster columns rise behind the judges' seats, while at the opposite end, above the door, there was a gallery, capable of accommodating 'certainly not less than a hundred people'.[57]

The oratory that had been a sanctuary of devotion and music was readily converted into a capacious judicial theatre, and, just as it had done in the seventeenth century, in the 1870s the space quickly drew in the Roman public. That early trial reported in *The Times* was not even particularly sensational, involving an inveterately crooked Italian widow who stood accused of stealing some diamond jewellery from an aristocratic lodger. Yet, the members of the public who congregated for hours in front of the hall's huge doors, as soon as they were opened, 'speedily filled the great space…without seeming to diminish the crowd outside'. Once all were settled, the journalist observed that 'the gallery and the two balconies…were crammed with fashionably dressed ladies to the exclusion of the stronger sex altogether.'[58] Italy's new legal system, installed in its lofty Baroque temple, was clearly embraced by Roman women from the outset. The enthusiasm generated by the banal story of some stolen diamonds was but a foretaste of the atmosphere to be experienced at the Court of Assizes during the trial for Giovanni Fadda's murder some eight years later.

## A Hungry Press

For days, weeks, and even months prior to the commencement of 'the Fadda trial' (as it was often called, using the victim's name rather than those of the accused), newspapers all over Italy advertised the event.[59] In Rome itself, walls were 'carpeted' with advertisements about the trial's coverage.[60] Newspapers offered discounted subscriptions and promised to out-do their competitors with the most exhaustive coverage of the proceedings. As Simpson has shown, directors

---

[57] 'Trial by Jury at Rome', *The Times*, 26 September 1871, p. 8.
[58] 'Trial by Jury at Rome', *The Times*, 26 September 1871, p. 8.
[59] Simpson reports that Rome's *Il Messaggero* first mentioned its intention to cover the Fadda trial in March 1879, *Murder and Media* (p. 32), well before a date had been fixed for the hearing.
[60] 'Il processo Fadda. La prima udienza', *Gazzetta Piemontese*, 2 October 1879, p. 1.

particularly of the capital's still neophyte liberal newspapers saw the trial as an opportunity to consolidate their sales nationally.[61] Their promotional tactics are exemplified by *Il Bersagliere*, an organ of the city's moderate progressives, founded in 1874 but from January 1878 owned by Hungarian financier and entrepreneur, E. E. Oblieght.[62] The newspaper boasted that it would offer 'the most extensive and exact accounts of this important trial', and would be sold for five cents throughout the kingdom for its duration—half the normal price outside Rome's city limits.[63] It is worth noting that, given average workers' wages of less than 2 lire per day (i.e. 200 cents), even the local and discounted prices were still quite high.[64]

The writer covering the trial for *Il Bersagliere* was Nicolò Coboevich, himself a trained lawyer. *Il Bersagliere*'s main competition in the capital was *Il Messaggero*, established as recently as January 1878, and representing a similar political position.[65] Its founding editor, Luigi Cesana, was quick to realize that lively reports of criminal trials were a key weapon in the competition to increase circulation. *Il Messaggero* had the advantage of a particularly talented journalist, Luigi Arnaldo Vassallo, who became the paper's editor from April 1879. Under the pseudonym 'Gandolin', Vassallo wrote extraordinarily evocative accounts of the Fadda trial which increased sales notably: the paper had to use two printing presses simultaneously to keep up with demand during the trial.[66]

Further testimony to the sales potential generated by the trial is that both *Il Messaggero*'s and *Il Bersagliere*'s daily reports were quickly compiled into printed volumes as soon as the hearing concluded.[67] Though each had a different style (Vassallo was more colourful, Coboevich more detailed), together these volumes amount to the closest available equivalent of a trial transcript. They are much more detailed than the official record of the trial, though the information contained in those documents corroborates the essential accuracy of both the commercially produced volumes.[68] Allowance for poetic licence must be made for the reporters,

---

[61] Simpson, *Murder and Media*, p. 2, but also chapter 2 and throughout.

[62] Olga Majolo Molinari, *La stampa periodica romana dell'Ottocento. Vol. 1, A–L* (Rome: Istituto di Studi Romani Editore, 1963), pp. 116–17.

[63] 'Avviso', *Il Bersagliere* (Rome), 30 September 1879, p. 1.

[64] Paolo Murialdi, *Storia del giornalismo italiano* (Bologna: Il Mulino, 1996), p. 65.

[65] Giuseppe Talamo, *Il «Messaggero» e la sua città. Cento anni di storia. Vol. I—1878-1918* (Florence: Le Monnier, 1979), pp. 38–9.

[66] Olga Majolo Molinari, *La stampa periodica romana dell'Ottocento. Vol. 2, M–Z* (Rome: Istituto di studi romani editore, 1963), p. 594.

[67] Vassallo's reports for *Il Messaggero* were compiled into the volume *Processo Cardinali e coimputati per l'assassinio del Capitano Fadda commesso in Roma il 6 Ottobre 1878 dibattutosi il giorno 30 settembre 1879 e seguenti davanti alle Assise di Roma*, 2nd edition (Rome: Edoardo Perino, 1879); Coboevich's accounts for *Il Bersagliere* were compiled as *Processo Fadda illustrato. Dibattimento alla Corte d'Assise di Roma dal 30 settembre al 31 ottobre 1879* (Rome: Giovanni Bracco Editore, 1879). Despite competition between the newspapers, portraits of the two journalists were chivalrously printed side by side in *Il Bersagliere*'s *Processo Fadda illustrato*, as a tribute to 'two of the principal reporters of this celebrated trial', pp. 180–1.

[68] An abbreviated account of the court proceedings appears at the end of the trial records at the Archivio di Stato di Roma, Tribunale Penale e Civile (henceforth ASR, TCPR), 1879, b. 3659, vol. IV, ff. 246–413.

but Coboevich's and Vassallo's volumes are a valuable source for any analysis of the trial proceedings. Both editions were augmented by lively engravings of scenes from the lives of the accused as well as the trial, and they sold quickly, with Vassallo's version soon requiring a second edition.[69]

One of Coboevich's early accounts in the *Bersagliere* evoked an important but forgotten aspect of the event by describing the city's distinctive soundscape during the trial. Newspapers hired criers (*strillari*), who wandered the streets stridently calling phrases such as 'Il processo del capitano Fadda!' to attract buyers. Peddlers even sold portraits of Fadda, his likeness being presented 'in a thousand ways and a thousand sizes'. They sang out 'Pictures of Captain Fadda', or 'Captain Fadda for a cent!'[70] At key moments in the trial there were reports of crowds of hundreds assembling at midnight outside *Il Bersagliere*'s offices in Piazza San Claudio, waiting to buy the latest account hot off the press. Once the crowds had bought their copies, newspaper boys ran up and down the Corso selling papers and making a 'hellish racket'. Eager customers lowered baskets on a string containing five cents from their apartment windows, then hauled up the newspaper like a prime catch.[71]

No matter what the hour, then, there was an appetite for news of the trial. Day and night the very air of the city rang with the sound of Fadda's name, reminding all and sundry that the trial was taking place. This no doubt helped to create an atmosphere similar to the 'garish sensationalism' that had so worried French conservatives during the Troppmann trial. In Rome, the Fadda trial was an event that all citizens, not just those who managed to attend the hearing, would have been aware of, and not only for a matter of days. As with other important trials in other major capitals, in Rome too, commercial imperatives allied with an official event to make it the talk of the town over several weeks.

Newspapers like *Il Bersagliere* and *Il Messaggero* had the advantage of being *in situ* in Rome, but interest was by no means limited to the capital. Papers published across the length and breadth of the peninsula also carried full accounts of the trial on a daily basis and vigorously staked their claims to the story, regardless of whether their cities had played a role in the events behind the trial.[72] Testimony to the recent modernization of communication techniques, as well as the intrinsic interest of the story, was the fact that even far-flung international newspapers reported the trial. These included not just a wide range of British and American newspapers, but even those of Australia and New Zealand. Foreign reports tended

---

[69] Giuseppe Fonterossi, *Roma fine Ottocento* (Rome: Edizioni Moderne Canesi, 1960), pp. 70–1.
[70] 'Processo Fadda', *Il Bersagliere*, 3 October 1879, p. 2.
[71] 'Il processo Fadda', *Gazzetta Piemontese*, 25 October 1879, pp. 1–2. This method of 'shopping' has still not completely disappeared in Italy.
[72] For example, *Il Piccolo* of Naples, *La Nazione* of Florence, the *Gazzetta Piemontese* of Turin, *L'Epoca* of Genoa, the *Corriere della Sera* of Milan, and all the Roman newspapers (although the papal *Osservatore Romano* gave only limited and very critical coverage).

to be revised versions of those by one or two key correspondents, but nevertheless, this was a trial that attracted international attention, suggesting almost universal interest in the events behind it.[73]

In Italy, the competition between regional publications and those of the capital was made most explicit by Genoa's *L'Epoca*, which began an intense advertising campaign almost three weeks before the trial commenced. From 11 September 1879, a prominent announcement appeared each day about the newspaper's coverage of the upcoming trial, which, by virtue of 'daily reports telegraphed by a special correspondent in Rome', would 'compete victoriously with the capital's newspapers'. Like *Il Bersagliere*, the Genoese newspaper was offered at a discounted price by mail all over Italy, and subscribers were even lured with the offer of a free book with each new subscription. They could choose between *The Battle of Legnano* (a famous Guelph-Ghibelline battle of 1176), the *Life of Victor Emmanuel*, or the *Life of Pius IX*.[74] Whether this range represented contemporary interests or the publisher's excess stocks is difficult to say, but what the offer makes clear is how vigorous editorial strategies sought to take advantage of sales opportunities presented by the trial.

*L'Epoca*'s production crowned these notably modern marketing tactics with a feature that represented a genuine victory over the capital's newspapers. During the hearing, each day's front page featured a superb full-size engraving of a scene from the story, and, as the trial progressed, key moments of the proceedings. The logistics of engraving and printing multiple large images in the 1870s were forbidding, and *L'Epoca*'s feat was unmatched by any other newspaper.[75] The reason a Genoese publication should have invested so heavily in the trial is not immediately obvious, given that the city was as geographically distant from the crime's orbit as it was possible to be. However, a clue lies almost hidden in tiny print about the newspaper's business office: like *Il Bersagliere*, *L'Epoca* was owned by the Hungarian E. E. Oblieght. It is very likely that his entrepreneurial vigour drove these singular efforts. Nevertheless, the example from Genoa suffices to underline how the Fadda trial made Italy, if only momentarily, into something of an imagined emotional community. All of Italy was united by excitement and curiosity about the murder, and the state's quest for justice.

---

[73] London's *Times* and *The Standard* reported on the trial, as did the *Illustrated Police News* (London) and a range of regional British newspapers. There are several reports on the Fadda trial in the *New York Times* and other US newspapers. Australasian newspapers generally reprinted stories from *The Times* with some delay, for example, 'Sensational Italian Murder', *New Zealand Herald* (Auckland), 13 December 1879; 'A Sensational Trial in Rome', *The Press* (Christchurch), 17 December 1879, p. 3; 'Crime in Italy', *The Press*, 8 May 1880, p. 5.

[74] *L'Epoca*, 10–11 September, 1879, p. 2.

[75] The first of *L'Epoca*'s full front-page illustrations was an artist's impression of Cardinali's attack on Fadda, his dagger plunged deep into Fadda's heart (*L'Epoca*, 30 September–1 October 1879, p. 1).

## *Il Processo Fadda,* Day One

Despite the inquisitorial confidentiality of the prosecution's investigations, by the time the trial began, on the morning of 30 September 1879, there was little doubt about who had murdered Giovanni Fadda. The public knew that the accusation against Pietro Cardinali would be the extremely serious one of premeditated murder. They also knew that, if found guilty, he could face the death sentence, even though there had been significant moves away from capital punishment after Italian unification. The Piedmontese criminal code, ultimately extended over all of Italy, provided for the death penalty except in Tuscany, where it had been abolished definitively in 1853, and was not reintroduced.[76] After unification, already strong ideological currents against the death penalty were intensified by the significant leftward political shift of 1876, and retrospectively, statistics reveal that by then, even though the nation's courts handed down between sixty-four and 102 death sentences per year, few if any executions actually took place.[77] However, Pietro Cardinali did not have access to those statistics, and the possibility of the death sentence must surely have struck fear into Cardinali's heart.

Similar fears no doubt affected the other two accused, though there was less certainty about the degree of their guilt. The figure over whom there was most public speculation was Raffaella Saraceni, accused of premeditating the crime with Cardinali, instigating him through a promise of marriage, and providing the financial means that supported his murderous mission. Technically, Saraceni was accused of being a 'principal agent' of the murder, which also had the potential to attract a death sentence. Antonietta Carrozza, Cardinali's adoptive sister and circus co-star, stood accused of having been 'knowingly involved' in the premeditative phase of the crime and facilitating the plan, but she was unlikely to face death.[78] The quasi-incestuous relationship between Cardinali and Antonietta certainly added a layer of piquant complexity to her position. But the mysterious veil the public most hoped the trial would lift lay over the intimacies of Fadda and Rafaela's superficially orthodox marriage.[79]

Given the inter-class relationships, the grave accusations, the immense media publicity, and the chance to hear about the main characters' desires and frustrations,

---

[76] John A. Davis, *Conflict and Control: Law and Order in Nineteenth-Century Italy* (London: Macmillan, 1988), pp. 128–9.

[77] Mario Da Passano, 'La pena di morte nel Regno d'Italia 1859-1889', in *Diritto penale dell'Ottocento. I codici preunitari e il codice Zanardelli*, edited by Sergio Vinciguerra (Padua: CEDAM, 1995), pp. 579–649. The statistical table referred to is on pp. 639–40, and appears to indicate that Italy's last executions took place in 1874. A completely revised Italian criminal code, which officially abolished the death sentence, was finally approved in 1889 and took effect from 1890. I thank Gian Marco Vidor for this reference. The most thorough recent work in English is Paul Garfinkel, *Criminal Law in Liberal and Fascist Italy* (Cambridge: Cambridge University Press, 2016).

[78] The official 'Atto di accusa' was reprinted in *Processo Fadda illustrato*, pp. 5–6.

[79] Pietro Lancia, 'Il processo Fadda', *L'Eloquenza*, vol. 2, nos. 7–8 (1929): 125–31.

**Figure 5.1** The crowd seeking entry to the Court of Assizes on the first day of the Fadda murder trial, Rome, 30 September 1879

Source: *Processo Fadda illustrato* (Rome: Giovanni Bracco Editore, 1879), pp. 164–5.

as well as the accounts of a menagerie of witnesses, it was no surprise that on the morning the trial began, a large crowd, animated and eager, gathered outside the court (see figure 5.1). A sense of the venue and its immediate surrounds as an arena in which emotions charged the air leaps out from all contemporary descriptions. As Vassallo reported, from time to time the crowd, with shouts of 'frenetic impatience', heaved against the vast double-doors of the building as if trying to burst through them. Within, the privileged but impatient throng of those already admitted filled the courtyard of the grand edifice. At the bottom of a stairway leading to the old oratory's upper balconies, large numbers of women jostled, many dressed in the sober garb of mourning. Yet among them, a few wore hats of such bright colours that they leapt out dissonantly 'amongst all this heartbreak'.[80] Even journalists of Vassallo's skill seem to struggle to find words for the strangely tragic yet excited mood generated by the trial.

The atmosphere was made even more interesting by the large number of witnesses called to Rome from southern Italy. The occasion brought Romans into

[80] Vassallo, *Processo Cardinali*, p. 6.

direct contact with citizens from some of the most isolated and rugged regions of the new nation. The ushers' call to assemble the witnesses, of which there were almost one hundred, gave rise to an 'endless stream of people', a 'variegated crowd of curious types, some of them picturesque'. One woman was wearing the costume of 'goodness knows what region', and its colours were so bright they hurt the reporter's eyes. The many Calabrian men present were said to be wearing a great deal of the corduroy that was their provincial custom, the very fabric that had distinguished Pietro Cardinali's stable boy in witness accounts collected mere hours after the murder. By contrast, some of the witnesses were true Romans, a notable example being a little old lady no more than 'four palms in height'. She told anyone who would listen that the murderer had been her lodger, adding that he carried a knife so fearsome-looking, the mere sight of it was enough to raise gooseflesh.[81]

If a Roman landlady's gooseflesh hinted at the visceral responses to come, that first morning the crowd already inside the court also witnessed less primal human emotions. After several hours of waiting, those within saw a group of dignified men, 'with the gravest expressions, all dressed in black', pass through a corridor. These were the defence lawyers, and they disappeared into the cells holding the accused. When the legal counsel re-emerged, looking even graver than when they had gone in, Vassallo asked one of them, 'And what of la signora Saraceni?' The lawyer answered that his client was in a pitiful state, one that inspired the 'deepest compassion'. Altogether he declared himself 'profoundly perturbed by the meeting'.[82] The image of several figures in black, gliding like grim reapers towards the meeting with their clients, foreshadowed an emotional mode that would soon be widely associated with courts and the legal profession: authoritative sobriety and restraint, in the face of deep perturbation.

For many, the robed lawyers must also have harked back to another Roman elite: the priests who, in their own way, were also interested in questions of guilt and its confession. The law, avowedly secular but no less laden with ritual than the religion whose regime it had supplanted, was a key pillar of the new state's efforts to assert its legitimacy over that of its venerable predecessor.[83] Not only that, but lawyers as a profession were deeply invested in the new state, representing by far the highest proportion of the professions in parliament.[84] Lawyers embodied, in a sense, the new government, and the atmosphere of this space for the law's 'performance' was crucial to the state's aspirations, just as churches were crucial to the religious hierarchy. The law's personnel emanated an emotional style appropriate to those who represented the reasoned use of power and authority. Their black

---

[81] *Processo Cardinali*, 6.   [82] *Processo Cardinali*, 6.
[83] Groppi, 'Il teatro della giustizia', p. 650.
[84] Fulvio Cammarano and Maria Serena Piretti, 'I professionisti in Parlamento (1861–1958), in *Storia d'Italia. Annali 10. I professionisti*, edited by Maria Malatesta (Turin: Einaudi, 1996), pp. 523–89. Table VII, p. 589, shows that lawyers were by far the most numerous profession, holding more than seven times the number of parliamentary seats than engineers or doctors in the first eight legislatures.

robes denoted a privileged position in a new hierarchy of knowledge, skill, and political legitimacy. The lawyers' grave expressions silently communicated the life-and-death seriousness of their business.

Trials as momentous as the one about to begin were to test the state's ability to control the emotional atmosphere of the legal arena. Ministerial directives to the presiding judges, known as presidents, of the nation's various courts several years prior to the Fadda trial reveal a conscious effort to establish emotional tenors commensurate with the legal system's role as a pillar of the new regime. In a memorandum circulated among the kingdom's court presidents in November 1874, the Minister of Justice, Paolo Vigliani, implored them to observe 'the example of other countries'. He lamented the high cost of Italy's justice system, in which the summoning of too many witnesses often caused hearings to become 'vast and complex'.[85] Instead, he helpfully urged the use of 'neither too many, nor too few witnesses', and stressed that each day's hearing should be used 'efficiently'. Clearly, that element of his request was not heeded in the calling of witnesses for the Fadda trial. But above all, Vigliani implored court presidents to create an atmosphere of 'order, calm and temperance', and to bar the 'excitement of passions and affects not compatible with the sober sentiment of justice'.[86]

As the minister's words imply, although the court was to be a place of utmost sobriety, passions and affect could not be banished. Rather, they should be expressed in a way that was compatible with the sacred ideals animating this novel hybrid of temple and arena. Those who represented the state or the legal profession were expected to stage their own emotions judiciously, setting an example for the audience. The carefully organized space of the court, whose unique choreography was carefully controlled by employees of the state, communicated the requirements of this particular emotional arena powerfully to all participants. Just as Taylor has argued in relation to the French case, there seems little doubt that in Italy too, rituals of the criminal courts were built over patterns that owed a great deal to those of the Catholic Church. As well as conferring gravitas, such ritualistic similarities facilitated the transition for a public mostly unfamiliar with legal proceedings. A parishioner who knew what to do at Mass would instinctively understand a court of law. The fact that in Rome the building itself had previously been a religious space would only have made the connections even clearer.

Conversely, there would inevitably be moments during this and other trials when proceedings generated an atmosphere more akin to a popular theatre. It was this possibility, inherent in the narrative about to be heard, that created so much excitement, expectation, and tension, on the morning of 30 September

---

[85] Paolo Onorato Vigliani (Minister of Grace and Justice), 'Circolare 10 Novembre 1874. Esecuzione della nuova legge sull'ordinamento dei giurati e sui giudizi innanzi alle Corti di Assise', *Raccolta circolari emanate dal Ministero di Grazia e Giustizia e dei Culti, anni 1871 al 1880*, vol. 2 (Rome: Regia Tipografia, 1881), pp. 332–7, here p. 332.

[86] Vigliani, 'Circolare 10 Novembre 1874', p. 335.

1879. Anticipating the appeal of these sentiments, not only had extra seating been set up, but a company of infantry to control the crowds had been ordered by the president of the court, Francesco Giordano.[87] In the early stages of the trial, the official hierarchy was still in control of the emotional atmosphere surrounding the event, and it has to be said that largely, they remained so. The fact that compassion was the first emotion verbally expressed by a lawyer taking part in the murder trial is emblematic. As Martha Nussbaum has pointed out, compassion, or 'pity that inclines to mercy', has long been held in high regard as a meeting place between emotion and ethical deliberation.[88]

Compassion had a clear place in legal processes, and not just in passionate Italy. As Thomas Dixon has skilfully detailed, the tears that sprang to the eyes of judges in Britain make particular sense if they are seen as expressions of this refined sentiment.[89] Involving both Christian and secular traditions, compassion was also an exemplary emotional response from those in positions of power in Italy's new courts of law. Like the legal professionals, the public and journalists attending the Fadda trial also felt and expressed compassion. But, less constrained by the professional requirements of the legal arena, both the public and reporters also experienced more intense feelings which may have been less filtered through 'ethical deliberation' before they were expressed. Such feelings reached a first peak when the accused were finally brought into public view.

## The Accused Appear

The audience, having heard, read, and talked so much about the lives of the accused, were hungry to see them in the flesh. They wanted to scrutinize their faces and bodies, to form opinions, to judge, and perhaps even to experience vicariously their desires, fears, jealousies. The men in the audience, *L'Epoca*'s columnist speculated—in an article placed under an idealized engraving of an alluring Raffaella Saraceni—burned with a desire to 'contemplate at their leisure the sad hero of this very sad drama, the horseman Cardinali'—not, somewhat surprisingly, the young widow. It was the women, he suggested, who could barely wait for the arrival of that figure.[90] In *L'Epoca*'s view, at least, members of the audience awaited those in whose shoes they could imagine placing themselves. What would upstanding men have to gain by imagining themselves in the shoes of a virile but unscrupulous womanizer? Why would the fine women of Rome be so

---
[87] 'Processo Fadda', *Corriere della Sera*, 30 September 1879, p. 2.
[88] Martha Nussbaum, *Upheavals of Thought: The Intelligence of Emotions* (Cambridge: Cambridge University Press, 2001), pp. 298–9.
[89] Thomas Dixon, *Weeping Britannia: Portrait of a Nation in Tears* (Oxford: Oxford University Press, 2015), pp. 169–82.
[90] 'Processo Fadda', *L'Epoca*, 1–2 October 1879, p. 1.

interested in the frustrations and desires of a woman who was outwardly so demure? *L'Epoca*'s speculations point to the fact that the trial promised the *frissons* of vicarious association with real-life figures whose deepest desires had escaped the usual emotional regimes.

On the first day of the proceedings, for those fortunate enough to have a seat within the court, the desire to see the accused first-hand was finally gratified at 11 a.m., after hours of waiting. An expectant hush fell upon the great space as the staccato notes of the guards' boots announced the arrival of the first prisoner.[91] It was Cardinali, dressed, like the lawyers, 'all in black', and, according to one report, 'almost pompously raising his hands' to the audience to reveal handcuffs.[92] It is unclear whether the gesture was the best the fettered circus artiste could do by way of saluting the public, or a deliberate revelation of his shackles. Reporters noted Cardinali's robust and well-proportioned figure, but spent more words describing his luxuriant though questionable *coiffure*. One described it as an 'interminable pony tail', while another mentioned a 'wave of carefully arranged black hair in the style typical of itinerant baritones'.[93] Between these condescending lines though, Cardinali seemed to radiate a certain vigour that the journalists chose not to dwell on.

It would be useful to have unmediated access to what women in the audience felt about Cardinali's appearance, but the views of male journalists are the only ones accessible to posterity. Making allowance for journalists' professional interest in fomenting intense reactions, their observations can still be revealing. Vassallo, displaying the insightful style that won him so many readers, wrote that Cardinali 'entered the court with a confident step, but you could see that he put great effort into appearing calmer than he really was'. The perspicacious journalist perceived a certain 'imperceptible' tremor in the eyelids, a certain 'rippling of the hands', which led him to conclude that Cardinali's flesh was rebelling against the man's desire to hide his true feelings.[94]

In another man, such efforts might have been admired as a variety of the very self-control that the Minister of Justice had urged senior legal staff themselves to embody. Later, Fadda himself would be extolled for his exemplary ability to restrain his true feelings. Yet, when Cardinali sought to do something analogous, he earned opprobrium. Vassallo epitomized the interpretation by writing that Cardinali's 'physiognomy was intelligent, but above all theatrical'.[95] The writer for Naples' *Il Piccolo* claimed that Cardinali's 'apocryphal lack of concern, the affected self-confidence', augmented by his 'permanent cynical smile', had succeeded only in winning the commentator's 'invincible repugnance'.[96] From the outset, Cardinali's

---

[91] 'Processo Fadda', *L'Epoca*, 1–2 October 1879, p. 1.
[92] 'Processo Fadda', *Il Bersagliere*, 1 October 1879, p. 2.
[93] *Processo Cardinali*, p. 7; 'Processo Fadda', *Il Bersagliere*, 1 October 1879, p. 2.
[94] *Processo Cardinali*, p. 8.   [95] *Processo Cardinali*, p. 8.
[96] 'Il Processo Fadda', *Il Piccolo*, 1 October 1879, p. 2.

performance in court was dismissed by those in a position to express judgement, from journalists to counsel to judges, as unattractive dissimulation.

Heinous as Cardinali's crime was, it is worth the compassionate historical gesture of imagining what it would have been like to be in his shoes; to seek to understand his dissimulation not so much as a revelation of low moral character, but the result of instinctive behaviour when confronted with a particular social space. Cardinali had spent his life making grand entrances into theatrical arenas. He was used to being the object of a public's gaze, particularly the keen glances of women in the front rows. Indeed, he had got into the habit of augmenting his standard of living by making intense eye contact with some of these women, and later reaping the material benefits that could flow as a result of their admiration. When, on 30 September 1879, he led the fearful trio of accused figures into an arena whose appearance was similar but whose purpose was altogether different from those he was so used to, he must surely have experienced a strange sense of déjà vu as the crowded audience came into his view.

After a year in a prison cell, Cardinali had finally returned to a public arena and, however anxious his mind, his long exposure to audiences prompted him to perform accordingly. He took his cue from the theatricality of the space, complete with eager audience; he probably raised his hands in habitual acknowledgement of those assembled. Just as he used to do in the circus, with his steady eyes he met the curious gaze of the public with equal curiosity.[97] Or, as Vassallo put it, he first looked pointedly at the president of the court, then moved his gaze across the crowd, 'with a slowness that did not lack dignity'.[98] Cardinali was not demure. As a circus performer, he had known how to invite the public to gaze at him, and now, through force of habit, he used the same technique in court.

Upon entering the court on day two of the trial, Cardinali tried to take a second opportunity to make a first impression. Presumably relieved of his handcuffs, but surrounded by four armed guards, 'he raised his hat, making an arc with his right hand until the hat came to rest on his thigh, and he placed his left fist on his hip, as if entering a dance hall.'[99] What might have passed for self-control on Cardinali's first appearance, now that he was unfettered, entered the realm of the inappropriate. This arena was fatally different from the ones he had known all his life, and ultimately, Cardinali's misjudgement of the court space and its audience did him few favours. An invisible line was crossed with his second, melodramatic entrance, and it was to be a steady slide downhill for Cardinali, to the nadir of the prosecutor's summing up, four weeks hence.

Returning to the first day, following Cardinali, Raffaella Saraceni was the next accused to appear. Her comportment was much more demure than Cardinali's, and the emotions she evoked in the journalists and among the public appear to be

---

[97] 'Processo Fadda', *Il Bersagliere*, 1 October 1879, p. 2.
[98] *Processo Cardinali*, p. 8.   [99] *Processo Cardinali*, p. 15.

far more sympathetic. She was accompanied from her cell by two guards. Vassallo described her as bent double, as if she wished to hide within herself, 'to be a fly or an ant, to be invisible to the hundreds of eyes fixed upon her with intense, shameless curiosity'. Unlike Cardinali, she was far from used to the public glare. Wasted, wrecked, aged, she was 'a woman destroyed'. She wept, sobbed, and hiccoughed continuously, her nose red, her eyes sunken, her lips damp, swollen, trembling. Her black widow's weeds and gloves only threw into relief her pallor.[100]

The great attention that all journalistic accounts gave to Raffaella's flesh was a proxy for reading her inner feelings, and, whether she felt it or not, she was read as expressing the deepest shame. Unlike Cardinali's body, which had given mere hints about his true feelings to the most perceptive observers, Raffaella's flesh left no doubts about her inner state. It pained everyone who witnessed her entrance: *L'Epoca*'s correspondent reported that her presence made a pitiable impression on all the assembled; *Il Piccolo*'s, who later claimed that the public expressed waves of compassion for Raffaella from the very beginning of the trial,[101] described her entry as one that 'wrought immense pity from the heart'. He concluded, 'Oh, if she is innocent, how miserable she must be; and if she is guilty, how much more so.'[102]

No such compassion was initially accorded to the third accused, Antonietta Carrozza. Vassallo reported that looking at her, no one would have guessed she was a circus performer. He described her olive-green dress as of 'equivocal taste', and her comportment as somewhere between embarrassed and indifferent.[103] By contrast, *Il Piccolo*'s more socially conservative writer was scathing. He described Carrozza as a strange 'human-bestial hybrid' who had sacrificed herself to 'the sensual appetites aroused in her man by other women'. He also perceived 'a strange resignation of character, the total silence of the sentiments and affects of a woman'.[104] The apparent lack of appropriate sentiment made her, in his view, unwomanly, and it seems that this made her guilty until proven innocent. The trial's findings, though, were not to be easily predicted by journalistic impressions of the crime's alleged perpetrators.

The three accused having taken their assigned positions, the jury of twelve men settled in, and the audience hushed, the president of the court, Giordano, flanked by two assistant judges, opened the trial. The imposing atmosphere of the Court of Assizes is illustrated by a contemporary impression shown in figure 5.2. The judge asked the accused to confirm their particulars. Cardinali did so with a steady voice; Raffaella's was barely audible; Antonietta followed. The president then ordered the full account of the charges, the 'atto di accusa', to be read aloud to all assembled. Much was already familiar, but the section that directly addressed the marriage relationship between Fadda and Saraceni must have particularly riveted

---

[100] *Processo Cardinali*, p. 7.   [101] 'Giustizia e legalità', *Il Piccolo*, 1 November 1879, p. 1.
[102] 'Il processo Fadda', *Il Piccolo*, 1 October 1879, p. 2.
[103] *Processo Cardinali*, p. 7.   [104] 'Il Processo Fadda', *Il Piccolo*, 1 October 1879, p. 2.

**Figure 5.2** The Court of Assizes of Rome during the Fadda trial

Source: *L'Epoca* (Genoa) 1–2 November 1879, p. 1, reproduced with permission from the Biblioteca di Storia Moderna e Contemporanea, Rome.

the audience. The *atto* claimed that a major motive for Saraceni to be rid of her husband was that she had allegedly often lamented publicly 'his complete impotence', claiming that he was, from her perspective, an 'inutile arnese', a 'useless tool'. The entire court listened to the full statement in 'maximum silence'.[105]

The stunned atmosphere was broken by the next step, when the president called in the witnesses and their presence was checked name by name. When the victim's father and brother, Giuseppe and Cesare Fadda, were called out, the public murmured in consternation and pity. The witnesses were sternly reminded of their duty to tell the truth, and then all were sent away until it was their turn to testify. The interrogation was about to begin. Vassallo noted that, as the reality of the trial became concrete in those stark seconds of silence, the 'imposing spectacle of the Assizes' finally got the better of Antonietta Carrozza. Her face reddened, her lips quivered, and she brought a handkerchief to her eyes. Her flesh

---

[105] 'Processo Fadda', *Corriere della Sera*, 1 October 1879, p. 2. This was one of the few newspapers to publish the full *atto di accusa*. Raffaella's alleged words about Fadda's impotence were presented in italics in the newspaper, though they were not emphasized in the original document. The word 'arnese' can mean tool, implement, gadget, and the like.

finally revealed that she had joined Raffaella in succumbing to her emotions.[106] Perhaps *Il Piccolo*'s stern journalist, who had found her devoid of sentiment, now thought better of her.

## Daily Hearings: Routine and Pathos

The trial consisted of an exceptional twenty-four days of hearings, spread over one month, from 30 September to 31 October 1879. Although the public and journalists assembled an hour or two before each day's hearing began, the personnel constituting 'the court', namely the three judges, the twelve jurors, and various ushers, formally entered at about 11 a.m. Proceedings were generally brought to a close by the late afternoon. Unsurprisingly, some days were rather routine, especially those involving the interrogation of the many minor witnesses. The trial's first phase, beginning with questions to the accused, and then nearly all witnesses, absorbed the first nine days' hearings. The remainder were dedicated to the great speeches made by the prosecution and the defence—though the unexpected appearance of new witnesses threw an exciting spanner into the trial's works shortly before its conclusion. This was just the most extraordinary moment among many that punctuated the trial's myriad details, during which heartstrings were pulled, beliefs beggared, eyes widened, ears strained, breath bated, then sharply drawn in, then exhaled in collective 'oohs' and 'aahs'.

The trial was long, but it was clearly engaging from beginning to end. Sometimes, beyond oohs and aahs, the audience expressed their feelings with bursts of spontaneous applause. When they did so, the president irritatedly and even angrily silenced them, using the effective threat of banishing sections of the audience from the room. Despite the trial's entertainment value, the participating public gradually learnt that the court was a very particular place when it came to expressing their collective emotions. Like other spaces with which most of the public would have had familiarity, such as the opera or theatre, the court was certainly one in which they experienced deep stirrings provoked by the highs and lows of an intense narrative. But they had to restrain and control their responses. Unlike other spaces in which gripping narratives unfolded, in court the public could not wear their hearts on their sleeves if they wanted to see the dramatic trial's finale.

Yet for the public and the accused, emotions, their expression, and their authenticity, while not the main object of the trial's scrutiny, quickly became key motifs. Cardinali's dubious affectations, already noted by many journalists, were thrown into relief by the president's initial interrogation, which forced the accused

---

[106] *Processo Cardinali*, p. 8.

to acknowledge his sexual relationships with Carolina and Antonietta and admit to courting admiration from women. Once that was out in the open, Cardinali was asked about his relationship with the unknown woman in Molise, from whom he had received so many letters, and even 'money, biscuits, and shirts'. The president reminded Cardinali that he had told the investigating magistrate he flattered the woman to solicit gifts. Cardinali shot back at the president that he would not be the first man to 'make love to women' (in the sense of flirting). 'No', agreed the president, 'but others do it because their hearts impel them; for you it is a profession.'[107] Cardinali was cast as emotionally inauthentic: he played on women's hearts even when his own was not in it.

Cardinali's self-gratification at the expense of others' purer sentiments was made even clearer by the way the president questioned Antonietta. According to Vassallo's account, Carozza was asked about the nature of her relationship with Cardinali, given that she had borne him two infants in 1870 and 1871, only to be cast aside when the artiste took up again with Carolina—with whom he had children both before and after the relationship with Antonietta. Did the 'relations' with Antonietta finish? 'No, sir', she answered, 'they continued'. 'Were you jealous of Carolina?' 'Oh yes!' 'Did you hate her?' 'Oh yes!' 'Would you have been pleased if she had left the company?' 'Oh yes!'[108] Curiously, while the two main published accounts of the trial generally corroborate each other, on this interchange they differed. *Il Bersagliere*'s report was much sparer. To the question of whether she was jealous of Carolina, Antonietta's reply was reported as a simple 'No'.[109] Clearly, the journalists took some poetic licence—Vassallo perhaps more than Coboevich. Even allowing for this, it is clear that the prosecution felt it was important to sound the emotional depths of intimate life within the circus.

Similarly, during Raffaella's first extensive interrogation, on day two of the trial, the prosecution delved into the details of her marriage in search of genuine feelings. Many of the couple's letters were read out loud, again as if inviting those present to assess the couple's emotional tenor. The prosecution sought to show that intense feelings on Raffaella's part were either sorely wanting, or expressed to inappropriate targets. To prove the point, the president focused on one particular moment: when Raffaella had been told by the police about her husband's death, why did they report that she reacted coldly? Why did she seem indifferent? Why had she not wept, as any other woman in her position would have done?[110] On that occasion, her apparent emotional containment, whatever its reasons, damned Raffaella. She should have wailed. She should have been distraught. Instead, she had been calm, and the police and other witnesses (a plasterer working in the house) had found that disturbing and revealing.

---

[107] *Processo Cardinali*, p. 14; *Processo Fadda*, p. 16.   [108] *Processo Cardinali*, p. 21.
[109] *Processo Fadda*, p. 24.   [110] *Processo Cardinali*, p. 18; *Processo Fadda*, p. 21.

Witness accounts of Raffaella's lack of reaction to the news of Fadda's murder fitted the prosecution's narrative well. The argument, effectively, would be that the linen of their marriage had actually remained too clean for Raffaella's taste. The president lost no time in coming to the delicate question of Giovanni Fadda's possible impotence. He read out the certificate attesting to the war injury and atrophied left testicle, and asked Raffaella, 'hesitantly', if her husband had been up to his marital duties. In contrast to her alleged coldness upon hearing about Fadda's death, in court Raffaella was frequently an emotional wreck, sniffling and whimpering under the prosecutor's questions. A full-page illustration of Raffaella in *Processo Fadda illustrato* shows her dabbing tears the size of pearls.[111] She was just able to assert having been unaware of her husband's physical impairments. The prosecution's argument would culminate in a claim that, even if Fadda had been sexually capable, he was not capable enough for Raffaella. Her desires and emotions were mismatched: on the one hand, she had appeared unmoved by the news that her husband had been murdered, and on the other, she seemed to desire more sexual satisfaction than he could give her.

The question of Fadda's sexual capacity surfaced regularly throughout the trial, though whose case the question best served was uncertain. The absence of children after seven years of marriage was its own poignant testimony, but it did not amount to hard evidence about the couple's sex life. Unable, or unwilling, to press Raffaella on the degree to which Fadda had been capable of the sexual act, the prosecution and the defence nevertheless raised the matter with any witness who had mentioned having heard rumours about it. There were many, but a particularly notable one involved some of the women of Cassano who recalled discussing the question while gathered to conserve tomatoes in the summer of 1878.[112] Such accounts took their place alongside other evidence. The court had heard the certificate of Fadda's groin injury read out earlier, and at the end of the second day, the report of the autopsy on Fadda's cadaver was also read aloud. The only transcript to report the reading compressed the long document into nineteen words. They focused on the twenty-three stab wounds and the fact of the atrophied testicle, but did not touch on the scalpel's journey down Fadda's urethra.[113]

Later though, one of the lawyers for the defence referred to Fadda's penile 'restriction', as if it were known to the court.[114] This suggests that the public, even with its high concentration of women, were not spared even the most specific details of the autopsy. What we cannot know, alas, is how the audience reacted to such details, let alone what they felt privately. The way the trial necessitated open

---

[111] *Processo Fadda*, p. 17.
[112] ASR, TCPV, 1879, b. 3659, vol. II, f. 263, 24 November 1878, verbal comparison, Maria Concetta Marino and Maria Ferraro. The women recalled discussing the matter during a ten-day session of making tomato conserve. The conversation was discussed in court—see *Processo Cardinali*, pp. 41–2.
[113] *Processo Fadda*, p. 24.   [114] Pessina's *arringa* on 30 October, *Processo Fadda*, p. 194.

discussion of aspects of sexuality in front of a female public is what most disturbed conservative elements of Italian society, and, judging by the desire of some men to protect the female public from such matters, it might easily be thought that there would be mass faintings and shock within the court. Nothing like that seems to have happened. Indeed, it was women's thirst to drink in such details that so alarmed some observers, from the poet Carducci to reporters for the Vatican's haughty newspaper, the *Osservatore Romano*.[115]

Popular attitudes to impotence in Italy await their historian, but many of the perceptive observations offered by Angus McLaren's general cultural history can be mapped neatly onto the Italian case. This is largely because the Church had so much early influence over those attitudes across all of Christendom. For hundreds of years, successful coitus had been a key factor in the validity of a marriage.[116] Although unstated, it was probably this that made the question central in the Fadda murder trial. The fact that it was discussed by women preparing tomatoes in 1870s Calabria, and by any number of others, underlines that in daily life such subjects were far from off-limits in women's conversations. On the other hand, as McLaren suggests, by the later nineteenth century, as sexuality became more medicalized, the problem of impotence was well on its way to being perceived by men as opening the undesirable possibility of public discussion of women's sexual needs.[117]

Judging by some reactions to the Fadda trial, this was a possibility that many in Italy strongly resisted. Yet the fact that the trial faced the question of Fadda's impotence and explored its implications, not over a kitchen table, but in a public arena before hundreds of men and women, was surely a key reason for the sensation generated by the event. By the end of day two, with an astonishing story having taken shape, the interrogation of Raffaella about her sex life, the reading of private letters, medical certificates, and autopsy reports, it was plain that the trial was not going to be a disappointment to the public after the enormous build-up. But the hearings did not only offer sensation by breaking taboos. There was much of deep human pathos, as well as humour, surprise, and other peaks and troughs of sentiment, to add flesh to the law's lengthy and sometimes dry deliberations.

The public was particularly moved on day three of the trial, when the murder victim's father, Giuseppe Fadda, a septuagenarian notary from Cagliari, took the stand as the first witness to testify. When the usher brought Fadda senior into the court, the audience paid 'profound attention' that signalled deep compassion.

---

[115] 'Cronaca cittadina', *Osservatore romano*, 22 October 1879, p. 3. The article reports the publication of Carducci's poem. Although the Church saw the poet as a 'Singer of Satan' and referred to the Fadda poem as one of his 'usual barbarisms', the *Osservatore* shared the sentiment that women ought not be witnessing 'the depraved episodes of this abominable trial'.

[116] Angus McLaren, *Impotence: A Cultural History* (Chicago: University of Chicago Press, 2007), p. xi, pp. 33–7, p. 73.

[117] McLaren, *Impotence*, pp. 109–10.

The president declared, 'You are the father of the victim', at which point, according to Coboevich, the old man simply broke down in sobs.[118] Asked if he preferred not to testify, he found the strength to whisper that he would abstain. At this point, according to Vassallo, 'Saraceni was weeping profusely' as well.[119] It was a brief but intense moment of pathos, where compassion for an old man who had lost his son to a violent crime was shared across the whole court. Focus on the facts was re-established by a long period in the witness box of the victim's younger brother, Cesare Fadda. Cesare provided so much information about the marriage, his feelings about the Saraceni family, and his conviction that Raffaella was to blame, that the raw emotions of the earlier moment were smoothed by procedure and the sheer weight of detail.

As well as routine and pathos, the trial also provided moments that fascinated the Roman audience, particularly when witness statements either corroborated or clashed with the claims of the official *atto di accusa*. The witnesses from Calabria were interesting in themselves, as they provided insights into life in a province with which most Romans would not have had personal experience. Among the first to be called was Rosina Pesci, a twenty-eight-year-old woman from Cassano who, under questioning in court, affirmed that Raffaella had once said to her that Fadda was impotent. Another early Calabrian witness was Leonardo Rizzo, conductor of an orchestra engaged to provide music for the circus. Rizzo repeated what he had said under interrogation nearly eleven months earlier: that the circus clown Carluccio had described Cardinali's friendship with the Saraceni family as one that allowed him 'to eat, drink, and f[uck]!'[120] It is unclear whether he pronounced the last word in full, but everyone knew that is what he meant.

Very early on then, the prosecution's witnesses reinforced to the court, jury, and public the idea that Fadda was sexually inadequate, that Raffaella had abhorred the vacuum, and that Cardinali had readily filled it. Even more damning was the testimony of a Castrovillari hairdresser, Rosina Garramone, who affirmed that the clown from the circus known as Carluccio had confided in her that Raffaella had offered him 100 piastre (about 500 lire) to go to Rome and kill her husband. Garramone reported that the clown had been extremely anxious, fearing that, if he refused, Cardinali would beat him up. She told the court that her advice to the clown had been to escape as quickly as possible. It was well known to all that Carluccio had done precisely this, because, since the murder, he had been the subject of a fruitless search by the police for months on end.[121] The prosecution's case would have been much stronger if they had not had to rely on a second-hand account of the allegation against Raffaella.

---

[118] *Processo Fadda*, p. 27.    [119] *Processo Cardinali*, p. 23.
[120] *Processo Cardinali*, p. 29; *Processo Fadda*, p. 31. Both reports use 'f...' instead of the word *fottere* (to fuck), so it is not known whether the full word was uttered before the court.
[121] ASR, TCPR, 1879, b. 3659, vol. IB, ff. 253–78, and ff. 316-8 testify to official attempts to find Carluccio, in a search that stretched from Naples and Bari to Milan and Turin.

As well as these notes of intense drama, the newspapers relished reporting clashes and disagreements between some of the Calabrian witnesses. An example involved Maria Ferraro, who had been Raffaella's wet nurse and remained her close confidante in adulthood. Suspected of having acted as a go-between in the plot to murder Fadda, Ferraro had figured in cryptic telegrams exchanged between Cardinali and Antonietta once the former had arrived in Rome. These referred to her by the code name *Mamma latte* ('Mother milk'). In court, Vassallo described Ferraro as having the appearance of a 'cunning peasant, energetic and malicious'.[122] Her testimony contradicted that of another local servant, who had told the investigators of banter among local women about how best to resolve Raffaella's unsatisfactory marriage. The two women were placed in front of each other to thrash out the truth. They 'exchanged threatening gestures and signs of anger', in 'pure Calabrian dialect', to the evident amusement of the journalists and, in all probability, the public.[123]

The fact that there was no clear resolution to the disagreement seems not to have been crucial. Of more concern were the telegrams themselves, whose secret language much vexed the authorities. Several of these miraculously fast missives had been exchanged between Pietro and Antonietta after he arrived in Rome to murder Fadda, only to find that Fadda was, in fact, in Calabria. Antonietta had already explained what the telegram's key code words meant to the investigating magistrate during the inquisitorial phase, but the court saw fit to invite a local expert to translate the telegrams before the public. The appearance of one Giuseppe Pinta, a prominent figure from the great Guillaume circus for which Cardinali himself had auditioned a few days before the murder, brought a note of burlesque to the sombre court rituals.

Pinta was widely known to Romans as the trainer of a beloved 'thinking donkey' named Marco. Vassallo commented wryly that the trainer's purplish face suggested strong 'oenological nuances',[124] while the rather light-hearted journalist for *La Capitale* could not resist an even more slapstick and probably fictional approach. His account noted that as Pinta entered the court, he shook hands with many old friends, who asked solicitously after Marco the donkey's health, reporting that 'readers will be relieved to know he is in top form.'[125] Pinta, answering the president's questions about the telegram language in all seriousness, affirmed that the key words, *Vasco* and *Vasca*, were circus jargon for husband and wife.[126] It was clear to all that Cardinali's and Antonietta's telegrams referred specifically to Fadda and Raffaella, and the superficially amusing episode ominously tightened the net around all three of the accused.

---

[122] *Processo Cardinali*, p. 41.   [123] *Processo Fadda*, p. 48.
[124] *Processo Cardinali*, p. 32.   [125] 'Processo Fadda', *La Capitale* (Rome), 6 October 1879, p. 2.
[126] *Processo Fadda*, p. 37; *Processo Cardinali*, p. 32.

## Moving Rhetoric

On 14 October, after nine days of questions to the accused and a wide variety of witnesses, the proceedings transitioned to a new and eagerly anticipated phase. The eminent lawyers for the prosecution and the defence were to deliver their *arringhe*, the speeches in which they would seek to persuade the jury of the guilt or innocence of the accused. The word *arringa* comes from the same root as the English 'harangue', but in Italian the term had (and still has) positive connotations, describing a heartfelt and often long address that sought to persuade an audience. The lack of an exact English translation for *arringa* is telling, while the French equivalent is *plaidoirie*. Like the Italian *arringa*, the *plaidoirie* is strongly associated with arousing emotions,[127] but in a very controlled way.[128] In Italy, as in France, *arringhe* could often last for several hours each, but the public looked forward to them with excitement for several reasons. One was that their commencement marked a turning point in the trial towards the final phase. Another was that skilled rhetoric was a much admired art, and, because the Ciceronian tradition of intertwining emotional and reasoned persuasion remained strong in Italian public speeches, everyone anticipated being gratifyingly moved by what they were about to hear.[129]

The sense of anticipation was heightened by the fact that these verbal contests were no mere theatrical performances. They were life-and-death appeals to the jury, the judges, and the public, and they would pave a path directly to the verdicts. Altogether, as well as the chief prosecutor, eight further advocates were due to present their *arringhe*: two on the prosecution side, appearing on behalf of the Fadda family (the *parte civile*); one court-appointed defence lawyer for Cardinali and one for Antonietta, and four privately engaged lawyers for Saraceni. As this new phase began, Vassallo estimated that at least two weeks of 'unbridled eloquence' should be expected.[130] Emotions were a key weapon in these carefully choreographed jousts between the legal arena's gladiators. It was almost *de rigueur* for each of them to open with a strong admission of how deeply moved they felt by the trial, the story behind it, and their own role in it. More than once, the lawyers even argued about who had the greater right to evoke emotions for the sake of their case.

Each side clearly concerted their presentations to work together as emotional crescendos. Early on, a quietly moving *arringa* for the prosecution was made by

---

[127] On the emotions engaged by French lawyers, see Gian Marco Vidor, 'Rhetorical Engineering of Emotions in the Courtroom: the Case of Lawyers in Modern France', *Rechtsgeschichte—Legal History* 25 (2017): 286–95. Nor was the duration and emotional intensity of these speeches characteristic only of Latin lawyers—on Irish courts, for example, see Barclay, *Men in Court*, pp. 131–2.

[128] Francesca Tacchi, *Gli avvocati italiani dall'Unità alla Repubblica* (Bologna: Il Mulino, 2002), p. 211.

[129] Franco Arato, *Parola di avvocato*, p. 14.

[130] *Processo Cardinali*, p. 63. Vassallo's phrase was 'eloquenza sfrenata'.

Antonio Ponsiglioni, lawyer, professor of political economy, and parliamentary deputy, born in Cagliari in 1842, the same city and year as Giovanni Fadda.[131] He knew the Fadda family personally, and as he commenced his address, the audience paid particular attention. Ponsiglioni announced that he had agreed to participate in this 'painful debate' not out of ambition or vanity, but 'as a friend of the lamented captain, and of the poor old man whose heart still feels the very stabs that slaughtered his beloved son'. He then referred to his own inner state: his 'veins and pulse trembled' as he faced his formidable adversaries.[132]

No doubt Ponsiglioni genuinely felt intense anxiety as the entire court's attention focused on him. But, as with any successful performer, he harnessed the trembling to give authenticity to what he was about to say. He tamed his anxiety with formulaic gentilities, paying homage to his learned friends on the other side. Ponsiglioni embodied a masculine ideal of intense but controlled emotion, just as his departed friend Fadda had done: they were of the same cohort, the same species of emotional man. Ponsiglioni explained that Fadda's was an honourable family of 'austere virtues', and that the soldier had turned his back on a 'splendid' civil career for loyalty and love of his country. In contrast to such disciplined and productive sentiments, Ponsiglioni portrayed Raffaella as vain, drawn to 'glitter, lust, and scandal'. The trial, he said, had revealed a 'trail of filthy affairs...all marked by an ostentatious cynicism'.[133] Unrestrained feelings, he implied, had been put scandalously on display.

The evocative narrative brought Raffaella and Cardinali together in a bold rhetorical flourish. Poor Fadda had probably been quite capable, Ponsiglioni suggested, of meeting his marital obligations, but Raffaella's insatiability made it difficult or even impossible for him to satisfy her needs. Cardinali, despite Carolina, despite Antonietta, was as free as any man of 'Muslim habits'. 'Raffaella had a choice: the captain or Cardinali. Which of the two men best satisfied her desires? There is no doubt.'[134] This was the *arringa*'s dramatic apex, portraying Raffaella's and Cardinali's greedy, unrestrained emotions as having led to unspeakable violence against a noble patriot. After this, having sought to win the audience to his view, the advocate proceeded ineluctably with a systematic rehearsal of the evidence against all three accused.

Ponsiglioni addressed his final, resounding words to 'that liberal institution', the jury, whose members, he said, 'would surely feel the sense of right and justice that was palpitatingly alive in this space'. Reining in the throbbing emotions of the arena back to the restraint of a hallowed temple, he concluded by telling the jury:

---

[131] http://notes9.senato.it/web/senregno.NSF/c9a692e20ea5e59dc125785e003c094c/c05353457231 71724125646f005ea3d7?OpenDocument (accessed 24 April 2018).
[132] *Processo Fadda*, p. 95.  [133] *Processo Cardinali*, p. 70.
[134] *Processo Cardinali*, pp. 69–73; *Processo Fadda*, pp. 95–102. Both Vasallo's and Coboevich's accounts corroborate each other well, though the reference to 'Muslim habits' does not appear in the latter's. Even if Ponsiglioni did not use it in court, Vasallo's use of the term as shorthand for sexual immorality is significant in itself.

'In pronouncing a verdict of guilty, you will be doing sacred work, for which society will be grateful in eternity.' His four-hour speech reportedly held the attention of the auditorium from beginning to end, at which point many lawyers, including those from the defence, gathered around to shake hands with and congratulate the orator.[135]

Next, the chief prosecutor, Ippolito Rutigliano, sought to clinch the prosecution's case. The reporter Coboevich, himself a lawyer, wondered whether the prosecutor would be able to add anything new, or whether this *arringa* would simply be a 'rifrittura', a refry, of earlier arguments.[136] Rutigliano also claimed, 'despite long experience', to feel unusual trepidation today. Whether this was due to 'the imposing crowd, the solemnity of the setting, or the brilliance of the defence lawyers', he could not say. Despite nerves, his mission was to render a 'sacrosanct' service in the name of justice. He claimed that he had repeated visions of the bloody cadaver of a proud soldier, and he would not rest until the authors of the crime were punished. It was clear that Rutigliano felt a heavy emotional investment in proving the guilt of those he accused, and he displayed his feelings as a badge of honour.

Rutigliano immediately took 'the jury back to Via dei Carbonari' to witness Fadda's final moments of life, when, with blood pouring out of him, the brave soldier sought to pursue his attacker. As Fadda expired, Rutigliano suggested, he must have known that 'his assassin had been armed by the woman to whom he had given his heart.'[137] This emotive exposition, delivered in 'a voice heavy with sentiment and with vibrant gestures', had a profound effect on the public. According to Vassallo, it was 'almost as if a shiver ran through the court.' Raffaella and Antonietta, he reported, were both 'agitated by convulsive gulps'.[138] Rutigliano underlined that Cardinali had 'coldly planned' the murder for weeks beforehand. He may have loved Raffaella, but, as the letters from his admirers showed, he loved for money and lust: 'he loved like a brute.'[139]

As for Raffaella, Rutigliano argued that she 'hated her husband', proven by her refusal to live with him and her malicious gossip about him. Rather than malign Fadda, Rutigliano claimed, she should have acknowledged that any shortcomings on his part were due to self-sacrifice on the 'altar of the *patria*'.[140] Instead, Rutigliano accused, Raffaella sought to do away with him, first by inviting the clown Carluccio to undertake the deed (and whose subsequent mysterious disappearance the prosecutor hinted was also foul play). Finally, Rutigliano claimed, Raffaella, 'between one kiss and another', had instigated Cardinali to carry out the murder.[141]

Raffaella's legendary coldness upon hearing the news of her husband's murder, her failure to shed one tear, found its corollary, the prosecutor argued, in her

---

[135] *Processo Fadda*, p. 102. [136] *Processo Fadda*, p. 102. [137] *Processo Fadda*, pp. 102–3.
[138] *Processo Cardinali*, p. 74. [139] *Processo Fadda*, p. 109.
[140] *Processo Fadda*, p. 111. [141] *Processo Cardinali*, p. 75; *Processo Fadda*, p. 108.

attitude in court: far from showing malice towards her husband's murderer and his accomplice, she sat there 'cold, taciturn, indifferent'. Her sentiments, in sum, were perverted: too passionate when they ought not to be, and too cold when she should have been moved. Possibly aware of incipient public sympathy for Raffaella, and knowing that his case against her was factually the weakest, the prosecutor urged the jury simply to find all three of the accused equally guilty.[142]

## The Defence

The prosecution's case now laid out, an advocate named Ercole Ranzi, a parliamentary deputy like several of the others, had the unenviable task of launching the defence by speaking for Cardinali. Ranzi began by 'permitting himself a frank word' to the prosecution, whose language he said had been 'abundant in sarcasm' towards those who, sitting on the 'bench of misadventure', nevertheless deserved respect. Ranzi warned the jury to guard themselves against exaggeration, imploring them to be 'as cold as the law'.[143] He was the first of several to criticize the emotive tactics of the prosecution, and he sought to return the proceedings to a cooler register. This suited his own task, which was to try to shift Cardinali's crime from the category of 'assassination' to a less serious one that would not carry the death penalty.

Yet, to do so Ranzi deployed arguments about passions and emotions to sow seeds of doubt about whether Cardinali really fitted the category of the 'assassin', whose distinctive feature was 'continuous cold premeditation'.[144] Cardinali's plan, he argued, had in fact been motivated by passion. The horseman was fanatically professional and intensely proud of his public admiration. Cardinali had clearly been moved, Ranzi reminded the court, when the circus experts Guillaume and Pinta assessed him as a first-class artist worth 400 lire a month despite his flaws.[145] Cardinali was similarly passion-driven, Ranzi argued, when it came to women. He 'was anything but a cold calculator', proven by the way Cardinali carelessly told friends in Bari of his lover's beauty and of his dreams. Was this, Ranzi asked rhetorically, the behaviour of a coldly premeditative assassin, or a man crazed by love?[146]

The prosecution had argued that the trail of witnesses Cardinali left in his wake was testimony to stupidity as well as calculation, but Ranzi's claim was that his client was motivated solely by an excess of passion and indignation on Raffaella's behalf. He echoed the prosecutor Rutigliano's powerful image of the illicit couple

---

[142] *Processo Fadda*, p. 120.   [143] *Processo Fadda*, p. 120.   [144] *Processo Fadda*, p. 127.
[145] Vassallo wrote that Cardinali wept upon hearing this assessment (*Processo Cardinali*, p. 86), while Coboevich wrote that he seemed irritated by the mention of professional flaws (*Processo Fadda*, p. 128).
[146] *Processo Fadda*, p. 128.

plotting 'between one kiss and another', suggesting how persuasive it might have been if, 'during amorous ecstasy', Raffaella had sighed, 'Ah, how happy we would be if only I were not married.' Ranzi proposed that she had uttered these words not as an instigation to crime, but as a fantasy about what might have been. Cardinali, driven by the trope of avenging a woman he thought duped by her husband, had made too much of his lover's sighs about a hypothetical situation. Guilty of the murder, no doubt, but driven by blind passion, Cardinali deserved a verdict, his defender urged, that would not involve the gallows, a verdict that was 'just, but human'.[147]

Ranzi concluded his *arringa* at 3 p.m. on Friday 18 October, and the hearing would resume the following Monday. The remainder of the trial was to be punctuated by two unexpected events. The first, on Sunday 19th, was the publication of Carducci's sensational poem, *A proposito del caso Fadda*, on the front page of the *Fanfulla della Domenica*.[148] When the hearing resumed the next morning, Carducci's verses provided Carlo Palomba, the advocate defending Antonietta Carrozza, with an appealing way to open his *arringa*. Expressing the conviction that 'Italy loves its army and is grief-stricken when one of its brave sons is barbarously murdered', the first figures Palomba defended were the mothers of Italy. The large number of women in the audience whom Carducci had so criticized had not come, Palomba said, 'to crumble pastries between the court and the prison'. They had been collectively moved to see that even a valiant soldier was not immune to an assassin's blade.[149] The mothers of Italy, he implied, were in court to pay homage to a martyred son of the nation.

After this strategic gesture to the maligned female public, Palomba settled in to the task of defending his client. Antonietta Carrozza stood accused of complicity in the crime, having 'knowingly assisted' the murderer. Her part in the coded telegraphic correspondence between Rome and Cassano just before the murder may be clear evidence of her involvement, but, as Palomba argued, she had suffered an entirely arbitrary arrest, at the behest of the local police rather than Rome's investigating magistrate. Building brilliantly on Carducci's poetic portrayal of the bloodthirsty matrons of ancient Rome, Palomba asked the court whether, as the prosecution claimed, Antonietta had really held Fadda's life in her hands, and whether it was really she who gave the fatal 'thumbs down that plunged the assassin's blade into Fadda's breast'. He was to paint an altogether more sympathetic portrait of Antonietta Carrozza.

To do so, Palomba developed the theme of maternal and family love he had introduced by defending the mothers of Italy from Carducci's pen. The prosecution had portrayed Antonietta, he said, as 'so cynical and indifferent as to play the

---

[147] *Processo Cardinali*, pp. 86–7; and *Processo Fadda*, p. 131.
[148] *Fanfulla della Domenica*, 19 October 1879, p. 1.
[149] *Processo Fadda*, p. 132; *Processo Cardinali*, p. 87.

part of matchmaker to her lover's paramour' (that is, matchmaker between Cardinali and Raffaella). That was all too easy a judgement, he declared.[150] Instead, he invited the audience to consider the life story of the woman before them: Antonietta had been 'torn' from her own family at the age of seven and placed in a circus. How would noble sentiments have been instilled in her heart? By the rider's whip? Thus she grew up, until Cardinali brutally snatched her honour, and she became a mother before she knew it. And yet, she never heard the word 'mother' pass over the lips of her little ones. She never saw them again, forced as she was by her bullying lover to give them up for adoption. This was a purely emotive argument, and unsurprisingly, the public's hearts melted into 'vivid signs of approval'.[151]

Palomba went on:

Antonietta cynical? No. She was a slave. She represents a stratum of society whose existence perhaps none of us knew about. In the hands of that man, she was an object, not a person. When I see such painful social phenomena I ask myself—given all these new societies for the protection of animals—whether there ought not to be one for humans whose lives are worse even than those of dumb beasts.[152]

This line too elicited warm *approvazioni* from the court. Palomba had clearly struck a chord, and he pressed his argument home. He demolished the idea, claimed by the prosecution, that there was something strange about the friendship between 'the gypsies' and the well-off Saraceni family. In small towns, where 'hospitality is a tradition and kindness an instinct', it was completely to be expected.[153] Moreover, Palomba suggested, in the Saraceni household, Antonietta had finally received the love and affection she had never found in 'Sultan Cardinali's harem'.[154]

The rest of Palomba's *arringa* was devoted to throwing doubt upon the prosecution's factual evidence. He did this creditably, even persuasively. But it was through his image of Antonietta's slavery, the tender affection she received in the Saraceni household, and above all the evocation of her own cruelly thwarted maternity, that he won the public's and the court's sympathy for his client. As he concluded, crowds rushed to the bench to shake his hand and congratulate him. They did this not because of the penetrating logic he employed in undermining the prosecution's evidence, but because of the way he had evoked primal sentiments about motherhood and family protection, and the abuse Antonietta had suffered without them. If the final verdicts can be taken to indicate the effectiveness of an advocate, Palomba's emotionally appealing address was the most successful.

---

[150] *Processo Fadda*, p. 132.    [151] *Processo Cardinali*, p. 88.
[152] *Processo Fadda*, p. 132. On the early animal rights movement in Italy, see Giulia Guazzaloca, '"In the Name of Justice and Compassion": Animal Protection in Italy during the Liberal Age (1861–1914)', *Modern Italy*, vol. 22, no. 3 (August 2017): 261–89.
[153] *Processo Fadda*, p. 133.    [154] *Processo Fadda*, p. 133.

The remaining hours of that afternoon were filled by the first *arringa* in Raffaella Saraceni's defence, presented by the young Saverio Tutino. Though a clever speaker who made stirring classical references, the court did not resonate with the intensity of his words as it had done for Palomba. For that, the public had to wait until the next day, when the thirty-four-year-old Neapolitan advocate, Pietro Rosano, took the stand. Even from the only traces of his words left to posterity, those printed on yellowing pages, it is clear why he attracted admiration. He began, as others had done, by declaring how 'profoundly *comosso*', how moved he felt, how close to the surface were his own emotions. Why so? It was not the gravest trial he had ever faced; it was not first time 'the executioner's axe glinted' over his client's head. No: the reason his heart beat so fast now, he explained, was the painful personal memory of a balmy May evening in 1871 when he had witnessed his friends Giovanni Fadda and Raffaella Saraceni joyfully marry. He then turned to Fadda's imagined ghost, asking ominously, 'who could have told you then that within a few years you would be dead, and that your wife would be the object of the most contumelious allegations?'[155] This imagery elicited another shudder from the court.[156]

Tutino then spoke directly about emotions in court, appearing to praise the prosecutors, particularly Rutigliano, for their evocative power and for the way they moved the audience, including himself. The compliment was a trick, for he quickly changed tack: 'But it is not for the prosecution', he announced, 'to accuse by emotion...they must be cold...they must not seek to convince through their own tears, nor by seeking to make others weep. That way, the verdict would be a consequence of emotion, not reason.'[157] Vassallo and Coboevich both reported this reprimand, but the former tellingly put words into Rosano's mouth that may never have come out of it: 'It is for us [the defence] to speak to the heart. You [the prosecution] represent society; we, the individual.'[158] Whether Rosano made the criticism so explicitly or not, it was implied, and he certainly accused the prosecution of evoking emotions, drawing critical attention to their potential misuse.

Emotions were weapons Rosano himself only made use of sparingly, relying more on eloquence and imagery to undermine the prosecution's case. He did not try to insist that Fadda was a paragon of virility, but suggested that if Raffaella had been forced to seek pleasure elsewhere, it was for those without sin to throw the first stone. In any case, he argued, Raffaella's alleged adultery was unproven: the prosecution's case was built on the hearsay of a small town, hearsay 'brewed in the local pharmacies and taverns'. The magistrate had put the brew into a bottle for the prosecutor to open in court. All that came out when the bottle was uncorked, he claimed, was 'insignificant froth, leaving no more lasting a mark than champagne on the fine dresses of lovely ladies.'[159]

---

[155] *Processo Fadda*, p. 139.    [156] *Processo Cardinali*, p. 98.    [157] *Processo Fadda*, p. 140.
[158] *Processo Cardinali*, p. 98.    [159] *Processo Cardinali*, p. 100; *Processo Fadda*, p. 142.

Shortly after Rosano tried to dismiss the prosecution's accusations, the proceedings were punctuated by something much more alarming than the pop of a champagne cork. As the speaker rested for a minute, a telegram was delivered to the president of the court. After reading it, he announced that the judicial authorities near Bari had finally found and arrested the elusive clown, Carluccio. The court was overtaken by sensation.[160] The subject of an exhaustive search all over Italy lasting months, Carluccio had almost been given up for dead. Having allegedly been commissioned by Raffaella to murder Fadda in return for 100 ducats, Carluccio was the prosecution's last hope of presenting evidence against her that Rosano would not be able to dismiss as small-town froth. The clown's discovery sparked profound surprise, or, as one reporter put it, 'universal stupefaction expressed by an "ooh," half a kilometre long'. Opera glasses were trained on Raffaella to see how she reacted to this threatening news, and within seconds, the sobriety of the court, hushed by Rosano's eloquence, became a rowdy arena, in which 'emotion took hold of everyone in the court'.[161]

## Intermezzo, with Clowns

Courts of law must often have encountered collective surprise for all sorts of reasons, particularly when witnesses or the accused revealed unexpected facts. Ideally, surprise would be muffled and absorbed by the court's serious atmosphere, but on this occasion, its magnitude was too great to be contained. The president indicated that he intended to use his discretionary power to allow the new witness to testify. Understandably, the defence was highly annoyed, and argued strongly for the trial to be deferred. There followed a heated though decorous argument about the extent of the president's powers, with the defence arguing that it was too late to introduce new witnesses. The court (presumably just the three judges) withdrew to deliberate, and the hall erupted into 'infernal discussion—like a nest of wasps'.[162] Soon the court re-entered, and the president announced that Carluccio would testify as soon as he arrived in Rome, the next afternoon. This caused enormous excitement that rippled out from the court and across the city.

The next day, hundreds and possibly thousands of Romans mobbed the station in the hope of glimpsing of Carluccio. A journalist writing for the serious Naples newspaper *Il Piccolo* lamented the decline of Rome from 'theatre of Caesar's triumphs to today's arena of clowns', and the way names like Cardinali and Carluccio eclipsed the great names of the day like Bismarck and Beaconsfield.[163] The scene

---

[160] *Processo Cardinali*, p. 100; *Processo Fadda*, p. 142.
[161] 'Processo Fadda', *L'Epoca*, 22–3 October 1879, p. 2.   [162] *Processo Cardinali*, p. 100.
[163] 'CARLUCCIO', *Il Piccolo*, 23 October 1879, p. 1 (upper case title original).

at the court immediately prior to Carluccio's appearance was one of pandemonium: *L'Epoca* suggested that if Vesuvius and Etna were to erupt together, their lava might have a faint chance of being compared to the human rivers flowing around the court.[164] *Il Piccolo* claimed that 'Deputies, senators, magistrates, professors, notables, men and women, have all been caught by the contagion of this judicial curiosity', and *Il Bersagliere* specified who some of them were, including the Turkish ambassador.[165] Even the eternally disdainful *Osservatore Romano* forgot its habitual condescension for a moment, reporting on the hearing's 'richness of incident', exemplified by 'two well-dressed ladies almost coming to blows in the reserved seating area'.[166]

Within the court, Vassallo described the atmosphere as delirious, with the immense crowd shouting, pushing, and squashing. He expressed relief that it would be his last day on the Fadda trial: tomorrow would see him bound for Tuscany, to report on another major case to be heard in Siena. Carluccio's appearance was a fitting climax for Vassallo's colourful pen. Running out of images to describe the suffocating crush, he said that even the moralists and puritans who normally sneer at these spectacles 'would conjure Jesus from their hands if it meant they could get a seat'. At 3 p.m. the court entered, to a prolonged 'Oh!' from the crowd. The president ordered the witnesses whose testimony made Carluccio a person of such interest—the hairdresser Rosina Garramone and the conductor Leonardo Rizzo—to be taken away. He then ordered Carluccio, whose full name was Carlo Bertone, to be brought in to the court. There was perfect silence. Then, everyone leapt up and craned their necks as Carluccio made his entrance.[167]

The clown was a disappointment. As Vassallo put it, 'Carluccio looked extremely common, both in dress and physiognomy. He looked like a peasant.'[168] Coboevich gave more detail: his face was pallid; he wore a suit the colour of lead; his face was thin, young and beardless; he had longish, lank brown hair.[169] Asked to state his details, the court heard that he was twenty years old, born in Contursi (about 100 kilometres east of Naples), of unknown paternity, and an entertainer by profession. Despite his disappointing appearance, his testimony entertained the public. He said he had come to know of the affair between Cardinali and Raffaella because late one night in Cassano he had witnessed her drop a rope for Cardinali to climb. He alleged that a few days after this, he had been summoned to Raffaella's house, where she, in the company of Antonietta, had offered him one hundred ducats to kill Fadda. He pretended to consider the proposal and accepted six ducats on the spot. He then became very anxious and decided to run away from the circus altogether. This he did in the company of a fellow clown, Federico Trebisondo.[170]

---

[164] 'Processo Fadda', *L'Epoca*, 23–4 October 1879, p. 2.
[165] 'CARLUCCIO', *Il Piccolo*, 23 October 1879, p. 1; and *Processo Fadda*, p. 147.
[166] 'Cronaca cittadina', *Osservatore Romano*, 25 October 1879, p. 3.
[167] *Processo Cardinali*, p. 101.     [168] *Processo Cardinali*, p. 102.
[169] *Processo Fadda*, p. 147.     [170] *Processo Fadda*, pp. 147–8; *Processo Cardinali*, pp. 103–4.

Yet Carluccio denied having told anyone about the proposal, including the hairdresser Rosina Garramone. He was then asked specifically if he had characterized the friendship between Cardinali and Saraceni as 'Eating, drinking and f…ing'? Yes, that he had said. How, the president asked, did he know about 'the third thing'? Carluccio retorted that Cardinali climbing the rope to her bedroom was one indicator, and he said he had also seen the pair in a garden 'in a wicked position'.[171] A long series of questions and answers then unfolded between the president, two defence lawyers, Carluccio, Raffaella, and, now brought back in, Rosina Garramone. Carluccio admitted that he recognized her but flatly denied he had ever told her anything about Raffaella's commission. The pair contradicted each other tit-for-tat, causing sensation in the audience. Both Vassallo's and Coboevich's reports convey scenes reminiscent of an operatic quintet where the performers sing together without hearing each other and are all at cross-purposes.

At the end of the day, which revealed nothing conclusive, the defence renewed its claims for a deferral. The president refused, and in fact complicated matters by ordering the appearance of two further witnesses to test Carluccio's claims. One was the other clown, Trebisondo, known within the circus as Bergamuccio.[172] Like Carluccio, Bergamuccio had to travel to Rome, in his case from Campobasso, southern Italy, which delayed the proceedings by a day. When he did appear, on the afternoon of Saturday 25 October, it was clear that the novelty of clowns had worn off, as the crowd lacked the intensity it had had for Carluccio's first appearance.[173] Bergamuccio began his story by claiming that he had assisted Cardinali to enter Raffaella's bedroom by means of a board perched between a windowsill and an adjacent rooftop, rather than a rope.[174] The audience ended after the two clowns had confronted each other in a welter of contradictions to the extent that ultimately their narratives lost all credibility.

## From Ridiculous to Sublime

Pietro Rosano, the young and talented Neapolitan advocate whose *arringa* had been interrupted by Carluccio's discovery, was now, after an interval of several days, able to resume the defence of his client Raffaella Saraceni. Recovering the disadvantage of lost momentum, Rosano drew the audience back in to his story by revealing his own emotions at the point when, a few days ago, just as he was overcoming his initial trepidation, the thunderclap of Carluccio's discovery had 'snatched the words' from his lips.[175] He told the court that he had

---

[171] *Processo Fadda*, p. 148.  [172] *Processo Cardinali*, pp. 104–8; *Processo Fadda* pp. 148–50.
[173] *Processo Fadda*, p. 155.  [174] *Processo Cardinali*, p. 110; *Processo Fadda*, p. 155.
[175] *Processo Fadda*, p. 167.

felt indescribable palpitations, and feared greatly for Saraceni's case. Turning the debacle to the defence's advantage, with sarcastic grace Rosano thanked the president for having called both Carluccio and Bergamuccio, declaring that 'the testimony of the lout from Campobasso had destroyed that of the bastard from Contursi.'[176]

The orator resumed a vigorous stride, and from there, over several hours across two days, he built a powerful defence of Raffaella Saraceni. He argued that there was absolutely no motive for his client to have sought her husband's murder. She might have done if Fadda had been tyrannical, but he was the opposite, and, as the prosecution themselves insisted, rightly or wrongly Raffaella had been tacitly permitted to gratify whatever desires she may have had. The prosecution had portrayed Raffaella as calculating. If so, Rosano asked, might she have calculated that her dowry, which yielded 80 lire a month after tax, would not have allowed her to live a carefree life with a retired acrobat? On the contrary, he claimed, the great 'calculatress's alleged plan would have forced her to don a leotard and descend into the circus ring herself', at which applause broke out in the court.[177] Though a clever image, above all the applause probably expressed the widespread sympathy for Raffaella's plight.

Rosano was once again moving his listeners emotionally, and the president threatened to move them literally if they continued to express their feelings with applause. The talented young advocate then pressed on to the finishing line with what he hoped would be a winning streak. He repeated that Raffaella had no motive to instigate the murder. Yes, she was a sensual woman, but she had been given a margin of tolerance by the most compliant of husbands. 'Jurors!', Rosano called out, 'Think of the civilizations of this cosmos: Egyptian, Greek, Roman. They have all fallen, leaving only one survivor among their ruins: justice; the sentiment of justice.'[178] Appealing to their pride, he proclaimed that the jurors would certainly do justice to their Roman origins as well as to Raffaella, by responding 'No' when asked if she were guilty. Thunderous applause broke like a wave over Rosano's final words, and it was some time before the long-suffering president was able to restore order.[179]

Rosano's was clearly an emotionally effective *arringa*. But the defence had an even more fearsome weapon in its armoury, in the form of the venerable professor of criminal law, Enrico Pessina. Born in 1828, Pessina's career was emblematic of the emergence of Liberal Italy. In March 1860, two months prior to the start of Garibaldi's conquest of the Bourbon kingdom in the name of Italian unity, Pessina had been exiled from Naples for his liberal views. In 1861, after unification, he returned home to take the chair in criminal law at the University of Naples. A passionate opponent of the death sentence, he was a parliamentary deputy from

[176] *Processo Fadda*, p. 168.
[177] *Processo Fadda*, p. 176.
[178] *Processo Fadda*, p. 177.
[179] *Processo Fadda*, p.177; and *Processo Cardinali*, p. 119.

1862 until 1879, when, shortly before the Fadda trial began, he became a senator (he would also be Minister of Justice briefly from late 1884 until mid-1885).[180] The day before his *arringa* in defence of Raffaella Saraceni, Pessina's eloquent adversary, Antonio Ponsiglioni, referred to him as a 'the prince of advocates'.[181]

Before Pessina spoke, the atmosphere in court, packed even more than usual with deputies, senators, ambassadors, and legal dignitaries, was reverential. In the words of the unnamed journalist who had stepped into Vassallo's shoes for *Il Messaggero*, the attention lent to Pessina's *arringa* was 'truly religious'.[182] The correspondent for Milan's *Corriere della Sera* used similar language, referring to the 'sepulchral silence' as Pessina rose, 'all practically holding their breath'. Once the revered advocate started talking, everyone 'hung off his lips'.[183] Yet, unlike some of his colleagues, including his protégé Rosano, Pessina did not open with emotional declarations. He admitted no nerves, and revealed nothing about his inner state. Pessina's technique was to use 'reason' first, and to save 'emotion' until last. He said he could not live up to the prosecution's overly benevolent characterization of him as a 'colossus', and warned the public that he was bound to fall short of the expectations that had been built up.[184]

But true eloquence, in Pessina's view, was not the ability to turn 'white into black, or change facts with the phosphorescence of words'. Rather, it had to be 'built on profound conviction'.[185] He began to dismantle the prosecution's case, element by element, leaving no doubt about the profundity of his own conviction of Raffaella's innocence. He threw a harsh light on various witnesses, particularly Rosina Garramone and Carluccio, underlining the questionable nature of the prosecution's evidence.[186] He argued that the existence of the telegrams exchanged between Pietro and Antonietta just before the murder was completely unknown to Raffaella, and therefore revealed nothing about her involvement in the plan.[187] He also threw doubt on the prosecution's claim that Raffaella had furnished Cardinali with over 500 lire before he departed for Rome.

Instead, Pessina argued convincingly that the possession of such a sum was not at all beyond a circus performer's means, as the prosecution had argued. He made these claims with reference to the circus's financial details discussed by witnesses early in the trial, in which it was revealed that the troupe earned 60 or 70 lire per day. And Pessina added convincing personal experience. He told the audience that in July 1878 he himself had spent fifteen days in Castrovillari at a trial, and happened to attend the Cardinali brothers' circus on several occasions.

---

[180] 'Enrico Pessina', *Il Parlamento Italiano, 1861–1988. Vol. V, 1877–1887: La Sinistra al potere. Da Depretis a Crispi* (Milan: Nuova CEI, 1988), pp. 500–1. See also Garfinkel, *Criminal Law in Liberal and Fascist Italy*, pp. 51, 183, and 186.
[181] *Processo Fadda*, p. 183.   [182] *Processo Cardinali*, p. 124.
[183] 'Processo Fadda', *Corriere della Sera*, 31 October–1 November, p. 2.
[184] *Processo Fadda*, p. 189.   [185] *Processo Fadda*, p. 189.
[186] *Processo Fadda*, p. 190.   [187] *Processo Fadda*, p. 191.

**Figure 5.3** An advocate addresses the rapt audience during the Fadda murder trial
Source: *Processo Fadda illustrato* (Rome: Giovanni Bracco Editore, 1879), pp. 196–7.

He affirmed that they were a high-quality act, perfectly capable of handsome earnings.[188] It was an appealing touch that underlined Pessina's authority to judge such matters, demonstrating that he was familiar with the world of popular entertainment as well as the arenas of political and judicial power. Something of the court's atmosphere of engaged attention as a lawyer for the defence, probably Pessina, made his speech, is captured in figure 5.3.

Pessina relentlessly pursued the events and facts laid out by the prosecution, casting doubt over them with, as some journalists put it, the keenness of a serrated blade.[189] It was only towards the end of his *arringa* that he added to these dry ingredients the leavening power of emotion. The subject here was Raffaella's motive, and the result took the audience's breath away. Pessina refuted the prosecution's argument that Raffaella hated Fadda because of her overdeveloped

---

[188] *Processo Fadda*, p. 194.
[189] A common image in the press—e.g. 'Processo Fadda', *Il Bersagliere*, 31 October 1879, p. 3, refers to Pessina's 'serrated dialectic'; 'Processo Fadda', *Corriere della Sera*, p. 2, refers to the 'extremely cutting blade' of his rhetoric.

sensuality. Fadda was almost certainly at least partially impotent, Pessina affirmed, but he asked the assembled if it was really wickedly sensual of Raffaella to yearn for the physical consummation promised by the sacred and indissoluble bond of marriage? He pressed the question home with the most memorable lines of his speech: 'And what if that indissoluble knot bears no fruit?', he asked, 'What is a house without children? Is it perhaps a Spring without flowers?'[190]

That phrase provoked gasps of admiration from the court. But Pessina did not stop to bask. He built the idea up into a powerful statement defending a woman's right to sexual gratification:

> You call her an adulteress! But think about the ideal of marriage: she wants to feel beautiful when she's embraced by her husband; she cradles the hope of a beautiful family to populate their home; she imagines her soul will become one with his. But fusing two metals into one needs fire! And if there is no fire? Love goes cold; the radiant conjugal home becomes a frozen cavern.[191]

Although the Rome newspaper from which these words are taken probably most faithfully reproduced Pessina's speech, it is worth noting that Milan's *Corriere della Sera* embellished its summary of his *arringa* with more suggestive phrasing. In those columns, Pessina portrayed Raffaella as a woman who deserved compassion, not disdain, because 'the torch of love never shone its rays into her home, over which reigned inertia, frigidity, impotence.'[192]

The notion of children was certainly there to appease Catholic consciences, but Pessina would not have sought compassion for Raffaella's yearning flesh if there had been any risk that the claim would fall on deaf ears. Throughout his speech at least one report claimed that Raffaella sobbed uncontrollably.[193] And it was to her, and her deceased husband Fadda, that Pessina addressed his closing words:

> Let me kneel and shed a tear on the tomb of Giovanni Fadda, thou valiant soldier whose noble existence was cut short by an assassin. And if the spark of your soul is somewhere in the ocean of light that is the spirit of the world, I know you will join me in recognizing the innocence of she who was your companion, and your spirit will enlighten the jurors in their deliberations.

> O Raffaella, kneel with me on that tomb, kneel and shed your tears, join me in asking for pardon from the husband you offended. Kneel in the dust before your judges, because you have sinned, and the shame of this public trial is the punishment that God has exacted for your sins.

---

[190] 'Processo Fadda', *Il Bersagliere*, 31 October 1879, p. 3.
[191] 'Processo Fadda', *Il Bersagliere*, 31 October 1879, p. 3.
[192] 'Processo Fadda', *Corriere della Sera*, 31 October–1 November 1879, p. 3.
[193] *Processo Cardinali*, p. 126.

But then, raise your brow, with confidence and with faith, and meet the eyes of those who judge you. For they will absolve you![194]

It had been a sublime defence, and if the applause that met Rosano's speech had been a wave, what met Pessina's was a tsunami, a colossal release of the emotional build-up of the entire trial. Pessina had released them by enlisting Raffaella to join him in acting out some very powerful cultural tropes. Histrionic as it might seem, the gesture of kneeling at Fadda's imagined tomb was highly operatic, easily visualized, and deeply evocative. Similarly, praying for pardon and redemption for sexual sin made the court into a vast Catholic confessional turned inside out. But in the end, the scene was enacted in a secular court, the death sentence glinting, and it was to the temporal judges that the final appeal was addressed.

The expectations of Pessina's speech had been immense, and the collective emotion that erupted at its conclusion showed that he had more than met them: he received a genuine ovation, and was 'suffocated with embraces'.[195] The applause was deafening, making a mockery of the president's vigorously shaken, but impotent unheeded bell. The scene was 'not far off delirium'.[196] Only the next day though, would the court, then Rome, then Italy and the world, hear whether Pessina and his colleagues had persuaded the jury that Raffaella was innocent.

## The Verdicts

On the morning of Friday 31 October, the twenty-fourth and final hearing of the Fadda trial began, as usual, at 11 a.m. Journalists were tired of trying to invent fresh ways to describe the intensity of the interest and the density of the crowd. Suffice it to say that never had such a crowd assembled for a trial in all of Italy's history.[197] For the last time too, reporters underlined that the public was largely composed of women.[198] The court entered to the usher's final cry of 'Laaaaa Cooooorte' at 11.30 a.m. and its first task was to establish the questions to be deliberated by the jury. A measure of the tension was the near breakdown of decorum amongst the lawyers, as Palomba, the advocate defending Antonietta Carrozza, sought the insertion of a question about whether she had been exposed to 'irresistible force'. The prosecutor, Rutigliano, leapt up out of order and launched into an imprecation to the jury to be on their guard about such questions, insisting that Antonietta acted out of cold premeditation. Pessina objected and the president reined in the prosecutor, but only after some confusion.[199]

---

[194] 'Processo Fadda', *Il Bersagliere*, 31 October 1879, p. 3.
[195] 'Processo Fadda', *Il Bersagliere*, 31 October 1879, p. 3.
[196] 'Processo Fadda', *Corriere della Sera*, 31 October–1 November 1879, p. 2.
[197] 'Processo Fadda', *Corriere della Sera*, 1–2 November 1879, p. 2.
[198] *Processo Fadda*, p. 193.   [199] *Processo Fadda*, p. 198.

The president spent some time summing up the arguments presented by the prosecution and the defence, but nowhere was this recorded, and indeed *Il Bersagliere*'s reporter declared that it had been impossible to follow the elaborate account. Instead, the journalist's report jumped to what his readers were waiting for: at 3.30 p.m., the accused were removed from the court, and the jurors withdrew to their chamber to deliberate. The court waited for one hour, during which the sense of anticipation was almost unspeakable. At 4.30 p.m., the jurors returned to the court. The head juror then rose, and, with his hand on his heart, he reported on the jury's majority-based verdict:

Was Pietro Cardinali guilty of murdering Giovanni Fadda? YES

If yes, was this murder carried out according to a premeditated plan? YES.

Was Raffaella Saraceni guilty of having induced Cardinali to murder Giovanni Fadda with a promise of marriage? NO.

If not, was she guilty of instigating him, or furnishing the means necessary to travel to Rome to commit the murder, or did she knowingly and consciously assist in the plans for the murder? YES.

If so, was her involvement such that without it, the murder would not have taken place? YES.

If in answer to either of the first two questions the answer is affirmative, had she formed a plan for the murder of Giovanni Fadda? YES.

And did Antonietta Carrozza help or assist or facilitate Pietro Cardinali in the murder? YES

If yes, did she do so under the influence of irresistible force? YES.[200]

The accused were brought back into the court to listen to the verdict, which was read out by a clerk. Antonietta was declared not guilty and was immediately released, to applause from the audience. Raffaella started to faint and was given succour by her legal team (see figure 5.4). The court officials withdrew to deliberate the sentences. After a mere twenty minutes the judges returned. The president pronounced that Pietro Cardinali would be sentenced to death, and that Raffaella Saraceni would do hard labour for the rest of her life. Public sentiment, to the minimal extent that it was recorded, lost the sense of chorus it had had during the trial. Opinion was strongly divided, and Italy's most sensational trial concluded in 'noises and agitation'.[201]

---

[200] *Processo Fadda*, pp. 199–200.   [201] *Processo Fadda*, p. 200.

**Figure 5.4** Raffaella faints during the reading out of the verdicts

*Source: L'Epoca* (Genoa), 6–7 November 1879, p. 1. Reproduced with permission from the Biblioteca di Storia Moderna e Contemporanea, Rome.

## Conclusion

The members of a public who, one month earlier, had heaved in unison against the great doors of the Court of Assizes in their eagerness to witness the trial, now dispersed for the last time. Like Dickens' audience after 'Jarndyce and Jarndyce', they were likely to have been 'flushed and hot' with sentiment, but they would not have been mistaken for those exiting from 'a farce or a juggler'. The Fadda trial may have had its farcical elements, but it concluded with one person sentenced to hard labour for life, and another, to death. For all the theatricality of the event, it concerned a cold-blooded murder, and life-and-death judgements by a court that represented Italian society as a whole. The trial, and the setting in which it was heard, constituted an emotional arena par excellence: a distinctive social space in which the emotions of those present were experienced, expressed, and staged according to formulae that would become a new norm. Emotions were essential to the spirit of the trial, but throughout, they took shape in ways that were specific to the arena in which it took place.

In the context of a developing relationship between nation-state and citizens, Rome's Court of Assizes was laden with significance in a way that makes it particularly worthy of detailed observation. Like Risorgimento battles, deceased kings, and martyred soldiers, the rule of law was a symbolic cornerstone of Italy's emerging liberal regime. After unification, phrases such as 'The law is equal for all', inscribed on the wall above the tribunal, became part of the new liturgies of daily life. Public spaces where citizens engaged with 'the law' were as important to Liberal Italy as temples and churches to a religious regime. But, compared with the spiritual depth of Catholic doctrine, and the stupendous temples in which it staged its own liturgies, Italy's courts did not necessarily augur a deepening relationship between citizen and nation. Dramatic cases such as the Fadda trial offered the state golden opportunities for 'spectacle, imagery and display', in which emotions might galvanize, even spiritualize, a tendentially indifferent set of citizens.

The state's officials quietly fostered such opportunities. Rome's Court of Assizes, a resonant former oratory originally selected for its scale and capacity, was specially fitted with even more public seating than usual for the Fadda trial. Throughout the hearings, the vast public was carefully controlled and invigilated, but never discouraged or barred—except when its members threatened to breach the rules appropriate to this emergent emotional arena. Journalists, harnessing their canonical reporting role in a liberal constitutional state to the interests of circulation and profit, strategically stoked the flames of public interest nationwide. It might even be argued that newspapers formed a vital part of a 'state–press complex': consciously or not, they circulated the oxygen of the Fadda trial's emotional highs and lows to the most distant citizens.

The operatic plot behind the trial inevitably lent a highly marketable theatricality to the proceedings. Italian women, who welcomed court hearings as one of the few opportunities they had to participate in the state's official activities, were particularly fascinated by the trial, at whose heart lay a failed marriage. The 'national poet', Giosuè Carducci, sowed the seeds of moral panic about Italian emotionalism by likening modern women to bloodthirsty spectators in Imperial Rome's Colosseum. In fact though, a comparative glance at legal spaces in England, France, and Ireland shows that the frequently alleged 'excessive theatricality' of Italy's courts was far from unique. Italy simply joined more mature political regimes in establishing the court of law as an arena where bonds between nation and citizen might be reinforced by the sharing of emotions according to a state-determined formula.

What made the phenomenon stand out in Italy, particularly in Rome, is that the public who wished to participate in trials were required to learn, more quickly than elsewhere, how a court differed from other arenas of Italian cultural and public life. Courtrooms, after all, were novel to most Italians in the 1860s and the 1870s. They may have resembled more familiar cultural spaces such as the opera theatre, and may have looked like places of worship. Indeed the fact that Rome's court once was such a place would only have added a sense of déjà vu to a public learning how to inhabit a new public arena. Courts may at times even have resembled a circus—particularly, as happened during the Fadda trial, when a donkey trainer or clowns took to the witness stand. But even if the court of law may initially have resembled a kaleidoscope of other social spaces, the public began to grasp that, as an arena of emotional expression, particular rules made it unique.

The *dramatis personae* of the court and the rituals they enacted signalled those rules and marked the arena's emotional boundaries. The entries and exits of the high officials recalled the entrances of priests in church, and marked the formality of the hearings. The lawyers for both prosecution and defence, in their black togas, represented a secular clergy. But the way they embodied and evoked emotions was different from their religious forebears. In court, the advocates were knights at arms. They judiciously used emotions as lances during their jousts, their *arringhe*. They even fought over who had more right to deploy emotional lances to move judges, jury, and public. The accused, closely scrutinized by the public, displayed their feelings too. Saraceni and Carrozza, with their bowed heads and demure tears, ultimately conformed to the rules. However, Cardinali, with his provocative eye contact, constant smirk, and proud gestures, badly misread the arena, and failed to win sympathy from the audience.

The public witnessed, and learned, new ideals about feelings that would ultimately engender a shift in the emotional standards of Italian public life. Its members knew they were expected to feel deeply, but they soon found that there were clear boundaries around how their feelings were to be revealed. Discreet exclamations, cries, and tears were acceptable, but a collective 'ooh half a kilometre long' was too long, and applause was for the theatre, not the court. Beyond the courtroom, newspapers, eager to tell the story, disseminated the rules of an emergent emotional arena to the furthest corners of Italy. A major affair in Rome, in national terms the trial marked a visible step in the development of the relationship between state and citizen. Emotions, during the Fadda trial, helped leaven an emerging national consciousness.

# Conclusion

## Reviewing Emotional Arenas

On Monday 3 November 1879, two days after the conclusion of the trial for Giovanni Fadda's murder, the Minister of Justice, Giovanni Battista Varè, issued a stern circular to the presidents of all of Italy's Courts of Assizes.[1] Couched in general terms and purportedly addressing the spiralling costs of justice, the circular was also undoubtedly a direct response to the cause célèbre that had captured the nation's imagination for the entire month of October.[2] This is clear partly from the document's timing. But it also made references to inordinately lengthy proceedings, to the inefficiencies of calling vast numbers of witnesses, to inappropriately impassioned exchanges between the prosecution and defence, to special one-off seating arrangements for the public, and to the accused being viewed by the public as if they were 'beasts on display in a circus'.[3] The minister's view, in short, was that Italian courts needed to be more efficient, less theatrical, and less emotional.

Varè made his points in chivalrous language that may have sought to spare the public prosecutor and president of Rome's court from too much direct embarrassment. Nevertheless, the thrust was clear. The high cost of justice in Italy compared to states with similar procedures could be reduced, the minister suggested, by making full use of each day's hearing, and by avoiding the 'indulgent luxury' of calling marginal witnesses who only muddied the waters. This was an obvious reference to the clowns presented unexpectedly during the final phase of the Fadda trial. Prosecutors, he warned (echoing claims made by Raffaella's defence lawyers), should also renounce ambitions to become famous orators and must avoid 'passionate rhetorical efforts to stir the souls' of those present. The prosecutor's role, he wrote, was to represent the 'impartial, serene, stable' aspects of the legal process. In the face of the law's 'simple and severe logic', he added hopefully, even advocates for the defence should curtail 'overly lengthy displays and irritating invective'.[4]

---

[1] Giovanni Battista Varè, 'Circolare 3 Novembre 1879. Giudizi innanzi alle Corti d'Assise', *Raccolta circolari emanate dal Ministero di Grazia e Giustizia e dei Culti, anni 1871 al 1880*, vol. 2 (Rome: Regia Tipografia, 1881), pp. 1172–4, here p. 1174.

[2] Several newspapers also commented on the circular, confirming that is was a direct response to the Fadda trial. See, for example, 'Echi del processo Fadda', *Il Bersagliere* (Rome), 6 November 1879, pp. 1–2; 'I giudizi penali', *Corriere della Sera* (Milan), 6 November 1879, p. 2.

[3] Varè, 'Circolare 3 Novembre 1879', p. 1174.

[4] Varè, 'Circolare 3 Novembre 1879', p. 1173.

The circular was, among other things, an instruction about emotional management of the legal arena, including the spectators. Varè warned that while public involvement in criminal trials was 'one of the great achievements of modern civilization', it would be a mistake to 'confuse publicity with spectacle'.[5] The minister added that he had even heard of 'special provisions for extra seating, with first- and second-class tickets offered for particular trials'—another clear reference to the Fadda proceedings. Such practices were to cease, he commanded, because they ruined the 'solemn tranquility' needed for justice. They encouraged 'expressions of sentiment from the crowds that distract the president from his main duties' by necessitating his intervention to 'maintain silence'.[6]

Varè's postscript to the Fadda trial, with its contrasts between soul-stirring rhetoric on the one hand, and on the other, the law's 'simple and severe logic' of serene, stable, impartiality, underlines that courts in 1870s Italy were spaces whose emotional dynamics attracted official concern, intervention, and shaping. It signals an Italian state still in the process of establishing its institutional and cultural contours. Hindsight does suggest that, in the case of the Fadda trial, officials overstepped the mark in their enthusiasm for public engagement in the Italian state's processes. The Minister of Justice's words represent an attempt to ensure that Italy's courts would be distinctive emotional spaces, where feelings were to be shaped and staged in ways that would augment the law's prestigious ideological mission, not distract from it. Varè's instruction points the way to the conclusion of this book's presentation of Fadda's life and death as a story in which the spaces, contexts, and characters of a still-fluid national community coalesce into a new paradigm for emotions history: the emotional arena.

The preceding chapters have shown how life in 1870s Italy—as in many other polities similarly conscious of their historical transitions—was experienced across a range of contemporaneously existing but defined social spaces. Within each, inner feelings, and their staging and shaping, followed patterns distinctive to that space. I have called these spaces emotional arenas partly because of the term's connotations of both boundaries and human scale. Even if 'emotional arenas' can be used metaphorically, and therefore without boundaries, the sense of scale and clear outer edges implied by the physical examples discussed in these chapters—a court of law, a circus, the private home, the theatre, places of worship, even the confessional—can help historians to contain and envisage an intrinsically evanescent historiographical quarry.

The 'emotional arena' idea emerged out of my own imagined presence during Giovanni Fadda's murder trial, a sense initially conjured by vivid contemporary newspaper reports. As I investigated further, Rome's Court of Assizes in 1879 appeared as a unique palimpsest of social spaces. The original, sacred purpose of

---

[5] Varè, 'Circolare 3 Novembre 1879', p. 1173.   [6] Varè, 'Circolare 3 Novembre 1879', p. 1174.

the building complemented the law's status in Liberal Italy. It was also a reminder of the way new regimes build upon the rituals of the old, and of the ambiguous ideological hegemony of a new Italian state as it sought to assert its identity in the nation's capital. Court proceedings supported the developing polity's quest for legitimacy based on the rule of law, and the story behind the Fadda murder created a golden opportunity for deep public engagement. But because so much of the trial's narrative revolved around a circus, because two of the three defendants were circus artists, and because witnesses included an impresario, a donkey trainer, two clowns, and other colourful characters, sometimes the boundary between 'publicity and spectacle' (as Varè put it) was ignored even by the elites who flocked to witness the proceedings, not to mention the more general public.

In retrospect, the narrative behind the trial, the architectural overlays, and the relative novelty of public criminal hearings in Rome make it easy to see how a neophyte public might occasionally have lost its emotional bearings. The audience was likely to have perceived the court as a kaleidoscope of the previously familiar: sacred spaces, theatres, circuses, even ancient amphitheatres. In 1879 though, this blurring of social and emotional boundaries prompted anxiety among some of the nation's opinion leaders. These are best represented by the prominent poet, Giosuè Carducci, who felt that the hallmarks of a mature nation should be rigour, sobriety, and clear separation between reason and emotion. Implicit in his poem about the Fadda trial was the assumption that reason was 'masculine' and emotions were 'feminine'. Moreover, in an unquestioningly patriarchal society, women's unabashed fascination with the trial's highly sexual themes only added to a broader sense of the event as grounds for moral panic.

Although the court is the most concrete of emotional arenas explored in this book, the documents brought together by the prosecution's investigation also provided the historiographical means to extend the notion outwards to less exceptional elements of life in 1870s Italy. Collectively, these rich sources not only shine light on unfamiliar aspects of Italian social history, they illuminate historical processes of emotional encounter, negotiation, navigation, experiment, management, and evolution, within a range of distinctive social spaces. Some of these arenas, such as Fadda and Saraceni's marriage, are clearly associated with the emergence of a new nation. The outwardly propitious match not only united representatives from distant geographical elements of a recently united Italy, it portended the movement of familial emotional regimes away from multigenerational families entrenched in local communities, towards more self-sufficient couples mobilized in service to the emerging nation.

In theory, the new couple should have been emotionally independent enough to support Giovanni Fadda's work administering and building the new state's infrastructure in its most distant parts. Alas, whether for insufficient sexual fire to 'fuse' the marriage's two elements (as lawyer Enrico Pessina suggested to the court), or for other reasons, Raffaella was perpetually drawn away from her marriage and back to the extended family of her childhood. Fadda's care in selecting and creating suitably decorous marital homes for his wife failed to persuade her to make a permanent transition from Cassano to wherever her husband was stationed. The couple's correspondence during their long periods of separation reveals deep feelings, but they are shaped and staged with utmost restraint. Even as their relationship unravelled—an almost unimaginably tragic matter in that period—their emotions were carefully contained.

In contrast to Fadda's and Saraceni's restrained style lay the altogether more chaotic, exuberant, and at times sinister emotional habits represented by the Cardinali Brothers' circus. Its public aspect was an arena of 13 metres in diameter, where performances evoked a complex mix of emotions. Chief among them were the public's empathetic senses of fear, relief, admiration, and joy when all went well for the daring artistes. These simple circus thrills were also leavened with a generous element of physical desire among at least some members of the public. It would be easy to assume that men monopolized these feelings, in relation to Antonietta. But as later events were to confirm, quite a few of the female spectators—even those who already had partners—ardently desired Pietro.

As long as such emotions were contained within the arena itself, where members of the public could and did monitor each other, the desires elicited in the circus remained innocent *frissons*, circumscribed within a very particular space. Yet, to judge by the energetic ways in which its artists socialized with townsfolk, the circus's boundary was more permeable than modern interpreters and contemporary locals might have expected. For the Saracenis and other families, the circus's innocent thrills regularly continued in glittering parties held at their private homes. Many townsfolk ended up imagining that after such gatherings, all semblance of innocence between Raffaella and Pietro Cardinali was lost.

Moreover, behind the scenes of the circus itself, its constituent families operated according to an emotional regime that was very different from Saraceni and Fadda's restrained and polite marriage. We know little about the emotional substance of Pietro's relationship with his main female partner, Carolina Misuraca, but it is clear that she tolerated the sexual relationship with his adoptive sister, Antonietta Carrozza, at close quarters. And while after the murder it was to Antonietta's legal advantage to claim that the circus's emotional ménage was marked by fear and jealousy, there is no reason not to believe her.

We also know that other women desired nothing more than to establish enduring emotional bonds between themselves and Pietro Cardinali. The court convicted Raffaella Saraceni on the suspicion that she was chief among them, so much so that she was willing to have her husband murdered in order to marry Pietro. Her sentence tends to confirm historical assumptions about the era's cultural concern with containing female desire, but that culture itself has successfully hidden significant female sentiments from historians of Italy. And while imaginative work on cultural texts about women's love and desire has underlined the interplay between cultural sources and everyday feelings among real people, the love letters written by Cardinali's admirers give us a sense of lived emotions in an unusually vivid and direct way. Their contents add considerably to the ways in which historians might understand the emotional and sexual desires of nineteenth-century Italian women.

Whether such desires were sufficiently strong to prompt Raffaella to commission the murder of her dutiful husband can never be known with certainty, but that is how Pietro Cardinali—and the jury—interpreted the matter. The resulting brutal assassination prompted the book's analysis of emotional arenas centring upon death. Prior to Italian unification, the Catholic Church had for centuries had a monopoly over concepts of death and the afterlife, the fate of cadavers, and the emotional succour offered to those left behind by the departed. After Italy was united, even if religion still dominated personal understandings of death held by most Italians, the Church's monopoly over mortality encountered competition from the new state. Novel 'arenas' for managing death and its emotions started to appear. The deaths in 1878 of Victor Emmanuel II, first king of united Italy, and Giovanni Fadda, one of the king's faithful lieutenants, are both exemplary of the way new emotional arenas centred on mortality began to take shape.

The king's death, in January, gave rise to Italy's first state funeral. A memorable historical turning point, the event and subsequent ritualistic commemorations harnessed the royal death's emotional potential to the aspirations of a secular governing elite. The funeral, minutely choreographed by the anti-clerical Francesco Crispi, Minister of the Interior and later prime minister, turned all of Rome into a secular arena of mourning. A cannon booming once per minute did not permit the population to forget its collective grief for more than a moment throughout the day. Regional arrangements were equally intense, though the population of Rome doubled in the days around the funeral as secular pilgrims descended upon the capital from all corners of the nation. The procession, involving representatives from all ranks of society, was more elaborate than anything Italians had ever seen. As well as being designed to honour the king, the event sought to reinforce popular emotional ties to the nation. In the sense that grief was evoked, shaped, and staged in new and spatially specific ways, Rome at the time of Victor Emmanuel's funeral constituted a novel emotional arena for Italy.

One eye witness to the funeral's distinctive sentimental register was none other than Giovanni Fadda, himself destined to follow his king into the afterlife nine months later. The violence and ignominy of Fadda's murder caused enormous indignation as well as grief, surrounding his death with an emotional tenor that was different from the king's. But it was also similar in that the emotions Fadda's death provoked were managed by secular authorities in distinctive ways. The clearest example was the autopsy on Fadda's corpse, performed in the hospital morgue by three doctors, in the company of the public prosecutor, his assistant, other state officials, and possibly even journalists. The post-mortem report's language, almost completely devoid of sentiment, embodies the emotional detachment that helped constitute the unassailable prestige that was secured by science towards the end of the nineteenth century. The fact that the autopsy was reported in the newspapers, albeit with only veiled reference to the more delicate anatomical aspects, indicates that the ideal of scientific detachment, even in the face of death, was well on the way to broad cultural dissemination.

The court of law in which the story of Fadda's murder finally culminated was also intended to be a space where reason and sentiment were ideally to remain separate. This was made clear in sources as diverse as Carducci's poem, and the Minister of Justice's circular of 3 November 1879. But for ideological reasons, the court, unlike the morgue, was very much in the public eye, and for this reason it gave rise to unprecedented challenges in terms of emotional management. As the trial unfolded, the presiding judge, ushers, advocates, defendants, jurors, journalists, and the public found themselves involved in a complex process of emotional negotiation within a novel and intense arena. In this space, detached forensic reason was frequently overwhelmed by emotional stimulation, so much so that the court was often thought to resemble a circus, or even an ancient Roman festival.

Tensions between these apparently opposed styles of emotional setting were enthusiastically described to those outside the court by eager though generally scrupulous journalists. Fadda's status as an official who had probably sacrificed his capacity to generate offspring to the cause of Italian unification raised the stakes on the court's judgment to an extremely high level. Ultimately, the forensic process redeemed Fadda's spirit by condemning Cardinali to death and Raffaella to hard labour for life. Notwithstanding the prominence of the public's involvement or the colourful witnesses, the verdicts left no doubt that the court was not a circus, nor even an amphitheatre, but a deadly serious legal arena.

By way of concluding this argument about emotional arenas in 1870s Italy, it is worth coming to the present briefly, to consider twenty-first-century phenomena that might be considered modern equivalents. The virtual spaces of social media, whose possibilities for unfettered emotional expression have been dizzying and even intoxicating, exemplify novel emotional settings for a hyperconnected world. In some sense such spaces might initially have been refuges, under the radar of existing emotions rules—but they also promise to become a form of regime in their own right. Ultimately, they may well lead to more enduring forms of emotional disorientation than that represented by the Fadda trial in October 1879, and they certainly portend even more in the way of political challenges. In comparison, the Fadda trial appears to be a relatively quickly achieved if minor triumph for an Italian state seeking to engage its citizens. For, although it was by no means the last sensational trial to be witnessed in Italy, to my knowledge, never again did an Italian court come so close to resembling a Roman amphitheatre. In this sense, the trial for Fadda's murder in 1879 had done its work for the new Italy.

## Epilogue

Once the case closed, the story naturally lost its thunder. But it was not forgotten, and the press kept the public informed about the defendants' fates for many years afterwards. Immediately after her release, Antonietta Carrozza was fought over by various circus impresarios.[7] She was quickly signed up by the great Suhr Circus, then performing in Rome's enormous Politeama arena, just across the Tiber River from the Court of Assizes.[8] Underlining that today's obsession with those who are famous merely for being famous is not a new phenomenon, the press reported that troops were required to stop the eager crowds from forcing entry to the overbooked Politeama on the evening of Carrozza's 'debut'. She only appeared for a few minutes, apparently, 'pallid and trembling' (see figure 6.1). Nevertheless, some of Rome's leading gentlemen, including a prince of the old Roman nobility,

**Figure 6.1** Antonietta Carrozza performing in the circus at Rome's Politeama, days after her release from the court

Source: *L'Epoca* (Genoa), 16–17 November 1879, reproduced with permission from the Biblioteca di Storia Moderna e Contemporanea, Rome.

---

[7] 'Processo Fadda (Echi)', *L'Epoca* (Genoa), 3–4 November 1879, p. 2.
[8] 'Echi del processo Fadda', *Il Bersagliere*, 6 November 1879, pp. 1–2. Reports on the phenomenon also appeared in various British newspapers and even the *New York Times*, 30 November 1879, p. 5.

CONCLUSION 211

**Figure 6.2** Raffaella bids farewell to her mother as her prison sentence begins
Source: *L'Epoca* (Genoa), 9–10 November 1879, p. 1 (owned by the author).

allegedly lined up outside her changing room afterwards in the hope of being presented to the humble artist.[9] Enjoying her short-lived celebrity, Carrozza was also reported to have made similar debuts in Naples and Florence (with an audience of over 3,000). But after the close of 1879, she disappeared from the historical record.[10]

Immediately after the trial, Raffaella Saraceni was moved to her permanent prison. On 10 November, Genoa's *Epoca* newspaper portrayed her in a poignant and tearful embrace with her mother at the start of her life sentence (figure 6.2). After that, nothing was heard of Saraceni until 1886, when the king conceded a royal 'grace' that reduced her sentence from life imprisonment to twenty years.[11] In 1891, false rumours that she was about to receive a royal pardon circulated in the newspapers briefly.[12] Then, towards the end of 1896, after seventeen years in prison, Saraceni was granted a full pardon on the basis of both 'exemplary conduct' and grave ill health. Doctors reported that she would die in prison if not released. Turin's *La Stampa* newspaper trusted that its readers would remember the 'noisy trial' that had led to her sentence all those years ago. Now aged forty-three, ill and ageing, with 'hair completely grey', Raffaella was finally released from prison on 25 November, 1896. She almost certainly returned to Cassano allo Ionio.[13]

Pietro Cardinali had been sentenced to death, though as mentioned in chapter 5, by the late 1870s few if any such sentences were executed. Nevertheless, shortly after the trial, the gravity of Cardinali's predicament was conveyed to readers of Genoa's *Epoca* newspaper with a full front-page illustration of the prisoner alone in his cell, contemplating his fate.[14] A few days earlier, the newspaper had reported that Cardinali had one final and emotionally moving visit from his eldest brother.[15] Three months later, in early February 1880, the king signed a decree that commuted Cardinali's death sentence into hard labour for life.[16] On 25 February 1880, Cardinali was transferred to the prison at Civitavecchia, a port city some 70 kilometres north-west of Rome. Rome's *Capitale* newspaper reported that at his departure from the capital's prison, the guards said goodbye to him with a certain affection, as if they were sad to see him go.[17] After that, Pietro Cardinali was not heard about in the public sphere again. In all probability he died in prison at Civitavecchia, aptly concluding this tale of life, love, and death in modern Italy.

---

[9] 'Da Roma', *Gazzetta Piemontese* (Turin), 13 November 1879, p. 1.
[10] 'La Carrozza al Politeama di Napoli', *Gazzetta Piemontese*, 15 December 1879, p. 5; on Florence, *Gazzetta Piemontese*, 18 December 1879, p. 2.
[11] 'Nostri telegrammi', *Gazzetta Piemontese*, 12 March 1886, p. 1.
[12] 'La grazia a Raffaella Saraceni', *Gazzetta Piemontese*, 7 March 1891, p. 1; and 11 March 1891, p. 1.
[13] 'La grazia a Raffaella Saraceni', *La Stampa* (Turin), 25 November 1896, p. 3.
[14] *L'Epoca*, 8–9 November 1879, p. 1.
[15] 'Processo Fadda (echi)', *L'Epoca*, 4–5 November 1879, p. 2.
[16] *La Capitale* (Rome), 3 February 1880, p. 2; 'La grazia al Cardinali', *Gazzetta Piemontese*, 3 February 1880, p. 3.
[17] 'Cronaca cittadina', *La Capitale*, 26 February 1880, p. 2.

# Bibliography

## Primary sources

Archives
Archivio di Stato di Roma. Tribunale Penale e Civile di Roma, 1879, busta 3659.

Newspapers
*Il Bersagliere* (Rome)
*La Capitale* (Rome)
*Corriere della Sera* (Milan)
*L'Epoca* (Genova)
*Il Fanfulla della domenica* (Rome)
*Gazzetta Piemontese* (Turin)
*Illustrated Police News* (London)
*La Nazione* (Florence)
*New Zealand Herald* (Auckland)
*L'Opinione* (Rome)
*L'Osservatore Romano* (Rome)
*Il Piccolo* (Naples)
*The Press* (Christchurch, NZ)
*The Standard* (London)
*The Times* (London)

Contemporary compilations of newspaper reports on the Fadda trial
*Processo Cardinali e coimputati per l'assassinio del Capitano Fadda commesso in Roma il 6 Ottobre 1878 dibattutosi il giorno 30 settembre 1879 e seguenti davanti alle Assise di Roma*, 2nd edition (Rome: Edoardo Perino, 1879). [Compilation from *Il Messaggero*, Rome].
*Processo Fadda illustrato. Dibattimento alla Corte d'Assise di Roma dal 30 settembre al 31 ottobre 1879* (Rome: Giovanni Bracco Editore, 1879). [Compilation from *Il Bersagliere*, Rome]

Official publications
*Raccolta circolari emanate dal Ministero di Grazia e Giustizia e dei Culti, anni 1871 al 1880*, vol. 2 (Rome: Regia Tipografia, 1881).

## Secondary sources

Alberti, Fay Bound. *Matters of the Heart: History, Medicine and Emotion* (Oxford: Oxford University Press, 2010).
Alessi, Giorgia. *Il processo penale. Profilo storico* (Rome-Bari: Laterza, 2001).
Alfieri, Fernanda. *Nella camera degli sposi. Tomás Sánchez, il matrimonio, la sessualità (secoli XVI–XVII)* (Bologna: Il Mulino, 2010).

Anderson, Benedict. *Imagined Communities: Reflections on the Origin and Spread of Nationalism* (London: Verso, 1991 [1983]).
Arato, Franco. *Parola di avvocato. L'eloquenza forense in Italia tra Cinque e Ottocento* (Turin: G. Giappichelli Editore, 2015).
Ariès, Philippe. *Western Attitudes toward Death: From the Middle Ages to the Present*. Translated by Patricia M. Ranum (Baltimore: Johns Hopkins University Press, 1974).
Ariès, Philippe. *The Hour of our Death*. Translated by Helen Weaver (London: Allen lane, 1981 [1977]).
Arpaia, Paul. 'Constructing a National Identity from a Created Literary Past: Giosuè Carducci and the Development of a National Literature'. *Journal of Modern Italian Studies*, vol. 7, no. 2 (2002): 192–214.
Assael, Brenda. *The Circus and Victorian Society* (Charlottesville: University of Virginia Press, 2005).
Association française pour l'histoire de la justice. *La justice en ses temples. Regards sur l'architecture judiciare en France* (Paris: Editions Errance, 1992).
Astarita, Tommaso. *Village Justice: Community, Family and Popular Culture in Early Modern Italy* (Baltimore: The Johns Hopkins University Press, 1999).
Babini, Valeria P. *Il caso Murri. Una storia italiana* (Bologna: Il Mulino, 2004).
Babini, Valeria P., Chiara Beccalossi, and Lucy Riall (eds). *Italian Sexualities Uncovered, 1789–1914* (Basingstoke: Palgrave Macmillan, 2015).
Bablitz, Leanne. *Actors and Audience in the Roman Courtroom* (London: Routledge, 2007).
Bablitz, Leanne. 'Roman Society in the Courtroom'. In *The Oxford Handbook of Social Relations in the Roman World*, edited by Michael Peachin (Oxford: Oxford University Press, 2011), pp. 317–34.
Bandes, Susan A. (ed.). *The Passions of Law* (New York: New York University Press, 1999).
Banti, Alberto Mario. *La nazione del Risorgimento. Parentela, santità e onore alle origini dell'Italia unita* (Turin: Einaudi, 2000).
Banti, Alberto Mario. 'The Remembrance of Heroes'. In *The Risorgimento Revisited: Nationalism and Culture in Nineteenth-Century Italy*, edited by Silvana Patriarca and Lucy Riall (Basingstoke: Palgrave Macmillan, 2012), pp. 171–90.
Banti, Alberto Mario. *Eros e virtù. Aristocratiche e borghesi da Watteau a Manet* (Rome-Bari: Laterza, 2016).
Barclay, Katie. 'Narrative, Law and Emotion: Husband Killers in Early Nineteenth-Century Ireland'. *The Journal of Legal History*, vol. 38, no. 2 (2017): 203–27.
Barclay, Katie. 'Performing Emotion and Reading the Male Body in the Irish Court, c. 1800–1845'. *Journal of Social History*, vol. 51, no. 2 (2017): 293–312.
Barclay, Katie. *Men in Court: Performing Emotion, Embodiment and Identity in Ireland, 1800–45* (Manchester: Manchester University Press, 2019).
Beaven, Lisa, and Angela Ndalianis (eds). *Emotion and the Seduction of the Senses, Baroque to Neo-Baroque* (Kalamazoo: Medieval Institute Publications, 2018).
Ben Amos, Avner. *Funerals, Politics, and Memory in Modern France, 1789–1996* (Oxford: Oxford University Press, 2000).
Berenson, Edward. *The Trial of Madame Caillaux* (Berkeley: University of California Press, 1992).
Betri, Maria Luisa, and Daniela Maldini Chiarito (eds). *«Dolce dono graditissimo». La lettera privata dal Settecento al Novecento* (Milan: Franco Angeli, 2000).
Bizzocchi, Roberto. *A Lady's Man: The Cicisbei, Private Morals and National Identity in Italy* (Basingstoke: Palgrave Macmillan, 2014).

Boschi, Daniele. 'Homicide and Knife-Fighting in Rome, 1845-1914'. In *Men and Violence: Gender, Honor and Rituals in Modern Europe and America*, edited by Pieter Spierenburg (Columbus: Ohio State University Press, 1998), pp. 128-58.
Bossy, John. 'The Social History of Confession in the Age of the Reformation'. *Transactions of the Royal Historical Society*, vol. 25 (1975): 21-38.
Bourke, Joanna. 'Fear and Anxiety: Writing about Emotion in Modern History'. *History Workshop Journal*, vol. 55, no. 1 (2003): 111-33.
Brookes, Barbara (ed.). *At Home in New Zealand: History, Houses, People* (Wellington, NZ: Bridget Williams Books, 2000).
Caesar, Ann Hallamore. 'Women Readers and the Novel in Nineteenth-Century Italy'. *Italian Studies* vol. 56, no. 1 (2001): 80-97.
Cammarano, Fulvio, and Maria Serena Piretti. 'I professionisti in Parlamento (1861-1958)'. In *Storia d'Italia. Annali 10. I professionisti*, edited by Maria Malatesta (Turin: Einaudi, 1996), pp. 523-89.
Carmeli, Yoram S. 'The Invention of Circus and Bourgeois Hegemony: A Glance at British Circus Books'. *Journal of Popular Culture*, vol. 29, no. 1 (1995): 213-21.
Cervellati, Alessandro. *Questa sera grande spettacolo. Storia del circo italiano* (Milan: Edizioni Avanti! Collezione 'Mondo Popolare', 1961).
Chartier, Roger, Alain Boureau, and Cécile Dauphin. *Correspondence: Models of Letter-Writing from the Middle Ages to the Nineteenth Century* (Cambridge: Polity Press, 1997 [1991]).
Chase, Karen, and Michael Levenson. *The Spectacle of Intimacy: A Public Life for the Victorian Family* (Princeton, NJ: Princeton University Press, 2000).
Chiavoni, Emanuela. *Il disegno di oratori romani. Rilievo e analisi di alcuni tra i più significativi oratori di Roma* (Rome: Gangemi Editore, 2008).
Clark, Anna. *Desire: A History of European Sexuality* (New York: Routledge, 2008).
Cohen, Deborah. *Family Secrets: Living with Shame from the Victorians to the Present Day* (London: Viking, 2013).
Cohen, Patricia Cline. *The Murder of Helen Jewett: The Life and Death of a Prostitute in Nineteenth-Century New York* (New York: Knopf, 1999).
Colao, Floriana, Luigi Lacchè, and Claudia Storti (eds). *Processo penale e opinione pubblica in Italia fra Otto e Novecento* (Bologna: Il Mulino, 2008).
Coleman, Kathleen. 'Entertaining Rome'. In *Ancient Rome: The Archeology of the Eternal City*, edited by Jon Coulston and Hazel Dodge (Oxford: Oxford University School of Archeology, 2000), pp. 210-58.
Coleman, Kathleen. 'Public Entertainments'. In *The Oxford Handbook of Social Relations in the Roman World*, edited by Michael Peachin (Oxford: Oxford University Press, 2011), pp. 335-57.
Connors, Joseph. *Borromini and the Roman Oratory: Style and Society* (New York: Architectural History Foundation, 1980).
Corbin, Alain. 'Backstage'. In *A History of Private Life. Vol IV: From the Fires of the Revolution to the Great War*, edited by Michelle Perrot, translated by Arthur Goldhammer (Cambridge, MA: Belknap Press of Harvard University Press, 1990), pp. 453-669.
Corbin, Alain. *Village Bells: Sound and Meaning in the Nineteenth-Century French Countryside* (New York: Columbia University Press, 1998).
Cornwell, John. *The Dark Box: A Secret History of Confession* (London: Profile Books, 2014).
Corrigan, John (ed.). *The Oxford Handbook of Religion and Emotion* (Oxford: Oxford University Press, 2007).

Corse, Sandra. '"Mi chiamono Mimì": The Role of Women in Puccini's Operas'. *Opera Quarterly*, vol. 1, no. 1 (1983): 93–106.

Cott, Nancy. *Public Vows: A History of Marriage and the Nation* (Cambridge, MA: Harvard University Press, 2010).

Cragin, Thomas. *Murder in Parisian Streets: Manufacturing Crime and Justice in the Popular Press, 1830–1900* (Lewisburg, PA: Bucknell University Press, 2006).

Croft-Cooke, Rupert, and Peter Cotes. *Circus: A World History* (London: Elek, 1976).

Da Passano, Mario. 'La pena di morte nel Regno d'Italia 1859-1889'. In *Diritto penale dell'Ottocento. I codici preunitari e il codice Zanardelli*, edited by Sergio Vinciguerra (Padua: CEDAM, 1995), pp. 579–649.

Dau Novelli, Cecilia. *La città nazionale. Roma capitale di una nuova elite (1870–1915)*, (Rome: Carocci editore, 2011).

Davidoff, Leonore, and Catherine Hall. *Family Fortunes: Men and Women of the English Middle Class, 1780–1850* (London: Routledge, 2002 [1987]).

Davidson, Jane W., and Sandra Garrido (eds). *Music and Mourning: Interdisciplinary Perspectives* (Abingdon: Ashgate Publishing, 2016).

Davis, John A. *Conflict and Control: Law and Order in Nineteenth-Century Italy* (Basingstoke: Macmillan Education, 1988).

De Giorgi, Fulvio. 'Forme spirituali, forme simboliche, forme politiche. La devozione al S. Cuore'. *Rivista di storia della Chiesa in Italia*, vol. 48, no. 2 (1994): 365–459.

De Giorgi, Fulvio. 'Note sulla modernizzazione ecclesiale'. *Rivista di storia contemporanea*, vol. 23-24, nos. 1-2 (1994–1995): 194–208.

De Giorgio, Michela. *Le italiane dall'unità a oggi. Modelli culturali e comportamenti sociali* (Rome-Bari: Laterza, 1992).

De Giorgio, Michela, and Christiane Klapisch-Zuber (eds). *Storia del matrimonio* (Rome-Bari: Laterza, 1996).

De Troja, Elisabetta. *My dear Bob. Variazioni epistolari tra Settecento e Novecento* (Florence: Società Editrice Fiorentina, 2007).

Diamond, Michael. *Victorian Sensation, Or, the Spectacular, the Shocking, and the Scandalous in Nineteenth-Century Britain* (London: Anthem Press, 2003).

Dixon, Thomas. *From Passions to Emotions: The Creation of a Secular Pyschological Category* (Cambridge: Cambridge University Press, 2003).

Dixon, Thomas. 'The Tears of Mr Justice Willes'. *Journal of Victorian Culture*, vol. 17, no. 1 (2012): 1–23.

Dixon, Thomas. *Weeping Britannia: Portrait of a Nation in Tears* (Oxford: Oxford University Press, 2015).

Duggan, Christopher. *Francesco Crispi 1818–1901: From Nation to Nationalism* (Oxford: Oxford University Press, 2002).

Duggan, Christopher. *The Force of Destiny: A History of Italy since 1796* (London: Allen Lane, 2007).

Durkheim, Emile. *The Elementary Forms of Religious Life*. Translated by Karen E. Fields (New York: The Free Press, 1995[1912])

Febvre, Lucien. 'Sensibility and History: How to Reconstitute the Emotional Life of the Past'. In *A New Kind of History: From the Writings of Lucien Febvre*, edited by Peter Burke, translated by K. Folca (London: Routledge and Kegan Paul, 1973), pp. 11–26.

Finlayson, Caitlin Cihak. 'Spaces of Faith: Incorporating Emotion and Spirituality in Geographic Studies'. *Environment and Planning A*, vol. 44 (2012): 1763–78.

Foley, Susan K., and Charles Sowerwine. *A Political Romance: Léon Gambetta, Léonie Léon, and the Making of the French Republic, 1872–1882* (Basingstoke: Palgrave Macmillan, 2012).

Fonterossi, Giuseppe. *Roma fine Ottocento* (Rome: Edizioni Moderne Canesi, 1960).
Foucault, Michel. *The History of Sexuality Volume I: An Introduction*. Translated by Robert Hurley (New York: Vintage Books, 1990 [1978]).
Frevert, Ute et al. *Emotional Lexicons: Continuity and Change in the Vocabulary of Feeling 1700–2000* (Oxford: Oxford University Press, 2014).
Gabaccia, Donna, R., and Loretta Baldassar. *Intimacy and Italian Migration: Gender and Domestic Lives in a Mobile World* (New York: Fordham University Press, 2010).
Gammerl, Benno. 'Emotional Styles—Concepts and Challenges'. *Rethinking History*, vol. 16, no. 2 (2012): 161–75.
Garfinkel, Paul. *Criminal Law in Liberal and Fascist Italy* (Cambridge: Cambridge University Press, 2016).
Gay, Peter. *The Bourgeois Experience: Victoria to Freud. Vol. 1, Education of the Senses* (Oxford: Oxford University Press, 1984).
Gentilcore, David. *Pomodoro! A History of the Tomato in Italy* (New York: Columbia University Press, 2010).
Ginzburg, Carlo. 'Microhistory: Two or Three Things that I Know about it'. Translated by John Tedeschi and Anne C. Tedeschi. *Critical Inquiry*, vol. 20, no. 3 (1993): 10–35.
Goffman, Erving. *The Presentation of Self in Everyday Life* (Woodstock, NY: The Overlook Press, 1973 [1959]).
Goffman, Erving. *Frame Analysis: An Essay on the Organization of Experience* (Boston: Northeastern University Press, 1986 [1974]).
Gordon, Eleanor, and Gwyneth Nair. *Murder and Morality in Victorian Britain: The Story of Madeleine Smith* (Manchester: Manchester University Press, 2009).
Gotti, Giulio. *Alcuni processi celebri e ricordi di vita forense* (Milan-Genoa-Rome-Naples: Società Editrice Dante Alighieri, 1935).
Graham, Clare. *Ordering Law: The Architectural and Social History of the English Law Court* (Aldershot: Ashgate, 2003).
Grendi, Edoardo. 'Micro-analisi e storia sociale'. *Quaderni storici*, vol. 12, no. 35(2) (1977): 506–20.
Groppi, Angela. 'Il teatro della giustizia. Donne colpevoli e opinione pubblica nell'Italia liberale'. *Quaderni storici*, vol. 37, no. 111 (2002): 649–79.
Guarnieri, Patrizia. *L'ammazzabambini. Legge e scienza in un processo di fine Ottocento*. (Rome-Bari: Laterza, 2006 [1988]).
Guazzaloca, Giulia. '"In the Name of Justice and Compassion": Animal Protection in Italy during the Liberal Age (1861–1914)'. *Modern Italy*, vol. 22, no. 3 (2017): 261–89.
Habermas, Jurgen. *The Structural Transformation of the Public Sphere: An Inquiry into a Category of Bourgeois Society*. Translated by Thomas Burger (Cambridge: Cambridge University Press, 1989 [1962]).
Hansen, Miriam. 'Pleasure, Ambivalence, Identification: Valentino and Female Spectatorship'. *Cinema Journal*, vol. 25, no. 4 (1986): 6–32.
Harris, Ruth. *Murders and Madness: Medicine, Law and Society in the* fin de siècle (Oxford: Oxford University Press, 1989).
Hay, Douglas. 'Property, Authority and the Criminal Law'. In *Albion's Fatal Tree: Crime and Society in Eighteenth-Century England*, edited by Douglas Hay et al. (London: Allen Lane, 1975), pp. 17–63.
Holloway, Sally. '"You Know I am All on Fire": Writing the Adulterous Affair in England, c. 1740–1830'. *Historical Research*, vol. 89, no. 244 (2016): 317–39.
Holloway, Sally. *The Game of Love in Georgian England: Courtship, Emotions and Material Culture* (Oxford: Oxford University Press, 2019).

Isastia, Anna Maria. 'La questione femminile nelle discussion parlamentari postunitarie: il Codice Cvile del 1865'. *Dimensioni e problemi della ricerca storica*, vol. 2 (1991): 162–84.
Jacob, Pascal. *The Circus: A Visual History*. Translated by Augusta Dörr (London: Bloomsbury Visual Arts, 2018).
Jalland, Pat. *Death in the Victorian Family* (Oxford: Oxford University Press, 1996).
Jando, Dominique. *Histoire mondiale du cirque* (Paris: Jean-Pierre Delarge, 1977).
Karant-Nunn, Susan C. *The Reformation of Feeling: Shaping the Religious Emotions of Early-Modern Germany* (Oxford: Oxford University Press, 2012).
Kertzer, David I. *Ritual, Politics and Power* (New Haven: Yale University Press, 1988).
Kertzer, David I. *Sacrificed for Honor: Italian Infant Abandonment and the Politics of Reproductive Control* (Boston: Beacon Press, 1993).
Kieschnick, John. 'Material Culture'. In *The Oxford Handbook of Religion and Emotion*, edited by John Corrigan (Oxford: Oxford University Press, 2007), pp. 223–38.
Kounine, Laura. 'Emotions, Mind, and Body on Trial: A Cross-Cultural Perspective'. *Journal of Social History*, vol. 51 no. 2 (2017): 219–30.
Kwint, Marius. 'The Legitimization of the Circus in Late Georgian England'. *Past and Present*, vol. 174, no. 1 (2002): 72–115.
Lancia, Pietro. 'Il processo Fadda'. *L'Eloquenza*, vol. 2, nos. 7–8 (1929): 125–31.
Laqueur, Thomas W. *The Work of the Dead: A Cultural History of Mortal Remains* (Princeton, NJ: Princeton University Press, 2015).
Lemmings, David (ed.). *Crime, Courtrooms and the Public Sphere in Britain, 1700–1850* (Farnham: Ashgate, 2012).
Levi, Carlo. *Christ Stopped at Eboli*. Translated by Frances Frenaye (London: Cassell, 1948).
Levra, Umberto. *Fare gli italiani. Memoria e celebrazione del Risorgimento* (Turin: Comitato di Torino dell'Istituto per la Storia del Risorgimento, 1992).
Leys, Ruth. 'The Turn to Affect: A Critique'. *Critical Enquiry*, vol. 37, no. 3 (2011): 434–72.
Lombardi, Daniela. *Storia del matrimonio. Dal Medioevo a oggi* (Bologna: Il Mulino, 2008).
Lucà Trombetta, Pino. *La confessione della lussuria. Definizione e controllo del piacere nel Cattolicesimo* (Genoa: Costa & Nolan, 1991).
Lyons, Martyn. ' "Questo cor che tuo si rese": the Private and the Public in Italian Women's Love letters in the Long Nineteenth Century'. *Modern Italy*, vol. 19, no. 4 (2014): 355–68.
Maggi, Stefano. 'I treni e l'unificazione d'Italia. L'epoca delle costruzioni ferroviarie'. *TeMA. Trimestrale del* Laboratorio *Territorio Mobilità e Ambiente*, vol. 4, no. 1 (2011): 7–14.
Majolo Molinari, Olga. *La stampa periodica romana dell'Ottocento* (Rome: Istituto di studi romani editore, 1963).
Malone, Hannah. *Architecture, Death and Nationhood: Monumental Cemeteries of Nineteenth-Century Italy* (London: Routledge, 2017).
Mazzonis, Filippo. *La monarchia e il Risorgimento* (Bologna: Il Mulino, 2003).
McLaren, Angus. *Impotence: A Cultural History* (Chicago: Chicago University Press, 2007).
Mitchell, Katharine. *Italian Women Writers: Gender and Everyday Life in Fiction and Journalism, 1870–1910* (Toronto: Toronto University Press, 2014).
Morris, Penelope, Francesco Ricatti, and Mark Seymour (eds). *Politica ed emozioni nella storia d'Italia dal 1848 ad oggi* (Rome: Viella, 2012).
Mulcahy, Linda. *Legal Architecture: Justice, Due Process, and the Place of Law* (Oxford: Routledge, 2011).
Mulvey, Laura. 'Visual Pleasure and Narrative Cinema'. *Screen*, vol. 16, no. 2 (1975): 6–18.
Muravyeva, Marianna. 'Emotional Environments and Legal Spaces in Early Modern Russia'. *Journal of Social History*, vol. 51, no. 2 (2017): 255–71.

Murialdi, Paolo. *Storia del giornalismo italiano* (Bologna: Il Mulino, 1996).
Murray, Marian. *Circus! From Rome to Ringling* (Westport, CT: Greenwood Press, 1973 [1956]).
Neale, Steve. 'Masculinity as Spectacle: Reflections on Men in Mainstream Cinema'. *Screen*, vol. 24, no. 6 (1983): 2–16.
Nussbaum, Martha. *Upheavals of Thought: The Intelligence of Emotions* (Cambridge: Cambridge University Press, 2001).
Painter, Borden W. Jr., *Mussolini's Rome: Rebuilding the Eternal City* (New York: Palgrave Macmillan, 2005).
Papaioannou, Sophia, Andreas Serafim, and Beatrice Da Vela (eds). *The Theatre of Justice: Aspects of Performance in Greco-Roman Oratory and Rhetoric* (Leiden: Brill, 2017).
*Il Parlamento Italiano, 1861–1988. Vol. V, 1877–1887: La Sinistra al potere. Da Depretis a Crispi* (Milan: Nuova CEI, 1988).
Pasi, Antonia, and Paolo Sorcinelli, eds. *Amori e trasgressioni. Rapporti di coppia tra '800 e '900* (Bari: Edizioni Dedalo, 1995).
Patriarca, Silvana. 'Indolence and Regeneration: Tropes and Tensions of Risorgimento Patriotism'. *American Historical Review*, vol. 110, no. 2 (2005): 380–408.
Patriarca, Silvana. *Italian Vices: Nation and Character from the Risorgimento to the Republic* (Cambridge: Cambridge University Press, 2010).
Pernau, Margrit. 'Space and Emotion: Building to Feel'. *History Compass*, vol. 12, no. 7 (2014): 541–9.
Peto, James. *The Heart* (New Haven: Yale University Press, 2007).
Pick, Daniel. *Rome or Death: The Obsessions of General Garibaldi* (London: Jonathan Cape, 2005).
Plamper, Jan. *The History of Emotions: An Introduction* (Oxford: Oxford University Press, 2015).
Porciani, Ilaria. *La festa della nazione. Rappresentazione dello Stato e spazi sociali nell'Italia unita* (Bologna: Il Mulino, 1997).
Reckwitz, Andreas. 'Affective Spaces: A Praxeological Outlook'. *Rethinking History*, vol. 16, no. 2 (2012): 241–58.
Reddy, William. *The Navigation of Feeling: A Framework for the History of Emotions* (Cambridge: Cambridge University Press, 2001).
Riall, Lucy. *Garibaldi, Invention of a Hero* (New Haven: Yale University Press, 2007).
Riall, Lucy. 'Martyr Cults in Nineteenth Century Italy'. *Journal of Modern History*, vol. 82, no. 2 (2010): 255–87.
Rifelli, Giorgio, and Corrado Giglio. *Per una storia dell'educazione sessuale, 1870–1920* (Florence: La Nuova Italia, 1991).
Romani, Gabriella. *Postal Culture: Writing and Reading Letters in Post-Unification Italy* (Toronto: University of Toronto Press, 2013).
Rosenwein, Barbara H. 'Worrying about Emotions in History'. *American Historical Review*, vol. 103, no. 3 (2002): 821–45.
Rosenwein, Barbara H. *Emotional Communities in the Early Middle Ages* (Ithaca, NY: Cornell University Press, 2006).
Rosenwein, Barbara H. 'Problems and Methods in the History of Emotions'. *Passions in Context: International Journal for the History and Theory of Emotions* [online journal], 1 (2010). http://www.passionsincontext.de.
Rosenwein, Barbara H. *Generations fo Feeling: A History of Emotions, 600–1700* (Cambridge: Cambridge University Press, 2016).

Rota, Arianna Arisi. *1869: il Risorgimento alla deriva. Affari e politica nel caso Lobbia* (Bologna: Il Mulino, 2015).
Russo, Angela. *«Nel desiderio delle tue care nuove». Scritture private e relazioni di genere nell'Ottocento risorgimentale* (Milan: Franco Angeli, 2006).
Rutherford, Susan. *The Prima Donna and Opera, 1815-1930* (Cambridge: Cambridge University Press, 2006).
Rutherford, Susan. *Verdi, Opera, Women* (Cambridge: Cambridge University Press, 2013).
Sala, Emilio. 'Women Crazed by Love: An Aspect of Romantic Opera'. *Opera Quarterly*, vol. 10, no. 3 (1994): 19–41.
Sbriccoli, Mario. 'Caratteri originari e tratti permanenti del sistema penale italiano'. In *Storia d'Italia. Annali, vol 14. Legge, diritto, giustizia*, edited by Luciano Violante (Turin: Einaudi, 1998), pp. 487–551.
Scheer, Monique. 'Are Emotions a Kind of Practice (and is That What Makes them Have a History)? A Bourdieuian Approach to Understanding Emotion'. *History and Theory*, vol. 51, no. 2 (2012): 193–220.
Schneider, Jane. 'Of Vigilance and Virgins: Honor, Shame and Resources in Mediterranean Societies'. *Ethnology*, vol. 10, no. 1 (1971): 1–24.
Schram, Albert. *Railways and the Formation of the Italian State in the Nineteenth Century* (Cambridge: Cambridge University Press, 1997).
Seymour, Mark. *Debating Divorce in Italy: Marriage and the Making of Modern Italians, 1860-1974* (New York: Palgrave Macmillan, 2006).
Seymour, Mark. 'Epistolary Emotions: Exploring Amorous Hinterlands in 1870s Southern Italy'. *Social History*, vol. 35, no. 2 (2010): 148–64.
Seymour, Mark. 'Emotional Arenas: From Provincial Circus to National Courtroom in Late Ninteenth-Century Italy'. *Rethinking History*, vol. 16, no. 2 (2012): 177–97.
Simpson, Thomas. *Murder and Media in the New Rome: The Fadda Affair* (Basingstoke: Palgrave Macmillan, 2010).
Sorba, Carlotta. *Teatri. L'Italia del melodramma nell'età del Risorgimento* (Bologna: Il Mulino, 2001).
Sowerwine, Charles. 'Channelling Grief, Building the French Republic: The Death and Ritual Afterlife of Léon Gambetta, 1883-1920'. In *Emotion, Ritual and Power in Europe, 1200-1920: Family, State and Church*, edited by Merridee L. Bailey and Katie Barclay (Basingstoke: Palgrave Macmillan, 2017), pp. 145–67.
Stearns, Peter N. *American Cool: Constructing a Twentieth-Century Emotional Style* (New York: New York University Press, 1994)
Stearns, Peter N. *Revolutions in Sorrow: The American Experience of Death in Global Perspective* (Boulder, CO: Paradigm Publishers, 2007).
Stoddart, Helen. *Rings of Desire: Circus History and Representation* (Manchester: Manchester University Press, 2000).
Tacchi, Francesca. *Gli avvocati italiani dall'Unità alla Repubblica*. Bologna: Il Mulino, 2002.
Talamo, Giuseppe. *Il «Messaggero» e la sua città. Cento anni di storia. Vol. I—1878-1918* (Florence: Le Monnier, 1979).
Taylor, Katherine Fischer. *In the Theater of Criminal Justice: The Palais de Justice in Second Empire Paris* (Princeton, NJ: Princeton University Press, 1993).
Taylor, Katherine Fischer. 'Geometries of Power: Royal, Revolutionary, and Postevolutionary French Courtrooms'. *Journal of the Society of Architectural Historians*, vol. 72, no. 4 (2013): 434–74.
Tellini, Gino, ed. *Scrivere lettere. Tipologie epistolari nell'Ottocento italiano* (Rome: Bulzoni Editore, 2002).

Thompson, E. P. *Customs in Common* (London: The Merlin Press, 1991).
Torselli, Giorgio. *Il Circo* (Rome: Fratelli Palombi Editore, 1970).
Tosh, John. *A Man's Place: Masculinity and the Middle-Class Home in Victorian England* (New Haven: Yale University Press, 2007 [1999]).
Trustram, Myna. *Women of the Regiment: Marriage and the Victorian Army* (Cambridge: Cambridge University Press, 1984).
Venzo, Manola Ida (ed.). *Scrivere d'amore. Lettere di uomini e donne fra Cinque e Novecento* (Rome: Viella, 2015).
Veyne, Paul. *Bread and Circuses: Historical Sociology and Political Pluralism*. Abbreviated and edited by Oswyn Murray, translated by Brian Pearce (London: Allen Lane, 1990).
Vidor, Gian Marco. *Biografia di un cimitero italiano. La Certosa di Bologna* (Bologna: Il Mulino, 2012).
Vidor, Gian Marco. 'Rhetorical Engineering of Emotions in the Courtroom: the Case of Lawyers in Modern France'. *Rechtsgeschichte—Legal History*, 25 (2017): 286-95.
Vidor, Gian Marco. 'The Press, the Audience, and Emotions in Italian Courtrooms (1860s-1910s)'. *Journal of Social History*, vol. 51, no. 2 (2017): 231-54.
Vidotto, Vittorio. *Roma contemporanea* (Rome-Bari, Laterza, 2001).
Wanrooij, Bruno P. F. *Storia del pudore. La questione sessuale in Italia, 1860-1940* (Venice: Marsilio Editori, 1990).
Wickberg, Daniel. 'What is the History of Sensibilities? On Cultural Histories Old and New'. *American Historical Review*, vol. 112, no. 3 (2007): 661-84.
Willson, Perry (ed.). *Gender, Family and Sexuality: The Private Sphere in Italy, 1860-1945* (Basingstoke: Palgrave Macmillan, 2004).

# Index

*Note*: Figures are indicated by an italic '*f*' following the page number. Footnotes are indicated by the letter n after the page number.

For the benefit of digital users, indexed terms that span two pages (e.g., 52–53) may, on occasion, appear on only one of those pages.

Albanesi, Albino  134–5, 140
Aloè, Giuseppe  42–3
Aloè, Raffaele  39
'Amalia' of Città Sant' Angelo  84, 92–4
amorous correspondence. *See* love letters
Anderson, Benedict  16–17
Angelo, Matteo  136, 141–2
anger  5, 13–14, 17, 25, 101, 161, 183
Antonietta (circus performer). *See* Carrozza, Antonietta
*A proposito del caso Fadda* (Carducci)  153–5
*arringhe* at Fadda trial
    for the defence  187–91, 196*f*
    for the prosecution  184–7
Astarita, Tommaso  7, 18
Astley, Philip  54–5
autopsy (of Giovanni Fadda)  18, 143–5, 180, 208–9

Baia, Rosina  73
Banti, Alberto Mario  23
Bari  128–32, 130*f*
Belli, Michele  131–2
Bellino-Rocci, Giovanni  43–4
Belmonte, Vittorio  138
Ben-Amos, Avner  121
Bergamuccio (circus clown)  193–4
*Il Bersagliere*  121, 139, 147, 165–8, 191–2, 199
Bertone, Carlo. *See* Carluccio (circus clown)
Bizzocchi, Roberto  125, 149
*Bleak House* (Dickens)  159
Borromini, Francesco  164
Bourdieu, Pierre  10–11
Brunetti, Maria  72–3

'C' of Catanzaro  87–93
Cagliari (Sardinia)  2–3, 21–2, 30–1, 181–2
Calabria  7 *see also* Cassano allo Ionio
Caltanissetta (Sicily)  28–32, 35
Campo Verano  146–7
Cannezzaro, Carmela  84, 96
*La Capitale*  212

Cardinali, Lorenzo  68–9, 75
Cardinali, Pietro. *See also* love letters: to Pietro Cardinali
    arrest for murder of Giovanni Fadda  1–2
    *arringhe* in defence of  187–8
    auditions for Guillaume circus  132
    cloak-and-dagger behaviour in Rome  134–6
    contemplates suicide  106, 109
    decoy letter  128, 129*f*, 131–2, 140
    as equestrian circus performer  56–9, 132
    erotic effect on audiences  60–1
    father's 'death'  105–6
    as inveterate womanizer  82, 87
    ménage à trois with Antonietta and Carolina  58–9, 66–7, 77, 207
    mission to murder Giovanni Fadda  3, 127–34
    murder enacted  128
    performance in court  174–5, 178–9
    portraits  57*f*, 130*f*
    relationship with Antonietta Carrozza  57, 64–7, 74, 133–4, 183
    relationship with Carolina Misuraca  66, 77, 81–2, 85–6, 93
    relationship with Raffaella Saraceni  3–4, 62–3, 68, 70–6, 133–4
    solicits money from admirer  102–5, 111–12
    telegrams to Antonietta Carrozza  133–4, 183, 195
    trial for murder  174–5, 178–9
    trial verdict and sequel  199, 212
Cardinali Brothers' Circus
    arrival in Cassano  50–2
    as emotional arena  76
    entourage and way of life  55–6
    erotic aspects  56–63
    intimacy with Saraceni family  67–70
    physicality of equestrian performances  56–60
    towns visited  50–1, 64–5, 68–9, 81–2, 95–6
Carducci, Giosuè  153–5, 158, 188, 202
Carluccio (circus clown)  74–6, 182, 186, 191–3
Carolina (wife of Pietro Cardinali). *See* Misuraca, Carolina

224  INDEX

Carrozza, Antonietta
   *arringa* in defence of 188–9
   as equestrian circus performer 57–60, 58f, 210f
   implicated in Fadda's murder 133–4, 186, 192
   in ménage à trois 50–1, 66–7, 77, 179, 207
   observes discovery of love letters 81–2
   portrait 58f
   relationship with Pietro Cardinali 57, 64–7, 74, 133–4, 183
   on trial for murder 169, 176–7, 179, 188–9
   trial verdict and sequel 210–12
Carta, Girolamo 148–9
Cassano allo Ionio (Calabria) 20–1
   arrival of Cardinali circus 50–2
   description 50–1
   *voce pubblica* in 70–6
Catanzaro (Calabria) 87–8, 96
Catholic Church
   influence in Italy 150–1
   on marriage annulment 27
Chieti (Abruzzo) 38–44, 125
church: as emotional arena 14–15
circuses. *See also* Cardinali Brothers' Circus
   as emotional arenas 17, 52–3, 63–4, 76–7
   English and French antecedents 54–5
   erotic aspects 56–63, 76–7
   Guillaume circus 55–6, 132, 183, 187
   Roman tradition 53–4
   Suhr Circus 210–12
Città Sant'Angelo (Abruzzo) 93
clowns. *See* Bergamuccio; Carluccio
Coboevich, Nicolò 166, 179, 181–2, 186, 190, 192
compassion 172–3, 176, 181–2, 197
confessional box: as emotional arena 14–15, 14n.48, 80
Corbin, Alain 90
Corigliano Calabro (Calabria) 81–2
*Corriere della Sera* 195, 197
Cosenza (Calabria) 36
Cotes, Peter 53
Cott, Nancy 23, 26, 41
Court of Assizes (Rome)
   architectural aspects 164–5, 177f
   as emotional arena 151
   public participation in trials 151–2, 169–70, 170f
courts of law. *See* law courts
Crispi, Francesco 121–2
Croft-Cooke, Rupert 53

D'Atri, Vincenzo 75
D'Azeglio, Massimo 153–4
death and deaths. *See also* funerals; morgue
   emotional arenas of 18, 113
   of Giovanni Fadda (*see* Fadda, Giovanni: death)
   of Giovanni Fadda's mother 45, 116–18
   of King Victor Emmanuel 114–15, 120–3, 149
   social meaning of death 113
death penalty 168–9
decoy letter 128, 129f, 131–2, 140
De Luca, Giuseppe 3–4, 74–5, 128–36, 140–2
desire
   elicited by circus performers 17–18, 56–61, 63, 76–7, 86–7, 207
   expressed in illicit love letters 5, 79–80, 82, 88–9, 207–8
   historiographical challenges 17–18, 25n.13, 80–1, 207–8
De Vincentis, Raffaele 74–5
Dickens, Charles 159
disappointment 5, 13–14, 105–6
Di Sciullo (hairdresser) 39
divorce law 124, 127
Dixon, Thomas 173
Donzelli, Edoardo 42, 125, 134
Duggan, Christopher 150–1
Durkheim, Emile 151

'Edoardo' 39, 40f, 48, 125
emotional arenas
   as concept 7–8, 12–16
   real *vs.* virtual 16–19
*Emotional Communities in the Early Middle Ages* (Rosenwein) 9
emotional refuge
   as concept 9, 13, 52, 79–80
   secret love letters as 95, 110–11
emotional regime
   as concept 9
   of circus troupe 52, 66–7, 111
   of confession 80–1
emotions
   as 'a kind of practice' 31
   historiographical challenges 5–6, 8–12, 80–1
   language and 11
   space and 11–16
emotive: as concept 9–10, 31
epistolary emotions. *See* love letters
*L'Epoca* 168, 173–4, 176, 192, 212
'exceptional-normal' events 4–5, 24n.10, 82

Fabiani, Vincenzo 71
Fadda, Cesare 39–41, 46–8, 177–8, 181–2
Fadda, Giovanni. *See also* Fadda murder trial
   —career
      as military officer 2–3, 21–4, 28, 35, 115

INDEX   225

postings 25, 28–31, 35–6, 38, 45
transfer to Rome 45–8
war wounds 21–2, 26–8, 39, 42–3, 122–3, 143–5, 148
—death
  assassination 1–4, 2f, 128, 136–8
  funeral 146–9
  national shock 115–16
  newspaper coverage 138–40, 145–6
  post-mortem examination 143–5, 180
—family connections
  correspondence with brother-in-law 44–8
  correspondence with father 45, 118
  correspondence with father-in-law 44
  correspondence with mother-in-law 29–34, 36–8, 45, 116, 119–20, 123–4
  family background 21–2
  mother's death 41, 114, 116–18
—marriage
  Cesare Fadda's account 39–41, 48
  Chieti residents' perceptions 38–44
  correspondence with Raffaella 5, 29–30, 35–6, 45–8, 116–18, 123–5
  early marital problems 36, 38–44, 40f, 48, 125–6
  marriage breakdown and separation 4, 48, 123–4, 126–7
  lived through letters 25
  local gossip and rumours 36–44, 70–6
  marriage agreement and wedding 2–3, 20, 26–7
  Raffaella's reluctance to cohabit 28–9, 46–7
  return of pianoforte 123–4
  sexual issues 27–8, 39, 42–3, 49, 145, 180–1, 196–7
  surprise visit to Cassano 33–5, 48
  as symbol of Italy's unification 22–3
—personality
  conscientious attention to extended family 32, 36–8
  duty to behave correctly 30–1, 119
  emotional self-restraint 117–18, 123–4
  fear of shame 36–7, 47–8
  impact of king's death on 123, 125–6
  jealousy 39, 40f, 42–4, 125–6
  suffers deep emotional crisis 124–6
—portraits 22f, 85f
Fadda, Giuseppe 45, 116, 118, 177–8, 181–2
Fadda murder trial
  autopsy report 143–5
  Carducci's poem on 153–6, 158, 188, 202
  closing speeches (arringhe)
    for the defence 187–91, 196f
    for the prosecution 187–91

conduct of the accused 173–6
emotional atmosphere 157, 169–73, 176–8, 184–6, 188–92, 194–5, 198
excessive theatricality 153–6
forensic groundwork 141–3
interrogation of the accused 178–80
interrogation of witnesses 181–3, 191–3
as national sensation 4–5
newspaper coverage 138–9, 153–6, 165–8
opening day 169–78, 170f
public participation in 151–3, 169–70, 170f, 177f, 196f
role of examining magistrate 141–3
sexual disclosures 144–5, 180–1
testimony of circus clowns 191–4
Varè's postscript 204–5
verdicts and aftermath 198–201, 200f
women's emotional engagement in 152–6
family/marital home: as emotional arena 12–13
  see also marital home
Fanfulla della domenica 153–4
Farghi, Vincenzo 134
fear
  in circus family 66, 77, 85–6
  of illness 34
  of judicial punishment 160–1
  of physical risk and danger 53–4, 56–9, 76, 207
  of public anger 161
  of shame 37, 39–41, 43–4, 78–80, 82–3, 92–3, 105
Febvre, Lucien 5–6
female gaze 60–3
Ferraro, Maria 183
Finizia, Michele 2–3, 82, 140–6
Fiore, Mariuccia 87, 90–2
Forleo, Giuseppe 130–1
Forum (Rome) 1–2, 141
Foucault, Michel 14–15
France
  circuses 55, 61
  law courts 151
  state funerals 121
  Troppmann trial 162–3
Franconi, Antonio 55
funerals and funeral processions
  as emotional arenas 146–7
  of Giovanni Fadda 146–9
  of King Victor Emmanuel II 114–15

Gandolin. See Vassallo, Luigi Arnaldo
Garibaldi, Giuseppe 8, 60–1, 114
Garramone, Rosina 73–4, 182
Gazetta della Capitale 139, 145–8

gender 12–13, 65–7, 105, 155–6, 163
    see also masculinity; women
Genoa 168
Ghenghi, Nicola 130–1
Gilbert and Sullivan 159
Giordano, Francesco 172–3, 176–7
*giudice istruttore* (examining magistrate) 141–3
Goffman, Erving 159
Graham, Clare 161
grief over death
    as emotional arena 18
    at king's death 114–15, 120–1, 149
    at Giovanni Fadda's death 146–9
Groppi, Angela 138, 155–6
Guillaume, Emilio 55, 132
guilt 14–15, 65, 77, 80, 105

habitus: as concept 10–11
happiness 39, 77, 108–10
Harris, Ruth 159–60
hate 179, 186, 197
Hay, Douglas 159–63
historiography
    of lived emotions 5–6, 80–1
    of sexual desire and intimacy 17–18, 25n.13, 80–1, 207–8
honour 37, 39, 65, 68, 78–9, 108
Hughes, Charles 54–5

*Imagined Communities* (Anderson) 16–17
impotence 27, 177–8, 180–1
Italy
    fostering of emotional allegiance to new liberal polity 150–2
    as 'imagined community' 114–15
    influence of Catholic Church 150
    legal system 157–9, 169
    liberal challenge to Catholic worldview 114, 149, 152
    marriage law 26–8, 86, 124, 127
    postal culture 29–30, 82
    public participation in trials 151–2, 157, 169–70
    railway development 50
    unification 22–3

Jalland, Pat 113–14
jealousy
    in circus ménage 66, 77, 85–6, 179, 207
    decoy letter and 128
    Giovanni Fadda and 39, 40f, 42–4, 125–6
    in love letters 5
    trials of crimes motivated by 159–60

Laqueur, Walter 113
law courts
    as both temples and theatres 151–2, 158–63
    Britain 159–61
    as emotional arenas 11–12, 15–16
    France 151
    Italy (*see also* Court of Assizes; Fadda murder trial)
        excessive theatricality 158–60
        international comparisons 157–61
        public participation in trials 151–2, 157, 169–70
        role of *la voce pubblica* 70–1
        sacred temples *vs.* rowdy circuses 19, 151–5, 171–2
Lemmings, David 161
Léotard, Jules 61
Levi, Carlo 50–1
Levra, Umberto 122
love letters
    as archival evidence of lived emotions 5–7, 80
    as emotional arena and refuge 17–18, 82, 95, 110–11
    to Pietro Cardinali
        anonymity and use of go-betweens 84, 96–8
        discovery of 81–2
        enclosed gifts 88, 93–4
        from 'Amalia' of Città Sant' Angelo 92–4
        from 'C' of Catanzaro 87–93
        from Mariuccia Fiore 87, 91–2
        from 'M.N.' of Larino (*see* 'M.N.' of Larino)
        as representing micro-historical 'exceptional-normal' events 82
        stationery, cryptic embellishments, spelling 82–3, 88–9, 89f, 98–101
lust 58–9, 63, 77, 186

Majo, Luigi 38–9
Marini, Carlo 135
marital/family home: as emotional arena 24–5
marriage
    as emotional arena 17, 23–6
    impotence as ground for annulment 27
    Italian marriage law 26–8, 86, 124, 127
    and nationhood 23
    promise of marriage 98–100
    Sphinx-like character 23, 41
marriage: Giovanni and Raffaella
    Cesare Fadda's account 39–41, 48
    Chieti residents' perceptions 38–44
    early marital problems 36, 38–44, 40f, 48, 125–6
    lived through letters 25

local gossip and rumours 36–44, 70–6
marriage agreement and wedding 2–3, 20, 26–7
marriage breakdown and separation 48, 123–4, 126–7
Raffaella's reluctance to cohabit 28–9, 46–7
sexual issues 17–18, 27–8, 42–3, 49, 145, 180–1, 196–7
as symbol of Italy's unification 22–3
masculinity 24–5, 60, 69, 163, 185, 206
McLaren, Angus 27
Menken, Adah Isaacs 59
Menni, Benigno 137–8, 143–4
*Il Messaggero* 166–8, 195
microhistory 4–5, 7, 24, 82
Misuraca, Carolina 66, 77, 81–2, 84–6, 93, 207
'M.N.' of Larino: letters to Pietro Cardinali 94–110
anguish on learning of Pietro's marriage 100–10
aspiration to marry Pietro 94–5, 98–101, 105–6
choice of stationery 98–101, 99f, 105–7
death as topic 105–6
distress on learning of Pietro's marriage 100–10
emotional vulnerability 105
feelings of attraction, desire and love 94–5, 98, 101–3, 105–6, 108–10
Pietro's pleas for cash 101–5
use of intermediaries 84, 96–8
as virtual emotional arena 95, 105
morgue: as emotional arena 18, 145
'Mother Milk' 172–3, 183
mourning. *See* funerals and funeral processions; grief over death
Mulcahy, Linda 160–1
Murray, Marian 53
Musmano, Luigi 75–6

Naples 2–3, 20–1
*Navigation of Feeling* (Reddy) 9
newspapers
reporting of Fadda's murder 138–9, 145–6
reporting of Fadda trial 138–9, 153–6, 166–8
Nola, Carolina (Raffaella's mother)
concern for daughter's marriage 27–8, 30, 33
correspondence with Giovanni Fadda 29–34, 36–8, 116, 119–20, 123–4
as family matriarch 33, 47
Nussbaum, Martha 172–3

Oblieght, E.E. 165–6, 168
opera theatre: as emotional arena 13–14
*L'Opinione* 121, 139
Oratory of the Filippini 164–5

Ospedale della Consolazione 2, 137–8
*Osservatore Romano* 180–1, 191–2

Pacchini, Teresina 42–3
Pachetta, Giulia 84
Paladini, Maria 134
Palomba, Carlo 188–90, 198
Panella, Rosa 42
Pantheon (Rome) 121–2
Panzi, Teresina 128, 136–8
Parissa, Antonia 96–7
Parma 35
Patriarca, Silvana 25–6
Pecia, Angelo 96–7
Pesci, Rosina 182
Pessina, Enrico 194–8
Piazza delle Chiavi d'Oro (Rome) 1, 134
*Il Piccolo* 155, 174–6, 191–2
Pietro (circus equestrian). *See* Cardinali, Pietro
Pinta, Giuseppe 183, 187
pity 172–3, 176–8 *see also* compassion
Plamper, Jan 9–10
Ponsiglioni, Antonio 184–6, 195
postal culture 29–30, 82
post-mortem examination 143–5, 180
pride 25, 141–2, 145, 194

Quartiere Alessandrino (Rome) 133

Raffaella. *See* Saraceni, Raffaella
Rago, Giuseppe 72
Ranzi, Ercole 187–8
Ravitti, Letizia 73
Reddy, William 9–11, 31, 52, 79–80
resentment 62–3, 75–7, 159–60
Riall, Lucy 60–1
Rizzo, Leonardo 75, 182, 192
Roman arenas 53–4
Romani, Gabriella 29–30
Rome. *See also* Court of Assizes (Rome)
as capital of Italy 4n.12, 111
as emotional arena 122–4, 149
Fadda's funeral 147–8
hegemony of Catholic Church 150
impact of Fadda trial on 167
king's funeral 121–2, 149
Quartiere Alessandrino 133
Rosano, Pietro 190–1, 193–5
Rosenwein, Barbara 8–9, 164
Rutigliano, Ippolito 186, 190, 198

sadness 77, 105–6
Salvatore, Felippo 96–7

San Martino battle  21–2, 27–8, 122–3, 143
Santi, Veronica  135
Saraceni, Giuseppe (Peppino)
   engagement announcement  44
   friendship with Pietro Cardinali  68–9,
      71, 73
   wedding delays  44, 46–8, 119–21
Saraceni, Raffaella. *See also* marriage: Giovanni
      and Raffaella
   alleged accomplice in husband's murder
      70–1, 74, 130–1, 140, 182, 192
   arrest for husband's murder  135
   *arringhe* in defence of  190–1, 193–8
   assiduous circus attendee  3–4, 62
   attachment to parental family  29
   conduct in court  175–6, 179–80
   correspondence with husband  29–30, 35–6,
      46, 119
   correspondence with mother  29, 34
   emotional coldness  146, 179–80, 186–8
   family background  20–1
   'immodest liaisons' in Chieti  38–44
   letter to 'Edoardo'  39, 40*f*, 48
   portrait  21*f*
   relationship with Pietro Cardinali  3–4, 62–3,
      68, 70–6, 133–4
   reluctance to cohabit with husband  28–9,
      46–7, 118–19, 123–4
   trial for murder  169, 175–6, 179, 190–1,
      193–8
   trial verdict and sequel  199, 200*f*, 211*f*, 212
Sardinia  2–3, 21–2, 38, 115–17, 157
Scheer, Monique  10–11, 31
Scorza, Gaetano  71–2
Servidio, Francesco  75
sexual desire and intimacy: historiographical
      challenges  17–18, 25n.13, 80–1, 207–8
   *see also* desire
shame and dishonour
   Antonietta Carrozza and  65
   Giovanni Fadda's fear of  37, 47–8
   marriage breakdown and  126
   Raffaella Saraceni and  176, 197
   women's sexual desire and  78–80, 82–3, 92–3,
      97, 108
Sharpe, J. A.  161
Sicily. *See* Caltanissetta (Sicily)
Simpson, Thomas  138, 155–6
Solferino battle  2–3

space: as analytical category  11
*La Stampa*  212
state funerals  114–15, 121–2
Suhr Circus  210–12

Taranto (Puglia)  50–1, 126–7
Taylor, Katherine Fischer  162–3
Teatro Politeama (Rome)  132, 210–12, 210*f*
'That daring young man on the flying trapeze'
      (song)  61
Thompson, E. P.  159–60
*The Times* (London)  139, 164–5
Tosh, John  24–5
Trebisondo, Federico  193
*Trial by Jury* (Gilbert and Sullivan)  159
Troppmann trial  162–3, 167
Trustram, Myna  23–4
Turin  4n.12, 21–2, 121–2
Tutino, Saverio  190

Varè, Giovanni Battista  204–5
Vassallo, Luigi Arnaldo  166, 169–71, 174–9,
      181–4, 186, 190, 192
Via Cremona (Rome)  1
Via dei Carbonari (Rome)  133–4, 139
Via della Testa Spaccata (Rome)  135
Victor Emmanuel II
   collective grief at his death  114–15,
      120–1, 149
   embodiment of Italian unification  114
   state funeral  121–2
'vigilance over virgins'  78–9
Vigliani, Paolo  172
*Village Justice* (Astarita)  7
*voce pubblica, la*  70–6, 78

women
   attendance at criminal trials  15–16,
      152–3, 165
   community scrutiny of women's lives  78–80,
      97–8
   female gaze  60–3
   involvement in Fadda trial  152–6
   resort to virtual emotional arenas  79–80,
      110–11
   sexual desire and shame  78–80, 82–3, 92–3,
      97, 108

Zaccari, Rosa  141–2